CAPITALIZING KNOWLEDGE:
ESSAYS ON THE HISTORY OF
BUSINESS EDUCATION IN CANADA

Capitalizing Knowledge

Essays on the History of
Business Education in Canada

EDITED BY BARBARA AUSTIN

UNIVERSITY OF TORONTO PRESS
Toronto Buffalo London

© University of Toronto Press Incorporated 2000
Toronto Buffalo London
Printed in Canada

ISBN 0-8020-4234-1 (cloth)

Printed on acid-free paper

Canadian Cataloguing in Publication Data

Main entry under title:

Capitalizing knowledge : essays on the history of business education
in Canada

ISBN 0-8020-4234-1

1. Business education – Canada – History.   I. Austin, Barbara J.

HF1131.C36 2000   650'.071'171   C99-932560-4

The University of Toronto Press acknowledges the financial assistance to
its publishing program of the Canada Council for the Arts and the Ontario
Arts Council.

University of Toronto Press acknowledges the financial support for its
publishing activities of the Government of Canada through the Book
Publishing Industry Development Program (BPIDP).

'Knowledge is the only real capital today.'
Peter Drucker, *Landmarks of Tomorrow*, 1957

Contents

Acknowledgments

The authors are highly indebted to Virgil Duff, Executive Editor, and Siobhan McMenemy at the University of Toronto Press for supporting the concept behind this collection and for shepherding the different drafts towards completion. We benefited enormously from the critical but constructive observations of several anonymous reviewers, especially two who remain known to us only as A and B. Frances Mundy oversaw the production of the book and we appreciate John St James for his meticulous copy-editing.

The contributors to this book have added a richness of detail and variations in attitudes that no single author could encompass. It has been a pleasure to work with this community of academics despite the thousands of miles that separate our universities. A special acknowledgment is due to Barry Boothman, who not only wrote two chapters from his research on the development of management education, but went well beyond the call of duty to help in the preparation of the manuscript – especially the tedious tasks of copy-editing and proofreading.

The Brock University President's Endowment Fund provided the grant that helped the editor bring this collection to publication.

BARBARA AUSTIN

Abbreviations

Text

AACSB   American Assembly of Collegiate Business Schools

ACSB   Association of Canadian Schools of Business / Association Canadienne des Écoles de Commerce (1963–72) became CAAS

ACSCBA   Association of Canadian Schools of Commerce and Business Administration (1957–62) became ACSB

ASAC   Administrative Sciences Association of Canada / L'Association des Sciences Administrative du Canada, beginning 1977

AUCC   Association of Universities and Colleges of Canada

CAAA   Canadian Academic Accounting Association

CAAS   Canadian Association of Administrative Sciences / Association Canadienne des Sciences Administrative (1972–77) became ASAC

CDDCSB   Council of Deans and Directors of Canadian Schools of Business (1970–6) became CFDMAS

CFBSD   Canadian Federation of Business School Deans (beginning 1995)

CFDMAS   Canadian Federation of Deans of Management and Administrative Studies (1976–95) later CFBSD

CIDA   Canadian International Development Agency

HÉC   École des Hautes Études Commerciales de Montréal

IFSAM   International Federation of Scholarly Associations of Management

SSHRC	Social Sciences and Humanities Research Council of Canada
SSRC	Social Science Research Council of Canada

Notes

AJS	*American Journal of Sociology*
AME	*Academy of Management Executive*
AMJ	*Academy of Management Journal*
AMR	*Academy of Management Review*
AO	Archives of Ontario
ASQ	*Administrative Science Quarterly*
BH	*Business History*
BHR	*Business History Review*
BJCS	*British Journal of Canadian Studies*
BQ	*Business Quarterly*
BW	*Business Week*
Calif.MR	*California Management Review*
CBR	*Canadian Business Review*
CEM	*Canadian Education Monthly*
CHR	*Canadian Historical Review*
CI	*Curriculum Inquiry*
CJAS	*Canadian Journal of Administrative Studies*
CJEPS	*Canadian Journal of Economics and Political Science*
CM	*Canadian Magazine*
CMR	*Canadian Management Review*
CPA	*Canadian Public Administration*
CUQ	*Columbia University Quarterly*
ER	*Educational Record*
HBR	*Harvard Business Review*
IM	*International Management*
JAS	*Journal of Administrative Studies*
JBE	*Journal of Business Ethics*
JBS	*Journal of Business Studies*
JEB	*Journal of Education for Business*
JEUC	*Journal of Education of Upper Canada*
JIBS	*Journal of International Business Studies*
JMD	*Journal of Management Development*
JMS	*Journal of Management Studies*
JOM	*Journal of Management*

JPE	*Journal of Political Economy*
JSBM	*Journal of Small Business Management*
JTIB	*Journal of Teaching in International Business*
MD	*Management Decision*
MR	*Management Review*
MS	*Management Science*
OS	*Organization Science*
PM	*Personnel Management*
PS	*Policy Sciences*
QQ	*Queen's Quarterly*
QR	*Queen's Review*
QUA	Queen's University Archives
QRE	*Quarterly Review of Economics*
SMJ	*Strategic Management Journal*
SMR	*Sloan Management Review*
UTP	University of Toronto Press
UTQ	*University of Toronto Quarterly*

CAPITALIZING KNOWLEDGE:
ESSAYS ON THE HISTORY OF
BUSINESS EDUCATION IN CANADA

Introduction

BARBARA AUSTIN

Management education in Canada has grown considerably since the Second World War. Canadian historians have frequently reflected upon the importance of professional disciplines like law, engineering, or education, but they have displayed scant interest in management as an academic subject. Most references in print to Canadian faculties of business administration have been oblique comments in the broad histories published about their universities. In contrast, numerous monographs are available for American developments, studies which survey general patterns or chronicle events at specific institutions.

Several issues probably account for the lack of published materials about Canadian practices. First, 'management education' can be defined in numerous ways: the design of curricula at the baccalaureate or graduate levels; the pedagogical practices employed in different courses; the evolution of schools of administration, their endeavours, and the various sub-areas in which their faculty members are engaged; the changing content of courses in distinctive aspects of management; or the development of institutional frameworks aimed at building professional norms and reputations. Second, modern programs in business administration really encompass a range of subjects and are staffed with faculty from different academic disciplines, a trait which can make it difficult to grasp the true scope of their activities. In theory, the general subject might be subdivided into disciplinary topics like accounting, marketing, or international business. As the papers in this volume also discuss, management educators have disagreed about the content of business curricula and the weights that should be attached to teaching, research, or community service. Third, because faculty and administrators at Canadian universities have traditionally emphasized organizational missions geared to the sciences or liberal arts, the development of professional studies in management has encountered considerable resistance. Despite the transformation of the corporate economy across the past century, some still think business administration is just experiential or is a vocation that belongs at community colleges or trade schools, not a field appropriate for university studies. Business faculties at numerous Canadian universities still cope on a daily basis with the legacy engendered by these misperceptions. Fourth, record keeping at most post-secondary institutions has not been well developed, and basic documents (course syllabi, committee minutes, and major reviews) often are shredded or memories are lost as the participants retire.

The essays in this volume record the treatment of intellectual preparation for business careers at several Canadian universities. The idea for a book grew from a request by the executive of the Administrative Sciences Association of Canada (ASAC), which is the scholarly association for the faculty members of Canadian business schools, for a history of that organization. During interviews with former deans and ASAC executives, it became clear that the evolution of the association was part of a much broader effort by professors and administrators to institutionalize management education in Canada. Many faculty members are nearing the end of their careers and research by scholars at different institutions appeared to be a valuable stance if the values and actions of those people were to be recorded. ASAC's Business History Division provided a forum for this expansion of the study. The deans of all Canadian business schools were contacted and asked whether any of their colleagues could prepare essays for presentation at the association's annual conferences following the normal peer-review processes. Several authors also were specially invited to prepare articles as the prospect for a compendium became realistic. Because the writing process was guided by personal or institutional interest, some readers may be disappointed that case studies of several faculties (such as those at British Columbia, McGill, or Western) have not been included. I hope the publication of this volume will stimulate additional endeavours or, at the very least, efforts to ensure the preservation of records in university archives.

This book enlarges our understanding by offering the first collection of papers dealing with the evolution of Canadian business schools, both large and small. As the essays indicate, the faculties have never operated as isolated academic communities. On the contrary, their curricula, organization, and research have been linked to the broader economies and societies in which they are located. The very character of management education requires faculty members to give concurrent attention to numerous issues, and their schools have handled these tasks in distinctive ways. Programs across Canada have been modelled after different schema from American and British universities, but there has never been total agreement about curricular design. The essays in this volume thus provide a form of picture book. Some are portraits that capture a discrete period in the history of a business school, while others are landscapes of a broader world.

The authors approach the subject with diverse viewpoints and methodologies, a consequence of their experiences, geographic locations, or intellectual orientations. Some have been administrators, all have taught and conducted research about different aspects of management, and several are historians who conduct their scholarly pursuits from inside the curious sphere of Canadian business schools. Not surprisingly, they interpret events differently and, if placed in a room with good wine and scotch, would strenuously argue about the development of different institutions. Although each author takes a specific approach to the subject, several common themes can be found in the essays. Every paper brings out the complexity of management education as an academic field, either by highlighting the interrelationships between business schools and their external environment or by chronicling the varied initiatives which faculties have undertaken despite scarce resources. Each also highlights both the difficulties associated with establishing a 'core body of knowledge' in business administration and the successive transformations of curricula. The case histories legitimately describe the dedicated efforts by personnel at different institutions, and a few bring out the petty concerns that are features of any form of human conduct. These studies, in particular, note the importance of organizational culture and values in moulding the actions of faculty members. Many of the practical matters, the failures as well as the accomplishments, associated with programmatic development are thereby revealed, along with variations from American policies. Management education has evolved along with Canadian business, slowly moving from an era dominated by personal administration to one characterized by professional executives. The problems encountered by the first commerce faculties, therefore, differed significantly from the issues faced by schools established after 1960.

Barry Boothman's two chapters act as bookends for the collection, providing overviews of the environmental contexts for the individual case histories. In the first chapter, 'Culture of Utility,' he describes how management education emerged and was transformed towards a university-level discipline. He teases out the complex threads of ideas, often from leading American programs, that offered an evolving canon about the appropriate dimensions of education for business. Boothman highlights the difficulties that management faculty members experienced in trying to broaden the definition of professional utility beyond the traditional trinity of divinity, law, and medicine. Their efforts were part of a general phenomenon during the late nineteenth and early twentieth centuries that included the professionalization of law, medicine, and engineering. Unlike these subjects, however, management education has lacked an external regulatory agency which appraises the body of essential knowledge and has not had well-defined criteria for accreditation or a cohesive set of occupational norms. Still, he argues, since professionalization has been at the centre of middle-class values, essentially defining middle-class status, management educators have increasingly tried to define a knowledge base through academic research and thereby claim a professional identity for their field. After a century of effort, some critics still have not been convinced. Recently, a reviewer for the *New York Times*, on Alan Ryan's book *Liberal Anxieties and Liberal Education*, noted during his discussion of specializations in the arts and sciences that 'the definition of these have been stretched in the United States to include some doubtful fields, notably business education, but this is not allowed in the better liberal arts colleges.'[1] Ouch – again!

Three distinct periods, each with a different emphasis, are reflected in the case histories. In the first phase, after 1900, Canadian business faculties gradually evolved from several different roots. With the exceptions of the École des Hautes Études Commercials de Montréal (HÉC) and the University of Toronto, the Canadian schools chose models of commerce programs from several variations found in American universities. Two reports, from the Ford and the Carnegie Foundations, both appearing in 1959, blasted the typical business programs taught in the United States. The criticisms began a second phase – of emphasis on management education. The two reports affected practices in all Canadian programs, but some faculties pushed for the reforms more energetically and effectively than others. In the early 1980s, the increasingly complex and diverse demands made on managers spurred divergent responses from different management faculties.

The quality of faculty members and the availability of resources help account for the current diversity in offerings.

The earliest commerce courses at Canadian universities were two-year diploma (not degree) programs. The department of political economy at the University of Toronto launched the first initiative in 1901. McGill's economics and political science department followed with a two-year commerce program in 1907. HÉC introduced the first commerce degree also during 1907. The school was created by the francophone Montréal Chambre de Commerce (not to be confused with the powerful and Anglo-dominated Montréal Board of Trade), and it used the European model of professional grandes écoles that operated separately from traditional universities. Pierre Harvey, a former dean of HÉC, describes these events in chapter 2, stressing the influence of the political context upon the school's formation. Interestingly, none of the other authors fully appraises this aspect in the histories of their organizations.

Queen's University pioneered correspondence courses in accounting and banking, beginning in 1914. From these initiatives, the university's department of political and economic science launched a bachelor of commerce degree in 1919. In chapter 3, Mervin Daub and Bruce Buchan consider the distinctive influence of American ideas, especially from Harvard and Chicago, upon the establishment of the Queen's business school, and trace the developments influencing their School of Business for almost a century.

The first four-year degree program in Canada was started at the University of Toronto by the department of political economy, which in 1909 began to offer a bachelor of arts degree in commerce and finance. Reflecting the liberal-arts orientation of the university, the course requirements included extensive obligations in economics, accounting, economic history and geography, English, and two modern languages. Toronto formally created a bachelor of commerce degree in 1920, a year after Queen's. Baccalaureate courses have remained joint offerings by the commerce and economics faculties, while graduate education was developed by a distinctive Faculty of Management, which was created in 1950. Professor Emeritus John Sawyer, in chapter 4, draws upon his experiences as a professor and an administrator for both the undergraduate and graduate programs to explain the evolution of this dual system.

Different concerns faced faculties, such as those at York and Calgary, that were created during the 1960s. The actions of their administrators were shaped by new ideas, especially by proposals advanced in two 1959 reports commissioned by the Ford and Carnegie Foundations.[2] In chapter 5, James Gillies, the founding dean of York's Faculty of Administrative Studies, describes how he imported a new framework for management education and the extent to which the university's administration was prepared to accept this. Since 1970 enrolment in the graduate program at York has been the largest among Canadian universities. Gillies reviews the practical problems which the faculty encountered in maintaining academic standards while meeting the escalating demand of students and companies for additional services.

Vernon Jones and former dean George Lane of the Faculty of Management at the University of Calgary have written the closest thing to a 'pure' case on the evolution of a Canadian business school, which they aptly title 'Development by Design' (chapter 7). The Calgary deans not only were heavily influenced by trends at leading American schools, but were able, not without considerable effort, to get their intentions enacted. In particular, the case study reveals some of the concerns which typified this period: the role of generalist versus specialist education, the weight of research versus teaching, and the appropriate balance of business and non-business courses in the curriculum.

These universities (like McGill and British Columbia) grew into large, traditional, full-service institutions. The three other case studies (Laurier, Saint Mary's, and Memorial) describe the growth of management faculties at smaller regional universities. Before the Second World War, the majority of commerce programs focused upon the accounting profession. During the 1960s the curricula were transformed to emphasize the concept of management, although a few faculties have retained a heavy emphasis upon accounting. Robert Ellis and John McCutcheon describe the development of the School of Business and Economics at Wilfrid Laurier University in chapter 6. Using an oral-history methodology, they uncovered the early history of business studies when, under the aegis of Waterloo College in 1937, a two-year program was launched from which students could transfer to the University of Western Ontario for additional learning. The Laurier faculty, through careful attention to course improvement, gained a reputation for supplying a quality program in management, while its neighbour, the University of Waterloo, specialized in accounting. Their findings led Ellis and McCutcheon to expand the research into a study of academic leadership.

Outside of the Maritime provinces, Saint Mary's is less well known than its Haligonian neighbour Dalhousie, but by meeting the needs of its regional constituents, Saint Mary's has come to have the largest business faculty in Atlantic Canada. Harold Ogden and Cathy Driscoll describe this persistent commitment to local service in chapter 8, and they highlight the efforts to reconcile professional education with the traditional liberal-arts mission of the university.

In chapter 9 Robert Sexty and Gina Pecore trace the growth of Memorial University's Faculty of Business. They employ Henry Mintzberg's methodology for tracking strategy formation to illustrate patterns of change. The authors have since reported that their charts have proved quite helpful during planning exercises within the faculty. After pestering from the editor for yarns from 'the Rock,' they have bravely included some anecdotes. Every university has gossip, odd personalities, and strange events – with stories that often grow larger in the telling. In a small institution, such phenomena are readily visible and a source of humour, but it is worth remembering that similar curiosities can be found in any organization. For example, from 1930 to 1959 the business school at Queen's was located in a former 'Home for Friendless Women and Children.' The well-liked and highly entrepreneurial dean during the late 1960s, Richard J. Hand, was known among his colleagues (but never, of course, to his face) as 'the invisible Hand.' To protect the guilty and avoid shaming the innocent, the rest of the authors have resisted the temptation to tell 'peachy' stories.

Crucial to the legitimacy of any profession is the construction of an association that represents its interests. Chapter 10 describes the evolution of the Administrative Sciences Association of Canada, which functions in a highly interconnected national and international organizational field. It has sought to build credibility for Canadian management professors by facilitating research-based knowledge as the core value of the profession. Like corporations in the private sector, ASAC has evolved through several strategic configurations from an informal framework characterized by personal interaction among deans to a large organization that sponsors annual conferences, lobbies governments, and provides collegial services. Despite major accomplishments across forty years, it has encountered substantive problems building professional legitimacy and facilitating coordination among Canadian business schools.

Barry Boothman concludes the book with his essay 'Canadian Management Education at the Millennium,' which assesses the 'state of the art' in curricular design and content. He surveys the different critiques which have been aimed at North American business schools since 1980 and argues that many Canadian faculties still have not adequately resolved those issues. Although the field in the United States has moved toward a core 'body of knowledge,' major gaps in curricular content still occur among Canadian programs owing to idiosyncratic interpretations by deans and committees. Boothman concludes by reflecting upon the factors which are likely to propel developments in the proximate future. Some readers will find his views critical and pessimistic, others realistic and forthright.

As Alice learned from her discussion with the Cheshire Puss, it helps to figure out where you are going if you know where you have been. Memory *is* identity: lose the one and you lose the other. This book examines some of the places Canadian business faculties have traversed in their search for professional legitimacy. We hope that by describing those efforts this volume will provide a basis for thoughtful discussions about how the knowledge base and its applications should be further elaborated.

NOTES

1 N. Glazer, 'Liberal Anxieties and Liberal Education,' *New York Times Book Review*, 26 July 1998, p. 6.
2 R.S. Gordon and J.E. Howell, *Higher Education for Business* (New York: Columbia University Press, 1959); F. Pierson, *The Education of American Businessmen* (New York: McGraw-Hill, 1959).

1

Culture of Utility: The Development of Business Education in Canada

BARRY E.C. BOOTHMAN

Angels and ministers of grace defend us!
Be thou a spirit of health or goblin damned,
Bring with thee airs from heaven or blasts from hell,
Be thy intents wicked or charitable,
Thou com'st in such a questionable shape
That I will speak to thee.

Hamlet, I, iv

Time, Time, my friend,
Makes havoc everywhere, he is invincible.
Only the gods have ageless and deathless life; ...

Oedipus at Colonnus

The emergence of managerial capitalism during the nineteenth and twentieth centuries was a complex form of social evolution. Modern corporate enterprise, which has internalized many of the functions previously carried out by small independent firms, has relied upon hierarchies of salaried executives to coordinate flows of goods or allocate resources among diverse operations, thereby substituting the visible hand of professional management for the invisible hand of market forces. Because this form of business requires more administrative positions than can be staffed by investors or entrepreneurs, the educational backgrounds of individuals have steadily assumed greater importance as criteria for hiring and promotion than personal connections or financial stakes. The effectiveness of the visible hand has required the formation of a class of administrators who are technically proficient and share fundamental norms about what constitutes 'professional' management. Although companies have carried out aspects of this process through seminars, conventions, or industrial associations, over time in North America much of the responsibility for management training has been delegated to colleges and universities.

Since the emergence of the first programs, business administration has represented one of the most dynamic fields of post-secondary education. It has proceeded through several iterations owing to shifting perspectives about the nature of management as an academic subject. The content, pedagogy, and academic status of this subject have received limited analysis, however, for diverse but mutually reinforcing reasons. First, histories about universities have tended to chart the parameters of institutional growth rather than the evolution of specific faculties. Most of the available chronicles simply note the dates and individuals associated with the creation of programs or the construction of the buildings housing those operations. Some authors still treat business as a subject which lacks the rigour appropriate to university studies and will not consider it a profession like law or engineering. Various historians also have confused the development of educational programs geared to the preparation of managers with commercial or industrial training, even though the objectives and intellectual content of each have been quite different. Second, although business history has attracted interest from scholars across North America, the locus of their investigations understandably has been upon corporate evolution. Educational innovations have not attracted attention except for a few officially sanctioned projects or overviews of intellectual trends. Third, most researchers within business schools have focused upon narrow areas of specialization and have displayed scant concern with the evolution of administration qua an academic field. Ironically, the faculties always have been portrayed as forward-thinking organizations that prepare individuals for the problems of modern enterprise. But while the members of business schools often stress the need to relate educational practices to environmental conditions, there has been a tendency to avoid historical introspection about their own activities. The attitude usually has been, 'If it's the past, you can forget it,' even though an understanding of longitudinal developments is essential for a realistic analysis of contemporary policies.

This essay consequently reviews the evolution of business education from the Victorian era to 1980, providing a background for the case studies that follow in this volume.[1] To anticipate the argument briefly, the field has been shaped by what can be characterized as the 'culture of utility.' During the nineteenth century, the emergence of the middle class and the transition towards an industrial economy stimulated demand for new forms of *useful knowledge*. Desires for vocational training were realized first in public schools and percolated towards the collegiate level. These goals conflicted with the emphases that had been placed upon liberal studies and the role of universities in preserving social order. Mounting demand from private-sector firms, however, led to the demarcation of business administration as a formal discipline between 1900 and 1930, a process which drew upon different models from the United States and Great Britain. Faced with continued opposition from other elements of the university community, the initial faculties legitimated their endeavours as the supply of *practical knowledge* and tried to rationalize the programs with the broader missions of their organizations. After 1960 Canadian offerings about administration multiplied and were reconfigured to meet demands for new types of administrative skills, as well as a drive by business faculty for academic legitimacy, shifts that entrenched the field as a form of *professional knowledge* geared to the preparation of managers and the elaboration of scientific theories about business affairs. This essay offers an exploratory synthesis, but it cannot appraise fully the intricacies of this phenomenon. The culture of utility did not so much represent an archetypal 'mind of an age' as an evolving set of beliefs about the appropriate dimensions of career-oriented learning. Over time, different choices were internalized in programs or habits of thought with a cumulative impact which shaped subsequent initiatives.

1. Useful Knowledge

The earliest forms of business education in Canada can be traced to the colonial era. During 1796 an evening school was opened in Niagara-on-the-Lake by a proprietor who offered instruction in 'any particular branch either in the practical or speculative mathematics,' including bookkeeping and writing.[2] Although citizens frequently professed a need for learning that was useful for day-to-day affairs, before 1850 similar private ventures were few in number and poorly attended, and rarely lasted more than a few months since formal education had limited value. Neither compulsory nor free, schooling was conducted within households by family members and tutors, or in towns by private ventures and religious societies. Children were brought together as individuals or groups when work was not required and given instruction about reading, writing, religious principles, and morals. The occasional student mastered more complex subjects and, if skilled or affluent, might seek higher learning in Great Britain or the United States.[3]

These simple arrangements were logical consequences of the character of British North American society. Population density, transportation networks, and income levels were not developed enough to support economic specialization. In most regions, settlers lived self-sufficiently as farmers or labourers in geographically isolated communities and, organized as families or with neighbours into productive units, laboured cooperatively to ensure their survival. They bought generic types of goods that required little special knowledge or skills. With the long-term expansion of settled territory, the colonies increasingly exported agricultural products or resources and imported manufactured or semi-processed goods. Merchants in villages or towns became key intermediaries for a complex system of exchange relationships, links in chains of capital and trade that bound Upper Canada, Lower Canada, and the Maritimes to Britain and its other colonies or the United States. They handled imports and exports, invested in new productive operations, and granted short-term credit for the right to sell the borrowers' output – sometimes gaining a dominant influence within local communities.[4]

Mercantile operations during this era typically were small proprietorships or partnerships located in a single geographic area and focused upon a single economic activity. Commercial enterprises often proved short-lived and, owing to a reliance upon long credit chains, had high carrying costs that left them exposed to economic fluctuations. With unreliable and slow modes of communications, prosperous merchants tried to minimize risk by elaborating contacts among different centres, networks of agents who collected information on business conditions and who built relationships with other companies. Management under these conditions was ad hoc, with success or failure considered a function of the owners' character – their acumen, probity, and caution. Record keeping, was employed as a means of bridging distances rather than a tool for coordinating productive activities. Accounting took the form of simple double-entry bookkeeping, with transactions recorded chronologically and with few attempts to collate data by subject or profitability. Clerks, 'black coat men,' were allocated minor positions and, if skilful, later might acquire equity positions or establish their own firms. Moreover, within these peripheral territories of the British Empire, norms about economic affairs were moulded by values disseminated from the imperial centre. The British economy experienced modest growth based upon industrialization via coal and water power during the nineteenth century. Technological development occurred as an accretion of improvements, often the recombination of known techniques, which restricted the need for organizational expansion or sophisticated practices. Business accordingly was perceived as experiential, a function of doing and not something which could be learned.[5]

The prestige of different occupations in Britain and Europe had been shaped by class origins and a loose set of cognitive assumptions. Trade and commerce, despite their importance, were viewed condescendingly by members of the upper classes, whose status was derived from agricultural property ownership or hereditary rank. For individuals originating from inferior positions, the primary route for advancement was to become professional gentlemen who, in the vernacular of the times, were 'regularly bred,' 'regularly taught,' and 'regularly educated.' This objective might be accomplished by attending institutions like Oxford and Cambridge, but the most utilized avenue entailed joining one of the learned or free professions: as divines, lawyers, or physicians. These occupations were treated as callings that served societal concerns versus self-interested vocational goals, and their members received honoraria or stipends rather than wages. A professional was considered an individual who conformed to norms of moderate behaviour and personal etiquette, not necessarily a person with expertise in a particular subject. A prerequisite for entry into the learned professions was a liberal education emphasizing the classical languages and humanities. These subjects conveyed knowledge about the past, mental discipline, and norms that gentlemen could apply (in conjunction with more specialized learning) for the welfare of society and thereby be entitled to assume positions of privilege.[6] Despite different environmental conditions, political authorities in British North America tried to elaborate an analogous system. A gentry class of office-holders and property-owners, along with a group of merchants and professional gentlemen, were to constitute the natural leaders, and below them stood an undifferentiated mass, 'men of the middling orders': yeoman farmers, shopkeepers, clerks, and artisans or manufacturers.[7]

By the middle of the nineteenth century, fundamental shifts in economic organization rendered moot the efforts to weave a traditional social fabric, a process that originated in the American republic and soon spread to central Canada. Urbanization and the construction of transport systems enlarged the size of markets, facilitating economic specialization and the growth of manufacturing. As the volume of transactions increased, general merchants, who had handled many goods within their localities, differentiated into brokerage, import or export operations, forwarding, banking, wholesaling, retailing, or commodities trading. Income disparities widened owing to the pace of development and concomitant shortages of skilled labour. The relative status of individuals frequently rose or fell even if they did not change their occupations or personal affiliations. Changes such as these were too vast to be accommodated within the traditional order and propelled an alteration of the social structure. Whereas an ill-defined continuum had existed between the ruling elite and the agricultural or labouring sorts, an identifiable middle class began to emerge, one which served as an escalator between societal levels. Members of this segment were recognized not by formal rank or wealth but by alternative (predominantly cultural) criteria: styles of consumption, assertiveness, and particularly a competitive ambition for *self*-distinction and *self*-betterment. Over time, individuals were perceived as belonging to the middle class because they had abilities or comprehended *useful knowledge* that generated respect from other citizens and that thereby permitted lifestyles approaching their aspirations.[8]

Trying to progress into the middle class, nearly every vocation sought recognition as a profession – including technicians, service functionaries like barbers or taxi drivers, and sports participants. Only a small minority succeeded, but by the close of the century government agencies acknowledged a broader range of salaried occupations including engineers, physicians, chemists, editors, miners, telegraph operators, public officials, academics, teachers, musicians, and even university students.[9] Given the growing levels of specialization, professionalism came to mean the mastery of esoteric knowledge about a complex subject by a sovereign individual. That person could release Nature's potential in constructive ways through the mental design of *scientifically* educated intelligence: the rules, theories, or principles that pertained to a specialty as opposed to an artisan's reliance upon mechanical procedures, anecdotal data, or instrumental applications. This reorientation required the supply of services based upon efficient methods and objective appraisals which provided value to clients. The members of professions increasingly claimed jurisdiction over different tasks because their knowledge was derived from prescribed regimens of learning. Social acceptance of their authority became strongest when a consensus emerged about the dimensions of that education and the relevant occupational norms.[10]

The number of professional associations grew sharply in North America after 1850 and their participants soon raised the criteria for membership or advancement. By organizing into associations, different occupational groups simultaneously attempted to control entry and competition, define standards for accreditation, and (through rituals, awards, or jargon) create an aura of exclusivity that reinforced their perceived authority to the uninitiated. Under ideal conditions, skills thus would matter rather than birth, knowledge rather than connection, competence rather than patronage. Higher education was particularly valued as a criterion for professionalism because it levelled a society vertically upward, allowing hard-working meritorious individuals to establish their credentials and gain positions in the middle class. Indeed, as the cachet became expert knowledge, aspiring individuals demanded learning that might be applied during their careers, and thereby broadened the intellectual foundations of professionalism from classical languages and humanities to other scientifically or rationally coherent programs of study.[11]

A greater role for formal education was concurrently propelled by industrialization. In traditional craft operations, workers had been pledged to masters and during their service learned about the varied activities of a trade: the supply of raw materials, the techniques of hand fabrication, and the distribution of finished goods. But across the nineteenth century a transition towards machine-based techniques and large batch output was facilitated by the exploitation of water and coal power. As factories expanded in size, machine workers tended to deal only with specific tasks. The owners of the larger factories usually did not feel they had obligations to ensure the education of their employees and often were able to employ forms of unskilled labour in productive operations. 'The old plan of apprenticeship, by which a young man was taught his trade, has disappeared and we have nothing in our industrial system to take its place,' noted the Royal Commission on the Relations of Labour and Capital during 1889. 'To be successful competitors with foreign manufacturers we must have workmen as highly skilled in their respective callings as those with whom they have to compete.' 'It would be a misfortune to the country at large to continue in the present line. An effort should be made to instil in the minds of the young a preference for industrial advocations rather than the over-stocked professional and commercial callings.' Reflecting the views of numerous witnesses, the commissioners suggested the introduction of practical subjects in the curriculum of public schools could enhance long-term economic growth. It 'will increase the prosperity of the working classes and will elevate their social position,' for 'the moral effects of such training are good. Improving a workingman's position will make him more contented and happy.'[12]

These social and economic concerns significantly influenced the efforts to construct an educational infrastructure, a phenomenon that first occurred in Ontario, the emergent heartland of the Canadian economy.[13] Like most Victorians, the promoters of this system assumed society would progress in a liberal manner with economic growth and the prospect of upward mobility. Canadians either would become 'a virtuous, intelligent, happy and prosperous people,' claimed Ontario's Superintendent of Schools, Egerton Ryerson, or 'the outskirt hewers of wood and drawers of water.' For 'these hard times of sharp and skilful competition and sleepless activity,' education as well as enterprise was required. Why should a mechanic be 'a mere operative at his bench or anvil, when by the higher powers of a cultivated mind, he might equally contribute to his country's wealth and advancement'?[14] The accumulation of property was equated with civilization and perceived as the means by which individuals might join the respectable classes. 'What are the Mechanical arts of a Country, but the very arteries and tissue of its prosperity and civilization?' Ryerson observed. 'Not an acre could be tilled, or a bushel of grain floured ... without the fruits of mechanical industry and, in several respects, of scientific mechanical invention. Without her mechanical arts, – nay, even without her coal mines, and the skill to work them, – Great Britain would be one of the poorest Countries in Europe, instead of standing at the head of human power.' With knowledge, literacy and manners, a father could earn more, educate his children to a higher level, and enable them to achieve a better life. Learning thus would propel a self-reinforcing cycle of social enhancement, consumption, and capital accumulation.[15]

At the same time, the conservatism and hierarchy associated with an agrarian regime were still valued. Social leaders in Victorian Canada often decried the apparent obsession with petty profit or the loss of collective values that seemed to accompany economic growth. Canadians, Lord Elgin declared at the 1849 convocation of the University of Toronto, lived 'in an age and in a condition of society, more favourable to the growth of what may be called "acquisitive propensities" to the exclusive growth of the commercial spirit than any ... before in the history of the world.' It was crucial that the pace of intellectual progress should match that of the economy lest wealth and luxury 'like rank and noisome weeds' spread through society. Divine Providence, Ryerson contended, had 'marked out Upper Canada for agriculture,' and manufacturing or commercial activities represented 'mere offshoots' of farming. Like many of his contemporaries, Ryerson's attitudes towards commercial interests were riddled with inconsistencies. He portrayed businessmen as social benefactors in speeches and textbooks, but at other times (reflecting popular stereotypes) complained about how merchants did not value the 'treasures and pleasures of the mind' and denounced them as selfish or irresponsible.[16]

The primary objectives of education were portrayed as mental discipline and personal improvement, that is, the inculcation of work habits, moral rectitude, and the mastery of general knowledge. Although commerce was conducted 'by isolated individuals, or in small shops,' Ryerson complained, Canada would remain a backwater unless the attitudes and skills necessary for economic progress were generated. 'Even a mechanic ought to combine in his own person, the qualifications and skill of the European manufacturing Superintendents and Operators.' Otherwise, the individual might be left a 'mere operative' unable to maintain his independence or status.[17] Education and social rank hence were inextricably linked. The lower classes would attend common schools where they could master reading, writing, and ciphering, a level of learning that was expected to be more than most citizens would ever need. The children of the wealthier parents had more extensive requirements 'according to their positions.' Many required secondary education and a small minority might even join 'a privileged class' by studying at a university. At the same time, the promoters of schooling accepted the idea that individuals should garner learning according to their abilities regardless of rank. 'The choicest intellectual marble must be dug out of obscurity, and polished and fitted for uses the most honourable and important to the Province.'[18]

These contradictory values moulded secondary education away from the simple distinctions advanced by provincial officials. Students often attended grammar schools for two or three years before departing for full-time employment, and many stayed just long enough to meet the obligations for a third-class teaching certificate. Data about high school leavers during the late nineteenth century suggests two-fifths intended to enter agricultural, commercial, or clerical positions; 25 to 30 per cent planned to become teachers; while approximately 20 per cent or less expected to undertake non-university (probably professional) education. Less than 10 per cent expected to attend university and a very small minority anticipated a career in the learned professions.[19] From the beginning, local school boards took these goals into account and designed curricula with optional streams that enabled individuals to establish backgrounds for their intended careers. Those expecting to enter medicine or law found classical studies valuable for entrance examinations or professional accreditation; individuals wishing to apprentice in surveying or engineering emphasized English and mathematics; others expecting to enter commerce could take bookkeeping, penmanship, and English; and the young men or women who wished to become teachers themselves took a range of subjects. During 1865, attempting to reverse this trend and entrench a dominant status for classical studies, Ryerson linked provincial funding with attendance in Latin or Greek classes. This constraint, which would have restricted secondary education to males and eliminated many optional streams, was opposed by citizens in local communities and, under repeated attack, was eased and then eviscerated. By his retirement in 1876, the high school curriculum in Ontario clearly had a utilitarian, not a liberal, orientation with subjects such as physical education, sciences, and commercial studies, which were rationalized as beneficial for all students.[20]

Bookkeeping was introduced as early as 1850, followed by courses in penmanship. These were legitimated initially as pragmatic topics that met the needs of middle-class male students, but were extended as the economy became more sophisticated, since farmers, lawyers, and other occupations had to keep records or engage in commercial transactions. Because 'the subjects of a commercial course are practical,' Ontario's education ministry remarked, 'many parents believe that if their children take them at school, they will be in a better position to earn a livelihood.'[21] Twenty-three per cent of the students in grammar schools took bookkeeping during 1867, a share that rose to 45 per cent by 1882 and 82 per cent by 1887. A two-year program leading to a commercial diploma (a terminal degree rather than university matriculation) was introduced during 1885, which later accounted for 14 per cent of all students. The Education Act of 1891 authorized commercial departments for secondary schools and the development of a commercial specialist's certificate that required the completion of nine papers for areas like stenography, banking, and drawing. The prompt acceptance of these topics was in stark contrast to the lengthy debates and resistance which greeted proposals for industrial or mechanical training well into the twentieth century.[22] However, the modifications continued to be framed by the goals of building mental discipline and personal ethics. The qualifications of a person in business, one observer noted, 'coincide in large measure with those which we associate with the ideal citizen ... honesty and integrity of character must be from first to last the distinguishing feature of the business man. Preparation for commerce will, therefore, insist with special force on all those elements in education which are closely bound up with the formation of character.'[23]

Similar initiatives were not launched in the Maritime or western provinces until the inter-war period, while extensive revisions were undertaken in Québec only after 1940, phenomena that reflected a slower pace of industrialization or clerical influence over schooling. In Ontario these actions soon proved inadequate for meeting the demand for business skills. Population growth, immigration, and the construction of railway systems expanded the size of markets, propelling firms to grow by expanding horizontally into new regions or by integrating vertically into marketing or resource control. Concurrently, new technologies based upon electricity and oil permitted greater economies of scale and scope in manufacturing and distribution. Firms became capable of dramatically increasing output, but this was not matched by administrative techniques, which had not significantly changed from the personal coordination associated with partnerships or proprietorships. Management, even for railways and the larger manufacturers, consisted of a few senior executives who emphasized financial issues or first-line supervisors who directed daily operations, and not the intermediary ranks of managers characteristic of modern firms. But effective administration of the larger enterprises required detailed records: cost analyses, productivity studies, and profitability assessments by markets, products, or services. As the volume of data accumulated, executives increasingly found it difficult to isolate relevant findings or to coordinate business units without rapid increases in administrative overhead.[24]

A partial solution was found in the redefinition of clerical services. Handwriting speed and the difficulties associated with making copies of correspondence had long represented practical restraints upon corporate size, but the invention of new types of equipment (typewriters, adding and punch-card machines) facilitated the mechanization of data recording and storage. Clerical functions then could be segmented into standardized tasks, with information compiled in organized systems and available in pre-determined formats. Among larger enterprises, white-collar activities assumed machine-like dimensions with bureaucracies for the processing of information. The total number of clerical workers grew from 2 per cent of the Canadian labour force in 1891 to 6.8 per cent by 1921. In particular, the share of clerical employment accounted for by women expanded from 14.3 to 41.8 per cent during this period.[25] Corporate officers perceived young women, with their longer attendance at high schools and superior literacy skills, as 'steadier than the boys' for clerical services. Moreover, reflecting gender stereotypes, they were paid less and treated as temporarily permanent employees who would later depart the labour pool. White-collar occupations thus not only expanded steadily but were segmented into two types of careers. Some men began in low positions but if skilful could expect promotion, while women and other young men remained at their tasks without realistic prospects of upward mobility.[26]

This change expanded the demand for functionaries capable of handling routine assignments like stenography, typewriting, and data storage – activities that could be learned as easily in a classroom as an office. Evening classes and lectures were available from Mechanics' Institutes, the Young Men's Christian Association, or religious schools, but the demand was serviced principally by private enterprises. 'Commercial colleges' emerged in American cities during the 1830s and the British Canadian Commercial College, the initial Canadian enterprise, opened in Toronto during 1860. By 1868 five more colleges had been set up in locations like Ottawa, Belleville, Hamilton, and London; and in 1887 the Central Business College was established in Toronto, the first of a successful chain owned by William H. Shaw. Few of the organizations operated outside central Canada before the turn of the century, but by 1910 they were well established in cities such as Vancouver and Halifax. Since clerical apprenticeship had declined with industrialization, the colleges offered a simple form of remedial supply. Initially catering to young men, the curriculum consisted of commercial arithmetic, elementary bookkeeping, or ornamental penmanship. After 1890 the majority of the enrolment was female and typewriting, phonography (shorthand), or secretarial services became the most popular offerings. Simple instruction was carried out by a teacher in a room filled with chairs and tables, often with materials prepared by local accountants.[27]

Commercial colleges claimed to offer distinctive advantages over public school education. 'No theory is learned that is not made a subject of actual business practice' owing to the presence of specialized instructors, a promotional brochure from one school declared. Another claimed that 'every dollar of tuition money paid to us will be refunded to any graduate whom we fail to place in a position.'[28] The Canadian Literary Institute, which was affiliated with the University of Toronto, supplied a course called 'Actual Business' as 'universal capital.' Students assumed the responsibility of conducting a business, including the handling of cash, blank notes, cheques, invoices, account sales, and certificates of deposit. Each student as a merchant bought and sold on an open account by giving and receiving notes and drawing or accepting drafts. Candidates received lessons in bookkeeping, arithmetic, penmanship, and commercial law. The aim was 'to impart such instruction as shall enable our students worthily to occupy the most responsible positions to which they may be called in the business world.'[29] Toronto's Central Business College was portrayed as a firm operated by entrepreneurs who had 'the spirit with which all successful businessmen and women are imbued.' Since the college was open all year rather than closed during the summer, students could take short flexible offerings with no requirements for entrance examinations or the completion of high school. Unlike the emphasis which public institutions placed upon mental discipline, the principal of the Central Business College declared, the organizations supplied training 'recognized as being of real practical value' to students 'who would qualify through it for a particular calling' and be ensured of employment through their placement services. 'So long as there are business positions to be filled and young people anxious to qualify for them, so long will there be business schools ... A boy leaves public school with a vague notion that he knows something, but he can do nothing. A six or twelve months' course in a business college fits him to take a position as a stenographer or as a bookkeeper at seven or eight dollars a month, and he is off to a good start. That boy will always be an advertisement for his school.'[30]

By 1900 approximately 400 commercial colleges operated in the United States with over 110,000 registered students, including 65,000 men and 35,000 women. Nearly four-fifths of the students attended day classes, indicating that the enterprises were considered reasonable alternatives to high schools or private academies. In Canada during 1921 (the first year the organizations were reliably surveyed), 140 colleges had an aggregate enrolment of 26,669 students, of whom 15,244 were female and 11,245 male.[31] Young men found them convenient vehicles for garnering rudimentary skills and access to employment. For young women, the colleges represented one of the few routes to office occupations that offered clean, safe environments and permitted the accumulation of savings. Wages for clerical employees were marginally adequate to support a middle-class lifestyle during the nineteenth century. Although earnings relative to other occupations deteriorated as the white-collar workforce expanded and the disparities between male and female employees widened, the average compensation for clerical occupations in Canada remained above that for employees of industrial firms until 1931 and it stayed higher than the labour average until 1941. Clerical work, the Minimum Wage Board of British Columbia thus noted, 'stands out above all others as offering the best wages to the greatest number of employees.'[32] Commercial colleges also attracted support from interests such as the Canadian Manufacturers' Association, the National Council of Women, and the Young Women's Christian Association, who promoted the services as means of preparing men and women for urban life and avoiding the crime, poverty, or degradation supposedly to be encountered there.[33]

Representatives of the colleges formed the Business Educators' Association during 1896 as a vehicle for standardizing courses, examinations, and diploma requirements, as well as garnering professional legitimacy. Only a small minority of the enterprises became affiliated with the organization, and professional educators were inclined to disparage the colleges because the instruction lacked intellectual content or was not subject to the review processes created for public schools. With scarce resources and low salaries for instructors, Ontario's Superintendent of Education suggested, the colleges had inconsistent standards and, in their zeal to attract students, advertised fictitious departments that promised better services than could be delivered.[34] By 1915, twenty-eight schools or colleges taught stenography in Toronto, producing over two thousand stenographers annually. Only 10 per cent of the candidates remained long enough to receive a certificate. The market was 'over-crowded with young, inefficient, poorly trained workers,' one study commented, 'since anyone could rent a room and start a business college.' With the greater complexity of corporate activities, employment agencies considered several years of high school inadequate even for secretarial work. 'The standard spoken of as desirable in order to secure the best advantages for the occupation is university matriculation, or three years in a high school, and nine months' or a year's training in a business college. The average girl requires one year's work in an office position in addition before she can be regarded as an efficient stenographer.' Employees who learned typewriting from public schools were 'not suited to office work, but can work in mail order departments and in other offices, fyling, addressing envelopes, etc.'[35]

Commercial training was never confused with the education of managers. Reflecting attitudes within the private sector, Edmund J. James, who founded the business program at the University of Chicago, noted the commercial colleges and secondary schools supplied knowledge that, 'however valuable in itself, does not suffice to fit a young man for the struggle of commercial life, for the wise management of a private estate or for efficient public service.'[36] By the turn of the century, especially in the financial sectors, Canadian firms launched their own initiatives to develop administrators. The life insurance companies, for instance, organized seminars and annual conventions to appraise financial or marketing techniques, while their executives coordinated courses and examinations for the accreditation of actuaries. Moreover, general publications increasingly characterized management as an intellectual endeavour where corporate officers had to eliminate confusion, oversight, or a lack of control among business units in order to achieve organizational efficiency. These goals could be accomplished if they stepped back from the normal preoccupation with daily tasks to consider the nature of management. By elaborating a system or method that monitored and evaluated performance at each level of an enterprise, executives could transcend individual activities for the achievement of collective efforts. Originating first in American engineering journals, these notions were popularized by Arch W. Shaw's *System*, the predecessor of *Business Week*, and appeared in Canadian publications after 1900. The *Monetary Times* regularly published articles about the need for professional management, especially in life insurance, while *Canadian Railroads* discussed ways of gathering, analysing, and transmitting information. This perspective, with its emphasis upon the roles of executives, was quite distinct from the concept of scientific management later advanced by Frederick Taylor, which stressed productive efficiency.[37]

Movement towards post-secondary programs that had an analogous orientation proved lengthy and difficult. Given the nature of economic activities, a high school education was considered sufficient for advancement even to the senior levels of firms. Only a very small minority of high school graduates, usually the children of wealthy or professional families, attended universities. With the conspicuous exception of the University of Toronto, most Canadian institutions retained religious affiliations that shaped their operations until the end of the nineteenth century. The central mission of a university was defined as the preservation of a morally sound social order, a goal accomplished not only through exposure to the 'culture of the ages' but by church sermons, fatherly lectures from professors, and detailed regulation of campus life. Each institution offered a curriculum, dominated by the humanities, aimed at developing mental discipline and balanced character. Courses followed a philosophical orientation and were handled by generalist faculty who had limited research obligations.[38] As Canadian society became more complex, university faculty repetitiously tried to legitimate this approach, claiming that they perpetuated cultural memory and kept alive 'the notion of a community of values' through a dissemination of the concepts and beliefs of major writers.[39]

Business-related courses hence were relatively unknown at the collegiate level. Ryerson had suggested political economy might be added to the curriculum as 'the science of national wealth or the means by which the industry of man may be rendered most productive of those necessaries, comforts and enjoyments which constitute wealth.' During 1844 a professorship in political economy was established at King's College, Toronto, to disseminate the 'theory of the pragmatic.' Instruction supposedly took an experimental 'practical' orientation versus theoretical 'book' learning, but the subject continued to be handled as training in logic, metaphysics, and moral philosophy. Occasionally bookkeeping was listed in a calendar or recommended as a prerequisite for entry. Victoria College, for example, characterized the availability of the course (along with astronomy, natural philosophy, and history) as 'proof of the eminently practical' instruction available to students.[40]

By the 1880s new beliefs began to reorient Canadian universities towards the pluralism of an industrial society. Philosophical idealists like John Watson of Queen's tried to reconcile the pace of social change with the Victorian notions of liberal progress and the importance of the individual as a moral agent. Those ends, they argued, might be realized through rational scientific inquiry aimed at discovering laws about environmental or social conditions, knowledge that individuals could apply to virtually all aspects of human existence. Concurrently, problems of civil disorder and class division stimulated popular demands for university faculty to investigate and find solutions for social issues. Under the combined influence of those expectations, subjects were fragmented into specializations and offerings steadily were elaborated in the sciences or new disciplines like engineering, architecture, and the social sciences. Whereas several professions had been considered suitable for collegiate education, services were supplied for more than fifty white-collar occupations by the 1920s. Various factors shaped the status achieved by each subject, but acceptance of its academic legitimacy required the establishment of a sound body of theoretical and professional knowledge.[41]

Queen's and Toronto established chairs in political economy during the late nineteenth century, the former appointing Adam Shortt and the latter William J. Ashley who was soon followed by James Mavor. An empiricist, Shortt did not believe 'in running a country or great organization on theory. You have to run it on the facts.' Ashley affirmed that political economy, if it was to have social utility, had to be predicative, using not 'the abstract, deductive method which had done as much service as it is capable of, but in the following new fields of investigation – historical, statistical, inductive.' Mavor similarly stressed impartial analysis that considered 'the dependence of the groups which constitute the commercial world upon each other and upon the public.'[42] They entrenched a more applied thrust for economics, placing an emphasis upon the study of institutional practices in the public and private sectors, but this did not translate into programs which provided training in business administration. Ashley later supported the concept of instruction for executives, wishing to 'make business a "learned profession" which would enable them to take a broad view of commercial operations,' but he took no action before leaving Toronto.[43] Adam Shortt feared the moral implications of segmenting political economy into components. Because economics dealt with production and the accumulation of capital, it could produce 'a tendency to regard wealth as in itself a kind of final object.' 'But it is not so desirable that this treatment should be elevated to the position of a separate science ... [T]he getting of wealth implies the using of man as one of the agents to that end, and we have constantly to ask to what extent this is justified. Thus the question of the production of wealth becomes but a subordinate part of some other subject concerned with the ulterior object of man in society.'[44]

Given these perspectives, the courses explicitly concerned with business remained limited. Dalhousie created and abandoned a two-year diploma during the 1890s, but substantive initiatives did occur in engineering faculties. Because of the strategic importance of new types of manufacturing technology, engineers often became middle or senior executives as Canadian big businesses first emerged. Courses about administrative issues accordingly were created as early as 1894, and thirty years later they represented a staple of the engineering curriculum.[45] For example, under the direction of Clarence Morgan of the New York Central Railroad, and with grants from the Canadian Pacific and Grand Trunk, a Department of Railway Engineering was created at McGill. Students took internships with the firms during the summer and were required to join one upon graduation. Although the program was terminated in 1916, it was considered a prototype by the founders of the Harvard Business School, 'just the sort of relation' they wished to establish with the business world generally, and 'a promising demonstration of the confidence of business men in the usefulness of university instruction.'[46]

The treatment of business courses at the post-secondary level was best encapsulated by the developments at Mount Allison in New Brunswick. Initially a small male academy (and later encompassing a women's college and a university), the institution was established during 1843 by Wesleyan Methodists to serve the Maritime region with instruction that might enable superior candidates to progress to collegiate studies. In 1874, in an attempt to strengthen enrolment, a commercial department was established under the direction of S.E. Whiston, 'a most skilful penman and accountant,' who provided instruction 'in the arts of merchandise, railroading, banking, &c.' Given a deep economic recession, one of the academy's publications declared, 'young men cannot employ these dull times better than in preparing to take full advantage of the revival of business soon to come.'[47] The department strengthened Mount Allison's revenues during the 1870s, but attendance dropped precipitously when Whiston resigned. With meagre resources, a limited program in bookkeeping and shorthand was supplied after 1880. A decade later, the ladies' academy introduced courses in shorthand and typing 'designed to meet the needs of those who wish to fit themselves for employment in business offices.' The commercial program was revived by a new principal with a 'business department' where students conducted imaginary transactions using Mount Allison currency and tokens representing merchandise. A one-year diploma course in commercial and secretarial topics was offered to men and women; but within five years the staff was reduced when new administrators configured the academy's mission back to liberal studies that would prepare students for university and prevent the emphasis upon religious values from being compromised. The commercial college remained as an adjunct, a source of supplementary revenues from certificate programs in finance, economics, or secretarial studies. Not until the 1950s, in response to growing demand from Canadian companies, was it abolished and replaced by a bachelor of commerce degree.[48]

2. Practical Knowledge

Although instruction about economics and business previously occurred in American engineering departments, the transition towards a scholarly treatment of management usually is dated from the establishment at the University of Pennsylvania in 1881 of the Wharton School of Finance and Economy, which was expected to provide business training for the city's social elite. Wharton, one brochure announced, would give 'young men special means of training and of correct instruction in the knowledge and arts of modern Finance and Economy ... [that] they might either serve the community skilfully as well as faithfully in offices of trust ... and aid in maintaining sound financial morality.' This message initially fell upon deaf ears. Only thirteen students attended during the first year and the program struggled for twenty years until operations were broadened to meet the needs of part-time candidates.[49]

After the turn of the century, offerings at American universities grew exponentially. Between 1898 and 1900 six institutions created business programs; 33 followed by 1917; 37 during the First World War; and 117 between 1918 and 1924. Many others added courses to existing operations, leading one observer to estimate that more than 400 American universities supplied business education by the middle of the 1920s. In 1915 there were 9000 students declaring the subject as a major; in 1920, 17,000; and during 1926, 58,000. The strongest indicator of programmatic expansion was the number of baccalaureate degrees awarded annually, which rose from 789 during 1916 to 1397 in 1920, 3205 in 1922, and more than 6000 by the late 1920s.[50] Moreover, at least ten engineering schools supplied management courses in 1922 and this number expanded to thirty-five a decade later. The scope of those offerings quickly broadened beyond production to include finance, office administration, law, personnel, and distribution. The Massachusetts Institute of Technology launched the most prominent initiative, Course XV, 'Engineering Administration,' which later became the Sloan School of Management.[51]

What forces shaped this phenomenon? During the emergence of managerial capitalism, aggressive individuals such as John Rockefeller, Andrew Carnegie, and Cornelius Vanderbilt successfully constructed giant business empires despite limited schooling. While prejudices against higher education took a long time to fade, these attitudes were less characteristic for succeeding generations of executives – especially among technology-oriented manufacturers. The growing importance of mass production and distribution had a dual effect. Through the exploitation of economies of scale or scope, goods and production processes became standardized, decreasing the use of skilled workers. But the construction of large companies also brought a rise in the proportion of jobs requiring advanced learning about scientific and managerial activities. The need, in particular, was for *practical knowledge*, learning that could be applied on a day-to-day basis. Higher education was indispensable for the new corporate hierarchies, observed the economist André Siegfried, and 'the time is past when a youth is initiated into business by sweeping out the office.' Wallace Donham, dean of the Harvard Business School during the 1920s, was blunter about the new reality. 'The banker today needs his trained statistician, his trained investment counsel, his advertising manager, and his men trained in engineering. He cannot wait for the long hourglass method of training these men by apprenticeship.'[52]

The development of business programs in the United States also was a consequence of a complex transatlantic intellectual exchange. During the closing decades of the nineteenth century a generation of young progressive intellectuals travelled to Germany for postgraduate education in economics. Having planned careers in the civil service, not in scholastic endeavours or the liberal professions, many found their preconceived notions overturned by German historical economists who dismissed the assumptions of laissez-faire economics. In particular, these economists argued for the positive role that government could play in industrializing societies and the ability of collective groups to overcome the 'inevitability' of natural forces. They also conveyed to their students respect for authority based upon expertise, the need for systemic research geared to improving social institutions, and the value of teaching techniques like seminars and case preparation. Upon returning to the United States, numerous graduates joined departments of economics and pushed for the revision and diversification of curricular offerings in order to better prepare the people who would handle public affairs. Their initiatives triggered extensive controversies among professional economists and were repeatedly derailed by older, more conservative academics. Many of the German-trained economists became convinced that a stronger social ethic within the business community and the development of research that might facilitate the accommodation of corporate and social concerns might be enhanced by the elaboration of courses concerned with 'business economics.' The supply of those courses, not coincidently, would also create a basis for an institutional framework from which they, as academic experts, could serve as consultants about social issues. Through personal action and lobbying, they thus propelled the establishment of new programs at institutions such as Harvard, Columbia, Chicago, Northwestern, and Wisconsin.[53]

Escalating attendance in accounting courses represented the immediate *raison d'être* for actually separating business-related offerings from departments of economics at many universities. Problems associated with corporate growth during the early decades of the twentieth century made the demand for personnel skilled in cost and managerial accounting seem unlimited. Strategic rivalry among large manufacturers was often driven by productive efficiencies that enabled firms to gain first-mover advantages. Successful implementation of those endeavours was contingent upon the elaboration of monitoring and control systems that employed a wide range of analytical techniques. Corporate growth strategies also compelled a greater reliance upon external financing of investments or acquisitions of other firms. To protect their financial stakes, investment bankers and securities dealers increasingly stipulated the periodic submission of financial and operating data. Regular statements and audits by independent agents were also mandated by legislative initiatives such as the Federal Reserve Act, the Federal Trade Commission, and income tax regulation. Financial accounting hence assumed a dominant status in the curricula of most American programs. Emulating other professions, accounting instructors quickly responded by elaborating a network of associations that stressed peer appraisals and technocratic expertise.[54]

During the 1890s in-house educational programs aimed at theoretical training and administrative practices were established by technological firms like General Electric and Kodak, ventures that later encompassed a broad array of efforts like General Motors Institute and the 'Flying Squadron' program of Goodyear. The National Association of Corporate Schools was formed as a clearing-house and medium for the exchange of information among these operations. Trying to delegate some of their educational services and to reduce the associated costs, business leaders soon lobbied universities for more symbiotic relationships. This did not amount to a sinister plot to suborn higher learning for a corporatist agenda, although some faculty certainly feared that might be the result. 'With the growth of the technical industries, the engineering side of the business was the first to wake up to the necessity of taking college, university, and technical school trained men into the business,' remarked Frank Jewett, the head of Bell Labs. 'The engineers were the first ones to organize college recruiting on a consistent basis, ... to create ... smooth working machinery for making contacts and getting in touch with the right type of men.'[55] In a modern economy, numerous executives believed, effective administration represented a means for achieving prosperity and harmony between labour and capital. Since colleges supplied training and research for other professions, analogous operations for business administration seemed logical. Affiliations with universities also might legitimate the claims of managers to hold specialized expertise and shared professional norms. Accepting these ideas, many of the self-made businessmen (including Carnegie, Vanderbilt, and Leland Stanford) who had disparaged higher learning became generous benefactors for new collegiate activities.[56]

American educators found these arguments hard to reject, especially as the children of middle-class families enrolled in ever greater numbers, and they responded with entrepreneurial fervour to realize the benefits that might accrue from a congruence of interests: higher enrolments, corporate donations, stable finances, diversification of curricula. Indeed, the pace of development was so rapid that in 1916 faculty from the leading universities organized the American Association of Collegiate Schools of Business (AACSB) to establish minimum academic criteria for business programs. By standardizing admissions policies and quality levels, they hoped to ensure that universities would retain a role as stewards for personal character and social values. This theme particularly characterized efforts undertaken by liberal arts colleges to reconcile the demand for vocational training with their traditional mission. The addition of business courses was rationalized as yet another form of preparation for careers and, in some cases, university strategies were totally altered. The most radical and popularly acclaimed innovation occurred at Antioch College – an elite cooperative program that mixed general education, self-directed courses, and employment at different firms. The school trained 'primarily for proprietorship and management, not for subordinate employment,' declared its president, Arthur Morgan. A college 'has certain points of resemblance to a factory,' and while 'the academic type of educator may object to this comparison, ... a study of the points of similarity might profitably be made.' Liberal arts colleges were especially well suited for preparing an output like senior executives. 'Violins can be made most cheaply in large factories but only the small shop could produce the Stradivarius.'[57] Some universities, of course, were not prepared to buy this boilerplate and faculty opposition repeatedly derailed proposals for business schools at Cornell, Yale, and Princeton. Nonetheless, Senator Robert La Follette of Wisconsin observed with considerable legitimacy that American colleges seemed to be 'cringing and fawning for the favors of predatory wealth. Big business must be cajoled and propitiated. Money however dirty or rotten is made a God ... it cannot be too vile or debased in its source to devote to the cause of higher education.'[58]

The concepts of Frederick Taylor also attracted the new faculties, especially after the 1911 publication of *The Principles of Scientific Management*. His work indicated the potential for research which would establish a theoretical orientation analogous to other disciplines. Since much of the business literature still took the form of anecdotes from executives or consultants, Taylor's work was especially valued since it offered a coherent schema. His emphases upon the specialization of labour, the roles of performance standards, along with the need for planning and communications had obvious implications for a curriculum. A brilliant publicist, Taylor popularized his ideas through books and speaking tours, generating legitimacy for the concept of scientific management. He was invited annually to lecture at the Harvard Business School and during 1913 more than five hundred students listened to his address at the University of Toronto.[59] The concepts from his publications were spasmodically integrated into programs, beginning with engineering faculties, then business schools at elite institutions, and radiating out to smaller colleges. But while instructors found the concept of scientific management useful, they dismissed many of Taylor's ideas as unnecessarily convoluted. In Canada, no university course focused purely upon Taylor's system, but his books were widely utilized in commerce, engineering, and mining.[60]

Considerable experimentation and little agreement occurred before 1930 about the design of business programs, the topics that should be included, or the content of courses. Even departmental titles varied: business, business science, business management, applied economics, commerce, administration, industrial management, and many others named after business functions.[61] Administrators at several universities (such as Harvard and Stanford) determined that management should be handled as a graduate subject, but this did not represent a practical option elsewhere. Most faculties were lineal descendants of economics departments, while their subject material and the attitudes of instructors encouraged close relationships with faculties of arts. As one study observed, private-sector support was essential, but the curriculum had 'to meet the demands or avoid the antagonism of the arts faculty.' The result was 'a compromise between liberal arts insistence and the business school judgment ... an academic structure lacking, in some cases completely and in other cases in certain respects, in coherence from either point of view.'[62]

In essence, baccalaureate programs had to provide a liberal education as well as career-oriented training. Curricula tended to stipulate extensive obligations in the liberal arts, and the key issue then revolved around the sequencing of subjects. The normal pattern followed a design elaborated at Columbia University that segmented baccalaureate studies into two years of non-business courses followed by one or two years devoted to management. The Amos Tuck School of Dartmouth College employed another popular format comprising three years of liberal arts, followed by one or two years of business. Comparatively rare was a design formulated at Wharton, which interspersed courses across an undergraduate education.[63]

Without a coherent body of theoretical knowledge, courses were added or deleted disjointedly. Often this proved to be a function of faculty whim, program size, or corporate interest rather than careful thought. Patterns can be identified among descriptive reviews of graduate programs, but the most detailed map of baccalaureate policies was a survey of thirty-eight AACSB schools published in 1931. Reflecting the importance of the finance function, 32.8 per cent of undergraduate class hours across the sample were devoted to accounting, finance, banking, and insurance. Economics accounted for another 11 per cent, while distribution (marketing, advertising, and selling) represented 13 per cent. The balance was fragmented across numerous subjects, but only 7.2 per cent were devoted to management (organization, personnel, production) and another 2.8 per cent to business and the public.[64]

Although perceived as avaricious money-grubbing even among business faculty, courses about investments usually were added to the curriculum by the First World War. Insurance tended to be a key component during the early 1900s, but appears to have dropped off after 1920. Courses dealing with foreign trade were available at California, Dartmouth, New York, and Northwestern, but the topic was rarer among Midwestern colleges and surprisingly not available at Harvard, Chicago, or Michigan. Only Wharton and Dartmouth apparently had courses on foreign exchange. However, many of the leading American schools stipulated courses about consular science since their graduates often joined the foreign service. Graduate programs also tended to require 'geography' or 'resources,' dealing with the raw materials and products from different countries. Law and marketing were normal parts of a curriculum, but many qualitative subjects later considered integral were unknown or rare: strategic management, communications, international business, labour relations, organizational behaviour, psychology, and sociology. In contrast, programs often included areas no longer handled by business schools: journalism, municipal governance, office and secretarial skills, railroad or utility management, and transportation. Numerous course titles would now seem bizarre to management faculty: 'National Efficiency' at Wharton; 'Industrial Values' at New York University; 'Materials of Commerce,' California; 'Drawings and Projections,' Michigan; or 'Household Accounts,' Oregon.[65]

During the formative period of management education, three alternative strategies shaped program development in the United States. Predicated upon the importance of the accounting profession, the exemplar of the first was Wharton, which shifted from an elite institution to a large operation with part-time candidates and extension services across Pennsylvania. Under the guidance of Dean Emory F. Johnson, the accounting faculty grew in size and distinction with highly specialized offerings. This pattern was then replicated for subjects like marketing and transportation. As one of most prestigious schools, Wharton was imitated by urban universities that serviced large populations of evening students and relied upon part-time instructors. Wharton graduates and former faculty members converted the programs at Columbia, New York, and Pittsburgh into virtual clones. Although the administrators of those business schools claimed to provide the best way for learning about the intricacies of modern business, critics often derided the emphases given to technical knowledge and courses designed for meeting the accreditation criteria of professions. When proposals for a similar curriculum were circulated at the Massachusetts Institute of Technology, an advisory panel dismissed it as 'largely devoted to accounting, and as such as little better than those given at the so-called "commercial colleges," whose principal province is to train clerks and amanuenses.'[66]

A second approach drew upon the notion that sound business practice followed basic laws. Recognizing the significance that scientific management gave to the division of labour and assuming business was really applied economics, various programs classified administration into different activities. For example, one schema, originally developed by the A.W. Shaw Company, divided operations into three divisions: production, distribution, and administration. Each was segmented into plant and production, which respectively had categories such as location, construction, and equipment; these were further split into topics like material, labour, agencies, and organization. Courses then were elaborated to examine the issues that occurred in the subareas for different industries. Assuming there was one best way to handle each task in a given sector, the pedagogy was descriptive and mechanistic rather than analytic. There tended to be considerable redundancy across courses, while the problems of a firm qua organization were rarely addressed.[67] The offerings steadily became more concerned with day-to-day operations, leading Arch Shaw to muse: 'I suppose, in a hundred years from now, when the work of the school is more specialized, we will have a professor of egg marketing, cabbage marketing, etc.' Major institutions like Harvard soon dropped this approach, but an emphasis upon narrow vocationalism became very popular among smaller colleges, where administrators wished to meet demands from local employers or students for job-related learning.[68]

A third strategy, which entailed an emphasis upon the development of professional executives and not the training of entry-level functionaries, emerged at the Harvard Graduate School of Business Administration. Executive conduct, noted Wallace Donham, the dean during the 1920s, was moulded by non-economic factors and entailed questions other than those dealt with by economists. 'We made the discovery that while two and two in mathematics may always be four, two and two plus the X of human relations and other "imponderables" involved in any situation is never four ... It gradually became obvious that a new conceptual framework was required.' Management education had to 'socialize the results of science' and create a 'social point of view,' which required a shift 'from the collection of materials for the illustration of known principles into the ascertainment of new principles.'[69] Leon Marshall, head of the Chicago program after 1910 and a student of the first business dean at Harvard, envisaged administration as a function of four interacting determinants: technical issues, value and price, social environment, and continuous change. Because these issues had to be organized simultaneously, executive action was analytical, not mechanistic, and education had to aim at, 'if not a science of administration, at least a scientific approach to the solution of administrative problems.' Since 'the individual will have little influence in determining any or all of the possible changes ... the slightest misjudgment of the actual course of events often means for the business but one outcome, failure. Woe to the business manager whose training gives him a static conception of business problems.'[70]

By the 1920s the orientations of Harvard and Chicago were almost indistinguishable. Each rejected vocational training in favour of the preparation of executives – with general management and marketing as the locus of the curriculum. Administration was presented as an art that relied upon cognitive judgment rather than technique. Characterized as an ongoing process, executive action entailed the pragmatic definition of objectives and the articulation of policies which directed corporate operations towards those aims. Since management was considered subjective and variable, the programs concentrated upon the appraisal of business problems, with courses that highlighted the scale of administrative questions, along with the need for creative thinking. Students examined case studies of different companies, industries, or business functions. This pedagogy was frequently misinterpreted elsewhere as non-intellectual and concerned with current practices. In fact, cases were not considered precedents (as occurred in a law school) but tools for training in logic and the use of information for decision-making. The method of analysis often was considered more important than the content of assignments: identify the true 'problem,' break it into constituent parts, assess the relevant factors, harmonize the decisions on the constituent issues, and reach appropriate conclusions for implementation. Business cases, Wallace Donham observed, did not lead to absolute conclusions but 'every fact of business which can be brought in is an asset to the student, giving him a broader foundation for executive judgement.' This pedagogy also had practical consequences, since it permitted faculty interchangeability among courses and larger classes than possible under a lecture format. By the late 1920s the small number of programs pursuing this orientation expanded the emphasis given to the human factor with courses in organizational behaviour and by importing faculty from sociology or psychology. The stature of these schools, especially Harvard, along with the body of research generated by their faculty, set an important foundation for the legitimacy of management as a collegiate discipline.[71]

Like their American counterparts, British universities also introduced a diversified set of offerings, but the acceptance of professional education for business remained limited. The two most ancient organizations, Oxford and Cambridge, had pursued narrow missions: cleric-run seminars for individuals intending to serve the Church of England or finishing schools for the children of the landed classes. Eschewing research and coherent academic standards, the universities were externally perceived as seats of idle frivolity, but lobbying from middle-class interests during the late Victorian era propelled extensive reforms that converted Oxford and Cambridge into professionalized institutions. Coordinated by career dons, educational activities were geared to the preparation of individuals for careers in the civil service at home or in India, colonial administration, and the liberal professions.[72] Not only did this reconfiguration fit the ideal of neutral service associated with pre-industrial concepts of professionalism, it also met a demand for competent administrators generated by Britain's imperial expansion, as well as the employment concerns of aspiring young men, who were able to garner a high-quality education but had little or no capital. Graduates from the institutions tended to originate from the middle-classes and to progress into public service. Initially, only a small minority went into 'trade,' but by the turn of the century the universities tried to attract candidates from business families and growing numbers of graduates undertook careers in banking, investment activities, and commodity or currency markets.[73]

Oxbridge remained firmly oriented towards the humanities, with an emphasis upon the delivery of a general education that would develop the leadership qualities of a social elite. From independent study under the guidance of tutors and an emphasis upon sport, collegial attendance was expected to impart grace, casual assurance, and a light touch of command. Selective recruitment practices facilitated a shift towards academically rigorous scholarship, but graduate programs remained comparatively undeveloped and studies that directly applied to business affairs were avoided. At Oxford, the economics faculty stressed economic history, classical theory, and the theory of wages. Alfred Marshall at Cambridge was able to segment economics into a separate course and a separate examination from the Moral Sciences and Historical Triposes. Determined to bring greater relevance and the use of scholarship for resolving social problems, Marshall introduced a curriculum for 'those looking forward to a career in the higher branches of business or in public life.' The program included political theory, the British constitution, economic history, law, money, and the conditions of employment, but Marshall dismissed accounting as intellectually disreputable and later questioned the value of applied subjects like commercial law. Concurrently, as researchers, Marshall and his successors slowly modernized their field by integrating classical economic theory with mathematical analysis and the abstract concept of marginal value.[74]

Demand for educational programs related to business, however, escalated owing to major disputes between employers and workers, housing and employment problems associated with urbanization, and deteriorating international competitiveness. This need was principally serviced by civic universities located in manufacturing and commercial centres. Institutions like the Universities of London, Manchester, or Bristol had established distinctive profiles from Oxford and Cambridge by emphasizing English and modern history, the sciences, or the development of expertise relevant to social problems. Their instructors began to service the niche of business education by the turn of the century. For example, the London School of Economics (LSE) was initially founded as an educational facility for potential politicians and not as a business school. Modelled after the École des Sciences Politiques in Paris, its programs were designed to produce graduates with the knowledge that would permit them to assume positions in governments and then tackle abuses generated by industrial capitalism. But, after lobbying by business interests, the London Technical Education Board tied funding grants to the supply of subjects like law, banking, or finance. A growing emphasis was placed upon the study of railway economics and the 'concrete facts of industrial life,' an orientation which was entrenched when the LSE became part of the University of London and assumed most of that institution's work in economics. Industrial relevance assumed greater significance with the formation during 1912 of the School of Social Science and Administration, which became a centre for a wide range of commercial subjects.[75]

The most prominent initiative, the Department of Commerce at the University of Birmingham, originated from demands by the city's chamber of commerce and followed a survey of American experiments in business education. The first professor, Sir William Ashley, an economic historian and the former chair of political economy at Toronto, believed the elaboration of university offerings might produce 'intelligent and public spirited captains of industry.' The Birmingham schema was concerned with educating 'principals, directors, managers, secretaries, heads of departments, etc. [who] will ultimately guide the business activity of the country.'[76] The program was focused upon students who were third-generation entrepreneurs who would inherit family businesses and might become the additional personnel necessary for those enterprises.

Ashley promised courses in 'commerce' or 'business economics' that dealt with trade or competitive issues and countered the anti-industrial bias often conveyed by public schools or Oxbridge. An emphasis was placed upon foreign languages and students were expected to graduate with a speaking knowledge in two or more languages. Commercial correspondence was introduced as a formal subject and students were made familiar with foreign economic literature and trade or technical publications. Birmingham was also the first British university to introduce accounting under the guidance of professional associations. Commerce courses examined geography, location of industry, advertising, and trade cycles in different countries. Other offerings included public finance, modern history, logic, ethics, and applied economics. Determined to strengthen the competitiveness of British industry, Ashley encouraged the development of courses that mixed economics and technology, and the school supplied tailor-made courses for specific firms. The staff produced numerous descriptive studies dealing with applied industrial and social questions, and Ashley was often quite blatant in his attempts to capture the interest of local manufacturers.[77]

The shift from economics to commerce was pursued at other civic universities with a diversity of offerings analogous to the range of offerings available at American institutions. Manchester had courses in banking, accounting, international trade, and railway economics that were taught by instructors who had been employed in those sectors. Leeds supplied a degree and diploma offerings with courses about languages, geography, accounting, and law in addition to economics. University College, London, had public finance, statistics, law, economic geography, competition, and combination. Liverpool stressed language and culture studies related to business with endowed chairs in Spanish and Russian.[78]

Despite these initiatives, programs about business administration remained limited in Britain until the latter half of the twentieth century. Enrolment was very low and graduates tended to go into teaching and research or government positions rather than business. Why did this occur? First, despite the spread of accounting courses, the subject did not evolve into a scientific tool for management but continued to be considered mere bookkeeping. Basic cost and managerial accounting techniques were ignored or not understood in British industrial practice until after the Second World War. Moreover, British accountants had organized into several respected and self-governing associations, but they usually were wealthy self-employed businessmen who, like lawyers, worked as consultants and not as staff for large manufacturers. Determined to preserve their quasi-monopolistic status, the societies resisted efforts to redefine accounting into an academically rigorous subject and insisted upon maintaining a system where several years of university studies were followed by a period of formal apprenticeship. Thus, most students continued to prepare for professional examinations through correspondence schools at night while also learning, willy-nilly, on the job as articled clerks.[79]

Accounting at British universities also was not linked up with a theoretical area like economics. Neither Cambridge nor Oxford would introduce courses owing to their supposedly 'vocational' character. Instead, an emphasis was placed upon neoclassical economic theory, which utilized a deductive form of logic and eschewed empirical research. Facilities for statistical research about industry also did not exist until the late 1930s and graduate students were rare because of a lack of employment opportunities. At the civic universities, scholars like Ashley produced numerous fine studies about business. These tended to be descriptive rather than analytical, and the applications often were presented in terms of their value for politics, not for corporate management. Even strong supporters of commerce courses like Sir Sydney Chapman at Manchester opposed 'trying to invent a new business science or ... teaching office technique on the lines of the "toy counting house."' As one economist noted, most of his colleagues caustically considered 'descriptive economics to be the domain of second rate minds, incapable of aspiring to the scholarly economist's highest level of activity: the development and perfection of the classic theory and the theory of distribution.'[80] This problem was reinforced by the strong sense of class elitism within Britain's system of personal or family capitalism, which impeded the acceptance of managers trained by universities. Promotion often was a function of status or of criteria like 'sound judgement,' 'courage,' and 'natural authority' rather than knowledge.[81]

The development of business education in Canada varied significantly among different institutions and was shaped by American and British phenomena. While lobbying by manufacturers for better executives and the need for accountants spurred the founding of business programs in the United States, north of the border the trend was shaped by the expectations of financial enterprises and their professional associations. Organizations like the Institute of Chartered Accountants of Ontario provided course syllabi and textbooks, but had left the learning process to individual self-instruction. Unable to meet the demand for better offerings and dissatisfied with the quality of candidates, they steadily delegated the responsibility for their programs to Canadian universities. For example, the impetus towards the creation of a commerce degree at Queen's was derived from a 1914 agreement with the Canadian Bankers' Association for the delivery of extramural diploma courses leading to accreditation as Associate (ACBA) or Fellow (FCBA). In 1921 the university also signed a contract with the Institute of Chartered Accountants that 'relieved the Institute of the labour of teaching students ... made the requirements for membership more uniform, and ... raised the education standards in the profession of Chartered Accountancy.'[82] Similarly, the Canadian Mens' Credit Association secured from Toronto's extension department the delivery of a three-year diploma course that led to professional accreditation. The Life Underwriters Association of Canada formed links with the University of Toronto and HÉC, while other initiatives were launched by the Society of Industrial Accountants of Canada, the Investment Dealers' Association of Canada (and its successor, the Investment Bankers' Association), along with the Certified General Accountants Association of Canada. These activities provided funds and markets for the universities, but when baccalaureate programs were elaborated they also propelled the curricula towards accounting, finance, and economics – a pattern replicated by follower institutions.[83]

Canadian faculties of management have long debated which institution established the first true university-level program. Queen's certainly launched the first degree at the baccalaureate level during 1919, but this should be understood as one step in an accretion that unfolded at several institutions. As had occurred in the United States, courses about administrative practices initially appeared in engineering faculties. The department at Queen's taught accounting and principles of employment for mining engineers during the 1890s. Toronto's Faculty of Applied Science and Engineering followed in 1906 with employment obligations that would convey 'some practical knowledge of the duties of the workman' for those intending to enter 'sales or other non-production departments.' Following the First World War, the curriculum was expanded to include economics, finance, law and management, subjects which were taught by the engineering faculty for several decades.[84] Across the twentieth century, those types of courses have remained an integral component of many engineering programs (as well as programs like nursing and kinesiology), but they have not been delivered by the instructors affiliated with business schools. Indeed, undergraduate commerce programs at English-language universities arose quite separately from the initiatives of political economy departments, and the approaches were institution-specific. Mervin Daub and Bruce Buchan carefully examine the origins of the Queen's business school in chapter 3, and therefore several other cases will be summarized to illustrate the variability of the endeavours.

A special committee of the Toronto Board of Trade during 1899 first suggested a major expansion of business and industrial education. Lobbying by the Board and the Canadian Manufacturers' Association led to the creation of a two-year diploma course at the University of Toronto in 1901. Rather than follow the emphases adopted by American universities, the bachelor of commerce degree at the University of Birmingham was employed as a model. There is no evidence of direct correspondence between James Mavor, the head of the department of political economy at Toronto, and William Ashley, but the Birmingham schema had been widely publicized. An emphasis was placed upon commerce, *not management*, with the expectation that graduates would be social leaders and proprietary owners – not salaried professionals, middle-level executives, or functional specialists. The Toronto diploma mirrored the Birmingham design with obligations in English, mathematics, physics and chemistry, economic theory, banking, transportation, public finance, the history of industry, commercial law, and two modern languages 'with exercises in commercial literature.' It supplied 'facilities for [the] training of young men who purpose entering upon a business career, especially domestic and foreign commerce, banking, or those branches of the public service ... in which a knowledge of business is essential.' However, the curriculum was less applied and retained a stronger emphasis upon public policy issues than its Birmingham counterpart.[85]

This program, one publication claimed, 'increased interest in the University on the part of the business community as manifested in many benefactions' organized by local bankers or members of the board of trade.[86] In fact, it was not popular since the course materials were handled in a traditional way with few variations for the candidates who planned to enter business. Only two or three diploma students enrolled annually, most of whom failed. Nonetheless, courses in actuarial science were established by the department of mathematics in 1906 and other options were added incrementally. During 1909 another two years of 'Honour Commerce' were authorized, a shift that triggered an expansion of courses in economic history, banking, and public administration. Political science candidates also had to sample these materials and were required to emphasize either accounting or actuarial science.[87]

Mavor was wary of proposals for greater specialization and insisted that the curriculum conform with the university's stress upon the liberal arts. Rapid increases in enrolment after the First World War compelled the organization of commerce and finance courses into a coherent program leading to a bachelor of arts degree. The university promised a mix of practical and intellectual development so students 'who look forward to banking, insurance or the work of any other financial institution, as well as those who propose to engage in some branch of commerce or manufacturing will each find among the options provided an appropriate theoretical training.'[88] In 1921 the Faculty of Arts also sanctioned a bachelor of commerce degree. The BA offered 'the advantages in general education of an Arts degree,' while the BCom. had 'instruction in those branches of education specially adapted to the study of business.' It supplied 'training for business and commercial life in general and at the same time to prepare applicants for the consular service, trade commissionerships abroad, for the foreign representation of Canadian firms as well as for the statistical and employment departments of large business houses.' Candidates were expected to demonstrate practical experience in business before the completion of their studies in the form of 'employment for a definite period in a commercial firm, public service or some business capacity.' A proposal to segment courses about commerce and finance into a distinctive organizational unit was rejected and the faculty decided 'it was not desirable to add technical or semi-professional subjects ... of a kind which would suggest any direct training in the actual conduct of business.' The program represented a major source of revenues for the department of political economy, accounted for one-fifth of its enrolment by the 1930s, and thereby facilitated an expansion of the number of instructors. Although courses were revised to reflect new theories and concerns, the design of the baccalaureate curriculum was not to be challenged seriously for eighty years: considerable economics and economic history, smaller amounts of accounting, language obligations, and few mandatory offerings in general management.[89]

McGill's initiative started analogously but then tacked towards the Wharton approach. During 1907 a two-year diploma course in commerce was established by the economics and political science department. 'Descriptive economics or commercial geography' familiarized students with 'the most important features of modern industrial and commercial organizations, including trade and transportation, the great wholesale markets, joint stock companies, monetary and banking systems.' Accounting courses provided 'a sound knowledge of the science of accounting' rather than training 'in the craft of keeping books.' Priority was also given to verbal and written skills in English and French, with an emphasis upon business correspondence.[90] The dean reportedly found this 'first plunge into business education academically disappointing,' owing either to a lack or preparation or to the course requirements vis-à-vis student capabilities.[91] Despite those problems, during 1911 a school of commerce was formed within the department and specialized courses for evening students were prepared despite 'protests from traditional faculties.' During 1918 a three-year program was approved leading to a bachelor of commerce degree. The orientation, the university declared, 'will be, as far as possible, of a practical nature,' with English courses supplying 'a drilling in letter-writing, precis-writing, and the preparation of reports,' while mathematical and scientific courses 'will deal in the fullest manner with applications to industry, commerce and finance.'[92]

At the small Western University (now the University of Western Ontario) the faculty tried to construct an undergraduate version of the

Harvard Business School. Although a philosophical course about economics and industry had been part of the undergraduate curriculum since 1902, the development of a baccalaureate program was a product of several reorganizations of the political science faculty between 1915 and 1919. These facilitated the creation of courses about commercial subjects and the formation of a separate department responsible for political economy, government, and law. The latter change permitted more applied courses to be elaborated, especially those dealing with corporate finance and stock market activities. Sherwood Fox, the dean of arts and sciences, commissioned a systemic appraisal of American programs, but was disappointed to find that the courses often 'were of a standard little higher than obtained in Canadian business colleges of secondary school level. No more than half a dozen appeared to belong to the university level.' Nonetheless, concerned that the university was 'losing students through not being able to offer a degree course in business,' he convinced the board of governors to sanction an undergraduate curriculum modelled after Harvard's.[93] A new department was authorized in 1920 after a meeting of the London Chamber of Commerce (attended by delegates from all of western Ontario's boards of trade and chambers of commerce) where the university's governors promised the 'most practical business education possible.' Fox declared the program would be similar to those at Toronto or Queen's but should stress areas like statistics and 'the principles of efficiency engineering.' Not only did full-time students want business education, 'there were doubtless many more that would eagerly embrace the opportunities offered in the proposed course.' With veterans and other young men seeking business careers, enrolment at Western could increase by 25 per cent.[94]

The department developed a program with courses in accounting, commercial law, business organization, efficiency, marketing, purchasing, advertising, credit and collections, and banking. A heavy emphasis upon practical learning soon became evident. University-educated businessmen, the university's *Calendar* explained, were not 'numbers' men who emphasized record keeping, since those bureaucratic matters could be handled by functional specialists. Rather, students were expected to master basic principles and comprehend the roles that each business function served in management activities. This pedagogical thrust became entrenched with the appointment of Ellis H. Morrow, a Canadian who had received an MBA from the Harvard Business School. Morrow immediately adopted the case method, a pedagogy which assured that Western graduates, one publication claimed, would 'fit into a business organization promptly and acceptably and with the ability to bring ... a university-trained mind that has been coached in the application of facts rather than theories.' The curriculum became far more applied than comparable efforts at Toronto or McGill – an orientation eulogized by the university's faculty and often disparaged elsewhere. Even theoretical materials like economics were 'not unduly stressed.' Instructors wrote cases about the problems of local firms, organized field trips, or enlisted executives as instructors. One course in marketing was advertised as 'largely handled by businessmen who will assign problems within their own experience,' while a finance offering had executives who would 'be frequently invited to lead the discussion on many of the problems submitted.' Studies in cost accounting would be carried out 'entirely in the field' and 'be of practical use to some business establishment.' This orientation created an organizational framework of mutual dependency. The cooperation of local firms was needed for the development of course materials and student employment, but the companies also gained access to the intellectual talents of Western faculty members.[95]

The program entailed work in all aspects of management including production, finance, marketing, and 'executive problems' (a precursor of strategic management). Morrow insisted that it lead to a bachelor of arts, not commerce, degree. Since the faculty operated within the Faculty of Arts, the students were expected to acquire a general knowledge of other subjects, and he opposed proposals for a three-year schedule that emphasized accounting. By dealing with actual business problems and reading the literature of business, Morrow insisted, students would 'cultivate a business point of view' and learn to 'think along sound and practical lines.' Ironically, at a time when other universities were deleting classical courses as entry requirements, Morrow demanded the retention of those prerequisites for commerce if the criteria were kept for other arts departments. 'With the elimination of the Latin requirements, every student in the high schools would automatically head for Commerce – "No, thank you."'[96] Increases in enrolment and faculty size permitted the establishment of a department of business administration during 1927. By 1931 students in professions like engineering could receive a business diploma after a year of intensive study. During the Great Depression the program was the largest offered by Western, one that was popularly ranked with medicine in status and reputation. 'More and more young men are entering univer-

sity hall with an idea of obtaining a practical training for a business
career' rhapsodized the *London Free Press*. Western's administrators
claimed that during the economic crisis almost all of the business graduates secured employment, a pattern that, they argued, demonstrated
the program's legitimacy.[97]

Owing to limited resources and internal resistance, most of the
attempts to establish baccalaureate degrees encountered significant
difficulties. A professorship in commerce was approved at Dalhousie
University in 1922 but was not properly staffed until 1930. The Vancouver Board of Trade unsuccessfully tried to mobilize support across
thirteen years for a program at the University of British Columbia. In
1929, finally convinced of the need for a commerce department, the
provincial government agreed to provide funding, but the operation
was so anaemic that when a new dean, Western's Ellis Morrow, arrived
in 1939 he did not realize there had been regular lecturers.[98] Most of
the other endeavours were geared to meeting the goals of accounting
associations. The University of Manitoba launched a two-year diploma
course in 1904 which ran intermittently with evening courses in 'practical' subjects and accounting. During 1917 an agreement was reached
with the Institute of Chartered Accountants of Manitoba for the examination of candidates seeking accreditation. Efforts to create a chair of
commerce were unsuccessful, and not until 1937 was a baccalaureate
program authorized with two departments: actuarial science and commerce. As part of a development of extension services and professional
faculties, during 1913 the Saskatchewan Institute of Chartered Accountants arranged for the provincial university to supervise its examinations, and a professor of accounting was appointed the following year.
Further discussions led to the creation in 1917 of a School of Accounting that had an annual enrolment of fifteen to thirty students, but by
1929 only fifteen degrees had been awarded. Despite requests for
courses in retail merchandising, accounting remained the only subject
until 1939. An analogous pattern unfolded at Alberta, which created a
two-year diploma in 1916 to satisfy the examination requirements of
the Institute of Chartered Accountants of Alberta. A commerce degree
was launched in 1926, but the offerings remained skewed towards
accounting until after the Second World War. A few of the religiously
affiliated universities (like Saint Mary's or Waterloo Lutheran) created
departments of business or secretarial studies to service local demand,
but these were clearly designated as ancillary to the basic missions of
the organizations.[99]

Since French-language universities emphasized classical studies as entry criteria for the free professions, few political science courses were available and even fewer in economics. Consequently, no obvious foundation existed for the construction of undergraduate business programs. As Pierre Harvey discusses in the next chapter, the founding of the École Hautes Études Commerciales, which was affiliated with the Université de Montréal, was quite distinctive, a case entangled with complex social and political issues. The school's design followed a European model – the grande école that prepared students for administrative positions in the public and private sectors. Here also, the problems of early development were replicated. Many of HEC's students, who came from the Ecole normale Jacques-Cartier and commercial or classical colleges, were described as 'assez mal préparés.' The lack of academically qualified candidates compelled the introduction of a one-year preparatory course in 1914. The school was perceived as a way not only of strengthening the French presence in the anglophone-dominated business sector, but also of preventing oversupply in the liberal professions. As late as 1921, the *Annuaire* of the Université de Montréal declared: 'L'enseignement de l'École s'addresse d'abord à tous ceux qui préfèrent se tourner vers les carrières commerciales ... au lieu d'aller se joindre à ceux déjà trop nombreux qui encombrent actuellement toutes les carrières libérales.' During the post-war period, HÉC (like McGill) garnered a secure market by replicating the Wharton approach, with evening classes and courses aimed at actuaries, accountants, and bank employees. The revised program promised that candidates would be able to resolve 'les grands problèmes économiques' confronting the commercial sectors after three years of studies 'spécialement réservées à la pratique des affaires et à la mise en application des theories étudiées précédemment.' Classroom learning would be reinforced with pragmatic lessons through visits to manufacturers, commercial museums, and conferences.[100] At Quebec the situation was even more difficult. A certificate in commercial law was introduced by Laval in 1908, but a 1913 plan to establish a chair in actuarial science was not carried out for eighteen years. An École Supérieure de Commerce de Québec was finally incorporated during 1937 and placed under the jurisdiction of Laval's Faculty of Social Sciences.[101]

As shown in table 1.1, enrolment grew across the interwar period, but certainly not at the American pace. By 1935 commerce majors represented only 2.3 per cent of baccalaureate students.[102] Without gradu-

TABLE 1.1
Canadian business programs: Annual full-time enrolment and degrees awarded,
1921–1991

	Atlantic Canada	Québec	Ontario	Western Canada	Total
Undergraduate enrolment					
1921	8	300	29	35	372
1931	108	416	222	137	883
1941	164	467	183	376	1,190
1951	444	1,388	838	754	3,424
1961	1,161	2,791	1,493	1,621	7,066
1971	3,483	9,833	3,615	5,122	22,053
1981	6,688	13,214	15,704	7,570	43,176
1991	7,498	17,606	19,435	10,268	54,807
Undergraduate degrees					
1921	0	10	2	0	12
1931	24	41	68	36	169
1941	24	58	82	99	263
1951	75	261	160	212	708
1961	143	485	280	235	1,143
1971	643	1,405	809	799	3,656
1981	1,018	3,432	2,992	2,058	9,500
1991	1,407	5,744	4,517	2,818	14,486
MBA enrolment					
1961	0	185	297	12	494
1971	63	325	680	240	1,308
1981	268	1,062	1,812	624	3,498
1991	463	1,714	2,359	1,048	5,584
MBA degrees					
1961	0	167	186	10	363
1971	21	252	641	221	1,135
1981	122	495	1,112	286	2,015
1991	220	1,051	1,679	475	3,425
Doctoral enrolment					
1961	0	0	0	0	0
1971	0	5	39	30	74
1981	0	79	67	18	164
1991	0	165	176	125	466
Doctoral degrees					
1961	0	0	0	0	0
1971	0	0	6	0	6
1981	0	4	14	5	23
1991	0	15	21	15	51

Sources: Compiled from the annual issues of Dominion Bureau of Statistics, *Chronicle of Higher Education*; Statistics Canada, *University Enrollments and Degrees* (Cat. 81-204) and *Education in Canada* (Cat. 81-211).

ate courses or a coherent body of intellectual knowledge, all universities encountered serious recruitment problems. The departments at Toronto and Western expanded in large measure by hiring their own graduates, while programs away from metropolitan centres relied upon part-time instructors or practitioners, but these patterns weakened the legitimacy of the subject for other faculty. Because the programs arose as extensions of economics departments and remained under the control of arts faculties, courses were weighted towards economic theory rather than business practice. Few faculty members were active researchers, and those who were tended to deal more with public-sector policy than private-sector experience. The bulk of the curriculum remained devoted to the liberal arts and did not allow the level of vocationalism that typified American programs. This orientation also matched a goal of the universities: character-building education for middle-class males. In the vernacular of the times, 'preparing the boy' remained the key concern. No university had a restrictive policy like the Harvard Business School, which banned women, but most faculty would have heartily agreed with Ellis Morrow that a 'Department of Commerce is designed primarily for men and in some respects is unsuitable for women.'[103]

Opposition to management education certainly was far more entrenched within Canadian universities than south of the border. At each institution, convoluted struggles unfolded between those who understood the desire for alternative types of 'disciplined intelligence' versus faculty who preferred to retain an aura of cultured exclusivity. For example, the principal of McGill, Sir William Peterson, noted in 1905 that the introduction of applied subjects was derived from a 'conviction that one of the most effective methods of strengthening industry by education is to provide the highest and most thorough scientific training for those who are to be the leaders of industry.' While the supply of those courses represented 'a good index of the marvellous development of the scientific and industrial activities,' no university 'can be in a healthy condition which is not spending a large part of its energies on those subjects which *do not* offer any preparation for professional life ... [W]e must not accept a purely utilitarian theory of education.' Many of his colleagues were less sanguine, perceiving the trend as just the thin end of the wedge. Sir Andrew Macphail, McGill's historian of medicine, complained about how the university 'has had hung upon it "faculties" of farming, commerce, music, education, dentistry, social service which is a kind of scavanging ... At one time McGill set the standard, now it is a mere imitation.' John MacNaughton of the Classics Department attacked the tolerance of 'crass utilitarianism ... The railway men are coming, it seems, into the academic fold; the bankers may follow – who knows where the process will stop.'[104]

The proliferation of offerings after 1918 intensified this angst. Reflecting the anti-corporate sentiments of many faculty members, the historian Frank Underhill claimed that only inferior students who had no cultural interests would take commerce, swelling the numbers of 'polished, well-behaved young Babbitts who are already so drearily a familiar sight on any big University Campus.'[105] Some administrators encouraged the programs as a new type of public service or as a means of enhancing revenues. Western's Sherwood Fox assured the Canadian Club that they would 'make a great contribution not only to Canadian business but to the life of our entire citizenship.' Others, like Hamilton Fyfe, the principal of Queen's, were caustically dismissive about the shift from older notions of collegial life. 'When a student comes to the university he doesn't know what he is or what he is going to be,' he told the Club. Tolerance of 'narrow vocational training ... may lead to serious mental and moral abnormalities. It may stunt his growth, and the whole object of university is to permit his growth ... The sham university that is out for immediate results and quick returns is like a glorified sausage machine which is going to chop and mould its product into various shapes.' Privately, Fyfe lamented to Queen's board of trustees that students perceived education as a mere business transaction, part of the process of building a career. 'The miasma of industrial commerce has soiled the face of many academies. They have adulterated the quality of their products and have tried to disguise the defect by advertisement.'[106] Dalhousie's principal, Carleton Stanley, cautioned against the deterioration of social values that would accrue from a decreased emphasis upon the liberal arts. 'We can and must wake up to the fact that this and other things of the kind – notably a similar dearth of Mathematics – means simply a lapse from civilization. Filling up our schools and colleges with alleged economics, alleged psychology, alleged sociology, in place of these fundamental studies is nothing less than the American "primrose path" to barbarism.'[107]

The faculties similarly faced scepticism from businessmen about the value of university studies. Not only were the education levels of Canadian executives appreciably lower than those of their American counterparts, many had strong biases against hiring college graduates and preferred individuals who advanced through corporate hierarchies by experience. Well into the second half of the twentieth century, Canadian banks accomplished this goal by selecting high school graduates and placing them in clerical tasks, while insurance firms recruited mature family men who had a background in sales. Letters to university administrators frequently complained about how graduates supposedly emphasized book knowledge, were unwilling to make commitments, or lacked patience.[108] Operating in a middle-sized and regionally divided economy protected by tariffs, domestically controlled enterprises were characterized by trailing-edge technologies and corporate concentration – traits which limited the need for best-practice techniques. Foreign companies dominated the leading-edge manufacturing sectors, and their Canadian subsidiaries often were branch-plant operations that lacked entrepreneurial functions like marketing and research. Paralleling British developments, the Canadian business elite itself consisted of a tight network of inter-locking directorships between a modest number of personal or family empires. It is important to grasp how small the number of managers and administrators remained. Census data for 1971 classified them as 2 per cent of all occupations, earning 2.6 per cent of employment income in Canada and 3.8 per cent in Ontario.[109] The growth of management education thus required a redefinition of the culture of utility aimed at strengthening its academic status *and* attracting support from private-sector interests.

3. Professional Knowledge

'We speak of "professional" education for business,' asked the authors of an influential 1959 study, 'but in what sense is business a profession?'[110] This question dominated the actions of management faculty members between 1945 and 1980, an era which differed significantly from the preceding period. It was characterized by a disappearance of overt debate about the value of administrative studies and a growing, if sometimes reluctant, acceptance of its academic legitimacy. Backed by government funding and driven by student demand, the number of programs, innovative course offerings, and enrolment grew quickly. Whereas the preceding period had been characterized by the lack of a consensus, debates during the 1950s shaped management education towards a form of *professional knowledge*. Business faculty seized the initiative in articulating a new scientific paradigm and successfully redeployed their activities with considerable autonomy from the influence of external interests.

Management programs had been geared to meeting the recruitment needs of corporate bureaucracies concerned with productive efficiency, but those endeavours fit poorly with the actual traits of business administration after mid-century. Large American enterprises were transformed in key ways between 1945 and 1970, patterns that later moulded big Canadian companies. In order to achieve satisfactory rates of growth and avoid reliance upon single product lines, many firms diversified into related or unrelated sectors. By 1968 fewer than 15 per cent of the two hundred biggest American firms had all of their operations focused upon one product class. The primary means for diversification was the acquisition of other companies, a strategy reflected in successive merger waves which have continued to the present day. Taking advantage of their unrivalled position after the war, many American corporations also rapidly expanded abroad.[111] Perhaps the most crucial long-term shift was a greater centrality for science and technology in all aspects of corporate behaviour. Wartime demands accelerated both the willingness and the ability to put science to daily business use. Nearly half of American scientific personnel were located in the areas of chemicals and electrical equipment before 1945, but during the next twenty-five years the scale of research and product innovation in other sectors widened substantially. Applications of new technology became key for successful companies: from research to production processes to administrative operations to distribution. Successful exploitation of those innovations required not only managers who were knowledgeable about scientific discoveries but also the elaboration of flexible administrative techniques capable of accommodating the faster pace of product development and strategic response. The strategic opportunities to make investments in production, marketing, and management tended to be short-lived. Once a opening closed, the managers of follower firms usually found the building of competitive capabilities vis-à-vis first movers quite difficult.[112]

These trends propelled a new phenomenon: the separation of top corporate officers (those responsible for coordinating and planning for an enterprise as a whole) from the middle-level managers responsible for different business units. As the complexity of corporate operations expanded, senior executives repeatedly suffered major problems of information overload. Before 1945, the head offices of diversified international firms rarely coordinated more than ten divisions and only the biggest handled as many as twenty-five. By 1969 numerous American and European firms operated forty to seventy divisions.[113] Since executives could not comprehend fully the markets or technological processes handled by many business units, quasi-autonomous subordinates occasionally invested in questionable ventures, rewarded themselves regardless of actual performance, or indulged in unrealistic perquisites. Corporate officers tried to avoid these problems by relying upon impersonal statistics but, owing to the intricacy of transactions among business units, cost-accounting data became less and less relevant for understanding competitive rivalry or for gauging performance. The problems arising from the separation of top and operating management was manifested by a logical concomitant: growing rates of divestitures.[114]

Moreover, before the Second World War, participation in securities markets was dominated by institutional investors (insurance companies, banks, or trust companies) and wealthy individuals. As late as 1952, only 4.2 per cent of the American public held corporate securities. Successive waves of mergers, acquisitions, and divestitures generated another phenomenon – an institutional market for corporate control that was characterized by purchases and sales of companies by investors who had not been owners or involved with specific industries. This development was facilitated by the growing importance of pension plans and mutual funds. Success for the managers of those funds was gauged by their ability to have the value of their securities portfolios outperform market indexes. To accomplish this goal, they traded securities in large blocks and made investment decisions on the basis of short-term performance rather than long-term competitive status. Those practices reshaped in like fashion the norms of the corporate officers who had to raise monies for acquisitions or investments.[115]

American firms compensated during the early 1950s for the problems generated by their growth strategies with executive development programs. At the leading universities, the changing shape of business therefore became a frequent subject for debate. A consensus rapidly emerged about the need for an analogous reorientation aimed at producing general managers rather than functional specialists. The apparent need was for a different breed, an individual educated with sophisticated analytical techniques and capable of seeing the problems of a corporation as a whole even if trained in a functional area. Peter Drucker, a popular management writer, best encapsulated the new wisdom by claiming that a leadership crisis confronted American enterprise. Promotion by experience simply took too long for individuals seeking to advance at a sufficient pace in corporate hierarchies, he argued. Senior managers were older than ever before, with an average age of sixty among corporate presidents and senior vice-presidents. The modern executive thus had to be made, not born. 'The analytical and theoretical knowledge which, in an earlier generation was possessed by only a few "scholars" in management, is a "must" today ... Yet, this knowledge and understanding are not normally acquired in the work through which the executive tends to come up as production man, salesman, accountant, or engineer.'[116]

This perspective was widely disseminated by the popular media, which quickly grasped the implications of the changing shape of strategic practices. 'The day of the truly professional general management man isn't here yet, but it's not soon far away,' suggested *Business Week*. 'That man will be trained for management in general, rather than in any one phase of business. He'll learn his technique in school, rather than on the job.'[117] The social turbulence associated with the Great Depression and wartime mobilization had created a wide gulf between the cognitive framework held by business leaders during the post-war years and that of the earlier generations. Numerous, previously extraneous, factors were cited as essential components for corporate decision-making by the 1950s. Extensive government intervention into economic or social affairs, for example, was widely acknowledged as inevitable, while organized labour had grown in scope and influence. Rising consumer expectations, ecological concerns, and the growing importance of international markets made earlier administrative practices or simple profit-maximizing objectives seem irrelevant. Rather, managers were portrayed as needing new psychological and political capabilities, and a baccalaureate degree hence was perceived as a minimum pedigree for entry into administration. This stronger emphasis upon education matched well the goals of the 'baby-boom' generation, whose members were looking for mechanisms that would ensure economic prosperity and their own career success.[118]

Proponents of reform argued that only a fundamental reorientation of the purposes and organization of business education would fit with this context. They derided the prevailing emphasis upon practical knowledge as reflecting a subjective and largely romantic view of administrative affairs. Instead, they assumed management could be developed as a scholarly discipline. Emulating sociology and psychology, business administration should be conceptualized as an academic science that employed objective techniques to identify systemic patterns and causal factors. If the locus of analysis was moved from individual cases to issues which confronted firms qua organizational systems, valuable results might be discovered that would abet corporate performance. The proponents of reform also assumed that the scientific study of management could be effectively taught at university if fundamental principles and theories applicable to all types of enterprises were disseminated. Faculty could best train students for their future responsibilities by conveying knowledge about quantitative or behavioural tools and by exposing them to economics, statistics, psychology, and sociology. Learning models and concepts from different disciplines, students then would be able to analyse relevant variables and identify solutions for organizational questions. To accomplish those goals, academic staffing priorities had to be redirected towards doctorates and the importation of faculty from other disciplines. With a shift towards a scientific paradigm, management educators thus expected simultaneously to achieve greater academic legitimacy, build a more exclusive profession, and satisfy the needs for private-sector utility.[119]

Owing to a growing wave of scholarship predominantly associated with Carnegie-Mellon, Chicago, and the Massachusetts Institute of Technology, many educators were persuaded of the potential for constructing a management science. Expanding upon techniques of wartime weapons development, scholars like Russell Ackoff and C. West Churchman advanced mathematical modelling as a way to achieve greater optimality in organizational actions. Operations researchers innovatively applied to decision-making situations previously esoteric techniques like probability theory, game theory, decision trees, and Monte Carlo methods. Unlike Taylor, even though his basic premises were retained, they tended to see a firm as an interrelated system rather than a series of isolated operations, and claimed to be uniquely qualified to integrate components into harmonious systems through the use of standardized statistical tools.[120] Observers thought this work might link up with a growing theoretical literature in organizational theory and behaviour. Drawing upon the ideas of sociologists such as Max Weber and Talcott Parsons, scholars began to probe the possibility that management was driven by identifiable and predictable factors (such as corporate size, administrative structure, technology, environmental conditions) or by fundamental imperatives (profit maximization, power, satisficing key organizational stakeholders). Herbert Simon of Carnegie-Mellon represented the pre-eminent theorist of this new perspective. Employing biology, economics, and computer simulations to develop a behavioural theory of the firm, he indicated how cognitive limits and different variables conditioned decision-making in systemic ways. Simon's research was paralleled by numerous other scholars, including Harold Koontz on general management, Douglas McGregor and Kurt Lewin on motivation, or Rensis Likert and Chris Argyris on job enrichment.[121]

Efforts to integrate these streams of research into the business curriculum were launched by various faculties, but the 1959 publication of two reports about management education accelerated the movement towards a new gestalt. The Ford Foundation commissioned and financed a study by Robert A. Gordon (University of California, Berkeley) and James E. Howell (Stanford), while the Carnegie Foundation concurrently sponsored a study by Frank C. Pierson (Swarthmore College). The authors exchanged information but reached independent conclusions that harshly indicted existing policies. Most business schools claimed to provide a professional education, but the studies found that curricular content and academic standards varied widely. Universities had not set clear prerequisites for admission to management programs, as they had for medicine or law. 'Business administration gets a much larger fraction of poor students and a much smaller percentage of the best students than do the traditional professional fields,' noted the Ford Foundation report. Indeed, 'the quality of a business school tends to vary in *inverse* proportion to the number of business courses it offers' Too many faculties concentrated 'their efforts almost exclusively on average or even mediocre students,' the Carnegie study claimed. 'Judged on intelligence test scores, undergraduate business students do not compare favorably with other important student groups.'[122] This situation was compounded by problems arising from inadequately trained faculty, especially the low percentage of doctorates and the use of improperly trained instructors. Many courses were handled by professors specializing in mathematics, economics, and statistics, even though they frequently had neither experience nor interest in management. Lacking qualified staff, universities also employed practitioners who supplied descriptive courses of low quality that stressed pragmatic guidance rather than theoretical analysis. Since enrolments would double or triple across the following decade, these problems were expected to worsen.[123]

A second line of criticism was aimed at the business curriculum. The number of mandatory business courses had expanded beyond justifiable limits, Frank Pierson contended, and standards for those offerings as well as electives should be tightened. Obligations for courses in liberal arts frequently were not enforced or students chose introductory-level offerings that had little relevance to business studies, thereby meeting institutional policies 'as quickly and as painlessly as possible.' In addition, while many faculties claimed to teach about fundamental principles of business, it was still possible to find ludicrously vocational offerings such as 'Principles of Baking: Bread and Rolls,' 'Freight Claim Procedure,' or 'Lumber Accounting.'[124] Gordon and Howell suggested executives needed 'breadth of knowledge, a sense of historical perspective, and flexibility of mind ... All this implies some familiarity with the more relevant branches of history, and perhaps philosophy, and some knowledge of the social sciences, particularly economics, political science, and sociology. Implied also is some appreciation of the nature and significance of scientific and technological developments.' A school that did not insist upon university-level science, mathematics, or English was 'simply offering a poor grade of education which inadequately prepares the student either for life or for a responsible business career.' Faculties had established dozens of minor fields of specialization 'that never should have been introduced at all.' 'It seems to us that the time has come to face up to the fact that "specialization has been running riot" in American business schools.'[125]

The reports advanced similar proposals for a curriculum consisting of three elements: a liberal education representing 50 per cent of studies, another 30 to 40 per cent geared to high-quality courses in administration, and the balance as a limited concentration in a subspecialty of management (preferably with half of that component in a complementary non-business subject). The mandatory component of business studies, approximately a year in duration, should provide a background in five subject zones: accounting and quantitative methods, finance and marketing, organizational behaviour, the environment of business, and administrative processes. Like others seeking reform, both reports were uncertain about the relationship between baccalaureate and graduate programs. Other faculties usually required training in a field before candidates could take graduate studies, but this conflicted with the preference of the authors to keep baccalaureate education pre-professional with a healthy dose of liberal studies.[126]

Each report was caustic about the research emanating from business educators. Gordon and Howell contended that 'more significant research of ultimate value has come out of nonbusiness departments of universities than out of the business schools.' Pierson suggested the research was 'heavily weighted on the side of description; much of it centers on particular companies or local trade groups; much of it is undertaken because of its practical usefulness; very rarely is emphasis placed on developing analytical findings which can be fitted into a general system of principles and tested in a scientific manner. This misplaced emphasis is almost as serious as the dearth of research itself.' The interviewees for the Carnegie study unanimously agreed that 'business schools have seriously underrated the importance of research.'[127]

Although some authors have portrayed the publication of the reports as a dividing point in the evolution of management education, it would be more accurate to state that these studies legitimated the direction already taken by leading faculties. Equally crucial were grants by the Ford Foundation for the development of programs at five universities. Although one (Columbia) proved an unmitigated failure, the projects provided models that other American faculties soon emulated.[128] After a burst of commendations from academics and practitioners, critics assailed the reports as unoriginal, overly critical, or biased in favour of the liberal arts. But the dimensions of curricula can be easily measured and the available data indicates a gradual re-orientation by American universities along the recommended lines. By the middle of the 1960s, most had increased social science, liberal arts, and science obligations to half of baccalaureate studies. They also reduced the number of mandatory business courses, along with the permissible levels of specialization. Descriptive and industry-related courses were phased out in favour of managerial courses that drew on the social sciences, quantitative techniques, and case analysis. To gain an aura of professional exclusivity, many universities adopted a proposal by Gordon and Howell that students apply for formal entry to management programs at the conclusion of their first or second year of baccalaureate studies. A handful of elite-aspiring faculties (including UCLA and Northwestern) went further and abolished their baccalaureate offerings in order to focus upon graduate education. The curricular guidelines were also adopted as membership criteria by the AACSB, thereby creating an institutional pressure for wider adoption.[129] The recommendations for new scholarly endeavours benefited from opportune timing. Within a decade, the construction of computing services triggered an eruption of positivist research predicated upon statistical modelling. Exploiting this new technology, management faculty in the United States redefined professional utility as meaning the production of scientific materials aimed at their academic colleagues – materials which steadily became esoteric and frequently inaccessible to business practitioners.[130]

These American developments occurred just before the scale of management education in Canada broadened dramatically. Between 1935 and 1960 offerings in business administration normally remained under the control of faculties of arts and, save for the addition of behavioural science courses at several institutions, neither their structure nor content experienced major alterations. Enrolment, nonetheless, grew across the period to 6 per cent of the undergraduate population at Canadian universities. Virtually every university created a business program by 1960, but only at Queen's, Saskatchewan, and British Columbia did the courses achieve faculty status, while at McGill, Western, Manitoba, and Alberta quasi-independent schools operated within the arts faculties. Twelve per cent of Canadian business academics had doctorates compared to a university average of 43 per cent in 1960. Somewhat younger and earning lower-than-average salaries, they were overburdened by teaching obligations and lacked support services such as graduate assistantships. Student-to-faculty ratios typically were twice the average level, a pattern which has continued at numerous universities to the present day.[131]

As shown in table 1.1, undergraduate enrolment in administration nearly doubled each decade between 1961 and 1991 until business accounted for 13 per cent of the full-time, and 17 per cent of the part-time, student population. Governments and university administrators anticipated the general growth that occurred during this time frame and responded with the construction of new facilities or universities. But, with few exceptions, such as the founding of York's Faculty of Administrative Studies, the development of Canadian business programs was not carefully planned. It was driven by escalating student demand and took the form of incremental additions of staff and courses that enhanced the capabilities of different schools. The number of management faculty members expanded from 107 in 1957 to 1100 during 1977, and to 2200 by 1991. Owing to institutional policies favouring other disciplines or the inability to recruit qualified staff, this represented a slower pace than the growth in student enrolment. Business schools frequently were treated by administrators as 'cash cows,' significant markets representing sources of revenues that might be employed for other initiatives. Even though 12 per cent of students were enrolled in commerce and administration by 1977, less than 5 per cent of the faculty, and 3 to 4 per cent of university budgets, had been so allocated. Business faculty still represented only 7 per cent of university instructors twenty years later and their operations probably received 5 per cent or less of university budgets. Indeed, course availability represented the main concern of administrators at many institutions, a goal manifested by a continued reliance upon part-time or less-qualified appointments. Despite these constraints, by the 1980s Canadian management faculty members tended to hold doctorates, although this trait was weakest among accounting instructors or schools located in geographically peripheral areas.[132]

The composition of the staff and student population of business schools altered in another notable way. Women represented fewer than 3 per cent of Canadian management faculty during 1961, but this share rose to 20 per cent by 1991. This proportion was close to the aggregate ratio of women to men across the instructional staff of Canadian universities, higher than the 7 per cent share that prevailed in the physical sciences, but lower than the 30 per cent rate that occurred in education and the social sciences. Most of the positions held by women in business schools were at the assistant professor level, however, and fewer than 2 per cent of full professors were female. The student population before 1961 was largely composed of white males, and women often were shuffled off to office management or secretarial studies. By 1991, women represented 45 per cent of undergraduate business students and 40 per cent of graduate candidates, ratios much closer to the actual composition of the workforce.[133]

The lack of planning associated with the elaboration of management offerings was a function of broader institutional goals. Between 1955 and 1970 administrators at Canadian universities took up the cause of general education that had been promoted at leading colleges in the United States. Trying to enhance access for more social groups, all universities abolished mandatory obligations for courses in classical studies and authorized greater student choice among programmatic offerings. Toronto, for example, eliminated its traditional honours program and increased resource allocations to general or pass courses. At the same time, to ensure conformity with the traditional function of preparing citizens for their social roles, the potential for specialization was restricted. Among business programs, this approach was reflected in regulations which tried to ensure students received a background in the arts and sciences and then a grounding in administration during the last two years of baccalaureate education.[134]

The executives of Canadian firms, which contributed extensively to the expansion of universities, saw no contradiction between this thrust and corporate needs. Most were convinced that an exposure to the liberal arts was as important for intellectual maturity as professional training. Growing rates of economic and social change appeared to suggest that no educational schema could fully prepare an individual for the unpredictable problems which might be experienced in the private sector. A 1964 survey by the Economic Council of Canada noted that 'companies are anxious that new employees have basic education which will permit training and retraining to meet continuing job requirements.' Reflecting a sentiment that often appeared in business publications, an article in the *Canadian Chartered Accountant* observed that 'in the future the profession will expect the chartered accountant to have acquired a broad liberal education through attendance at university.'[135] Rapid job growth seemed to ensure the career success of university graduates regardless of which subjects attracted their interest. Hence, while business leaders backed an expansion of management programs, they expressed little, if any, interest about the design or content of curricula. Those issues were usually left for resolution by business faculty. The major issues at most universities entailed practical matters: introducing courses, upgrading staff, strengthening curricular content, and raising entry criteria as well as academic standards. For this author, the case studies in this volume (particularly for smaller schools like Memorial, Saint Mary's and Wilfrid Laurier) summarize well some of the real difficulties the faculties had to tackle.

Within this context, did American developments, particularly the Foundation reports, have a significant influence? Curricular adjustments were consistently made on an institution-specific basis. The available records suggest that business schools, at a maximum, considered three or four 'comparable' programs when making their choices. While the Foundation reports were sometimes cited during strategy reviews, the adoption of their recommendations appears to have been an issue of whether those ideas matched the directions that faculties already wished to pursue. Among the case studies in this volume, the strongest influence occurred at Calgary and York where the faculties had recruited heavily from the United States and, not surprisingly, the reports were considered reasonable advice about what constituted a professional endeavour. The original design for the York program was modelled after the schema at UCLA.[136] Calgary, like Alberta, adopted the reports' guidelines and sought accreditation with AACSB as ways of building a stronger reputation. Publication of the reports was used to legitimate the need for program reviews at British Columbia, Concordia, and McGill, which led to an expansion of general management courses and areas like organizational behaviour, business policy, or marketing. In contrast, no real impact occurred upon the baccalaureate degrees at Toronto and Western.[137]

Among small institutions, which were concerned with meeting demand for entry-level positions, an emphasis upon accounting and finance was retained but was mitigated by the formation of new qualitative areas. This aspect is particularly highlighted in the articles about Saint Mary's and Wilfrid Laurier. In a similar vein, St Francis Xavier introduced a commerce degree in 1948 that emphasized accounting, finance, and economics. It underwent an explicit shift towards a managerial emphasis during the 1970s. Acadia also launched a baccalaureate program in 1953 that stressed accounting. The faculty changed the curriculum because 'a clearly perceived danger in teaching accounting was that of a drift to instilling a technical competence only, losing sight of any humanistic value-content and in so doing, separating Commerce students from the rest of the University and its Liberal Arts tradition.' They felt it necessary 'to balance the obvious need for a degree of considerable technical competence with a code for professional conduct and the realization that Business reflects expectations and attitudes that are not quantifiable.'[138] Among schools located away from urban centres, emphases upon accounting and economics often were retained owing to student demand or an inability to recruit instructors. Several other faculties (like Brock, Mount Allison, or Waterloo) have backslided to narrow functionalism and the supply of entry-level accountants.

Perhaps no development proved as intractable as the transition towards management as a science, a process which took fifteen to twenty years longer in Canada than in the United States. The European historian Robert Locke has legitimately noted that 'the new management studies paradigm is as much a cultural as a scientific expression.'[139] The traditional culture at Canadian universities was not supportive of scholarly research before the 1960s. As Claude Bissell, president of the University of Toronto, observed, the 'Canadian academic tradition was amateur and genteel; if you did not expose yourself in print, you were in a strong position to comment freely and sharply on those who did so.'[140] The practical difficulties associated with constructing management offerings compounded this tendency, since many faculty members lacked the time or resources for scholarly investigations, especially at smaller institutions. If a broad curriculum was to be supplied, then faculty had to be recruited from numerous disciplines: industrial psychology, sociology, law, management science, marketing, finance, and management. Lacking large indigenous sources of doctoral candidates until the 1980s, schools responded in two ways. First, during the rapid growth of programs, hundreds of potential positions could not be staffed owing to a lack of qualified faculty. In contrast, other departments had underutilized resources and, understandably, administrators hired individuals with doctorates from other disciplines to supply management courses, sometimes with deleterious results, since many did not understand the new theoretical literature or were unsympathetic to business interests. Second, some universities stressed the recruitment of individuals who earned their doctorates in the United States, but this generated an additional complication. Those faculty members usually maintained their professional credentials through American academic societies. Not surprisingly, their research appeared in American conferences or journals, concentrated upon American practices, and applied models or theories based upon American experiences. Management was researched as generically North American with the traits of Canadian business conveniently dismissed, a tendency reinforced by a lack of financial support for Canadian texts, readings, or cases.[141] The development of a Canadian association representing administrative studies, which Barbara Austin discusses in chapter 10, was essential for building professional legitimacy, but it proved quite troublesome.

Following a design from the Harvard Business School, Western authorized a doctorate of business administration degree in 1961. By 1969 Toronto and British Columbia established PhD programs, with specializations in business economics, finance, marketing, and organizational behaviour. York and the four Montreal universities followed during the 1970s, but the output of doctoral candidates extremely small until the late 1980s (see table 1.1). Most of the programs were not properly funded, with the consequence that less than one-fifth of the candidates ever graduated and often after a much longer period than anticipated.[142]

In no single area did management faculties establish their professional legitimacy as effectively as the supply of master of business administration degrees. Approximately one-fifth of the six hundred colleges and universities in the United States during the late 1950s offered business degrees at the master's level, but most of the enrolment was located at a small number of institutions. Nine universities accounted for more than half of the MBAs awarded annually, and approximately one-quarter of the degrees were conferred by Harvard and New York University. The number of MBAs awarded annually in the United States then mushroomed from 4500 during 1956 to approximately 60,000 in 1986.[143] As shown in table 1.1, Canadian full-time enrolment at the master's level in business expanded between 1961 and 1991 from 494 to 5584 students, or about one-fifth of all graduate students. The degrees conferred annually grew from 363 to 3425. Many of the leading faculties (notably York, Western, Toronto, Queen's, and British Columbia) put their best instructors and the bulk of available resources into those endeavours. If calendars and course syllabi from different universities are surveyed, it becomes apparent that after 1970 Canadian MBA programs tended to be the first locations for curricular innovations, the creation of new topics, and the dissemination of new theories or models. Between 1971 and 1991 the institutions offering MBA degrees nearly quintupled to thirty-three as even weakly endowed faculties attempted to tap a seemingly unlimited market. While this trend was propelled by business needs for professional managers, students increasingly perceived the MBA as the minimum educational pedigree for a career, a viewpoint fostered by the popular media.

The design of the programs closely followed the guidelines of the Ford Foundation report. Gordon and Howell identified three types of master's offerings: integrated two-year programs by universities focusing exclusively upon graduate studies that assumed candidates had not received baccalaureate management courses; hybrid programs that required one to two years of studies; and one-year programs built upon a set of undergraduate prerequisites in management. Both studies recommended the first option, which had a managerial orientation and stipulated a mandatory curriculum during the first year with analytical, quantitative, and behavioural components. Institutions offering graduate and undergraduate degrees, the reports asserted, had failed to differentiate course content between the levels. While graduate education had to cover similar subjects, the Ford Foundation study contended, greater emphasis should be given to problem-solving, integrative courses, and rigorous analysis. Paralleling their proposals for baccalaureate education, the authors advised against specialization (except for accounting) and suggested the elimination of vocational courses.[144]

Two cases illustrate the diverse issues associated with a transition towards a professional paradigm at Canadian universities. From its formation as a department in the Faculty of Arts, business education at Western had stressed several years of liberal studies followed by learning about administration via the case method. Graduate work for an MA degree with a thesis and a diploma offering for engineering students were introduced during the 1930s. Despite a growing significance within Western's baccalaureate offerings, the program was comparatively insignificant relative to the large institutions south of the border. As enrolment swelled after 1945, the university's president, Edward Hall, became convinced of a need to separate business administration from the arts and science faculty, but he also wished to ensure the program would remained balanced with studies in humanities. Concurrently, a report from the business faculty noted that other schools 'will establish leadership unless we take positive action.' Toronto would offer a 'full list of courses leading to a Master of Commerce degree,' Queen's 'has already established itself in the field of accounting and is consolidating its position in industrial relations,' and 'other universities are awakening to the possibilities of business training.'[145] A conference during 1948 brought together more than a hundred executives from different firms, and the participants agreed that a severe shortage of skilled managers had occurred. They called for graduate-level training in administrative affairs and suggested Western would be a 'natural location for a national school.' A 'concentration in one spot appears to be the sensible proceeding. Having regard to Canada's size, duplication of effort would be weakening.' The participants proposed the creation of a School of Business Administration as a distinct but constituent part of the university. If Western was to secure a leadership status, rapid action appeared warranted since Toronto intended 'the creation of an outstanding school of business administration' modelled after the revised curriculum at Chicago.[146]

The close relationship between the business community and the university was exploited to mobilize resources for new initiatives including new teaching facilities, residences for students, recruitment of faculty, and executive development programs. Formal establishment of a separate business school permitted the introduction of graduate training, and the first MBA degree was awarded in 1950. By 1956 approximately 100 students were enrolled annually. The number of students grew to 270 by 1966 and 500 by 1976, when Western accounted for half of all MBA enrolment in Canada, a share that then decreased as offerings were expanded by other universities. The Western MBA degree was explicitly modelled after the Harvard program, employed the case method, and heavily relied upon the American school for academic staff well into the 1970s. The graduate program eventually had nearly twice the enrolment of the 'pre-professional' baccalaureate degree as the faculty tried to position Western as a school known principally for MBA education. They portrayed the operation as 'Harvard North,' but elsewhere the appellation often was used derisively (sometimes unfairly) to denote a lack of originality in academic approach or a perceived weakness of theoretical research.[147]

Given a lack of Canadian programs designed to train instructors, the university was encouraged by the Association of Canadian Schools of Commerce and Business Administration to launch an advanced degree. Authorized in 1961, the doctoral degree in business administration was the first initiative of its kind in Canada and represented an internal source of supply for an expansion of the business school. However, it attracted considerable opposition within the university, including one prominent member of the arts faculty who claimed '[t]here wasn't enough substance to warrant a degree at this level in management.' Funds to launch the DBA had been expected from the Ford Foundation but initially could not be secured. Again the school drew upon its connections with the business community to garner sponsorship, arguing that contributions from 'associates' for research and development about business would be akin to the aid that the Canada Council provided to the humanities. After 1970 the Western business school's activities were expanded through the supply of research opportunities for business faculties in Canada, the preparation of teaching materials for academic programs and continuing-education, and the endowment of research professorships.[148]

Defining professional utility as the elaboration of applied services, the Western faculty elaborated a complex series of continuing-education programs in management training, sales management, production and operations management, management information systems, and international business. Teams of faculty members also offered executive programs in countries such as Brazil, Kenya, and China. Another well-attended activity, the London conference, was inaugurated to bring together academics and practitioners around specific themes. Nonetheless, by the late 1970s the Western business school still was known predominantly for the commitment of its faculty members to teaching and the development of course materials, not for scholarly research. A strategic plan proposed the formation of a centre to stimulate intellectual vitality and to attract the best faculty, but the necessary funding was not available from the university. After protracted negotiations and delays, a joint funding arrangement between the federal government, corporate sponsors, and the university led to the establishment of the National Centre for Management Research and Development, an institute that has since become known for support of investigations into areas like corporate governance and women in management.[149]

The commerce program elaborated at the University of British Columbia also had followed the philosophy and methods of the Harvard Business School, but slowly shifted towards a much greater stress upon scientific research. The curriculum after 1950 was reorganized to permit specialization in different sub-areas of business, although policies to maintain intellectual breadth in business and non-business subjects were retained. As at Western, the faculty launched a range of offerings aimed at meeting the post-war demand for skilled managers: executive development seminars; professional courses in accounting and real estate management; and specialist diplomas in hospital management, insurance, and sales management. A general course leading to an MBA degree was also approved and, in conjunction with other western Canadian universities, a residential institute for training middle and senior managers was established, the Banff School of Advanced Management. By 1955 the programs represented the third largest degree group at UBC and nearly 10 per cent of total enrolment. A distinctive Faculty of Commerce was formed, since the pattern and intent of those initiatives diverged to a degree that the arts faculty could not be expected to maintain interest over the complex range of commitments. Informally, a growing level of specialization was achieved through an ad hoc segmentation of the staff into divisions, each with a recognized leader.[150]

Across the post-war era, the senior administration at UBC strongly encouraged the development of research as a way of achieving academic legitimacy and of serving external interests. During the 1960s the commerce faculty nearly tripled in size, and increasingly doctoral-level staff were recruited from the United States. In response to the Foundation reports, the objective of the undergraduate program was shifted 'to prepare a student both for a future role in decision-making, and for professional responsibility in the supporting activities of administration.' During 1969 the undergraduate and graduate programs were awarded recognition by the AACSB, the first time a double recognition was granted to a Canadian university by the American association. Concurrently, some of the applied programs aimed at external client groups were phased down or transferred to an extension department. Although faculty policies continued to allow instructors different emphases upon teaching effectiveness and community service as criteria for tenure or promotion, revisions to the guidelines steadily placed a greater weight upon research and scholarly attainments. Crucial to a reorientation was the approval of a PhD degree. The program was explicitly intended to prepare candidates who could 'carry out research which contributes to theoretical knowledge or leads to practical improvement in business methodology.' Through training in the behavioural sciences, economics, and quantitative methods, students were 'expected to make a significant contribution to the literature of the discipline.' This shift was reinforced by the creation of an M.Sc. degree that permitted specialization in areas like quantitative methods and finance. The different initiatives converted UBC into not only one of the biggest business schools in Canada but also, by the early 1980s, an institution with a reputation for excellent scholarship in finance, transportation economics, business-government relations, and marketing.[151]

After 1975 the orientation of Canadian business programs shifted measurably, this time in the direction of overt vocationalism, a pattern that has continued unabated to the present day. The trend, manifested by reductions in non-business obligations and increased levels of academic specialization, unfolded incrementally as faculties successively revised their curricula. Discussed more fully in chapter 11, this trend was driven by student demand for skills which would ensure them entry into an increasingly restrictive job market. During the 1960s Canadian companies began to diversify extensively, and as tariff barriers were reduced over the following twenty years exposure to international competition led to a substantial turnover of the leading firms.[152] Under these conditions, corporate hiring practices were reconfigured to stress technical specialization (especially in areas like finance and marketing), even though senior executives continued to call for the preparation of general managers. This trend matched the interests of many Canadian faculty members since, with the new paradigm of scientific management, they could validate their professional credentials by broadening the mandatory curricula and adding options in ever more specialized areas. But in one sense, the faculties who took this path seemingly went back to the future, since the new curricula looked like the approach developed by Wharton during the early twentieth century. Predominantly intended for entry-level functionaries, the programs had sharply reduced obligations for non-business courses. Business courses dominated the curricula with high levels of permissible specialization, albeit in analytically intensive offerings.

Of course, not all universities followed this transition. The faculty at the University of New Brunswick retained a curriculum that mandated a general background in business and non-business subjects. At Trent, a liberal arts institution, a solid program in administration was created to round out the university's services and to attract good students, but it was delivered with an interdisciplinary orientation, usually by non-business faculty.[153] In a few cases, institutional inertia drove organizational conduct. Perhaps the best illustration has been the baccalaureate commerce degree at Toronto, which remained a joint offering of the management and economics faculties. In comparison with the degrees supplied by other universities and unlike the MBA program delivered by the Faculty of Management, the curriculum's design has not been significantly adjusted and has not required various topics in administration usually deemed essential elsewhere. As the history of the department of political economy noted, 'In very truth one could describe the B.Com. as an Honours Degree in economics, accounting and foreign languages, with options in finance, economics, general business, and liberal studies of many sorts.'[154] One of the heaviest course of studies at the university, the program became notorious on campus for chronic understaffing and a reliance upon part-time lecturers as the department diverted revenues to build up its research-oriented political science and economics personnel. The economics faculty has retained an effective veto over curricular modifications since the disestablishment of the department of political economy in 1982. Consequently, despite lengthy and repetitious debates, the only substantive adjustment has occurred at a separate division, the University of Toronto at Scarborough, where a provostial review sanctioned changes intended to give students a more holistic view of organizations.[155]

4. Capitalizing Knowledge

In this essay, I have argued that management education has evolved through three distinctive periods. The types of programs developed during each reflected the nature of business enterprise, the state of intellectual enquiry about commercial affairs, the goals of educational institutions, and the petty concerns of faculty members and students. Needless to say, the essay has highlighted overarching patterns and has not probed the more sophisticated issues. For example, there is little research yet available dealing with how fast ideas and concepts developed by American or British academics were actually disseminated in Canada. An extended analysis could also bring out more fully the comparative accomplishments and failures.

What implications can be drawn from the issues which have been probed? First, the development of management education has encountered considerably more resistance in Canada than south of the border. Canadians, it has been sometimes suggested, share less of the 'acquisitive materialism' associated with American culture, and this may be one factor that slowed the introduction of business offerings at the post-secondary level. On a more pragmatic level, vocational-oriented programs threatened the beliefs held by many academics about the proper roles of higher learning. Given the lack of a theoretical literature and a concise set of occupational norms, many members of the university community had trouble accepting the very notion of business as a profession. At numerous universities, despite advancing to the formal status of a 'school' or 'faculty,' Canadian business schools continue to deal with the practical consequences of this institutional resistance: archaic budgetary formulae, discriminatory resource allocations or research support. In contrast, their counterparts at American universities sometimes were created as quasi-independent units that could fully reap the rewards of their growth.

Each faculty passed through its own idiosyncratic evolutionary pattern, and cooperation in curricular development between business schools has always been rare. Canadian management education by 1980 had evolved into several generic orientations and curricular content varied widely. Ironically, by importing staff from other disciplines and the United States, management faculties may have perpetuated perceptions within Canadian universities that their field lacked coherence and definable standards. Unlike engineering or law, a Canadian association analogous to the AACSB did not garner the status which would allow the delineation of minimum criteria, or consistency, among business programs. Only in the latter half of 1990s, as the perceived legitimacy of domestic programs came under sustained challenge, was there a decisive movement towards accreditation or affiliation with the AACSB, a policy shift that included major institutions like Laval, Queen's, and Toronto.

Was Canadian management education truly professional as the millennium approached? Faculty members generally would have agreed that significant progress had occurred and the value proffered by most programs was being raised, but that systemic problems remained. Business administration was really a fragmented field consisting of overlapping subjects, since the curriculum had to cover a wide range of issues. The rigour of theoretical knowledge and quality of research varied significantly among those subjects, well advanced in some (like organizational behaviour, finance, and marketing), emergent in others (strategic management, international business), and still poor for some (management information systems, entrepreneurship, human resource management). The potential for inter-changeability of instructors among subjects decreased as the level of scholarly endeavour in each subject rose. Capabilities also varied widely among institutions, and finding an equipoise among the competing demands of research, teaching, and service proved elusive for most faculties. Canadian business schools had avoided direct challenges to their activities owing to the autonomy they enjoyed during the era of expansion. But the path to academic legitimacy *and* professional relevance rested upon two implicit assumptions: the scientific study of management could be taught effectively at university; and management could become a scholarly discipline that would benefit the private sector. By the 1980s numerous observers expressed grave concerns about the prevailing wisdom as scholarship became more esoteric and disconnected from business practice. By equating professional identity with academic legitimacy, schools of business administration successfully capitalized knowledge to build positions within the university community, but in the process they inevitably sowed the seeds of discontent.

NOTES

1 The author expresses his thanks for the generous assistance provided by the staffs of the libraries of the University of New Brunswick, the University of Toronto, and the State University of New York at Buffalo. All costs for the project, from which this essay and chapter 11 are derived, have been covered from personal funds and were not subsidized by any government agency or public institution.

2 Quoted in F. Vernon, 'The Development of Adult Education in Canada, 1790–1900,' unpub. PhD thesis (University of Toronto, 1969), 95.

3 See S.E. Houston and A. Prentice, *Schooling and Scholars in Nineteenth-Century Ontario* (Toronto: UTP, 1988), chapters 1 and 2.

4 D. McCalla, 'Rural Credit and Rural Development in Upper Canada, 1790–1830,' in R.E. Otter, ed., *Merchant Credit and Labour Strategies in Historical Perspective* (Fredericton: Acadiensis Press, 1990), 255–72. D. Sutherland, 'Halifax Merchants and the Pursuit of Development, 1783–1850,' *CHR* 60 (1978), 1–17. T.W. Acheson, 'The Great Merchant and Economic Development in Saint John, 1820–1850,' *Acadiensis* 8 (1979), 3–27.

5 P. Mathias, *The Transformation of England: Essays in the Economic and Social History of England in the Eighteenth Century* (New York: Columbia University Press, 1979), 94. S. Pollard, *The Genesis of Modern Management* (Cambridge: Harvard University Press, 1965), 90–1. D.S. Landes, *The Wealth and Poverty of Nations: Why Some Are So Rich and Some So Poor* (New York: W.W. Norton, 1998), 213–23, 282–3.

6 This discussion is, of course, a severe reduction and the following sources will be useful for those wishing more extensive appraisals. E. Friedson, *Professional Powers: A Study in the Institutionalization of Formal Knowledge* (Chicago: University of Chicago Press, 1986), chapter 2. S. Rothblatt, *Tradition and Change in English Liberal Education: An Essay in History and Culture* (London: Faber and Faber, 1976), chapters 3 and 5. R.D. Gidney and W.P.J. Millar, *Professional Gentlemen: The Professions in Nineteenth-Century Ontario* (Toronto: UTP, 1994), esp. chapters 8, 13, and 17. S.M. Blumin, *The Emergence of the Middle Class: Social Experience in the American City, 1760–1900* (New York: Cambridge University Press, 1989). A valuable discussion of pre-industrial attitudes is J.E. Crowley, *This Sheba, Self: The Conceptualization of Economic Life in Eighteenth-Century America* (Baltimore: Johns Hopkins University Press, 1974).

7 See J. Errington, *The Lion, the Eagle and Upper Canada: A Developing Colonial Ideology* (Montreal: McGill-Queen's University Press, 1987); J.K. Johnson, *Regional Leadership in Upper Canada, 1791–1841* (Montreal: McGill-Queen's University Press, 1989); F. Ouellet, *Lower Canada, 1791–1840: Social Change and Nationalism* (Toronto: McClelland and Stewart, 1980); and P.A. Buckner and J.G. Reid, eds, *The Atlantic Region to Confederation: A History* (Toronto: UTP, 1994). The emergence of the middle-class in Canada has not been well explored, but see D. Gagan, 'Class and Society in Victorian English Canada: An Historical Reassessment,' *BJCS* 4 (1989), 74–87.

8 Blumin, *The Emergence of the Middle Class*, 108–229.

9 AO, RG 49-19, 'Report Relating to the Registration of Births, Marriages and Deaths for the Province of Ontario for the year ending 31 December 1890,'

1892 Sessional Paper no. 10, table 26. Business people were not considered professionals by the Registrar-General and were placed in a distinctive category.

10 H.I. Wilensky, 'The Professionalization of Everyone?' *AJS* 70 (1964), 137–58. E. Durkheim, *The Elementary Forms of the Religious Life* (Glencoe, Ill.: Free Press, 1947), 208.

11 B.J. Bledstein, *The Culture of Professionalism: The Middle Class and Higher Education in America* (New York: W.W. Norton, 1976), 87–99, 106–13. D. Ross, *The Origins of American Social Science* (New York: Cambridge University Press, 1991), 159–62.

12 J. Armstrong et al., *Report of the Royal Commission on the Relations of Labor and Capital in Canada* (Ottawa: Queen's Printer, 1889), 119–21.

13 The issues are excellently covered by R.D. Gidney and W.P.J. Millar, *Inventing Secondary Education: The Rise of the High School in Nineteenth-Century Ontario* (Montréal: McGill-Queen's University Press, 1990). Developments outside Ontario remain poorly researched and the available studies focus upon religion and schooling.

14 AO, Pamphlet series, 1867 no. 1, E. Ryerson, *The New Canadian Dominion: Dangers and Duties of the People in Regard to Their Government* (Toronto, 1867), 7. E. Ryerson, 'The Importance of Education to a Manufacturing and Free People,' *JEUC* 1 (October 1848), 299.

15 E. Ryerson, 'Nature and Importance of Education to Mechanics,' in J.G. Hodgins, ed., *Documentary History of Education in Upper Canada* [hereafter *DHE*] (Toronto: L.K. Cameron, 1900–10), 11: 45, 50. See also A. Prentice, *The School Promoters: Education and Social Class in Mid-Nineteenth Century Upper Canada* (Toronto: McClelland and Stewart, 1977), 75–84. The roles of school reforms in social discipline and the transition to a print culture are well explored by Houston and Prentice, *Schooling and Scholars*, 189–309.

16 E. Ryerson, 'The Importance of Education to an Agricultural, a Manufacturing and a Free People,' *DHE*, 7: 148. 'Lord Elgin at the Toronto University Convocation of 1849,' *DHE*, 8: 264.

17 Ryerson, 'Education to Mechanics,' 45, 42.

18 *Christian Guardian*, 28 April 1841, quoted in Gidney and Millar, *Inventing Secondary Education*, 151.

19 R.M. Stamp, *The Schools of Ontario, 1876–1976* (Toronto: UTP, 1982), 8. J.A.C. Ketchum, '"The Most Perfect System": Official Policy in the First Century of Ontario Government Secondary Schools and Its Impact on Students Between 1871 and 1910,' unpub. PhD dissertation (University of Toronto, 1979), appendices D6 and D9.

20 R.D. Gidney and D.A Lawr, 'Egerton Ryerson and the Origins of the

Ontario Secondary School,' *CHR* 60 (1979), 442–65. Gidney and Millar, *Inventing Secondary Education*, chapters 11 and 12, provide a comprehensive analysis.

21 Province of Ontario, Department of Education, *Annual Report, 1886,* 326.
22 Stamp, *The Schools of Ontario,* 42–3, 80–4. See also R.M. Stamp, 'Technical Education, the National Policy, and Federal-Provincial Relations in Canadian Education, 1899–1919,' *CHR* 52 (1971), 404–23.
23 A. Kahn, 'Commercial Education in Secondary Schools,' *CEM* 22 (1900), 216.
24 See J.R. Benniger, *The Control Revolution: Technological and Economic Origins of the Information Society* (Cambridge: Harvard University Press, 1986); and J. Yates, *Control Through Communication: The Rise of System in American Management* (Baltimore: Johns Hopkins University Press, 1989). Studies of the emergence of managerial techniques in Canada have not been published, but quite useful is O. Zunz, *Making America Corporate, 1870–1920* (Chicago: University of Chicago Press, 1990), 37–66.
25 Dominion Bureau of Statistics, *Occupational Trends in Canada, 1891–1931* (Ottawa: King's Printer, 1939), Table 5.
26 Zunz, *Making America Corporate,* chapters 4 and 5. Canadian variants are reviewed by G.S. Lowe, *Women in the Administrative Revolution: The Feminization of Clerical Work* (Toronto: UTP, 1986), esp. chapters 4–6.
27 N.S. Jackson and J.S. Gaskell, 'White Collar Vocationalism: The Rise of Commercial Education in Ontario and British Columbia, 1870–1920,' *CI* 17 (1987), 186–7.
28 W.H. Shaw, *The Story of a Business School* (Toronto: Central Business College of Toronto, 1903), 6. Central Business College of Toronto, *Prospectus* (Toronto, 1910), 42.
29 McMaster University, Special Collections, *Woodstock College, Woodstock, Ontario, in Affiliation with the University of Toronto, Announcement, 1883–4* (Woodstock, Ont.: Pattulo & Co. Sentinel-Review Steam Book & Job Printing Office, 1883), 37.
30 Central Business College of Toronto, *Prospectus of the Central Business College of Toronto* (Toronto, 1905), 43. P.D. McIntosh, 'Why Business Colleges Succeed,' *CM* 21 (1903), 316–17.
31 The American data are from M.W. Sedlak and H.F. Williamson, *The Evolution of Management Education: A History of the Northwestern University J.L. Kellogg Graduate School of Management, 1908–1983* (Urbana: University of Illinois Press, 1983), 2. The Canadian data are from Dominion Bureau of Statistics, *Statistical Report on Education in Canada, 1921* (Ottawa: F.A. Acland, 1923), 124–5.

32 British Columbia Department of Labour, *Report of the Minimum Wage Board* (Victoria: King's Printer, 1923), 8.

33 See C. Strange, *Toronto's Girl Problem: The Pleasures and Perils of the City, 1890–1930* (Toronto: UTP, 1995). American experiences are best covered in S.H. Strom, *Beyond the Typewriter: Gender, Class, and the Origins of Modern American Office Work, 1900–1930* (Urbana: University of Illinois Press, 1992); and Zunz, *Making America Corporate*, 103–48.

34 John Seath, *Education for Industrial Purposes* (Toronto: King's Printer, 1911), 325. For analogous observations relating to the Maritimes, see part V of R.M. Dawson and H.M. Tory, *Report of the Royal Commission* (Halifax: King's Printer, 1944).

35 AO, RG 49-19, *Report of the Ontario Commission on Unemployment*, 1916 Sessional Paper no. 55, 181–2, 184.

36 Quoted in Sedlak and Williamson, *The Evolution of Management Education*, 2–3.

37 R.D. Cuff, 'Strengthening Proprietary Capitalism in a Corporate Age: The Case of Arch W. Shaw,' in P.B. Buchan, ed., *ASAC Proceedings: Business History* 18: 24 (1997) (St John's: Memorial University), 35–43.

38 For more extensive treatments, see A.B. McKillop, *Matters of Mind: The University in Ontario, 1791–1951* (Toronto: UTP, 1994), chapters 4 and 5; and M. Gauvreau, *College and Creed in English Canada from the Great Revival to the Great Depression* (Montréal: McGill-Queen's University Press, 1991).

39 Rothblatt, *Tradition and Change*, 46.

40 'Proceedings of the King's College Council in 1844,' *DHE* 5: 145. N. Burwash, *The History of Victoria College* (Toronto: Victoria College Press, 1927), 85.

41 McKillop, *Matters of Mind*, 187–94. C.H. Judd, *Problems of Education in the United States* (New York: McGraw-Hill, 1933), 76.

42 W.J. Ashley, Inaugural address of 9 November 1888, quoted in A. Ashley, *William James Ashley* (London: King, 1932), 49. Shortt quoted in S.E.D. Shortt, *The Search for an Ideal: Six Canadian Intellectuals and Their Convictions in an Age of Transition, 1890–1930* (Toronto: UTP, 1976), 103. Mavor quoted in P. Craven, *An Impartial Umpire: Canadian Industrial Relations and the State, 1900–1911* (Toronto: UTP, 1980), 47.

43 A.P. Usher, 'William James Ashley: A Pioneer in the Higher Education,' *CJEPS* 4: 2 (1938), 161.

44 A Shortt, 'The Nature and Sphere of Political Science,' *QQ* 1: 2 (1893), 95–6.

45 N.J. Pupo, 'Educational Promises and Efficiency Ideals: The Development of Management Education in Ontario, 1900–1960,' unpub. PhD thesis (McMaster University, 1984), 192–200.

46 S.B. Frost, *McGill University, For the Advancement of Learning, 1895–1971* (Montreal: McGill-Queen's University Press, 1984), 2: 40–1. J.D. Greene to H.L. Higgenson, April 1908, quoted in J.L. Cruikshank, *A Delicate Experiment: The Harvard Business School, 1908–1945* (Cambridge: Harvard Business School Press, 1987), 43.

47 *Catalogue* (1875), 33, quoted in J.G. Reid, *Mount Allison University: A History* (Toronto: UTP, 1984), 1: 146.

48 Reid, *Mount Allison University*, 1: 215–17; 2: 256.

49 Quoted in Sedlak and Williamson, *Evolution of Management Education*, 3.

50 J.H.S. Bossard and J.F. Dewhurst, *University Education for Business: A Study of Existing Needs and Practices* (Philadelphia: University of Pennsylvania Press, 1931), 253–5. D.O. Levine, *The American College and the Culture of Aspiration, 1915–1940* (Ithaca: Cornell University Press, 1986), 59. S.A. Sass, *The Pragmatic Imagination: A History of the Wharton School, 1881–1981* (Philadelphia: University of Pennsylvania Press, 1982), chapters 2 and 3.

51 D.F. Noble, *America By Design: Science, Technology and the Rise of Corporate Capitalism* (New York: Alfred A. Knopf, 1977), 312–13.

52 Siegfried quoted in Bossard and Dewhurst, *University Education for Business*, 9. Harvard Business School, Donham Papers, 'Training for Business,' 26 February 1929, quoted in Levine, *American College*, 48.

53 D.T. Rodgers, *Atlantic Crossings: Social Politics in a Progressive Age* (Cambridge: Harvard University Press, 1998), 76–111. The conflicts within the economics profession have been surveyed by M.O. Furner, *Advocacy and Objectivity: A Crisis in the Professionalization of American Social Science, 1865–1905* (Lexington: University Press of Kentucky, 1985), and by D. Ross, *The Origins of American Social Science* (Cambridge: Cambridge University Press, 1991).

54 Bossard and Dewhurst, *University Education for Business*, 43. H.T. Johnson and R.S. Kaplan, *Relevance Lost: The Rise and Fall of Managerial Accounting* (Cambridge: Harvard Business School Press 1987), 128–30. See also P.J. Miranti, Jr, 'Associationalism, Statism and Professional Regulation: Public Accountants and the Reform of Financial Markets, 1896–1940,' *BHR* 60 (1986), 438–68.

55 F.B. Jewett, 'Dinner Address,' *Bell System Educational Conference, 1924*, 192, quoted in Noble, *America By Design*, 170.

56 J. Weinstein, *The Corporate Ideal in the Liberal State* (Boston: Beacon Press, 1968). M.J. Sklar, *The Corporate Reconstruction of American Capitalism, 1890–1916* (Cambridge: Cambridge University Press, 1988), 1–40.

57 'The Antioch Plan,' *Engineering News-Record*, 96 (January 1921), 108–11, quoted in Noble, *America by Design*, 201.

58 Quoted in M. Curti and V. Carstensen, *The University of Wisconsin: A History, 1848–1925* (Madison: University of Wisconsin Press, 1949), 2: 244.

59 D. Nelson, 'Scientific Management and the Transformation of University Business Education,' in D. Nelson, ed., *A Mental Revolution: Scientific Management Since Taylor* (Columbus: Ohio University Press, 1992), 77, 82. M.T. Copeland, *And Mark the Era: The Story of the Harvard Business School* (Boston: Little Brown, 1958), 26. D. Nelson, *Frederick W. Taylor and the Rise of Scientific Management* (Madison: University of Wisconsin Press, 1980), 180.

60 Nelson, 'University Business Education,' 83–7. Pupo, 'Educational Promises,' chapter 5, surveys the adoption of scientific management at Western, Queen's, Toronto, and McMaster.

61 In *New York Life Insurance versus Deer Lodge* (1913), the United States Supreme Court declared that insurance was not 'commerce.' Since the subject was widely considered essential for a curriculum, alternative designations were adopted by many institutions for the titles of their programs.

62 Bossard and Dewhurst, *University Education for Business*, 318.

63 Ibid., chapter 10. Discussions of the issues can be found in E.R. Seligman, 'A University School of Business,' *CUQ* 18 (1916), 241–52; H.S. Person, 'Amos Tuck School of Dartmouth College,' *JPE* 21 (1913), 117–26; L.C. Marshall, 'The College of Commerce and Administration of the University of Chicago,' *JPE* 21 (1913), 97–110; and W.E. Hotchkiss, 'The Northwestern School of Commerce,' *JPE* 21 (1913), 196–208.

64 Bossard and Dewhurst, *University Education for Business*, 291.

65 L.C. Marshall, 'A Balanced Curriculum in Business Education,' *JPE* 21 (1917), 86–7. C.A. Daniel, *MBA: The First Century* (Lewisburg: Bucknell University Press, 1998), 52–7. Daniel has provided a useful overview, but many management educators will find his views mercurial and the narrative incorrectly mixes developments in American baccalaureate and graduate programs.

66 'Engineering and Business Administration,' *The Technology Review*, 1913, 391, quoted in Nelson, 'University Business Education,' 81.

67 Marshall, 'A Balanced Curriculum,' 84–8.

68 Shaw to Gay, Spring 1914, quoted in Cruikshank, *A Delicate Experiment*, 81.

69 W.B. Donham, *Administration and Blind Spots* (Boston: Harvard Graduate School of Business Administration, 1952), 13–14. Donham quoted in Cruikshank, *A Delicate Experiment*, 155.

70 L.C. Marshall, 'A Balanced Curriculum,' 89, 91.

71 A.N. Whitehead, *Aims of Education* (New York: Free Press, 1967), 5. Donham quoted in Cruikshank, *A Delicate Experiment*, 139.

72 The reform movement has been extensively surveyed: W.R. Ward, *Victorian*

Oxford (London: Frank Cass, 1965); D.A. Winstanley, *Later Victorian Cambridge* (Cambridge: Cambridge University Press, 1947); and especially S. Rothblatt, *The Revolution of the Dons: Cambridge and Society in Victorian England* (Cambridge: Cambridge University Press, 1981).

73 C.A. Anderson and M. Schnaper, *School and Society: Social Backgrounds of Oxford and Cambridge Students* (London: Public Affairs Press, 1952), 6–7.

74 P. Deane, *The Evolution of Economic Ideas* (Cambridge: Cambridge University Press, 1978), chapters 7 and 8. A.W. Coats, 'Sociological Aspects of British Economic Thought, 1880–1930,' *JPE* 75 (1967), 706–29.

75 M. Sanderson, *The Universities and British Industry, 1850–1970* (London: Routledge and Kegan Paul, 1972), 190–3.

76 Ashley, *William James Ashley*, 88.

77 W.J. Ashley, *Commercial Education* (London: Williams and Norgate, 1926), chapter 4.

78 Sanderson, *The Universities and British Industry*, 205–10.

79 R.H. Parker, *Management Accounting: An Historical Perspective* (London: Macmillan, 1969), 17. R.R. Locke, *The End of the Practical Man: Entrepreneurship and Higher Education in Germany, France and Great Britain, 1880–1940* (London: JAI Press, 1984), 128–32.

80 S. Chapman, 'Some Memories and Reflections,' unpub. manuscript quoted in Sanderson, *The Universities and British Industry*, 207. J. Jewkes, 'L'Université de Manchester,' in *Cinquartenaire de la revue d'économie politique 1937*, 112–13, quoted in R.R. Locke, *Management and Higher Education since 1940: The Influence of America and Japan on West Germany, Great Britain, and France* (Cambridge: Cambridge University Press, 1989), 99.

81 D.F. Channon, *The Strategy and Structure of British Enterprise* (Cambridge: Harvard University, Division of Research, Graduate School of Business Administration, 1973), 42–6. A.B. Thomas, 'Management and Education: Rationalization and Reproduction in British Business,' *International Studies of Management and Organization* 10: 1–2 (1980), 71–109.

82 D.D. Calvin, *Queen's University at Kingston: The First Century of a Scottish Canadian Foundation, 1841–1941* (Toronto: Hunter-Ross, 1941), 159.

83 Pupo, 'Educational Promises,' 92–118.

84 University of Toronto Archives [hereafter UTA], *Calendar of the University of Toronto, 1915–1916* (Toronto: University of Toronto, 1915), 396. See also Pupo, 'Educational Promises,' 196–8.

85 UTA, *Calendar for the University of Toronto for the Year 1906–1907* (Toronto: The University Press), 403.

86 W.J. Alexander, ed., *The University of Toronto and Its Colleges, 1827–1906* (Toronto: The University Press, 1906), 96.

87 I.M. Drummond, *Political Economy at the University of Toronto: A History of the Department, 1888–1982* (Toronto: UTP, 1983), 39–40.

88 UTA, *Calendar for the University of Toronto for the Year 1920–1921* (Toronto: UTP, 1920), 200. Mavor's values and their influence are explored in Shortt, *The Search for an Ideal,* chapter 7, and in Drummond, *Political Economy,* chapter 3.

89 UTA, *Calendar for the University of Toronto for the Year 1921–1922* (Toronto: UTP, 1921), 292. UTA, Department Records, file 17, box 1, A65–005: R. MacIver to O.D. Skelton, 22 March 1923; MacIver to M.A. Mackenzie, 16 Oct. 1925. File 18, box 1, MacIver to R. Falconer, 5 Nov. 1925.

90 McGill University, *1907 Calendar,* quoted in Frost, *McGill University,* 2: 29.

91 Quoted in E.D. McPhee, *History of the Faculty of Commerce and Business Administration, The University of British Columbia* (Vancouver: University of British Columbia, 1974), 9.

92 Frost, *McGill University,* 2: 54. McGill University, *1920 Calendar,* quoted in R.S. Harris, *A History of Higher Education in Canada, 1663–1960* (Toronto: UTP, 1976), 243.

93 W.S. Fox, *Sherwood Fox of Western: Reminiscences* (Toronto: Burns and MacEachern, 1964), 42.

94 *London Free Press,* 2 April 1920.

95 Western University, *College of Arts Calendar, 1921–1922* (London: Western University, 1921), 77–8.

96 E.H. Morrow, '... Finally the call came and I started to work in 1922,' in D. Saunders, ed., *Learning to Lead: In Celebration of Seven Decades of Business Education at Western, 1923–93* (London: Western Business School, 1993), 18. Although it contains numerous insights, many readers will find this volume disappointing, with an annoying amount of self-congratulatory propaganda.

97 J.R.W. Gwynne-Timothy, *Western's First Century* (London: University of Western Ontario, 1976), 464–5. *London Free Press,* 17 May 1930.

98 McPhee, *Faculty of Commerce,* 3–23.

99 W.L. Morton, *One University: A History of the University of Manitoba, 1877–1952* (Toronto: McClelland and Stewart, 1957), 120–1, 162. M. Hayden, *Seeking a Balance: The University of Saskatchewan, 1907–1982* (Vancouver: UBC Press, 1983), 123–7. Harris, *Higher Education,* 243.

100 Université de Montréal, *Annuaire, 1921–1922,* 223, 227. P. Harvey, *Histoire de l'École des Hautes Études Commerciales de Montréal, 1887–1926* (Montréal: Presses HÉC, 1994), 1: 292–4.

101 R. Rumilly, *Histoire de l'École des Hautes Études Commerciales de Montréal* (Montréal: Beauchemin, 1966), 15–26, 47. J. Hamelin, *Histoire de l'Université*

Laval: Les péripéties d'une idée (Sainte-Foy: Les Presses de l'Université Laval, 1995), 193.

102 Statistics Canada, *Historical Compendium of Educational Statistics* (Ottawa: Information Canada, 1975), 216.

103 E.H. Morrow, 'Aims and Objectives' (1940), 24, quoted in E.D. McPhee, *Faculty of Commerce*, 24.

104 'The Place of the University in a Commercial City,' in W. Peterson, *Canadian Essays and Addresses* (London: Longmans Green, 1915), 260. Others quoted in S.B. Frost, *McGill University* 2: 54–5, 58.

105 F. Underhill, 'Commerce Courses and the Arts Faculty,' NCCU *Proceedings*, 1932, 62–3, 69, quoted in Axelrod, *Making a Middle Class: Student Life in English Canada During the Thirties* (Montréal: McGill-Queen's University Press, 1993), 60.

106 Canadian Club of Toronto, *Proceedings, 1930–1931*, 153; *Proceedings, 1931–1932*, 94–5. Fyfe to the trustees quoted in F.W. Gibson, *Queen's University: To Serve and Yet Be Free, 1917–1961* (Montréal: McGill-Queen's University Press, 1983), 2: 129.

107 Dalhousie University Archives, Principal's Office Correspondence, A-736, 'Dougald Macgillivray, 1926–1938,' Carleton Stanley to Macgillivray, 24 Nov. 1931, quoted in P.B. Waite, *The Lives of Dalhousie University: 1925–1980, The Old College Transformed* (Kingston: McGill-Queen's University Press, 1998), 2: 51.

108 Axelrod, *Making a Middle Class*, 60–1. The educational background of Canadian executives was examined in several studies commissioned by the Economic Council of Canada. The best overview is in D.J. Daly and S. Globerman, *Tariff and Science Policies: Applications of a Model of Nationalism*, Ontario Economic Council Research Studies (Toronto: UTP, 1976), 32–9.

109 B.E.C. Boothman, 'The Foundations of Canadian Big Business,' Fifth Canadian Business History Conference, October 1998. *Census of Canada, 1971* (Ottawa: Information Canada, 1974), 14-1, 14-2, 17-71, 17-72.

110 R.A. Gordon, and J.E. Howell, *Higher Education for Business* (New York: Columbia University Press, 1959), 69.

111 B.R. Scott, 'The New Industrial State: Old Myths and New Realities,' *HBR* 51 (1973), 133–48. M. Leontiades, *Strategies for Diversification and Change* (Boston: Little Brown, 1980), 7–14. The internationalization of American firms during this period is best captured by M. Wilkins, *The Maturing of Multinational Enterprise: American Business Abroad from 1914 to 1970* (Cambridge: Harvard University Press, 1974) and R. Vernon, *Sovereignty at Bay: The Multinational Spread of U.S. Enterprises* (New York: Basic, 1971).

112 A.D. Chandler, *The Visible Hand: The Managerial Revolution in American Business* (Cambridge: Harvard University Press, 1977), 472–6.

113 A.D. Chandler and R.S. Tedlow, *The Coming of Managerial Capitalism: A Casebook of American Economic Institutions* (Homewood, Ill.: Irwin, 1985), 709–16, 765–75.

114 For a full appraisal, see Johnson and Kaplan, *Relevance Lost*, chapters 6 and 7.

115 T. Hikino, 'Managerial Control, Capital Markets, and the Wealth of Nations,' in A.D. Chandler, F. Amatori, and T. Hikino, eds, *Big Business and the Wealth of Nations* (New York: Cambridge University Press, 1997), 480–96. T.K. McCraw, *Creating Modern Capitalism: How Entrepreneurs, Companies, and Countries Triumphed in Three Managerial Revolutions* (Cambridge: Harvard University Press, 1997), 336–8.

116 P. Drucker, 'Executives are Made ... Not Born,' *Nation's Business*, 40 (October 1952), 36. The comprehensive version of Drucker's argument was published in *The New Society: The Anatomy of Industrial Order* (New York: Harper and Brothers, 1950), chapters 21–4.

117 'Can You Teach Management?' *BW*, 19 April 1952, 126.

118 H.I. Ansoff, 'The Changing Shape of the Strategic Problem,' in D.E. Schendel and C. W. Hofer, eds, *Strategic Management: A New View of Business Policy and Planning* (Boston: Little Brown, 1979), 30–44. Education and postwar values are enjoyably appraised by D. Owram, *Born at the Right Time: A History of the Baby Boom Generation* (Toronto: UTP, 1996), esp. chapters 4 and 5.

119 S. Schlossman and M. Sedlak, *The Age of Reform in American Management Education* (Los Angeles: Graduate Management Admission Council, 1988), 45. These arguments were similar to those elaborated by participants in other professional disciplines. See C. Jencks and D. Reisman, *The Academic Revolution* (Garden City, NY: Anchor, 1968), 252–4.

120 G. Burrell and G. Morgan, *Sociological Paradigms and Organizational Analysis* (London: Heinemann, 1979), 118–81. Locke, *Management and Higher Education since 1940*, 30–55. S.P. Waring, *Taylorism Transformed: Scientific Management Theory since 1945* (Chapel Hill: University of North Carolina Press, 1991), 20–77.

121 Waring, *Taylorism Transformed*, chapters 3–6, provides a useful, if occasionally superficial, overview of this literature. A thoughtful analysis of the theoretical logic can be found in Burrell and Morgan, *Sociological Paradigms and Organization Analysis*.

122 Gordon and Howell, *Higher Education for Business*, 136. F.C. Pierson, *The Education of American Businessmen* (New York: McGraw-Hill, 1959), x, 55.

123 Gordon and Howell, *Higher Education for Business*, 341–6. Pierson, *Education of American Businessmen*, 270–3. The proportion of doctorates in Amer-

ican business schools was estimated at 40 per cent and expected to drop to 21 per cent by 1969.

124 Pierson, *Education of American Businessmen*, 164, 196.

125 Gordon and Howell, *Higher Education for Business*, 13, 174–5, 217. The concern about specialization can be traced back to the 1930s, when the first survey of management education questioned the practice. 'One wonders whether much of the purported specialization in the collegiate business schools, most of it perhaps, is not mere window-dressing designed to impress students and businessmen ... For the most part, the real reasons for the development of any extensive specialization have to do with matters other than that of the educational interests of the students.' Bossard and Dewhurst, *University Education for Business*, 313.

126 Pierson, *Education of American Businessmen*, 164. Gordon and Howell, *Higher Education for American Business*, 126.

127 Gordon and Howell, *Higher Education for Business*, 380–1. Pierson, *Education of American Businessmen*, 311–13.

128 A different perspective can be found in S.A. Aaronson, 'Serving America's Business?: Graduate Business Schools and American Business, 1945–1960,' *BH* 34 (1992), 160–82. This paper considers developments at Harvard and Columbia, neither of which were on the leading edge of the new trend, but does not probe the outcomes of curricular experiments funded by the Ford Foundation at those institutions.

129 J.J. Clark and B.J. Opulente, *The Impact of the Foundation Reports on Business Education* (Jamaica, NY: St John's University Press, 1963), 5–7. See also S. Schlossman, M. Sedlak, and H. Wechster, *The 'New Look': The Ford Foundation and the Revolution in Business Education* (Los Angeles: Graduate Management Admissions Council, 1986).

130 Locke, *Management and Higher Education*, chapters 1 and 2, provides a comprehensive survey of the intellectual logic.

131 Harris, *Higher Education*, 512–13. Enrolment data were calculated by the author from Statistics Canada, *University Enrollments and Degrees* (Cat. 81-204) and *Education in Canada*, (Cat. 81-211). Statistics Canada segmented enrolment and degrees for business from those for the social sciences beginning with the 1967–8 academic year.

132 M. von Zur-Muehlin, *Enrollment and Graduation Patterns in Management and Administrative Studies at Canadian Universities* (Ottawa: Statistics Canada, 1981). A. Chaiton, *Role of Management and Management Education in Meeting Rising Expectations: A Canadian Perspective* (Toronto: CFDMAS, 1979). Estimates for 1998 were supplied to the author by Statistics Canada, July 1998.

133 Statistics Canada, *A Statistical Profile of Education at the University Level*

(Ottawa: Statistics Canada, 1996). E.J. Mighty, 'The Responsiveness of Management Education to Workplace Diversity,' in A. Lapointe and G. Gorman, eds, *ASAC Conference Proceedings: Management Education 16* (1995), part 11 (Windsor, University of Windsor), 46. Canadian Federation of Deans of Management and Administrative Studies, *Guide to Canadian Management and Administrative Studies Programs* (Ottawa: Author, 1991).

134 P. Axelrod, *Scholars and Dollars: Politics, Economics, and the Universities of Ontario, 1945–1980* (Toronto: UTP, 1982), 100–5. For the rationales behind the changes, see C.B. Macpherson et al., *Undergraduate Instruction in Arts and Science: Report of the Presidential Advisory Committee on Undergraduate Instruction in the Faculty of Arts and Science*, University of Toronto (Toronto: UTP, 1967), esp. Part II.

135 Quoted in Axelrod, *Scholars and Dollars*, 107, 108. chapter 5 excellently captures the relationship between private-sector goals and university education during this period.

136 See L.T. Hosmer, *Academic Strategy: The Determination and Implementation of Purpose at New Graduate Schools of Administration* (Ann Arbor: Division of Research, Graduate School of Business Administration, University of Michigan, 1978). Comparing the graduate programs at York, Manchester, and Vanderbilt, he appraised the start-up of the York initiative very critically.

137 Johns, *University of Alberta*, 332. McPhee, *Faculty of Commerce*, 106–7. S.I. Anand, 'The Faculty of Commerce and Administration: An Historical Documentary of Its Origins,' unpub. monograph (Montréal: Concordia University, 1993). Frost, *McGill University*, 2: 312.

138 K.A. Lannon, 'A Documented History of Business Administration at Saint Francis Xavier University,' unpub. monograph (St Francis Xavier University, 1993). J.D. Cameron, *For the People: A History of St. Francis Xavier University* (Montréal: McGill-Queen's University Press, 1996), 272–4. Personal communication, Berry to B.J. Austin, based upon an unsigned and undated document in the commerce department files likely authored by Professor Nijs de Vas. Dr Berry was head of the commerce department of Acadia at the time of writing and I am grateful to Dr Austin for this quote.

139 Locke, *Management and Higher Education*, 52.

140 C. Bissell, *Halfway Up Parnassus: A Personal Account of the University of Toronto, 1932–1971* (Toronto: UTP, 1974), 71.

141 M.B.E. Clarkson, 'The Alien MBA,' *CBR* 6 (Spring 1979), 24.

142 This is the author's estimate based upon discussions with the respective universities. The program at York University, for example, was not funded until 1987, and unless they had partners who could shoulder some of the costs, doctoral students survived only by taking on exten-

sive teaching or consulting obligations, which had serious implications for their academic careers.

143 Daniel, *MBA*, 149–50, 264–5.
144 Gordon and Howell, *Higher Education for Business*, 257–69. Pierson, *Education of American Businessmen*, 258.
145 Quoted in Saunders, *Learning to Lead*, 38.
146 Gwynne-Timothy, *Western's First Century*, 464–5. *Globe and Mail*, 15 May 1950.
147 Saunders, *Learning to Lead*, 60–1, 70–1.
148 Ibid., 35. Gwynne-Timothy, *Western's First Century*, 473.
149 Saunders, *Learning to Lead*, 82–6.
150 McPhee, *History of the Faculty of Commerce*, 41–79.
151 Ibid., 116–20.
152 Boothman, 'The Foundations of Canadian Big Business.' Only half of the top 100 Canadian-controlled companies of 1973 were still among that group by 1988.
153 A.O.C. Cole, *Trent: The Making of a University, 1957–1987* (Peterborough: Trent University, 1992), 138–9.
154 Drummond, *Political Economy*, 121.
155 Ibid., 118, 160, 162. S.F. Borins, 'Duet with Business: How Scarborough College Got Serious about Its Commerce Program,' www.scar.utoronto .ca/acad/mgmt-eco/mgmt/duet2.htm.

2

The Founding of the École des Hautes Études Commerciales de Montréal

PIERRE HARVEY

The École des Hautes Études Commerciales de Montréal (HÉC) has been affiliated with the Université de Montréal since 1915, but remains an autonomous institution funded by Québec's Ministère de l'Éducation in the same capacity as a university. The director of HÉC is a member of the Conference of Rectors and Principals of Québec Universities (CREPUQ). The school's enrolment now exceeds 9000, including 7000 undergraduates, some 550 MBA students, and about 105 Ph.D. students.[1] The HÉC faculty consists of 170 full-time professors supported by 250 part-time lecturers. Ever since its founding in 1907, the school was designed to have a university status with a permanent faculty and to be housed in a building the government had built especially for this purpose. This chapter does not attempt to trace the whole of HÉC's long history,[2] but focuses instead on its inception, beginning in the latter part of the nineteenth century, and also explains how this project, which was finally brought to fruition in 1907, was unique within the North American context of the day. To understand the early history of the École des Hautes Études Commerciales de Montréal, one must examine the circumstances surrounding the founding of the Chambre de commerce de Montréal, for the birth of HÉC should be viewed as a direct continuation of the Chambre de commerce's own creation.

In the last quarter of the nineteenth century, the French-speaking population of Montréal had gradually consolidated its majority status, thanks to the influx of francophones from the surrounding countryside and the early stages of the annexation of neighbouring villages. Although the English-speaking minority still dominated economic life in what was then Canada's uncontested metropolis, the French-speaking population was gradually carving out a more prosperous place for itself, especially in commerce. However, tension between the two linguistic communities sharing the city remained high, and eventually came to the surface on the hanging of Louis Riel in November 1885. The situation was exacerbated with the outbreak of a smallpox epidemic in the fall and winter of 1885–6.[3] It is against this unstable background that the idea of founding a francophone chamber of commerce in Montréal was first conceived.

Since 1822, English-speaking businessmen had organized their own association, the Committee on Trade, which later became the Montréal Board of Trade in 1842. Although some French-speaking businessmen belonged to the Board of Trade in the last quarter of the nineteenth century, their numbers were few. The vast majority chose not to join an organization where they did not feel at ease or play a significant role. This sentiment was clearly expressed in the first issue of the *Bulletin de la Chambre de commerce* in 1899.[4] It should be noted that there already existed two French-language weekly business magazines in Montréal at this time: *Le Moniteur du Commerce* and *Le Prix courant*. It was in the 26 November 1886 issue of *Le Moniteur du Commerce* that a letter called on Montréal's businessmen to found a French-language chamber of commerce that would operate parallel to the Board of Trade. This idea could not have been totally unexpected, since the project was quickly endorsed by over 130 people. A few weeks later, the Chambre de commerce du district de Montréal received its charter and began its operations.[5] Although the new organization was concerned with the same issues as the Board of Trade – customs, strikes, navigation, canals, and so on – it soon developed an interest in another crucial area, business education.

By the 1890s, Québec had a number of primary- and secondary-level institutions dedicated to teaching business, and most collèges classiques began offering courses in commerce. However, the Chambre de commerce was not entirely satisfied with the quality of this teaching. In 1893, Damase Parizeau,[6] one of the founding members of the Chambre, recommended that a committee be appointed to look into improving the quality of business teaching in Québec. Nevertheless, between 1893 and 1900, the Chambre did little more than set up the committee; a few visits to business colleges were organized, and one or two reports were prepared for the government of the day.

In February 1900, however, the secretary of the Chambre de commerce de Montréal reported, with no further comment, having been sent the program and regulations of the École des Hautes Études Commerciales de Paris by Joseph-Xavier Perrault, Canada's representative at the 1900 Paris world's fair.[7] An agronomist, writer, member of the pre-1867 parliament, and staunch opponent of Confederation, Perrault was the author of the open letter that had led to the founding of the Chambre de commerce du district de Montréal in 1887. Although the Chambre's records of proceedings make no mention of any discussion of the HÉC de Paris documents, Perrault's message played an instrumental role in the school's founding: indeed, for the first time the Chambre de commerce addressed, at least implicitly, the issue of business teaching in higher education.

Another year would pass, however, before the issue would arise again – this time thanks to a message from south of the border. In early December 1900, another member of the Chambre de commerce, Georges Gonthier, sent a copy of the entire program offered by a new American institution, the New York University School of Commerce, Accounts and Finance, which was primarily dedicated to training accountants. Gonthier was himself a public accountant, a small profession practised by very few francophones in Montréal. Although he served as treasurer of the Chambre de commerce in 1902 and as Auditor General of Canada in 1924, Gonthier had interests outside the field of accounting, and education was one of them. The explanation included in his lengthy covering letter is an eloquent illustration of this interest. In his words, the Chambre de commerce 'has for some time been concerned with establishing technical schools in our city. Would it not be fitting to also address the important issue of advanced commercial studies?'[8] To my knowledge, this is the first time the expression hautes études commerciales (advanced commercial studies) was specifically used in the Québec context. Perrault's message from the previous year had pointed in the same direction, albeit implicitly. Gonthier's, however, was clear and direct.

Despite the efforts of these two members, the Chambre de commerce du district de Montréal showed little eagerness to promote the development of advanced business teaching in the early years of the twentieth century. With the Boer War heightening tensions between Québec's francophone and anglophone population, especially in Montréal, there was little time to focus on the need to provide the younger generation with post-secondary training in business. The issue was not addressed in a meaningful way until 1904 – when, strangely enough, the issue was raised in the House of Commons during a debate on the settlement of the Alaskan border. It will be remembered that the border dispute arose for the first time in the summer of 1896 with the discovery of gold in the Klondike. The settlement reached through arbitration between the English and American governments in the fall of 1903 was criticized by Canadians who felt that one of the English representatives on the arbitration tribunal, Lord Alverstone, had betrayed domestic interests. The event led to a lively debate in Ottawa, and elsewhere in the country, that did not spare the British magistrate. On 23 October 1903, Henri Bourassa, the fiery MP from the Québec county of Labelle, asked to voice his opinion on the Alaska boundary issue before the end of the fall session.[9]

Bourassa was well versed in the matter, for in 1898–9 Laurier had appointed him secretary to the Canadian delegation in charge of discussions with the Americans about the Alaska boundary. In his long, well-documented speech Bourassa had argued that Lord Alverstone was not to be blamed for the settlement conditions, since Canada could not legally claim the contested territories owing to decisions made by England years before. According to Bourassa, the situation clearly demonstrated that Canada's international interests could be properly defended only if it were free to direct its own foreign policy, and to achieve this the country needed to have its own diplomatic corps. After a brief exchange of views in response to Bourassa's presentation, the parliamentary session ended and the matter remained dormant.

During the summer of 1904, the issue of foreign representation resurfaced as the House of Commons debated the budgets to be granted to the commercial representation provided by the British Crown. This commercial representation was not held in high esteem: it was very small, inefficient, and treated with little consideration by the British civil service. In the first week of August, a Montréal MP, Honoré Gervais, raised the same concerns as those addressed ten months earlier by Bourassa.[10] As a loyal supporter of Prime Minister Laurier, Gervais was careful not to mention Bourassa in his argument, for the latter had had a falling out with the Liberal party in 1900 over the prime minister's interventionist policy in the Boer War.

In his speech, Gervais explained how, in his view, the British foreign service did not serve Canada's interests well, and why Canada should obtain the right to employ its own foreign affairs staff and the power to sign its own treaties. Gervais suggested a gradual transfer of powers, beginning with consular services. He also emphasized the need to properly train the new Canadian consuls to the same level of competence as their international counterparts. To this end, Gervais recommended that each province create a school for advanced commercial studies (école des hautes études commerciales) similar to those in Europe. After citing the examples of the École des Hautes Études Commerciales de Paris, the main Écoles Supérieures de Commerce in France, and the Institut Supérieur de Commerce in Antwerp, Gervais presented a detailed description of the program offered at Germany's Leipzig business school.

Jurist Honoré Gervais was an important figure in Montréal, with degrees from Université Laval and the Albany law school. Gervais taught civil procedure and international law at Université Laval à Montréal,[11] was a member of the university's board of directors, and entertained close ties with certain intellectual milieus in Europe, especially in Paris. Apparently, Laurier had personally recruited Gervais to run as a federal MP. Despite his prestige, Gervais's address to the House of Commons fell mainly on deaf ears. But he would soon have another opportunity to express his ideas – and this time under more favourable conditions.

A few months after Gervais's speech, a major event occurred in Québec politics that had important repercussions for the founding of HÉC. Subsequent to a 'palace revolution' in the Liberal party, in the spring of 1905, Premier Parent was forced out of office and replaced by one of his ministers, Lomer Gouin. Because of parliamentary rules of the day, Gouin was obliged to call a by-election after his ascendance to power. On 5 April 1905, during the election campaign, Gouin held a large public assembly, presided over by Honoré Gervais, to unveil his party's platform. Gervais was the federal MP for Montréal–St Jacques, the same county that Gouin represented in the legislative assembly. The two local politicians were thus members of two Liberal majorities (one in the federal capital, the other in the provincial capital) and, given the customs of the day, worked closely together. In his speech, the new premier clearly expressed his commitment to making education a top priority: 'We must ... soon establish in this province ... schools for advanced commercial studies like the 100 or so that exist in Europe, [since] economic and social developments in recent years ... have forced us to become, more than ever, better equipped for the struggle.'[12]

A few days later, on 10 April, an editorial in the Liberal newspaper *Le Canada* reported on the new premier's remarks, casting them in a more firmly nationalist light. The editorialist reminded his readers that as a result of the conquest of New France by Britain, the French-speaking population had, for all intents and purposes, been excluded from major commercial activities. He went on to explain how the commercial interests of the population had changed over time. 'But our merchants,' he added, 'have a great deal of catching up to do, at least in certain areas, to compete with their English-speaking counterparts.' The editorial concluded by commending the premier for his project to 'create the instrument (a school for advanced commercial studies) that is needed to turn our aspiring merchants into men who are as informed and up-to-date about global economic issues as their opposite numbers in the English-speaking community.'[13] This nationalist overtone – which Gervais had carefully avoided as a loyal supporter of Laurier – played a pivotal role in the events leading up to the founding of business-administration teaching at the post-secondary level in Québec.

On 29 November of the same year, Honoré Gervais was given a second opportunity to present his proposal to create a post-secondary institution to train the consuls he believed Canada needed. He took advantage of an invitation to speak at a large banquet of the Retail Merchants' Association of Canada to briefly outline the themes of his 6 August 1904 speech in the House of Commons,[14] and to address the more general issue of the need for adequate business training in Québec. According to Gervais, there was an urgent need to develop a university-trained business elite to deal with the new economic reality and, consequently, to establish institutions capable of providing the required knowledge. On this occasion, Gervais found himself speaking to a much more receptive audience than in the House of Commons, where the majority of MPs, especially anglophones, did not take kindly to a proposal aimed at reducing (even if only slightly) Canada's role as a colony of the Empire. The captive audience included not only some of the most eminent members of the Chambre de commerce, MLAs, cabinet ministers, but also Premier Gouin himself, who obviously shared some of Gervais's views.

From late 1905 on, events unfolded rapidly: barely one year later, the École des Hautes Études Commerciales de Montréal was created. However, a few significant episodes that occurred along the road to the school's founding deserve to be mentioned. The last phase in this long process took place at the Chambre de commerce, which had done little since the interventions of J.-X. Perrault and Georges Gonthier in 1900. Perrault – who passed away in April 1905 following a brief illness – devoted many of the last years of his life to the Société Saint-Jean-

Baptiste, a nationalist organization of which he was president. Gonthier, however, kept up the battle at the Chambre de commerce. One might say that the year 1906 belonged to him, for he never abandoned his efforts until the school was finally founded. Throughout this pivotal year, Gonthier took advantage of every new story, every rumour (both ill- and well-founded) to keep the issue in the forefront. He managed to win the firm backing of Université Laval à Montréal and of Monsignor Bruchési – who as archbishop of Montréal was rector of the Université. However, despite its keen interest in the project, the Université had to withdraw its participation, in the autumn of 1906, owing to a lack of funds. Still, the vice-rector strongly recommended the creation of the institution, which was now avidly promoted by the Chambre de commerce, and proposed that the new institution be affiliated with Université Laval à Montréal, while having administrative autonomy. In light of the Université's inability to ensure funding for the institution, the Chambre de commerce turned to Premier Gouin. Intense negotiations lasted until the end of the year.

On 15 January 1907, Lieutenant-Governor Jetté publicly announced the founding of the École des Hautes Études Commerciales in the speech from the throne that opened the 1907 legislative session. A bill tabled five days later was given royal assent on 14 March. The École des Hautes Études Commerciales was thus established as a legal, independent corporation, free to establish its own programs, hire faculty, and recruit students as had been the wish of the vice-rector of Université Laval à Montréal. The school, which received direct funding from the government, was recognized as an institution of higher education, but not affiliated with the Université for reasons that will become clear later. The newspapers referred to it as a 'nouvelle université' with no denominational ties – a fact that led to a number of problems for both the school and the government in subsequent years. As many as three years would pass before teaching would actually begin at HÉC. First, a new building needed to be built, a qualified faculty hired (in Montréal and in Europe), programs prepared, regulations drafted, and students recruited. All of this would finally be accomplished in the fall of 1910, when HÉC welcomed its first thirty-two students, nine of whom would successfully complete the next three years of classes to obtain the degree of Licence en sciences commerciales (licentiate in commercial science) in the spring of 1913 – the first graduating class in HÉC's history.[15]

The first years of its existence were by no means easy for the institution. However, it is not my intention to discuss the events marking this period. Instead, I would like to devote the rest of this essay to a comparison of the circumstances surrounding the creation of HÉC in March 1907 with those that prevailed in the rest of the continent at the time. In terms of the events taking place in other parts of North America at the turn of the century in this field – which had not yet been termed sciences de la gestion (business administration) by the French-speaking community, but was still referred to as hautes études commerciales (advanced commercial studies) – the École des HÉC is a unique case. English Canada cannot be factored into this comparison, since business institutions were not created there until years later. But a number of differences between the environment in Montréal and in the United States can be underlined here.

First, beginning with the ground-breaking case of the Wharton school in 1881, almost every American business teaching institution was created within a 'college' or department by developing a special program comprising a number of 'classical' courses drawn from college programs and an array of business-related electives. Several years, even decades, would pass before these programs could separate from their college or department of origin to become business schools in their own right. In contrast, the École des Hautes Études Commerciales de Montréal was founded as an independent institution with a comprehensive legal profile, safeguarded by a Québec government charter. The school immediately received the funding it needed to construct a building to house its activities. The state also promised an annual grant to provide HÉC with the means – so the school's administrators had been led to believe – required to ensure its proper operation as a university institution. Under these conditions, it is almost impossible to draw a parallel between the beginnings of the École des Hautes Études Commerciales de Montréal and those of American business schools. HÉC began as a full-fledged, independent organization – probably the first of its type in North America, with the possible exception of the Tuck School in Dartmouth, which acquired the more ambiguous status of an 'associated' school.

A second major difference between the École des Hautes Études Commerciales de Montréal and the first American business schools should be pointed out here: almost all the American schools were limited to undergraduate education, while HÉC has always offered teaching beyond the bachelor of arts. Third, in the United States, new business schools often had to contend with indifference, sometimes even hostility, from the university community and, especially, from college faculty members.[16] Young professors who, upon completion of their PhD, agreed to begin their careers in these schools – which were almost openly discredited – had to develop the syllabi of the newly created business programs. To achieve this, they established close ties with the business community, which in return provided the support they needed.

In Montréal, the situation could not have been more different. Although certain members of the Chambre de commerce played an active role in convincing the government to create the École des HÉC, the Chambre subsequently almost completely lost interest in the school's fate. Neither the Chambre, its member firms, nor individual members intervened on its behalf to help overcome the school's financial hardships. Moreover, the Chambre and the Montréal business community did not support HÉC when it was under attack from opposition MLAs and certain ultra-Catholic elements of society, primarily represented by the unofficial journal of the archbishop of Québec City, L'Action. For almost a decade, the École and the Chambre would each conduct their affairs independently.

Contrary to its American counterparts, HÉC was widely accepted from the outset by the university community. For instance, although the March 1907 law granting the school's charter made no mention of an affiliation with Université Laval à Montréal, Monsignor Bruchési launched a discrete, yet tireless, ten-year campaign to affiliate the two institutions. And Édouard Montpetit – a young professor at HÉC since its founding who later became secretary general of the Université de Montréal – enjoyed immediate prestige among the university community, where he felt greatly at ease. However, the École was long ignored by the collèges classiques, though this should not be interpreted as a form of protest against the institution's university status.

Thus, the conditions prevailing in the United States had almost no influence on the creation or the structure of the École des Hautes Commerciales de Montréal. The institution was fashioned after European models – the French schools, of course, but mainly the Belgian. The non-Québécois teaching staff, including the school's first two principals, were recruited in Belgium. Many of HÉC's first career professors acquired their training in France, and, as early as the first year of the institution's existence, the first chairman of the board, Isaïe Préfontaine, went on a lengthy journey to study the operation of French, Swiss, and Belgian business schools, even German ones. But, of all the differences between the École des Hautes Études Commerciales and American business schools at the turn of the century, the most striking was in their objectives. The schools south of the border evolved in the same direction as the rest of American society: they were structured in response to a demand that was first expressed by businesses, but that gradually became widespread as a new industrial order began to take root. This demand, however, was expressed not only by the business world, but also by the younger generation, who wished to take advantage of business career opportunities created by the emerging modern economy in the United States. The main thrust behind this demand was pure nineteenth-century liberalism and, as such, was dictated by the free market. The situation was entirely different in the case of the École des Hautes Études Commerciales.

While it benefited from the growing prosperity of the world at the turn of the century, the Canadian economy did not experience the process of industrialization at the same pace as the United States. As a result, there was at the time little demand for graduates with post-secondary education in business administration from Montréal's French-language business community. Although this community was not without influence in terms of its numbers and scope, it was small and compact enough to continue the traditional practice of apprenticeship for training its new managers. In this context, the creation of the École des Hautes Études Commerciales corresponded to what may be viewed as a collective, perhaps even a 'national,' project – the school was established as a response to pressure on the government from a group of citizens, the members of the Chambre de commerce du district de Montréal. Funding for its facilities and operations was provided by the public purse. What is more, the new institution was assigned a complex mission: to relieve overcrowding in the traditional liberal arts professions by offering graduates of collèges classiques new avenues into the job market; and, above all, to promote the creation of a new class of francophone executives able to compete with their English-speaking counterparts and to enhance their compatriots' influence in the economic life of Montréal, Québec, and even Canada.

The École des HÉC was therefore not a response to business imperatives, unlike the schools in the United States. It was mandated to make an essential contribution to the economic development of the francophone collectivity. Joseph-Xavier Perrault (the founder of the Chambre de commerce de Montréal), Georges Gonthier (the most tenacious and effective proponent of the school in the critical year of 1906), and Premier Lomer Gouin expressed this sentiment time and time again. Essay writer Errol Bouchette went even further when he argued that the entry of HÉC graduates in the job market demanding employment opportunities worthy of their training would force the government to adopt, at long last, an industrial development policy.[17] For Bouchette, HÉC was never intended to meet a demand from business, since such a demand did not exist at the time; instead, the school could create a supply of professionals that would fuel the implementation of an aggressive industrial policy, which Bouchette wholeheartedly believed would ensure Québec's economic progress.

In short, the creation of the first American business schools at the turn of the century and the founding of HÉC in 1907 entailed two almost entirely different processes. The École des Hautes Études Commerciales constituted a unique case in North America. Its style was European, though marginally adapted to suit the Montréal environment. In fact, the promoters of the project and the school's founders, including J.-X. Perrault, Honoré Gervais, and Lomer Gouin, made almost exclusive reference to European establishments. The sole exception to this rule was Georges Gonthier, who in his 1900 letter referred to an American example, that of the New York University School of Commerce, Accounts and Finance.

While Europe served as a model for the school, the prevailing conditions on the old continent still differed from those in Montréal. For instance, although the local chambers of commerce played a significant role in the early affairs of the business schools in both Montréal and Europe (especially in France), the nature of this role was far from being the same. In France, the chambers of commerce enjoyed a quasi-public status and even had a degree of fiscal authority – they could collect a special tax in exchange for their role in establishing and managing a certain type of technical and professional training. Thus, the École des Hautes Études Commerciales de Paris was created by the Chambre de Commerce de Paris, and was entirely dependent on it for both funding and management. The government's role was limited to recognizing its degrees by declaring the institution a 'public utility.'

In Québec, as in the rest of Canada, chambers of commerce have always been mere business associations with no financial resources other than those raised internally from their members. When the École des HÉC de Montréal was created in 1907 at the request of the Chambre de commerce de Montréal, the business association had promised the school an annual grant of $5000. Moreover, the original charter stipulated that every officer of the school, with the exception of the principal, should be members of the Chambre and recommended by this association.[18] However, the Chambre de commerce never paid this grant and its commitment was eventually cancelled through a charter amendment. In fact, after the first few months of hardship preceding the school's creation and the first few years of its operation, the Chambre de commerce and HÉC almost completely ignored each other and have long followed separate paths. The school thus increasingly became a concern of the government, especially that of Lomer Gouin.

If the École des Hautes Études Commerciales de Montréal was developed along European lines, its syllabi were by no means a mirror image of those of the École des Hautes Études Commerciales de Paris, despite their similar acronyms and the numerous references to the Parisian institution made by the major proponents behind the Montréal institution's founding. The block of courses dedicated to business teaching accounted for almost two-thirds of the total class time of the school's initial program, compared with 30 per cent at the Paris institution at the same time. Moreover, language teaching, which accounted for over 25 per cent of the activities at the Paris HÉC, represented only 7 per cent of class time in Montréal.[19] Finally, the Paris program lasted only two years at the time, while the Montréal HÉC offered a three-year post-B.A. program.

The École des Hautes Études Commerciales de Montréal was first and foremost inspired by the Belgian model. The school's first principal, Auguste-Joseph de Bray, was Belgian (and a graduate of Antwerp), as was the second, Henry Laureys (a graduate of Louvain). Several members of the original faculty were also recruited in Belgium, and various aspects of the school's initial program (developed by de Bray) appear to have been borrowed directly from the program of the Institut Supérieur de Commerce in Antwerp. In 1910, Premier Gouin himself noted to the members of the legislative assembly the fact that he had 'visited ... in Antwerp the world's first school for advanced commercial studies ever to be built.'[20] Finally, in 1925, Belgian universities granted the École des Hautes Études Commerciales de Montréal 'the equivalent status of Belgian and Canadian licentiate in commerce.'[21]

With time, however, the École des Hautes Études Commerciales de Montréal lost much of its European character and gradually acquired a North American identity. This transformation, however, occurred over several decades, and was not completed until after Québec's entire education system was completely revamped in the 1960s.

NOTES

This essay was translated by Benoît Ouellette.

1 The PhD program is offered jointly by the École des Hautes Études Commerciales, McGill University, Concordia University, and Université du Québec à Montréal (UQAM).

2 For an account of the early years of HÉC see Pierre Harvey, *Histoire de l'École des Hautes Études Commerciales de Montréal, Tome I : 1887–1926* (Montréal: Éditions Québec/Amérique–Presses HÉC, 1994).

3 See Michael Bliss, *Plague: A Story of Smallpox in Montreal* (Toronto: HarperCollins, 1991).

4 For a week-by-week account of the events surrounding the founding of the Chambre de commerce, please refer to *Le Moniteur du Commerce*, whose owner and publisher, F.D. Shallow, was one of the principals behind the project.

5 *Bulletin de la Chambre de Commerce du district de Montreal* 1:1, 1 May 1889, 12.

6 Former deputy and an important businessman at the time, Damase Parizeau was the great-grandfather of Jacques Parizeau, the former premier of Québec.

7 It is believed that these documents were obtained at a booth operated at the fair by the Chambre de commerce de Paris at the 1900 Paris world fair, which showcased the programs and accomplishments of the École des Hautes Études Commerciales de Paris.

8 Although the letter from Gonthier is no longer in the archives of the Chambre de commerce, the full text was published in *Bulletin de la Chambre de commerce du district de Montréal*, 1 December 1900, 97; our translation.

9 *House of Commons Debates* 6 (23 October 1903), 14774–93.

10 Ibid. 5 (6 August 1904), 8753–72.

11 At that time, Université Laval à Montréal was a branch of Université Laval in Québec City. The branch obtained its own charter in 1920 only, and became the Université de Montréal.

12 Translated from an article in the 6 April 1906 issue of the newspaper *Le Canada*. The premier was citing a 'French author,' whose name he did not reveal. In all probability, this author was Georges Blondel, a professor at the École des HÉC de Paris and a friend of Gervais.

13 Our translation.

14 The full text of Gervais's speech was published in French in the magazine *Le Prix courant* 50, 26–9.

15 In 1910, the main program of study at HÉC was the Licence en sciences

commerciales et maritimes (licentiate in commercial and maritime science) – a three-year program with the bachelor of arts degree as a prerequisite. The PhD program launched at the same time was not as successful.

16 F.C. Pierson, *The Education of American Businessmen: A Study of University College Programs in Business Administration* (New York: McGraw-Hill, 1959), 40–1.

17 Errol Bouchette, *L'Indépendance économique des Canadiens-Français* (Montréal: Wilson & Lafleur, 1913), 199.

18 The Chambre de commerce de Montréal still plays a role on the board of directors of the school's corporation, together with the alumni association, the Government of Québec, the faculty association, and the student association.

19 HÉC archives, Jouy-en-Josas, France.

20 *La Presse*, 4 June 1910; our translation.

21 *Livres de minutes* (École des Hautes Études Commerciales de Montréal, 22 October 1925); our translation.

3

Business Education at Queen's, 1889–1988

MERVIN DAUB and P. BRUCE BUCHAN

This chapter examines the development of educational programs for business at Queen's University. The university introduced political and economic science as a component of undergraduate education during the late nineteenth century, and in 1919 it became the first Canadian institution to supply a complete baccalaureate program in commerce. Across the following eighty years, the faculty members developed a complex set of intramural offerings and extension services despite small size, limited resources, and a lack of close proximity to the commercial centres of Canada or the United States. Despite the broader reputation of Queen's as an educational institution, in many ways this essay thus is about 'the little business school that could.' The development of programs about commerce and business, therefore, has been, and remains, no mean feat.

Their evolution has been quite distinct from the experiences of other Canadian universities. Although partially conditioned by institutional goals, the process was heavily shaped by the conduct and objectives of different faculty members as the varied operations of the business school were propelled through several stages. The first section of this chapter briefly reviews the institutional background, as well as the factors and personalities that shaped the emergence of studies in economic and social affairs. The establishment of the baccalaureate degree in commerce between 1919 and 1937 is then considered. The narrative appraises the intellectual sources of the program and how the course of study was geared to the practical study of business problems. The third section highlights the accomplishments and problems that unfolded during the intermediate period following, as the faculty strived to maintain a viable operation. The final part summarizes the fundamental transformation towards a professional orientation, which unfolded between 1963 and 1988, a period when the school became a major supplier of business education in Canada.

Antecedents, 1889–1919

The earliest origins of the study of business or commerce are difficult to designate. Certainly, there are some very early references from the classical period, including Plato's *Republic* or various writings of Aristotle, while commentaries occasionally surface in documents from the Roman and medieval eras. This reference to ancient philosophical sources might initially seem inappropriate, but the business program at Queen's was a product of the political economy department, which had emerged from the university's original emphasis on classical studies and moral philosophy as the appropriate subjects of higher learning.

Founded in 1841 as a Presbyterian college for theology and arts studies, Queen's served as the post-secondary institution for the eastern district of Ontario and remained a denominational college until 1912. During the early years it was a tiny enterprise, perpetually near bankruptcy owing to the low income levels of the surrounding region and the unwillingness of the Presbyterian synod to fund activities other than the faculty of theology. Under Principal George Munro Grant (1835–1902), who was determined to block takeover attempts by the University of Toronto and efforts by the Ontario government to centralize control over post-secondary education, the university was redirected, albeit with considerable internal and external turmoil. Grant rebuilt Queen's through numerous endowment campaigns and slowly converted it into a diversified institution similar in form to, although much smaller than, Toronto and McGill. Not only did he push for a formal separation from religious control, he sought to strengthen the social legitimacy of the university by redefining its mission in secular terms as a provider of educational activities that could meet the needs of different interests and aid social development. Characterizing the University of Toronto as 'the provincial university,' Grant aspired to make Queen's 'a national institution' that serviced interests beyond those in its geographic hinterland, a goal that was realized through selective expansion into applied sciences, medicine, and mining engineering. Secularization also permitted application for special appropriations from the provincial government and private foundations that were rationalized as support for the university's service ideal, although Grant and his successors had to work assiduously to minimize the potential for government interference. Extramural or extension courses were initially offered in eastern Ontario and after 1900 were extended to the provinces and territories in Western Canada. Concurrently, research in different aspects of the liberal arts was increased through the efforts of people like the philosopher John Watson and the literary critic James Cappon. A new publication, *Queen's Quarterly,* was a convenient vehicle for publicizing their observations. The first university-based intellectual journal in Canada, it also was one of the few in existence before 1920.[1]

As discussed in chapter 1, economic affairs in North America underwent a dramatic transformation during the second half of the nineteenth century. The growing importance of industry, along with the associated division of labour and the emphasis upon functional specialization, spurred the growth of academic interest in business and commerce. University-based programs initially developed at Wharton and after 1900 at a select group of institutions like Chicago, Wisconsin, and New York University. At other universities, while many faculty members recognized the importance of business affairs, they did not share a 'pragmatic persuasion,' that is, they did not fully accept an emphasis on practical subjects or a shift from the traditional role that universities had carried out for training young gentlemen. Without stooping to 'in-tradeism' or a tolerance of the 'nouveau riche,' they were prepared to accept limited innovations in curriculum design and efforts to differentiate economics from moral or political philosophy, subject to the proviso that a significant role for liberal studies would be retained. This second approach was the pattern that unfolded at Queen's, partially because during the late nineteenth century the university had been staffed largely by academics recruited in England and was anglophile in many respects.

Political economy was introduced during 1878, but as a branch of mental and moral philosophy with a course taught by John Watson. The subject traditionally had lacked theoretical rigour, and participation by faculty members in debates about public policy questions had been deemed unacceptable despite the growing importance of issues like tariffs, taxation, banking, or public finance. An idealistic philosopher who believed that human sciences and human reason could triumph over natural forces and mechanistic notions of society, Watson extensively reshaped the curriculum and made Queen's one of the few

Canadian universities that dealt with politics and economics as regular components of undergraduate studies. He encouraged teaching and applied research about Canadian issues, not just economic methodology. The classes, for the first time in Canada, were delivered by a 'Political Science Department' that was separate from philosophy.[2]

With Watson's support, during 1888 Adam Shortt was appointed as John Leys lecturer in political economy and in 1892 became the Sir John A. Macdonald professor in political science. The son of a miller in the pioneer district of Ontario's Bruce County, he had been educated by a Presbyterian clergyman who had been the first graduate of Queen's and was a member of its governing board. Shortt began the arts course at the university expecting to emphasize theology, but shifted to secular fields, especially philosophy. He attended Edinburgh and Glasgow universities but did not earn a degree; upon his return to Canada, on the basis of his work in the United Kingdom, Queen's awarded him an MA in 1885. His initial appointment to teach political economy had been with the expectation by George Grant that Shortt would give the course a decent internment, but instead he resuscitated the subject.[3]

During the 1890s Shortt carried out a lengthy series of empirical investigations into banking, history, and public policies that, despite the brevity of his academic career, later led economists to see him as the founder of their discipline in Canada. He also served as an expert consultant for governments, chairing a dozen conciliation boards set up under the federal Industrial Disputes Investigation Act. In 1908 he resigned from Queen's to accept a position on the new Civil Service Commission, one of the first social scientists hired by the federal government to solve social problems using technical knowledge. A pragmatist and not a social theorist, he shared Watson's belief that general laws governed the evolution of civilizations, but perceived an industrial society as a complex set of semi-autonomous relationships. Shortt became convinced that careful analysis would allow the identification of malleable components that, through public action, could then be transformed to enhance social welfare. His classes were devoted to practical questions about Canadian society and, reflecting his own ambitions, Shortt encouraged his students to continue research at American graduate schools. Over time he inspired an impressive group of students, many of whom shared his faith in public service, and the network that formed among these individuals later was key for the development of business education at Queen's.[4]

The courses delivered during Shortt's era were essentially economics, but were supplemented with readings that included precursors of business textbooks such as Cunningham's *The Growth of English Industry and Commerce* and Brentano's *Guilds and Trade Unions*, or political volumes like *Theory of the State*. As early as 1900, honours students were offered courses like Political Economy or Society and the State. Classes explored the need for government to take a balanced role in the regulation of capital or labour relations, and discussions centred around the problems associated with laissez-faire economics or excessive state intervention. Students read Plato, Locke, and Socrates in the former course and Adam Smith, John Stuart Mill, and Aristotle in the latter.[5]

There is little question that the direct father of business studies at Queen's was Oscar Douglas Skelton. Born in 1878, Skelton completed high school at Cornwall, an eastern Ontario town within the traditional hinterland of Queen's and attended the university, where he was an enthusiastic student of classics, winning an award as outstanding Latin scholar and receiving an MA with first-class honours in 1899. He then pursued graduate studies at the University of Chicago, a small Baptist college that had been transformed into a major institution by endowments from the Rockefeller family. He dropped classics after a year and departed for Britain to make his fortune. Skelton became the first known Canadian to pass the examinations for the Indian Civil Service, but was denied an appointment owing to his poor eyesight. After several years of working for a popular journal in Philadelphia, he returned to the University of Chicago in 1905, this time as a doctoral candidate in political economy. He studied with the economist J. Laurence Laughlin, who played a key role in establishing a commerce program at Chicago and later had a pivotal role in the formation of the Federal Reserve system. At the urging of Adam Shortt, Skelton returned to Kingston as a lecturer in 1907 and the following year became the Macdonald professor of political science, rejecting more lucrative offers from American universities and a position as deputy minister of labour in Ottawa. He normally taught political science and sociology – especially courses about government and the economy, labour problems, socialism, public finance, and constitutional theory. Author of seven books and numerous essays, editor of the *Canadian Bankers' Journal*, and a frequent consultant for the federal government, Skelton became one of the most prominent persons at the university and his rising status led to an appointment as dean of arts from 1919 to

1924. After serving as a special counsellor with the Department of External Affairs, he chose to remain in Ottawa and from 1925 until his death in 1941 was Canada's undersecretary for external affairs.[6]

Upon his appointment as head of the department of political science, Skelton immediately sought an assistant to build up the teaching areas that complemented his interests. His initial appointment was William Swanson, who had received an MA from Queen's in 1904 and also attended Chicago for doctoral studies under Laughlin. Swanson returned to Kingston and handled the economics courses of the department, along with a burgeoning group of correspondence offerings, until he departed in 1917 to become professor of economics at Saskatchewan. Of equally good fortune was Skelton's ability to convince W.C. Clark to return to the university during 1916. Born in Glengarry County of eastern Ontario, Clifford Clark had studied languages, literature, history, and political economy before leaving for Harvard, where he pursued post-graduate work in economics under F.W. Taussig, one of the co-founders of the Harvard Business School. He received an MA degree but never finished a dissertation on the marketing of prairie grain. Clark rapidly progressed and became a full professor by 1923, but he altered his career objectives repeatedly. During 1918 and 1919 he took a leave of absence to serve with the federal department of labour, but in 1923 resigned to join a firm of real estate developers with operations in Chicago and New York. He taught economics part-time at the University of Chicago during this period and, after the collapse of his business prospects in 1929, returned to direct the Queen's commerce program. In 1932 he resigned to become a deputy minister in Ottawa, a position he held for the next two decades.[7]

Skelton, Swanson, and Clark believed, like Shortt, that an understanding of social science was important to public affairs and business. The head of the department was particularly impatient with the 'backwoods preachers' who still dominated the university. While still at Chicago, he had written to Shortt that 'strikes, trusts, taxes, socialism, tariffs, banking, bulk a great deal larger in the public mind than the authenticity of St. John's gospel or the wheretofore of the whyness of Hegel. Possibly they shouldn't, but here for once Providence and the stream is with the righteous, otherwise the political sciences.'[8]

The influence of economists and other social scientists had rapidly been extended within American universities and governmental activities after 1900. Through new modes of theoretical analysis, along with the formation of professional academic associations or by adopting the guise of neutral expertise, many academics had been able to shape the elaboration of public policies aimed at controlling the problems associated with industrialization and urbanization. However, despite intensive efforts by teachers of the liberal arts, Canadian universities still had comparatively little influence in the larger society and were ignored by political authorities. To extend their autonomy and status within the university community, Skelton and his colleagues pushed for a secularization of the institution, while concurrently proposing programs that would meet the demands of external interests for useful education. As early as 1909, Skelton began to lobby for a distinctive school of commerce. He argued that this initiative was necessary 'because there was much scope for improving the education of people going into business both to provide specific tools of business management and to provide a broader educational background.' Although it might be too expensive to establish a full operation, 'there were a large group of employees in the banks that could benefit from extension courses in economics.'[9]

Although the proposal was rejected, through careful planning Skelton was able to build up the department and by the outbreak of the First World War it had an enrolment of 303 students, which included 79 candidates majoring in economics and 100 in political science. A social-problems perspective was applied in a range of courses. An introductory course in sociology was abolished in favour of one on Labour Problems that dealt with questions like profit-sharing as a solution to employee relations, the legality of sympathetic strikes and picketing, or legal liability in industrial accidents. Skelton offered a course about Social and Charitable Work that dealt with the 'principles and methods of present day social betterment activities.' The department supplied courses in Principles of Economic Theory, Economic Geography, Corporation Finance, Public Finance and Taxation, and Economic Geography. Even supposedly abstract courses like Principles of Economic Theory leaned towards the practical with a promise that the concepts could be applied in such 'concrete problems as money, banking, the tariff, transportation, the distribution of wealth, and the labour question.'[10]

After three years of protracted negotiations, Skelton launched an initiative to meet the educational needs of external interests. Under a contractual arrangement with the Canadian Bankers' Association, a program of correspondence courses was created during the autumn of 1914. The university was responsible for preparing the syllabus of study, conducting examinations, and awarding diplomas at two levels designated as 'Associate' (ACBA) and 'Fellow' of the Canadian Bankers' Association (FCBA). Aimed at 'men already in the service of the Canadian banks,' the program covered 'both practical and theoretical aspects of their work.' Instruction for the associate's course was handled by the Shaw Correspondence School in Toronto and the subjects included commercial and foreign-exchange arithmetic, English composition, bank correspondence, and bookkeeping. Students periodically took examinations that were administered by staff at the university. All aspects of the fellow's course were handled through correspondence operations conducted by the university. The offerings included courses in economic theory, corporate finance, money and banking, advanced accounting, and auditing. Although wartime conditions might have interfered with the venture and Skelton had initial problems gaining support from some banks, it was a large operation from the start. By November of 1915, 685 people were enrolled in the associate's course and 315 in the fellow's. Students utilizing the service were located from Dawson Creek to Newfoundland.[11]

Establishing the Bachelor of Commerce, 1919–1937

As outlined in the first chapter, in Canada post-secondary education for business emerged incrementally during the first two decades of the twentieth century. The University of Toronto during 1901 launched a two-year diploma course modelled after the commerce degree at Birmingham. The program was extended to four years in 1909 and reorganized as an honours baccalaureate degree in arts in 1919. McGill during 1907 created a similar diploma that was more practical and intended as preparation for certain professions, especially accounting. HÉC has long claimed to have been the first business school in Canada, 'le doyenne des écoles d'administration,' but it was not then an established university and only gave diplomas. Queen's, in fact, was the first Canadian *university* to offer a complete *degree* in commercial or business studies, even though a separate school was not created to handle that endeavour.

It might seem that the establishment of a degree was inevitable but, as occurred elsewhere, the initiative reflected institutional concerns and was quite distinctive. The financial status of Queen's after 1914 was strained by the costs associated with the formation of new departments, and enrolment declined, a phenomenon that occurred at other post-secondary institutions during the war. Despite increases in government funding, the loss of tuition revenue became so severe that in 1917 the senior administrators were forced to approach the chancellor, James Douglas, for a million-dollar donation to stabilize the institution's financial position. The small size of the university, however, compounded the situation. Salary scales were less than half of the prevailing levels of Toronto or McGill, and the lack of resources blocked the development of essential services, such as an expansion of the library collection. The principal, not surprising, emphasized the importance of extension services since they had helped the institution's cash flow. Concurrently, manufacturers based in Ontario demanded greater research services by Canadian universities and an expansion of programs geared to the careers of returning veterans. A proposal that could simultaneously provide greater revenues, meet the needs of external groups, and fulfil the university's service goals would thus have obvious appeal.[12]

Near the end of the war, Skelton prepared a lengthy memorandum for Principal R. Bruce Taylor about 'suggestions as to the best way in which Queen's can meet the new calls being made upon the universities in consequence of the growing pressures of our economic and social problems.' Canada, he argued, could no longer escape the difficulties of 'an advanced industrial system,' which included 'the burden of taxation, the insistent demands for social reconstruction, the dangers of class and sectional cleavage, the problems of land settlement and of provision for returned soldiers, the task of keeping and extending the share we have won in the world's trade, our modest part in the problems of international reorganization – these and many more such issues demand all the thought and study we can give ... The days of happy-go-lucky ease, the days when we had a continent to burn, are gone for good and all.' Universities had to introduce 'semi-professional instruction for many of the new tasks,' while concurrently encouraging scholars to research and communicate information about those questions to students and the general public. Educational services for business or public and social administration could allow 'systematized deductions from experience ... Just as the training of the doctor and the engineer, formerly obtained wholly by practice and apprenticeship, now is based on extensive college study, so will the preparation for these other activities more and more be given in the universities.'[13] Taking this logic much further, Clark subsequently argued that only the spread of a managerial ethic could offset some of the problems associated with industrialization. 'If we are to be saved from the dangers of a crudely acquisitive society, this professional point of view must be spread among business men as widely and as rapidly as possible. The task in so far as it can be performed by education is one which only the University can perform, and it is one which will call for the best which the University can give.'[14]

Skelton proposed, as a first step, a degree course in commerce that would be delivered by the Faculty of Arts. The trustees appointed him chair of a special committee of senior professors and in March 1919 that group recommended a major increase in the emphasis given to research, the creation of graduate fellowships, and a four-year program leading to a bachelor of commerce degree, with provision for a fifth year of work qualifying for a master of commerce degree. Approval was complicated by considerable opposition, which took some time to die away. The initiative, James Cappon, the outgoing dean of arts, publicly declared, was just 'another instance of the extension of Vocational Education in the University. The instruction in these courses includes a few humanistic subjects but is mainly economical, commercial and actuarial.' 'It must be kept in mind, however, that in the Arts Faculty at least education should always have more than a merely vocational purpose ... In the midst of all our practical modern developments this original and most characteristic function of the University, that of training a large-minded citizenship, remains properly the chief function, the function which distinguishes it from a Technical or Business College.' Privately, he characterized the introduction of business-related courses as a capitulation to material values. 'We seem to have reached the decadent days of that great middle-class mercantile civilization that was so proud of itself ... even twenty years ago ... Quite a half of the legislation and movements we think progress ... are merely the movements of a sick man tossing on the bed.'[15] One trustee, J.M. MacDonnell, a successful businessman who later became chair of the board, claimed that commerce courses had a 'questionable value' since they 'circumscribed that latitude of the mind which is the real spirit of learning.' Rather, he asserted, the vocational spirit that was invading universities should be 'eradicated as speedily as possible.'[16] Skelton and Clark, with help that included Shortt and other sympathetic representatives, carried the day. Ironically, while the trustees felt there was a legitimate need for the commerce program, opponents within the academic community assured each other that it would flounder. One story that has long circulated, probably apocryphal, is that Skelton himself told Cappon that the degree would not attract too many students.[17]

In fairness, some would argue that the debate has never died away and has formed the basis of an ongoing tension about the 'legitimate' character of academic endeavours, not only between the commerce faculty and the rest of the university but also within the business school itself. As in other professional faculties of law, medicine, and engineering, there have been uneasy and repetitious arguments about the relative merits of theoretical versus practical education, the appropriate emphases for research versus teaching, or the degree of intellectualism versus professionalism. Business education at Queen's, like the endeavours at other institutions, periodically shifted according to the influence exerted by proponents of those alternate perspectives.

Skelton and Clark were aware of the objections aimed at collegiate business education. Programs that employed more theoretical and broad-based learning had been frequently criticized by business practitioners who wanted graduates with useable skills. To practitioners, Skelton argued that commerce frequently was no different from law or medicine, that 'the fledgling [graduate would] profit by his early experience more rapidly and less painfully than is commonly the case' without higher education. To academic opponents, he declared a need 'to see retained in the course of the commercial student a substantial measure of literature and history and science, in order to open up interests and phases of life that may otherwise be barred to the business man. It is for the same reason that I believe instruction in economics and social relationships, the specific study of the ways and principles of commerce are essential in a business man's training and superior for this purpose, other things being equal, to instruction in subjects of only remote and indirect bearing.'[18]

Skelton and Clark argued, on every occasion possible, that the need for business education had become a matter of social urgency. In a special calendar published for the degree, Skelton observed: 'Business affairs and social relationships are taking on a new complexity. Broad issues of economic justice have grown insistent. The scope of public activity has widened. New international relations impose new tasks and offer new opportunities alike in private industry and in public service. With this development there has come, particularly in the United States and latterly in the United Kingdom, a recognition that the university must take a greater part in preparing men for these wider tasks.'[19]

The format of the program was based upon their understanding of other degrees in America and Europe. Skelton segmented these into three forms: narrow, specialized vocational courses; broad, liberal arts–based schema; or curricula lying between those two extremes. He cited New York University as an example of the first, the Harvard Graduate School of Business Administration as representative of the second, and the University of Chicago and others as examples of a compromise between those extremes, adding that the third was 'the plan which we have followed in Queen's.' Skelton admired the Harvard program because it restricted business to graduate studies, afforded 'a longer period of study, a more comprehensive and thorough training and ... unusual opportunities for special investigation.' However, Queen's could not cover the financial costs associated with that orientation and Canadian demand was almost exclusively for baccalaureate offerings. Hence, the university should supply a broader foundation 'than the purely technical school can do, without requiring the six or seven years of graduate school.'[20]

Moreover, many American programs were launched to meet the needs of manufacturing companies, while the Queen's initiative was intended to prepare candidates for entry into Canadian banking and insurance. This thrust also fit the intellectual orientation of the faculty and the public-service concerns espoused by Shortt and Skelton. Although his vision of business education was more influenced by pedagogy and philosophy of science, Clifford Clark's views were, not surprisingly, similar to those of Skelton, and he distinguished between two academic models. The first consisted of 'highly technical, highly specialized subjects ... designed to give the specialized skill necessary for a particular business or a particular "job."' The second was 'designed to teach the principles which underlie business administration in general and to give the business training necessary for any business career ... In the technical type of school, the courses are primarily descriptive; by lecture and drill the student is taught what to do in a given position, is given the detailed technique necessary for a particular business. In the other type of course, broad mental training, not specialized routine knowledge, is the object aimed at and hence the development of principles inductively from the results of observation, comparison and reflection takes the place of the dogmatic presentation of facts.'[21]

Clark and Skelton appreciated the pedagogical orientation of the Harvard Business School (founded in 1908) which treated management as a profession, an art, and a science. Harvard's first dean, Edwin F. Gay, believed that the 'teacher of business ... must discover the fundamental principles of business system, and then, in a scientific spirit, teach not only those principles, but the art of applying them after investigation, to any given enterprise. Generalizations and concepts could be induced from observation through experience and the accumulation of facts about firms and their activities.'[22] One of the ways in which that knowledge could be acquired was through a structured analysis of case materials. Although the origin of the case method has often been attributed to the Harvard Law School, the technique drew upon the German model of teaching natural sciences, which had been commonly described as a 'laboratory method.' American economists who had undertaken doctoral studies in Germany during the late nineteenth century imported the technique. At Harvard, the pedagogy had been applied as a seminar approach by F.W. Taussig of the economics department and then was refined into a sophisticated pedagogy by Melvin Copeland and other instructors in the business school.[23]

Skelton was most heavily influenced by the philosophy of the College of Commerce and Business Administration at the University of Chicago. The baccalaureate degree educated students both culturally and professionally with an emphasis upon managerial rather than technical issues. The course was not vocational in orientation or geared to turning out semi-skilled functionaries like bookkeepers, stenographers, or clerks. Rather, it was 'aimed at enrolling ambitious young men, the future executives of American business, and giving them an education that would fit them for positions in management.'[24] Just eleven of the thirty-six credits required for the bachelor of philosophy (in commerce) degree were business subjects, and the other courses were taken from the faculties of arts and science. The program, observed Leon C. Marshall, dean of the college after 1910, conveyed 'a broad cultural foundation in the main divisions of human knowledge. Above this foundation is placed a broad survey of the social sciences ... Even after the social science survey has been completed, narrow specialization may not occur.' Courses explored different types of business problems via the case method to reinforce pragmatic decision-making and keep a focus upon thinking rather than doing. Through field trips, outside lecturers, and obligations for summer employment with firms, students engaged in 'a considerable amount of contact with actual conditions' and avoided 'the academic spirit' in their work.[25]

Skelton's experience at Chicago, his senior position, and political antennae were the deciding factors when the parameters of the Queen's program were defined. Clifford Clark probably favoured an approach that explicitly followed the Harvard schema, but no records have survived that indicate a serious disagreement. The schedule leading to a bachelor of commerce required the equivalent of nineteen full-year courses if one entered with 'junior matriculation' (the equivalent of Grade 12 in Ontario high schools). It was expected a student would normally take four years but, as with other arts programs, the work was not rigidly divided by year, so that a candidate could take a longer period if necessary. Students had to achieve 'second division standing (54% or better) in ten courses or their equivalent – the pass mark at that time being 40%.'[26]

The curriculum could be tailored to fit career interests, with streams in general business, banking and finance, accounting and auditing, and foreign trade. Students were provided with the options of specializing in public service or social service. Brochures described the degree as suitable for 'a large and increasing number of positions, especially in such departments as those dealing with Labour, Trade and Commerce, Finance, Railways, Agriculture, and Natural Resources.' Upon graduation, students were promised a higher probability of gaining 'entrance and promotion' in the civil service, and university publications suggested their prospects would be improved by courses in municipal and federal government, law, office management, socialism, or industry-government relations. The social-service option was 'designed for work in philanthropy and community service.' The offerings for a public service specialization could be supplemented with courses like Economic Theory of Distribution, Labour Problems, National Problems, Social Problems, Psychology and Supervised Field Work, Methods of Social Amelioration, and Methods of Social Investigation. A commerce degree thus would strengthen the intellectual background of social workers and, in line with Skelton's political philosophy, would help them to abet social harmony and the environmental conditions associated with industrial capitalism.[27]

An examination of the curriculum reveals several other issues. First, 'General Subjects' (English, French, and mathematics, which were normally taken during the first year of studies) actually were intended to bring candidates up to the level of senior matriculation or Grade 13. Second, all courses supplied by the department of political economy were labelled as 'economics' regardless of their economic, political, or commercial content, a policy that remained in place until 1933. Third, nearly three-quarters of the required courses were taken in the arts and sciences. All university candidates, regardless of professional aspiration, had to take Introduction to Economics and Introduction to Politics (each a full-year course).[28]

From the beginning, the program sought to inculcate a 'cultural and professional background,' along with leadership skills and the knowledge of business skills. An emphasis had been given by the department of political science to the study of management issues even before the new degree was established. A course in Labour and the State was regularly offered, along with another entitled National Problems, which covered imperial relations, post-war reconstruction, language and racial issues, immigration, and community organization. Students were required to submit annually essays on designated topics like 'Unemployment, Its Causes and Remedies' and 'The Working of the Canadian Industrial Disputes Investigation Act.'[29] Once the program was under way, special courses in management were created for the optional streams such as Factory Management, Employment Management, and Office Management. Industrial Management used Frederick Taylor's *Shop Management* as a textbook and sought to 'acquaint the student with some of the problems to be met in industrial plants.' By learning theories and skills in scientific management, students considered the issues confronted by the 'machine shop type of factory' rather than the problems characteristic of specific industries. By 1924 the course was redesigned to provide 'a study of the organization and the factors in industry and of the relations and labour problems involved.' Problems of Labour considered questions 'arising out of the wage system, and their attempted solution by legislation, organization and internal management.'[30]

The commerce degree was established, its director noted in 1923, 'with the definite belief that principles of business are capable of being taught as Law has come to be taught.' It was not possible to substitute instruction for practice, but 'it is definitely assumed that the discussion of business principles and the study of business cases will help to make trained and competent business men.' 'There seems to be little doubt that the case method of teaching business will assume as large proportion as has been in the teaching of Law.' To ensure that a managerial perspective was fully inculcated, every effort had been made to restrict enrolment 'to those who are definitely looking forward to business as a profession; and any attempts to look on ... [commerce] as merely an Arts Course with an overdose of Economics are consistently and on the whole successfully discouraged.'[31] Indeed, as the curriculum was successively revised, greater attention was placed upon the development of managerial characteristics. Professionalism and professional conduct had assumed greater importance, noted the director in 1928, since business was 'becoming more a matter of planning, organizing, and accurate analysis, and less a matter of mere bargaining.'[32] Pedagogical pragmatism and a positivistic philosophy of science were expected to give the degree both academic legitimacy and practical relevance. The art, science, and profession of business received equal importance since, as described in the Queen's *Calendar*, the mission was 'to unite a general cultural foundation with a study of economic principles and an introduction to the technique of the various professional occupations to be followed.'[33]

The development of a managerial focus was systemic with courses using the case method. This instructional technique was presented as the 'problem method,' whereby 'the student will have constantly presented to him by the Instructor or by practical business men, problems that have actually arisen in business.' Although most of the graduates entered private-sector firms, concepts and skills learned through the case approach were presented as transferable to public bureaucracies, health services or other not-for-profit organizations. By solving business problems inductively, students would learn 'a systematic body of principles underlying business activity,' 'the power of investigation and analysis,' and 'the habit of thinking systematically on business subjects.'[34] Students were given actual business problems from Canadian companies, and courses like marketing, business finance, and industrial management were often handled by outside lecturers from the business community. The visiting speakers constituted a veritable *Who's Who?* of the Canadian private and public sectors. The lecturers during the 1922–3 academic year, for example, included senior officers from Canadian Locomotive, the Canadian Pacific Railway, Imperial Oil, and the Dominion Bureau of Statistics. To reinforce the practical side of business affairs, classes were supplemented with visits to plants near Kingston, and students had to submit investigative reports based upon those trips. Students also were obligated to work for a minimum of one summer in 'approved business establishments or in public offices' in order to collect data for a thesis and to gain insights for their areas of specialization.[35]

How many students were there in the first year? Skelton reported at the end of the 1919–20 academic year that 'no separate registration was made, as the work is not distinct from the regular Arts work in the early stages, but twenty students have expressed their intention to proceed to the Bachelor of Commerce degree. From enquiries which have been made it is clear that a very considerable number of men and women will wish to avail themselves of the new opportunities if adequate instruction is provided.' Until the 1960s commerce students were registered in the Faculty of Arts and enrolment data appeared intermittently in university publications. The only measure of program size for which complete data are extant has been an output factor: the number of degrees conferred annually. Two degrees were granted in the autumn of 1921 and the annual number of degrees awarded increased from seven to seventeen between 1922 and 1925. In the first graduating class were William Edgar Black and Thomas William Oates. Black, the first graduate, went on to a teaching career in Montreal at Westmount High School and Sir George Williams (which became a part of Concordia University). Among the fifty-four graduates during those years were six women, including Beatrice Eakins, who in 1922 became the first woman in Canada to receive a baccalaureate degree in commerce.

Who were the professors to whom these students were exposed? The entire department in the autumn of 1919 consisted of Skelton, professor and head of department; Clark, associate professor, director of banking and commerce courses; and L.I. Shaulis, a junior instructor. The following year Shaulis was replaced by J.W. Ballard, an appointment in accounting, while Ellis H. Morrow and R.E. Burns served as part-time lecturers in accounting. Morrow left in 1922 to head the business program at Western and later the commerce faculty at the University of British Columbia. The key appointment of this early period was W.A. Mackintosh, an outstanding student of Skelton's. Born in 1885 in the eastern Ontario town of Madoc, he had attended Queen's and received a BA in political economy during 1916. Macintosh followed Clark's lead and pursued graduate work in economics at Harvard under F.W. Taussig. Returning to Kingston after the completion of his doctorate, Macintosh, like Clark, advanced quickly and became professor in 1928. Author of three major works on the development of the prairie wheat economy, he also later succumbed to the lure of government. Between 1936 and 1946 he served as an adviser to several royal commissions and the federal ministries of finance and reconstruction. Macintosh returned to Queen's to serve as the dean of arts and quickly rose to the principalship, a post that he held for a decade.[36]

Skelton had to recruit staff not only to deliver the new degree and run the bankers' courses but also to handle a correspondence arrangement for the preparation of accounting students. After internal deliberations over two years, the Canadian Institute of Chartered Accountants of Ontario approached him during the summer of 1921 for help in designing a program. Skelton developed a schema where the Institute 'would choose the textbooks, register the students, collect the fees and set the syllabus,' while 'Queen's on its part would act as the educational agency of the Institute in carrying out the details of this policy.' As one observer later commented, the 'energetic and optimistic Mr. Skelton' indicated the university could start this program immediately, in the autumn of 1921, but developments soon indicated that 'he and, through him, Queen's, had bitten off far more than they could possibly chew ... During the first year it became obvious that Queen's simply did not have the manpower to handle the weight of the correspondence courses. The lesson exercises started flooding in and almost immediately there were delays in returning the graded exercises.'[37] During the first year 275 students enrolled, virtually all from Ontario, for what was initially intended as a four-year series of courses. The requirements were later raised to five years and the program eventually encompassed all of Canada. By the end of the Second World War, there were 1400 students enrolled annually.

Skelton advertised extensively for accountants and secured two lecturers from Western Canada. He recruited in England during the summer of 1922 and hired two young CA graduates who exerted a strong influence on accounting education across the next half-century: C.A. Ashley, who stayed briefly at the university and then joined the department of political economy at Toronto, and R.G.H. Smails, who never left. They arrived 'late in September, just in time for the fall term to open. There they found the chartered accountants' course of instruction in what can reasonably be described as a shambles. Smails used to claim that he was unable to enter his new office at Queen's, because the unmarked exercises were stacked so thickly on the floor that he could not push the door open.'[38]

However, perhaps because of their youthful energy as much as anything else, the commerce faculty dug their way out over the next several years. Registration in the baccalaureate program expanded from 114 candidates in 1923 to 215 by 1929 (out of a total enrolment of 3000 students at the university), while the number of degrees conferred annually ranged from 21 to 27. In contrast, the students registered in the correspondence courses grew from 487 to 629 across that time period.[39] Macintosh became director of the commerce program after 1923 and the accounting instructors remained a steady cohort. Non-accounting courses in business were handled by a mix of part-time and term appointments. But Clark and Skelton departed after lengthy battles with the principal of the university and in frustration over the limited scope of the commerce activities. Despite considerable efforts, the initiatives did not generate the coherent program of academic study and research that they had planned. The courses in commerce and accounting, quite vocational in orientation, were loosely related to the arts curriculum and staffing requirements for the areas of public policy and social services were never fulfilled owing to budget constraints. Salaries remained a mundane but telling issue as Queen's paid the political economists well below the compensation levels received by their colleagues at Toronto or in the federal civil service. Both Skelton and Clark more than doubled their salaries when they moved to Ottawa.[40]

The curriculum during those years evolved towards a formal year system and the establishment of an honours program. Smails later noted that students were advised 'to take only arts subjects in their first year, then two economics and two accounting courses in second year, and in the third (and the subsequent) year(s) courses in regular order.' This schema was 'made rigid' in 1929 along with a requirement for 'a total of twenty courses with a minimum of 50% in each general course, and in each course or half-course in economics numbered 10 or higher a minimum of 55% with an average of 66%.'[41] A three-year sequence of courses in either mathematics or a modern language also was imposed. This basic design remained relatively constant across the next fifty years despite later additions to the mandatory component of the curriculum.

By the conclusion of the 1920s, a viable undergraduate program had been firmly established, accompanied by a steady upgrading of academic standards and an expansion of extramural operations. The temporary return of Clifford Clark coincided with the entry of the first candidates to a fifth year of studies leading to a master of commerce degree. Queen's might, he speculated, 'look forward to the time when the Commerce Courses can be put wholly on a graduate basis.' The 'ideal training for business consists of two years of advanced work in a professional school following four years of liberal arts.' However, 'in this young country we may have to be content with a second best, say, two years of Commerce training open to men who have completed their third year in Arts.' William Macintosh, who became the head of the department in 1928, was prepared to accept a vocational thrust in commerce courses but was unwilling to sacrifice the traditional goals of university education. Separating business into a graduate program, he noted, was likely to make undergraduate courses even more narrow and technical. An emphasis on the liberal arts component, in contrast, might propel a long-term shift by business leaders from limited profit-seeking objectives toward greater creativity and social cooperation.[42]

The weakening of the Canadian economy during 1928 presaged a global collapse of stock markets and international trade, which triggered a deep downward economic spiral. Across this period to 1937, the commerce program and the extramural activities continued relatively unchanged. The Institute carried out a full-scale review of its courses and requirements during 1931, but the university's role remained secure. Enrolment in the accounting courses fluctuated from year to year but usually varied between 350 and 400 students per year. By the end of the 1930s, the Institute program supplied by the university had been adopted by other provincial chartered accounting associations except for Manitoba, Saskatchewan, and Québec. Aggregate undergraduate registration varied from 200 to 240 students during the early years of the Depression, leading Macintosh to complain about 'classes still large enough to tax our resources.' During the latter half of the 1930s, as employment opportunities remained limited, enrolment ranged from 160 to 180 candidates. An average of 27 degrees was conferred each year between 1930 and 1937.[43] Low salaries, the reluctance of the university administration to hire permanent new staff, and a heavy workload triggered considerable personnel turnover; but during this time frame two key faculty members joined, J.L. McDougall and Lawrence Macpherson.

The physical facilities available for business studies also represented a continuing issue. Smails later noted that the bankers' and chartered accountants' services

> involved the department in the big job of administration as well as teaching. Administration must be housed, at least after fashion, and so quarters were provided in the New Arts Building by turning Room 313 into a general office and a small adjacent room, built at the end of the corridor, into an 'executive office' ... It contained no office furniture and was not equipped with so much as one telephone. In April 1922 Clark was writing plaintively to the Treasurer, 'May I suggest that one of the sundries [in the

budget] might well be a telephone. There is, I believe, a real need for a telephone service for the banking and accounting office; the continual running up and downstairs is not only annoying but represents a serious waste of my time and the time of my staff.' Well in that 'executive' office the Director and his team of C.A.'s, seated on kitchen chairs at two collapsible tables worked many hours a day for two years, in an atmosphere which would now be regarded as one of incredible noise and confusion.

During 1924 the completion of the Douglas Library allowed space for several accountants including Smails, the clerical staff, and the director of the commerce program – 'no doubt to the envy of our scattered and unhoused colleagues in the department and elsewhere in the university.' Six years later, Mackintosh persuaded the university administration to let the department use the recently acquired Home for Friendless Women and Children at 75 Union Street. This, Smails later commented witheringly, was understood to be 'a wholly temporary arrangement.'[44]

The faculty, in fact, stayed in the Home for Friendless Women and Children for nearly three decades, until the autumn of 1959 when Dunning Hall opened. Ironically, despair over government funding reductions during the 1990s, along with the 'temporary' location of the National Executive MBA program just blocks from the original location of 'the House,' triggered frequent gossip that the school might be once again destined for physical facilities of this type. Fortunately, the original was torn down long ago to make way for campus expansion.

An Intermediate Stage, 1937–1963

Major changes came during 1937 with the formal establishment of the School of Commerce and Business Administration. Although enrolment in the baccalaureate program and the correspondence courses held up across the Depression, the university suffered serious financial difficulties as the crisis deepened. Treasurer William McNeil was notoriously tight-fisted, but the administrators still constantly had to seek out sources of new funds. One initiative came from Mackintosh, who had organized a well-attended conference about labour relations at the university during 1936, the first of its kind in Canada. He proposed 'a scheme for an industrial relations unit at Queen's which would teach, conduct research, and act as a clearing-house of information.'[45] Not only did this fit with his concerns about the effects of industrial capitalism, but the subject of labour relations was a major public-policy issue during the 1930s. Unemployment reached approximately a third of the male working population in southern Ontario, while strikes and violent clashes with authorities were all part of an abysmal labour scene.

Robert Charles Wallace, the new principal, quickly endorsed the concept. Macintosh and Wallace then approached Clifford Clark, then a deputy minister of finance, and Norman Rogers, a former member of the department and the federal minister of labour. They similarly conducted discussions with Bryce Stewart, a Queen's graduate and former director of the National Employment Service who had become research director of Industrial Relations Counsellors Inc. of New York, a not-for-profit enterprise funded by John. D. Rockefeller, Jr, which conducted research and consulting services about labour questions. Arguing that Queen's could be a 'neutral ground' for conferences and the collection of statistical data, Macintosh and Wallace sought contributions from leading Canadian firms. 'Constructive methods of cooperation,' the principal observed, 'have been developed and are operating in many of the Canadian industries and more will undoubtedly be established in the future. We could hope to assemble all such methods and plans in order that, instead of the whole problem being a matter of fighting for ground and for face on both sides, it can be looked at by our students and by all who are interested to get information as a problem of co-operative wisdom.'[46] Grants from the firm of James Richardson and Sons, along with donations from other enterprises, provided sufficient funds for a five-year operation by the summer of 1937. J.C. Cameron, a Queen's commerce graduate who worked for Canada Packers, was chosen as the first director.

Few changes were made to the curriculum during the 1930s. Macintosh had refused to add courses about industrial psychology or human relations, although those subjects could be explored in the offerings of other social science departments. In the area of management, one course, Industrial Management was consistently listed in the annual schedules, while several electives about general management were sporadically available. After the new unit was established, the course was substantially modified and described as 'a study of the application of the principles of management in industry' that gave special attention to employer-employee relations.[47] This change indicated an early recognition of the importance of human relations and presaged the introduction of other offerings geared to qualitative or general management issues.

The commerce faculty had been part of the department of economics and political science headed by William Mackintosh, who also served as the director of courses in commerce and business administration. In the spring of 1937, when the board of trustees approved the formation of an industrial relations unit, on Wallace's recommendation it also amalgamated undergraduate and graduate business courses, the correspondence courses, and the new unit into a 'School of Commerce.' This was described as 'an administrative organization to serve under the Faculty of Arts ... with Professor W. A. Mackintosh as Director of the School with an honorarium of $500 per year in addition to his salary as Head of the Department.'[48] The reorganization might have been expected to resolve a high level of bureaucratic confusion, but the School of Commerce effectively remained part of the department of economics and political science. The surviving documents shed little light on this issue except for suggestions that the new structure could simplify administrative procedures. Separating the growing volume of extension work and other business-related subjects from economics and politics certainly made sense. However, Mackintosh and Wallace probably wished to establish a distinctive 'School of Commerce' when the industrial relations unit was created in order to present a balanced proposition, especially to prospective corporate donors. Otherwise, external observers might have perceived the initiative as one that tilted the department and the university in favour of labour or the left. This rationale is necessarily speculative, but it seems likely given Mackintosh's administrative skills. He certainly kept control of all business-related courses and operations! The steady monies derived from the extension courses gave him greater influence than any other individual within the university. In addition, the initiative matched other efforts by Wallace to expand the research orientation of the university, and analogous units were established within a decade at Laval, McGill, and the Université de Montréal.[49]

The Second World War brought considerable changes for the new school. Unlike what happened in the Great War of 1914–18, the federal government encouraged men who were already at university to complete their studies. Thus, graduations from the commerce program ranged from 27 to 36 per year across the period of 1939 to 1943. But undergraduate registration dropped from 178 in 1938 to 113 in 1940 and 87 in 1942 as young people enlisted in the Canadian armed forces or undertook war-related jobs. Annual graduations between 1944 and 1946 therefore declined to a range of 14 to 19.[50] There was also considerable turnover as faculty members entered and returned from service with the federal government. Smails characterized the period as 'for the most part, [one] of weary improvisation.' Mackintosh, for example, remained in Ottawa as a member of the team in the finance ministry that was responsible for the management of economic affairs. During his absence, different individuals served as acting heads of the department, while Smails became acting director of the commerce and correspondence programs.

The return of members of the Canadian armed forces, who were supported by subsidies from the Veteran's Educational Funding Act, triggered a massive increase in enrolment, which Smails and others referred to as 'the great surge.' Undergraduate registration doubled to 199 candidates in the autumn of 1945 and then expanded to 444 students during the following year and 431 in 1947. Graduations increased to 34 in 1947, 78 in 1948, 111 in 1949, and 78 in 1950. Approximately 86 per cent of these students were former servicemen. None of the classrooms was large enough to accommodate the sessions, and the acute staffing shortage could not be eased despite the return of faculty members who had been seconded to public service and the hiring of new instructors. Several policy changes thus were instituted to ameliorate the situation. The entrance requirements for women and veterans were lowered to junior matriculation or the equivalent of Grade 12, thereby eliminating the original first year of studies and reducing the completion time for a degree. The thesis obligation also was made optional between 1948 and 1952 in order to keep the workload of faculty members manageable. However, the curriculum then reverted to the four-year design, which stipulated senior matriculation and a thesis. The extra year was again rationalized as necessary for 'a more cultural Commerce course' that would incorporate 'liberal arts options in History, English, Psychology, Philosophy, Religious Knowledge, Sociology, Drama and Art.'[51] In addition, there was considerable pressure from elsewhere in the university for conformity with the traditional standard of four years of studies if a candidate wanted to claim an honours versus a pass baccalaureate degree.

During the post-war era, the school assumed further responsibilities, which included new extension courses for the Society of Industrial Cost Accountants of Ontario and the Trust Companies Association of Ontario. These were natural extensions of the correspondence programs, but they increased the demands upon the faculty and support staff. Nonetheless, the personnel complement was not large during the post-war years, especially considering their obligations. Mackintosh, while the titular leader, was really an economist and full-time administrator. In practical terms, Smails, Cameron, and six other faculty members had to handle the intramural courses, the industrial relations unit, and the portfolio of extension offerings. One instructor who joined the group was J.E. Smyth, who later became a noted figure in the accounting field and a co-author (with Daniel Soberman of the law faculty) of the first major Canadian textbook about law and business administration.

After 1951 the pace slackened as the business programs moved into a period of maturity. During 1951, Mackintosh was appointed principal of the university, with J.A. Corry as the vice-principal, while Smails took over as director of the commerce school. New instructors and staff were occasionally added as circumstances permitted and the members of the school of commerce struggled to address the many needs of their stakeholders from the confines of the Home for Friendless Women and Children. For example, Edgar J. Benson, who later became the federal minister of finance, was hired in 1952 as a part-time lecturer in public finance and as an assistant for the director of the correspondence courses. Daniel Monieson also was hired as a sessional appointment in marketing and later returned to spend much of his professional career at the school. Others made brief appearances, such as Ian Stewart, later a deputy minister of finance in Ottawa, who temporarily helped with the banking courses.

Enrolment in and graduations from the baccalaureate program declined across the 1950s despite steady economic growth. In 1948, the last year with a large number of returning veterans, 298 candidates were registered in commerce. The following year, classes returned to the 'regular' pre-war size of 30 to 40 students in each year of the program. Annual graduations dropped to 18 by 1952 and remained near that level for the rest of the decade. Smails publicly observed that the size of the 1952 graduating class was 'only one-third to one-half of what it should be' and that the 'School will not be making the contribution which it should make to the supply of potential business executives ... Commerce at Queen's is losing ground not only absolutely, but relatively to other Schools of Commerce.' In 1957, he felt the baccalaureate degree still was 'barely holding its relative position' and did not expect an improvement before 1960. Smails blamed 'aggressive salesmanship' by other institutions, especially the University of Western Ontario, which had created a Harvard-inspired MBA program, for this development.[52]

Equally important was the focus on extension courses and the school's position inside the department. Although the number of part-time students had dropped off during the war, it increased sharply during the 1950s for all faculties at the university. Registration in the extension courses more than doubled, from 2111 to 5051 candidates, dwarfing the intramural offerings. The subject matter of the courses and the need for personnel to service those activities kept the commerce faculty focused upon banking and accounting. The economists tended to be involved with the banking courses, but most of the business-related faculty still were accountants by training. Cameron and the industrial relations staff were physically separated from the rest of the staff, with their operation in the Old Arts Building and not in 'the House.' To a large degree, the school of commerce was geared to the delivery of instruction in accounting, but course requirements and overall control remained under the jurisdiction of the economics faculty. Although offerings in organizational behaviour were phased into the curriculum, Smails was quite conservative and strong emphases were not placed upon general management; business policy, or marketing even though those subjects had emerged as major business concerns. The degree, therefore, looked stodgy and dated. Indeed, the most prominent innovations came from the faculty's political science colleagues, who created a new specialization in public administration. To widespread acclaim, courses about municipal government and the politics of democracy were introduced during the 1940s, along with an Institute on Local Government, which conducted research into urban affairs.

Mackintosh, who was by nature an entrepreneurial bureaucrat, might have been able to change this situation, but upon returning after the war he served as vice-principal and then aggressively sought the principalship. Upon appointment to the senior position, he had more pressing obligations. Full-time enrolment at the university grew by 50 per cent from a post-war low in 1951 to 3100 students by 1960. Realizing that after twenty years of neglect the university's physical plant had seriously deteriorated and anticipating a massive wave of students during the 1960s, he concentrated upon fund-raising for capital projects and an expansion of graduate studies or research-oriented faculties. Mackintosh became known as a 'building Principal' and his term of office later seemed a veritable golden age to Queen's. He did not moreover forget his colleagues in the department or the House. Government and corporate support was sought for an overdue modernization of their facilities. A significant contribution came from Charles Avery Dunning, who had been premier of Saskatchewan and then the federal minister of railways and minister of finance. At the time of his appointment to the latter post, Clark had been a deputy minister in the finance department. Named chancellor of the university after his retirement from politics in 1940, Dunning held the position until his death in 1958; his son was a graduate in the commerce class of 1941. Dunning's ties to the university were thus deep and, in keeping with the practice of naming buildings after important 'friends' of the institution, a large new facility was dedicated in his memory. Dunning Hall opened in November 1959 and housed a collection of departments including economics and political studies, geography, sociology, and industrial relations, along with the extension operations.

During the autumn of 1958, a new director for the school, Lawrence G. Macpherson, took office. Smails had been at the university for over thirty-five years without leave and had carried a heavy administrative and teaching load. He was very tired and much in need of a change, his colleagues later recalled. Macpherson, although he also was an accountant, indicated a need for a basic transformation. The school could easily and profitably accommodate twice the existing number of students, he reported, and the consolidation of the faculty in Dunning Hall enhanced the prospects for new activities. Macpherson's term of office also coincided with the release of two influential studies, commissioned by the Ford and Carnegie Foundations, which contained many suggestions for the reform of business curricula. With the turnover of directors, the faculty quickly moved to launch a graduate program and enter executive education.

Key to the development of an MBA degree was Richard J. Hand, who had joined the school early in the 1950s and who worked in the 'newer' subject of marketing. Hand had retained important relations with American universities, especially Chicago where he had completed all but his dissertation. He also built strong personal links with many of the more powerful individuals within Queen's. The immediate result of his efforts was a two-year MBA degree, based upon the program at Chicago. Launched during the 1960–61 academic year, it put an emphasis on three underlying disciplines of management during the first half of studies: economics, behavioural science, and statistics. Students took major functional courses for areas like marketing, finance, production, or accounting. During the second year, an integrative course in business policy (a precursor of strategic management) was required and they could choose electives in areas of special interest. Following the recommendations of the foundation reports, the program marked a shift towards a paradigm that overtly treated management as a science. 'The student will develop his appreciation of the principles and processes of business administration, the functional operations of individual firms, the analytic and decision process leading to successful management,' one brochure declared. But, reflecting the efforts in the baccalaureate program to balance theory and the practical, it promoted the need for administrators to act 'skilfully and humanly' and restricted the possibility of narrow specialization.[53]

Concepts from other academic areas were integrated into an array of courses and, as the degree was revised, greater emphases were placed upon quantitative techniques and business organization as a system. Marketing courses, for example, taught patterns of consumer behaviour, the psychology of advertising, and techniques of selling. Students learned about the 'contributions made by the social sciences (such as psychology and sociology) towards the understanding of human behaviour in a marketing sense.' Thus, they assumed the role of 'the marketing manager' and understood 'the significance of retailers, wholesalers, the role played by manufacturers ... and the whiles of the consumer as they affect the firm's operations.'[54]

Executive education initiatives, which were begun during the winter of 1959–60, were logical extensions of the correspondence courses in banking and accounting. Three programs were offered: an evening session during the regular academic year (primarily for the local Kingston market); 'Perspectives on Management' (a one-week program with invited professors from other institutions); and an executive summer school (which met for three weeks during the spring and summer, normally used in-house faculty, but did engage instructors from locations like Harvard). The programs were well attended, made money, raised the faculty's profile in the business community, and complemented the extension courses.

There were administrative changes as well. Cameron, the head of the industrial relations unit, retired at the end of the 1959–60 session, and coincident with the appointment of a new director, the unit was spun off as a separate entity, the Industrial Relations Centre. At the same time, the university also decided to rename the school. When the official title 'School of Commerce and Business Administration' had been adopted in 1937, it was commonly shortened to 'School of Commerce.'

This designation did not conform to the practices of American universities, increasingly seemed anachronistic, and was simplified during the autumn of 1960 to 'School of Business,' the name by which it remains known. The entity was not immediately segmented into an operation with its own faculty board and remained a part of the economics department, reporting to the principal, the Senate, and the trustees through the Faculty of Arts and Science.

Years of Expansion, 1963–1988

During May 1963, the School of Business finally became de jure what it had been de facto, namely, a separate faculty with a dean reporting directly to the principal. J.A. Corry, the new principal, explained the move to the trustees as consistent with a 'program of decentralization of administration which had been commenced some years ago.' But the appendix to the Senate's report in support of the recommendation was more to the point. It spoke of the 'complex nature' of the school's activities, which had various 'ill-defined lines of responsibilities.' For example, the commerce program reported through the head of political and economic studies to the dean of arts and science and on to the principal; the MBA administrator was accountable directly to the Senate; the professional and executive programs reported to the principal or vice-principal. Because the same faculty members were engaged in most of these endeavours, a common grouping with a dean seemed obvious.

In marked contrast to developments at Toronto during the same period, the economics faculty gave up the direct control of the business curriculum it had held for nearly forty-five years. This decision, in retrospect, might be surprising, because it had profited from the cash flow associated with the extension programs and the internal budgetary credits earned for the mandatory enrolment in economics courses by undergraduate commerce students. During the early 1960s, revenues from the professional programs declined as a steady source of funds and were overtaken by special contributions and the new executive education programs (which were not offered as regularly). The budget of the economics department could not be based on those two sources with any confidence. Moreover, the executive programs emphasized instruction in management and marketing and therefore represented an intellectual movement away from the subjects of accounting, banking, and finance that the economics faculty had partially supplied. Student credits from required economics courses became a part of the arrangement between the new school and the department, but intermittently became a bone of contention in subsequent years. Registration in the commerce program slowly increased from 108 candidates in 1958 to 135 by 1963 and was expected to jump by 50 per cent within several years. The economics faculty understandably felt assured about the future of their resources and therefore agreed to turn the school loose financially and administratively.

The school continued to be administered by Lawrence Macpherson, now as dean, who coordinated a varied collection of faculty, programs, and staff. The traditional group, with an accounting and economics emphasis, consisted of Macpherson and six other instructors. Six other faculty members, and particularly Richard Hand and Daniel Monieson, represented the newer influences of management and marketing. But it was still a small operation; only twenty-eight candidates graduated at the spring convocation in 1964. The commerce degree had acquired a good record for post-degree employment placement and achievement, but the curriculum had essentially remained the same since the 1930s.[55] There was a broad first year, a heavy emphasis on economics and accounting, and a smattering of courses in management and marketing. These were delivered by faculty whose academic preparation varied widely, with some particularly effective in the classroom or consulting. Research was almost non-existent. The personnel did not change significantly for two years after the divorce of the business school from the economics department. Several interviewees for this paper who were present at the time described the organizational climate as characterized by lethargy, considerable confusion, and a sense of frustration among those who wanted to get on with new initiatives but were being obstructed by the inclinations of the senior faculty.

The stalemate began to break in the middle of 1965, when Macpherson was promoted to vice-principal of finance for the university. This appointment precipitated a search for a new dean, a process that required more than the time available before the succeeding academic year. Hand and Monieson were the two leading candidates for the position. Monieson held a doctorate, had taught at Wharton, retained good links with the business community through his consulting practices, and could have gone elsewhere had he chosen. Hand had received some doctoral training at Chicago, acquired brief teaching experience at Northwestern, but was better connected with the local community and the power structure of the university. Although either would have been an excellent choice, the search committee and the principal chose Hand, who became dean in July 1966. His term of office coincided with an exceptional growth in the demand for higher education in Ontario. Registration in the baccalaureate program rose to 170 students in 1967 and to 411 by 1969. In the MBA program, the student population expanded from 33 in 1963 to 82 in 1967 and 122 by 1969. Hand was a 'new broom,' but a sufficiently experienced one to be effective at bringing about the changes that he and the other younger faculty believed were overdue. Seven instructors, all with solid research credentials, were added within two years in the areas of operations research, production, marketing, and accounting.

Hand's vision of the school was consistent with the conclusions of the Foundation reports, as opposed to the emphasis that had been placed upon correspondence courses and vocational training. It was also distinct from the applied-management orientation of Harvard. Instead, he tended to follow the approach of Chicago, especially the new curriculum that institution elaborated during the 1950s with financial support from the Ford Foundation. This curricular orientation placed an emphasis on the theory behind management – especially economics, social psychology, and mathematics. It also stressed a need for faculty to research how that growing body of academic theory could be applied to accounting, finance, marketing, production, and other aspects of business. Hand then sought out personnel who fit with this perspective. He was particularly diligent about this activity and started a regular schedule of recruiting visits to major American business schools for expatriate Canadians who had undertaken doctoral studies. His diligence was rewarded with the hiring of an important number of new faculty members between 1969 and 1972.

The MBA degree had been steadily revised since 1960 and was the area where curricular modifications were tested out. The chairs for the program retained close contacts with the business community from their consulting and other activities. Under their guidance, the course of study assumed a modern appearance aimed at creating a 'professional foundation' with such innovations as detailed instruction in statistical techniques, the use of computers, and interactions with important business firms. Sometimes the latter were arranged by members of the school's Advisory Council, which was expanded to include the representation of different interests from the private sector.[56]

During 1967 a major review led to a reorganization of the undergraduate curriculum, changes that drew upon the concepts developed in the graduate program. The nature of the shift was highlighted in university publications. While the orientation towards business problems had been retained, potential entrants were assured, the school would 'introduce the student to the most modern management techniques, particularly the application of mathematics to problems of business in Operational Research and in the use of computers.' Courses in calculus and computer science were added to the first half of the study schedule, along with requirements in marketing, management science, production, and human behaviour during the latter half. The requirement for a graduation thesis was terminated.[57] These changes also were propelled by lobbying from the undergraduate business students. Concerned about the uneven quality of instruction, in 1967 they organized a Commerce Society, which operated separately from the Arts and Science Undergraduate Society. Their representatives demanded 'a program of course evaluations' and 'a program for relating academic courses to the business community.'[58] While the new student association did not acquire an official status until 1968, it had an important influence on the faculty and their perspectives about the undergraduate degree.

The early years of Hand's deanship were not expansionary in all dimensions. In one area there was 'a drawing to a closeness,' to use the term of one contemporary. During the 1969–70 academic year, the school and the university quietly, but officially, chose to withdraw from all professional, correspondence-based courses, although it took until 1971 to close down the interrelated activities. Several factors contributed to this decision. The bankers' and accountants' professional associations wanted the delivery of a large amount of material, much of it overtly vocational in nature. These activities did not match the shift towards a research and academically rigorous orientation or the growing emphasis upon general management. Efforts were made to hire part-time instructors but they were expensive, often unreliable, and of uneven quality. With the rapid growth of intramural enrolment after 1965, Hand enjoyed a level of financial flexibility that earlier administrators like Smails could only have dreamed of.

The pace of development accelerated during the next decade as the school was fundamentally transformed. Between 1969 and 1972, fifteen new faculty members were permanently added. Several others stayed temporarily and went on to important academic careers elsewhere, while a few departed for graduate studies in the United States and later returned to assume staff positions. By the spring of 1972, the size of the faculty had virtually doubled from the complement when Hand took over six years earlier. In comparison with the problems experienced by other Canadian business schools during this period, his success in building a highly qualified staff was quite extraordinary. With very few exceptions, most of them remained at Queen's for the rest of their professional lives and made important contributions to its reputation through research, teaching, or administrative activities. The university administration abetted his efforts to create new positions and was able to offer competitive remuneration. The Vietnam War ironically facilitated his task because it made American academic postings problematic for expatriate Canadians, with the possibility of forced induction into the armed forces, an issue that some faculty members have since cited for their decision to return to Canada.

Most of those who came have attributed the real explanation for Hand's success to the man himself. He had the singular ability, in a kind of self-effacing way, of making the person he spoke to feel like 'a potential Nobel laureate' whose opinions were valued highly. As one faculty member later recalled, 'he made me feel "special" somehow.' In part, this was a direct reflection of his personality, for Hand was an intellectual and perceptive teacher. It was also a deliberate device, for he had, no doubt, learned that nothing works better with an academic than flattery. The dean read widely and could intelligently converse about most areas of business studies.

These capabilities were particularly valuable during the 1970s as aggregate enrolment at the university continued to increase. The university's administration, now under the guidance of John Deutsch (a commerce graduate in 1935), expressed concerns that the scale of the expansion might overwhelm the capacity of Kingston to handle the student population. As a result, during 1971 the principal announced that a cap of 10,000 students would be placed on the total size of enrolment at the university, a policy that naturally required quotas on admissions into individual departments and faculties. Approximately one hundred people completed the baccalaureate commerce program annually, and about sixty the MBA. Growing enrolment in each year of the programs had required the creation of multiple sections for required courses. Initially, the new policy had little effect on the size of those activities since, as the undergraduate chair later noted, with Hand's full support, he regularly exceeded the official quota by amounts that drew the attention of the senior administration but 'could always be negotiated.'[59] Hand was thus able to add another thirteen faculty members between 1973 and 1975, while other individuals were hired for the support system that handled the operations of the business school. To have managed nearly doubling the complement yet again over a three-year period, while at the same time managing the growth in enrolment, must have seemed a Herculean task. Those who knew Hand well report he was constantly on the road.

Dunning Hall simply could not accommodate all of the new people, since the economics department (which shared the facility) also grew rapidly during this period. Nor, for that matter, could it provide sufficient classrooms, a commodity that was at a premium everywhere on campus. A centralized and judicious course-scheduling arrangement (which included evening and Saturday classes) was just able to deal with the problem. The university's administrators had anticipated the shortage of office space a decade earlier and began planning to convert the area that the football stadium had occupied since 1921. A complex of buildings and parking facilities was constructed for all of the social sciences, including part of the business school. The story of how this was accomplished, and the consequent nostalgic ill will it spawned, has been told elsewhere.[60] Macintosh-Corry Hall, named after the two former principals, was completed during the early 1970s, and the business school has occupied a portion of the building ever since. The lack of an appropriate place to run the executive education courses also was a practical problem. These sessions required special seminar and lecture rooms that were of higher quality than those employed to service the normal student population, with contiguous accommodation space and 'break-out' rooms to facilitate discussions, scheduling, or meals. Hand and other faculty members pushed for a new facility, which the university eventually provided. The Donald Gordon Centre, named after the former chief executive officer of Canadian National Railways, was opened during September 1974 in a renovated old-stone home called 'Roselawn,' originally built in the 1840s. Symbolically, H.D. Helmers, its first director, and the individual who supervised all of the early work on the facility, was a relatively new member of faculty who had been hired in 1969.

With the growth in the number of young personnel, the school was regularly animated by new ideas and academic debates. A workshop series, where faculty could discuss their research with colleagues or invited visitors could present papers, was started during 1971. A movement to mount a doctoral program was linked to the new emphasis upon research. Hand realized that an ability to hire and keep research-oriented faculty members was contingent upon the existence of this option. Otherwise the school would simply be perceived as 'small-time.' Since he also considered the dominant goal of universities to be intellectual development, the development of this initiative was seen as essential if the professional legitimacy of business studies was to be strengthened. The faculties of law, medicine, and engineering had already moved in that direction. Between 1972 and 1974, tentative discussions were held about the dimensions of an appropriate curriculum and the type of specializations that might be offered.

Throughout this period there were also discussions about the two mainstream programs, particularly the baccalaureate degree. The major innovation was a conversion to single-term or half-year courses whenever possible in order to provide greater flexibility in offerings and scheduling. The policy change met with considerable opposition from other departments, particularly economics, but it eventually was adopted by much of the rest of the university. Some of the traditional obligations, such as a politics and/or English course in first year were also dropped, while new requirements in computing and international business were added.

After this frenetic pattern of growth, a hiatus set in during the 1974–75 academic year. This pause partially reflected a natural desire by the faculty to pause and integrate operations, but it was also compelled by the realization that the principal was serious about an enforcement of the enrolment cap. Government grants also began to slow after a decade of heavy spending on post-secondary education. Enrolment and graduations for both programs reached a more or less steady state. Seven hundred were registered across the different years of the commerce program and about 160 graduated annually after 1974. Approximately 200 students were registered in, and 90 graduated from, the MBA program annually, a level that was maintained until the two-year degree was phased out during 1994.[61]

At the same time, the plans for a doctoral degree ran into significant obstacles. The program chair and Hand had managed to convince a sceptical Senate that the school needed and could mount the venture. The exact structure had deliberately been left vague, except for a promise that the business faculty would work closely with the economics department, which had an established reputation in graduate studies. The key problem was with securing financial support from the provincial ministry of colleges and universities. With shrinking appropriations, numerous applications from different institutions, and concerns about the potential quality of those offerings, it withheld funding approvals for new initiatives. The doctoral proposal languished for two years before faculty demands and bureaucratic infighting brought approval from the university. Nevertheless, as Hand observed, 'we will have to pay for it ourselves in the early years.' A new chair and committed faculty outlined a curriculum that included compulsory courses in different business subjects, obligations for a double-major field (with comprehensive exams in both), and an original dissertation. Six fields were planned: finance, marketing, accounting and information systems, organizational behaviour, management science, and managerial economics. This represented a distinctive program among the PhD degrees available at the time, although other Canadian business schools have elaborated similar options since then. Candidates were admitted in 1978, and the first two students graduated during the spring of 1984.

Despite the growing restrictions, Hand tried to expand the instructional staff. Eight people were hired between 1975 and 1978, but only three stayed on at Queen's in academic positions. Research output (in the form of books, articles in learned journals, presentations at academic conferences) steadily expanded. The scholarship of the faculty appeared in diverse publications like *Management Science*, the *Canadian Journal of Economics*, the *Journal of Marketing Research*, the *Journal of Accounting Research*, the *Journal of Business*, the *Canadian Banker*, and *Financial Management*. In addition, a working paper and a reprint series were launched. Not surprisingly, the subjects were highly varied and included railroads, profit-sharing schemes, professional licensing, forecasting accuracy, police colleges, and multivariate approaches to consumer behaviour.[62]

Hand ran the entire operation on a personal basis, literally out of his own pocket. He maintained exclusive control of the budget, had little time for committees, and preferred to consult faculty members on a one-to-one basis. However, as general university matters occupied more of his attention, he spent less time at Dunning Hall. As a result, it was during this period that the sobriquet by which he became best known, 'the Invisible Hand,' came into general use. On one occasion, a graduating class even provided him with an empty picture frame emblematic of this cognomen. The dean could be notoriously hard to find if a person wanted to speak with him, and yet he seemed to be constantly stopping in to an office or pausing in a corridor to talk. Usually he was looking for an opinion on something or other – a new appointment, a promotion, or an argument he had read. In this way, faculty morale remained high. Thanks to the diligent work of the program chairs, most of the school's operations proceeded smoothly. While this management style was appropriate for the earlier, smaller scale of educational activities, it did not fit well with the complex character of the organization by the middle of the 1970s. Besides the emerging resource constraints, internal affairs were affected by the younger faculty members, who were more outspoken and activist than those of earlier times.

For those reasons, the dean was pressured for greater openness and collegiality in decision-making processes – particularly in the areas of budgets, appointments, and reviews for promotion or tenure. Before he was forced to deal with these issues, however, Hand was appointed the vice-principal of resources. Like the promotion of Macpherson a decade earlier, the move came as a surprise. C.A. Lawrence, chair of the undergraduate program, took Hand's place while a search committee was organized to find a permanent administrator. He used the opportunity to open up the administrative processes and, for the first time, presented the budget publicly. After considerable discussion, formal committees and standardized procedures for promotion and tenure assessments were also introduced. By the time a permanent successor, John R.M. Gordon, took office in the autumn of 1978, the organizational climate had been significantly altered.[63]

Gordon's term was characterized by a noticeable change in philosophy. This was a deliberate choice, but also was part of a dialectical process that has been characteristic of professional schools, a periodic shift between the relative emphases given to a theoretical versus applied orientation. Gordon was the clear favourite of the business community, as well as of those faculty members who believed there had been an excessive movement towards an academic approach and who feared the school was losing touch with the interests of its basic stakeholders. He also did not have the intimate familiarity with the university administration that Hand had enjoyed. A graduate of the University of British Columbia in mechanical engineering, Gordon took his MBA at Queen's on a part-time basis before moving to the Sloan School at MIT for doctoral studies. While his specialization was in operations management and production, he became involved with the initial summer program in executive education offered by Queen's. This activity led to extensive consulting assignments and case-writing, which became permanent traits of his academic endeavours. After graduating from MIT, he spent several years teaching at Western before moving to IMEDE in Switzerland, where he helped to establish an MBA program. He returned to Kingston in 1975.

Gordon had always been interested in academic administration and had nearly done his dissertation on the subject before changing to another topic. He lost little time in putting some of his thinking into action, including the creation of a revitalized Advisory Council, a new emphasis on continuing education, and efforts to strengthen alumni relations through the organization of chapters of business graduates in places like Montréal and Toronto. He planned a consulting program for small firms as a way of strengthening links with the local business community. In addition, the dean supported the Queen's Business Environment To-day conference, which had been started in 1977 by the Commerce Society, as an annual enterprise that would bring business, labour, and government leaders together at the university. He also supported efforts by the students to organize the Intercollegiate Business Competition, which was first held at Queen's during 1979 and involved teams from across the country. Both initiatives brought favorable media coverage, which the school had not previously enjoyed. Finally, Gordon set up the office of associate dean to handle internal administrative affairs so he could concentrate upon fund-raising and relations with external stakeholders.

Curriculum reviews were undertaken in part at the dean's urging, but primarily as a response to a 1980 conference of North American business school deans. The participants endorsed greater emphases upon non-cognitive or affective skills (such as group work and leadership), communications skills, internationalization of the course of studies, the inclusion of liberal arts subjects like business history, and provision for lifelong management education. These goals were fundamentally different from the themes underlying the commerce and MBA programs, and as a result triggered a lengthy and soul-searching review.[64] After a careful review of the market possibilities, an in-residence program for executive education was restarted during the spring of 1981. Although this operation began on a small scale, it grew in size and reputation to become one of the foremost in North America, and has represented an important source of discretionary funds. Gordon also made good on his intentions to reactivate the Advisory Council. Beginning in 1978, and eventually expanding to about eighteen individuals, each of whom had a three-year term, the council acted as a two-way street, bringing ideas on the curriculum or research and taking back to the business community information about the school.

Gordon's first term of office not only followed a period of rapid expansion but coincided with significant restraints owing to cutbacks in operating or research grants from public authorities. He accordingly did not have the manoeuvring room of his predecessor. The number of publications and conference presentations still expanded and the placement success of graduates for both programs continued, but these phenomena were largely functions of earlier efforts.[65] The total number of faculty remained quite stable through his first term. The second term began with high hopes, since the university launched a major fund-raising campaign that Gordon believed would supply new monies to the school. He was most concerned with support for faculty research projects and an expansion of the computer facilities, along with the physical plant.[66] The dean could take heart from an expansion of the executive program of short courses, which had been limited to 65 candidates. By 1984, the school increasingly had to turn people away, and the following year a second three-week session was added. By the late 1980s, it also was oversubscribed, forcing the creation of additional sessions. The initiative steadily became known as one of the foremost in North America. However, Gordon was largely stymied in his initiatives to develop new facilities or to gain the number of faculty members he believed were essential for the different operations. It came as a surprise to some that he chose to step down as dean when his second term expired, but this decision followed a convention that had developed at the university. The dean felt he had exhausted the lines of development that he had intended. A final factor in the decision was probably a sense that the pendulum had begun to swing back towards a greater emphasis upon research and intellectual development.[67]

In stepping down, Gordon could take quiet satisfaction from having completed the transformation towards a professional and managerial orientation. His emphases on links to the business community, executive education, teaching, and case-based research raised the external profile of the school. As the chair of the Federation of Deans for Canadian Schools of Business, Gordon also built formal relationships with institutions across the country, something that had not occurred previously. These initiatives affected subsequent developments and, by 'opening to the world' in a different way, complemented the reconfiguration pursued by Hand. In retrospect, both were necessary, vis-à-vis the older, more provincial 'commerce' character of the school, to meet the changing times.

Although the period falls outside the scope of this essay, during the past decade the business school has again experienced a new wave of transformation. The design of the commerce program has been changed in several ways, but would still be recognizable to administrators like Smails. However, in 1994 the two-year MBA degree was closed. With the concurrence of the university, graduate studies were privatized and placed on a full-fee basis. The finances of the business school have since prospered or lagged according to the market demand for its services. Two degree programs were instituted: an MBA in Science and Technology, delivered in Kingston, and a National Executive MBA, which has been supplied by video-conferencing and has competed against initiatives by other universities such as Western. In addition, there have been a variety of initiatives aimed at advancing the research and international profile of the faculty. These efforts culminated in November 1998 with the announcement that Queen's had received an unconditional accreditation for all of its business programs by the American Assembly of Collegiate Schools of Business. 'This accreditation is a shining example of what the faculty, staff and students can achieve when we work together,' declared Dean Margot Northey. With an eye on the next century, the faculty would endeavour 'to be at the forefront of business thinking by challenging the status quo and offering bold, innovative programs for business education.'[68]

Conclusions

What conclusions can be drawn from this case study? As noted in the introduction, one theme has been the business school's ability to do a lot with limited resources. Historically the school has served a diverse collection of internal and external groups with a very small complement. In part, this was a result of a distinctive strategic evolution that unfolded incrementally rather than through explicit planning. The faculty originated from the social objectives of the early political economists, but until the 1960s essentially functioned as a correspondence school attached to the economics department with a small intramural effort. The approach was intended to fulfil the university's service goals and to overcome the natural disadvantage of not being located in a commercial centre. At the same time, the intellectual and personal connections of the faculty facilitated the development of links to the business and political communities, and the emphasis on research endeavours has varied both in volume and form over time. Accordingly, the school has been perceived both as an 'insider' and an 'outsider' to the academic operations of Queen's.

Another theme has been the impact of intellectual trends, especially ideas and concepts derived from the United States, that repeatedly shaped the character of business education. 'Schools of thought' organized around somewhat different philosophies occasionally were espoused as faculty members joined from universities like Berkeley, Harvard, Michigan, Minnesota, or MIT. But the most significant 'external' influence, through the line of succession from Skelton to Hand, was the business administration program at the University of Chicago, which was frequently utilized as a model. Equally important was a periodic evolution through the addition of new functional disciplines. Beginning with a focus on accounting and banking, the school was reconfigured through the inclusion of industrial relations in the 1930s, marketing in the 1950s, management science in the 1960s, and more recently subjects like organizational behaviour, management information systems, and finance. This development not only matched trends elsewhere, but transformed the faculty from a liberal-arts to a professional orientation.

The authors are inclined to gauge organizational success according to output measures. Between 1919 and 1988, Queen's provided education for over 4500 undergraduates and MBAs, several thousand candidates who took correspondence courses, along with the participants in its executive education programs. The cumulative numbers of these individuals has undoubtedly had an impact. A 1952 study that surveyed graduates from the baccalaureate program noted, '[W]hether it be a profession, a manufacturing enterprise, or the Civil Service, Queen's Commerce has its representatives.'[69] This continues to be the case to the present day. There have been presidents of corporations, ambassadors and senior bureaucrats, judges, lawyers, professors, medical doctors, ministers of the Crown, several ministers of the cloth, and one priest (who took his vows *after* graduating from commerce). All passed through the School of Business at Queen's. To this contribution must be added the impact of many publications and the active role in public and academic life by the professors. Together the evidence points to the conclusion that there has been a sizable achievement over a long period by the 'little business school that (always) could (and did).'

NOTES

1 For a full study of the nineteenth-century institution, see H. Neatby, *Queen's University, 1841–1917*, vol. 1 (Montréal: McGill-Queen's University Press, 1978), esp. chapters 12–13, and 15. A useful comparative analysis can be found in A.B. McKillop, *Matters of Mind: The University in Ontario, 1791–1951* (Toronto: UTP, 1994), chapter 8.

2 Neatby, *Queen's University*, 217–22, 275–8. Watson's intellectual approach has been explored insightfully by A.B. McKillop, *A Disciplined Intelligence: Critical Inquiry and Canadian Thought in the Victorian Era* (Montréal: McGill-Queen's University Press, 1979), 171–203.

3 S.E.D. Shortt, *The Search for an Ideal: Six Canadian Intellectuals and Their Convictions in an Age of Transition* (Toronto: UTP, 1976), 95–7.

4 B.G. Ferguson, *Remaking Liberalism: The Intellectual Legacy of Adam Shortt, O.D. Skelton, W.C. Clark, and W.A. Macintosh, 1890–1925* (Montréal: McGill-Queen's University Press, 1993), 14–22. Shortt, *The Search for an Ideal*, 98–102. The cross-relationships among these individuals, many of whom attended the University of Chicago, were extremely important for the early study of economics and business in Canada. Stephen Leacock (McGill), H.A. Innis (Toronto), and O.D. Skelton received doctorates from that university. Clifford Clark and William Mackintosh were encouraged to undertake doctoral studies at Harvard. An outline of those developments can be found in D.G.B. Jones, 'Origins of Marketing Thought,' unpub. PhD dissertation (Queen's University, School of Business, 1987).

5 Queen's University Archives, Queen's University, *Calendar of Queen's College and University for the Year 1900–1901*, 80, 81–2.

6 J.L. Granatstein, *The Ottawa Men: The Civil Service Mandarins, 1937–1957* (Toronto: UTP, 1982), 28–44. W.A. Macintosh, 'O.D. Skelton,' in W.A. Mackay, ed., *Macmillan Dictionary of Canadian Biography*, 4th ed. (Toronto: Macmillan, 1978), 115.

7 W.A. Mackintosh, 'William Clifford Clark and Canadian Economic Policy,' *CJEPS* 19 (1953), 411–13; 'William Clifford Clark – A Great Civil Servant,' *QR* 28 (January 1953), 12. R.B. Bryce, 'William Clifford Clark,' *CJEPS* 19 (1953), 413–23. Granatstein, *The Ottawa Men*, 44–9.

8 QUA, Adam Shortt Papers, O.D. Skelton to A. Shortt, 24 November 1910, 27 July 1907, quoted in Ferguson, *Remaking Liberalism*, 27.

9 QUA, *Report of the Principal to the Board of Trustees for 1910–1911*, 9.

10 QUA, *Calendar, 1910–1911*, 96; *Calendar, 1913–1914*, 124, 126.

11 QUA, Board of Trustee Minutes, 16 October 1914. *Principal's Report, 1914–1915*, 9, 11–12.

12 QUA, *Principal's Report, 1919–1920*, 16–17. W. Eggleston, *National Research in Canada: The NRC, 1916–1966* (Toronto: Clarke Irwin, 1978), 1–19.

13 QUA, D.M. Gordon Papers, box 2, file 9, 'Memorandum on Economic Research and Social Business Training,' 15 October 1918, unsigned.

14 W.C. Clark, 'University Training for Business – A Reply,' *QQ* 30 (January 1923), 332.

15 QUA, *Principal's Report, 1918–1919*, 15. Cappon to W.L. Grant (Autumn 1919), quoted in F.W. Gibson, *Queen's University: To Serve and Yet Be Free, 1917–1961* (Montréal: McGill-Queen's University Press, 1983), 2: 39.

16 J.M. Macdonnell, 'The Decline of the Arts Faculty,' *QQ* 30 (January 1923), 310–18.

17 Gibson, *Queen's University,* 39. R.M.G. Smails, 'The Story of Commerce at Queen's,' unpub. paper (Queen's University, Dept. of Political and Economic Science, 1949), 4 . Another version of this paper was published in *QR* 28 (October 1953), 448–55.

18 O.D. Skelton, 'University Courses in Commerce,' *Proceedings of the 59th Annual Convention of the Ontario Educational Association* (Toronto: Ontario Educational Association, 1920), 451.

19 QUA, *Courses in Commerce and Business Administration, 1919–1920*, 1.

20 QUA, Principal's Files, 'Report of Committee on Research and Commercial Courses,' 24 March 1919. Skelton, 'University Courses,' 453.

21 Clark, 'University Training,' 327.

22 Edwin Francis Gay, 'The New Graduate School of Business Administration,' *The Harvard Illustrated Magazine* 9 (1908), 161, quoted in D.G.B. Jones and P.A. McLean, 'Ahead of the Class: The Founding of Commerce at Queen's,' in B. Austin, ed., *ASAC Proceedings, Business History* 16: 15 (Windsor: University of Windsor, 1995), 83.

23 D.G.B. Jones and D.D. Monieson, 'The Origin and Early Development of the Case Method in Marketing Pedagogy,' in K.D. Bahn, ed., *Developments in Marketing Science* (Montreal: Academy of Marketing Science, 1988), 156–60. See also J.L. Cruikshank, *A Delicate Experiment: The Harvard Business School, 1908–1945* (Cambridge: Harvard Business School Press, 1987), chapters 2–4.

24 R.H. Turner, 'A History of the School of Business of the University of Chicago, chapter 1: J. Laurence Laughlin and the Early Years,' unpub. manuscript, University of Chicago Archives (undated), 55–7, quoted in Jones and McLean, 'Ahead of the Class,' 82

25 L.C. Marshall, 'The College of Commerce and Administration of the University of Chicago,' *JPE* 21 (February 1913), 100–1.

26 QUA, *Queen's Calendar, 1921–1922*, 9–10. Smails, 'The Story of Commerce,'

6. QUA, W.A. Mackintosh Papers, 'Courses in Commerce and Administration 1919–20 – The School of Business 1969–1970.'

27 QUA, *Courses in Commerce and Administration, 1919–1920*, 19, 21.

28 M.D. Nicholson, 'Queen's Commerce Graduation,' unpub. BCom. thesis (Queen's University, 1952), 3. Smails, 'The Story of Commerce,' 5.

29 QUA, *Calendar of the Faculty of Arts, 1919–1920*, 152–3.

30 QUA, *Calendar of the Faculty of Arts, 1922–1923*, 114; *Calendar, 1920–1921*, 133; *Calendar, 1921–1922*, 113.

31 QUA, *Principal's Report, 1923–1924*, 40. *Principal's Report, 1925–1926*, 39–40.

32 QUA, *Courses in Commerce and Administration, 1928–1929*, 7.

33 QUA, *Courses in Commerce and Administration, 1919–1920*, 2.

34 QUA, *Calendar, Faculty of Arts, 1921–1922*, 9–10; *Courses in Commerce and Administration, 1921–1922*, 8.

35 N.J. Pupo, 'Educational Promises and Efficiency Ideals: The Development of Management Education in Ontario, 1900–1960,' unpub. PhD thesis (McMaster University, 1984), 148. QUA, *Courses in Commerce and Administration, 1921–1922*, 10.

36 Granatstein, *The Ottawa Men*, 44–9. Ferguson, *Remaking Liberalism*, 32–3.

37 P. Creighton, *A Sense of Yesterdays* (Toronto: Canadian Institute of Chartered Accountants, 1983), 108.

38 Creighton, *A Sense of Yesterdays*, 109.

39 QUA, *Principal's Reports*, 1923–4 to 1920–30.

40 Ferguson, *Remaking Liberalism*, 36–8.

41 Smails, 'The Story of Commerce,' 6.

42 Clark quoted in *Principal's Report, 1931–1932*, 52. W.A. Macintosh, 'The Curriculum of a Course in Commerce,' *Papers and Proceedings*, Canadian Political Science Association, 2 (1930), 95–8. The theme of business education as an element in social transformation was highlighted by Macintosh in 'The Psychologist and Economics,' *QQ* 30 (January 1923), 299–310.

43 Creighton, *A Sense of Yesterdays*, 150.

44 Smails, 'The Story of Commerce,' 9.

45 Gibson, *Queen's University*, 2: 149.

46 Richardson Papers, Wallace to Richardson, 2 July 1937, quoted in Gibson, *Queen's University*, 149–50.

47 QUA, *Calendar of the School of Commerce and Administration, 1938–1939*, 25.

48 QUA, Board of Trustees Minutes, 7 May 1937, 4.

49 The authors are veterans of many bureaucratic discussions over their years at the university. They are both struck by how this 1937 arrangement represented a typical Queen's solution.

50 Interestingly enough, the proportion of women in the classes rose dramati-

cally, at least in the school, unlike the First World War when it remained relatively constant. Only 23 women graduated between 1939 and 1946 out of a total of 199 degrees conferred.

51 Nicholson, 'Queen's Commerce Graduation,' 7.

52 QUA, *Principal's Report, 1951–1952,* 31. *Principal's Report, 1956–1957,* 19.

53 QUA, *Courses for the Degree of MBA, 1961–1962,* 5.

54 QUA, *School of Commerce and Administration Calendar, 1957–1958,* 34.

55 See, for example, D.A. Wilson, 'Graduates' Page – What Are You Doing?' *The Commerceman* 18 (1963), 65–6.

56 QUA, *Courses for the Degree of MBA, 1964–1965,* 7. The graduate degree went through subsequent reorganizations in 1967 and 1971 aimed at creating a professional orientation.

57 QUA, *Courses for the Degree of Bachelor of Commerce, 1968–1969,* 10.

58 B. LeRoy, 'Commerce at Queen's: A Professional Student Society,' *The Commerceman* 22 (1967), 47–8.

59 The constraints ironically had the effect of increasing the quality of incoming students. Queen's quickly had the highest proportion of Ontario Scholars of any university in the province.

60 See M. Daub, *Gael Force – More than a Century of Football at Queen's* (Montréal: McGill-Queen's University Press, 1996).

61 QUA, *Principal's Reports,* 1977 to 1994 annually published the registration data. The undergraduate enrolment was officially capped at 720 but temporarily was allowed to rise to 800. After 1980 it was held at 750 candidates.

62 School of Business, *The Inquiry* 1 (1977), 27–30. This publication replaced the *Commerceman,* which had been moribund for several years. With a more alumni-focused approach, modelled on the University of Chicago's School of Business publication, *The Inquiry* has continued down to the present.

63 The reader is referred to a new book by the authors entitled *Getting Down to Business: A History of Business Education at Queen's* (Montréal: McGill-Queen's University Press, 1999), which contains the full history in an expanded form.

64 See 'Managers for the XXI Century: Their Education and Development,' Report of the Annual Meeting of the American Assembly of Collegiate Schools of Business, Chicago, 1981.

65 *The Inquiry* 2 (1977–8), 14, 16.

66 'Looking to the Future,' *The Inquiry* 8 (1983–4), 1, 4–5.

67 *The Inquiry* 12 (1987–8), 1–3.

68 www.business.queensu.ca/new, 'Queen's Accredited by Prestigious U.S. Business Assembly,' 12 November 1998.

69 Nicholson, 'Queen's Commerce Graduation,' 31.

4

From Commerce to Management: The Evolution of Business Education at the University of Toronto

JOHN A. SAWYER

The Joseph L. Rotman School of Management of the University of Toronto has evolved into a full-service business school. Its roots can be traced back to the Diploma in Commerce established by the Department of Political Economy in the Faculty of Arts during 1901. It now supplies a full-time and a part-time MBA program, an Executive MBA degree, an MMPA (Master of Management and Professional Accounting) program, a PhD program, various executive development initiatives, joint responsibility with the Faculty of Arts and Science for two undergraduate commerce and finance programs (BCom. or Major in Commerce taken as part of a BA or BSc. degree program), and a joint MBA/LLB degree with the Faculty of Law. This chapter explains the evolution of the offerings in commerce and management, their underlying philosophies, and the institutions that administer them.[1]

Origins and Staffing of the Bachelor of Commerce Program[2]

The bachelor of commerce degree at the University of Toronto has its roots in the appointment in 1888 of William Ashley, an Englishman from Oxford University, as the first Professor of Political Economy and Constitutional History in the Faculty of Arts of the University of Toronto. Ashley left Toronto in 1892, spent a few years at Harvard University, and then returned to England to the new University of Birmingham. There he founded the School of Commerce and began the program leading to the first bachelor of commerce degree – the forerunner of many BCom. degree programs throughout the British Empire. Eighteenth-century economists had divided the English economy into three sectors: agriculture, manufacturing, and commerce.

Commerce included the transportation, marketing, and financing of goods. The Birmingham program included economic geography, economic history, general economics, modern languages, and accountancy. This education was designed to produce cultured men who would become leaders in the world of commerce.

The Wharton School of Finance and Commerce was founded in 1881 as an undergraduate school at the University of Pennsylvania, and a number of American universities formed business schools around the turn of the century. The faculty at the University of Toronto chose, however, to follow the Birmingham, rather than the American, model. Ashley's successor at the University of Toronto, James Mavor, a Scot from Glasgow University, followed Ashley's lead in a modest way. In response to requests from the Canadian Manufacturers' Association and the Toronto Board of Trade, he arranged for the Department of Political Economy to offer from 1901 to 1911 a two-year diploma course in commerce. Students studied English and any two modern languages, mathematics applied to commerce, inorganic chemistry and physics, drawing (optional), commercial law, economic theory, industrial history, banking, public finance, and transportation.[3] The course was not popular, with an enrolment of only two to three students a year.

In 1909 the department began to offer a four-year honours course in commerce and finance that led to the degree of bachelor of arts. Across the period of 1913 to 1926, there were 82 graduates from this program. The Commerce and Finance degree followed the Birmingham model: it contained considerable economics, economic history, accountancy, financial subjects (including corporation finance and actuarial science), some economic geography and commercial law, and a foreign-language requirement. In 1921 a course in business administration was added, and in 1922 an elements of commerce course. A businessmen's committee was created to advise on the programs, help place graduates, and propose speakers for the course in business administration.

In 1920 the first students were admitted to a very similar schema that led to a bachelor of commerce degree. The program remained in the department of political economy and was not placed in a separate school of commerce as had been done in Birmingham. During 1931 a proposal was made by the head of the political economy department to the university's president for the creation of a Faculty of Economics separate from the Faculty of Arts. Presumably there would have been a distinctive department of commerce within that faculty. The proposal was not acted upon. Until the 1960s, with the exception of law, all instructors in commerce were either in the department of political economy or in the department of mathematics. Accounting was taught by the mathematics faculty until 1926, when the courses and staff were moved to the department of political economy. 'Interest and Bond Values' and 'Actuarial Science' remained subjects taught in the mathematics department.

A significant addition to the commerce staff was made during 1911, when Gilbert Jackson (a Cambridge graduate) was appointed. He became the supervisor of studies for commerce in 1922, and held the position until he left the university in 1934. C. Alan Ashley (a Birmingham graduate, not related to William) joined the staff to teach industry and trade, auditing, and corporation finance. He succeeded Jackson as supervisor of studies, a position he held for about twenty-five years. In many respects, Jackson and Ashley shaped the character of the bachelor of commerce program, which also drew on economists in the department for courses such as transportation, labour economics, and managerial economics. The staff in accounting was built up from the 1940s, and courses in finance, marketing, and administrative sciences were later introduced. Beginning in the 1960s, the latter courses were staffed mainly by what is now the faculty of the Rotman School of Management.

During the 1930s there was pressure from the business community to make the bachelor of commerce program more *practical*. The department of political economy responded by creating a master of commerce degree in 1938. This was a two-year program in which the first year comprised courses about subjects that a student would have studied in an undergraduate commerce program. Students with a BCom. who had studied those subjects were exempted from the first year. The second year began as a program similar to an MA in economics and gradually became an advanced program in commerce.

The Bachelor of Commerce Program in a Liberal Arts Environment

Vincent Bladen, the first director of what is now the Rotman School of Management, expressed in 1957, when he was Dean of the Faculty of Arts and Science, the following belief:

> In these days of pressure for education *in* business administration, it is well to consider whether the university in performing its ancient function of liberal education may not in fact provide a better education *for* business

than can be provided by ... courses in Business Administration ... I am, of course, presenting a justification of the policy of the University of Toronto in maintaining the liberal arts character of its Commerce course and in developing a professional course in Business Administration in the Graduate School ... The object of university work in industrial relations, for example, is to turn out men 'suitable to become' rather than 'made' industrial relations officers.[4]

What was meant by the *liberal arts* and how did they originally fit into the role of the university? Has the University of Toronto been successful in maintaining the BCom. program as a liberal arts program? The first of the medieval universities, the University of Bologna founded in 1088, evolved from a law school begun during 890. The university became in the twelfth and thirteenth centuries the principal European centre for civil and canon law. Around 1200, faculties of medicine and philosophy were added. The second great medieval university, the University of Paris founded about 1150, originally had three 'superior' faculties: theology, canon law, and medicine, and one 'inferior' faculty: arts. In the faculty of arts, the trivium of grammar, logic, and rhetoric and the quadrivium of arithmetic, geometry, music, and astronomy were taught. These seven sciences constituted the liberal arts.[5] They were intended to serve as a preparation for more advanced studies or for later life. The third of the early medieval universities, the University of Oxford founded during 1167, was modelled on the University of Paris, with initial faculties of theology, law, medicine, and the liberal arts.[6]

It is noteworthy in the context of a study of modern schools of management that the early medieval universities were designed primarily to train people for the professions. The first non-ecclesiastical civil service began to emerge. Claude Bissell, president of the University of Toronto, observed: '[G]rammar and rhetoric were the prologue to law ... and dialectics was the prologue to theology ... or to medicine ... To the three basic professions – law, medicine, and the church – the twentieth century has added a host of others, fruits of the demand for specialization, of the rise of the social sciences and the flourishing of the natural sciences, and of the steady expansion of the state. Even the business man, traditionally a rough diamond and proud of it, has capitulated to professionalism.'[7] To the three original professional faculties, a fourth, the faculty of business or management, has been added, along with several other professional faculties.

The Renaissance of the 1400s revived the interest in Greek and Roman philosophy, however, and the liberal-arts curriculum gradually became the central focus of the universities. Bissell, in 1955, stated that, unlike the early medieval universities, the foundation of the University of Toronto was liberal-arts studies and these were 'firmly founded on a series of carefully constructed honours courses, where intensive work in one or two subjects was thought of as the best way of giving minds depth and flexibility.'[8]

How does the University of Toronto's BCom. program fit into the University of Toronto's liberal arts scheme? Alfred North Whitehead described the importance of the liberal arts to business education thusly: 'The universities have trained the intellectual pioneers of our civilization – the priests, the lawyers, the statesmen, the doctors, the men of science, and the men of letters ... The conduct of business now requires intellectual imagination of the same type as that which in former times has mainly passed into those other occupations ... The way in which a university should function in the preparation for an intellectual career, such as modern business or one of the older professions, is by promoting the imaginative consideration of the various *general principles* underlying that career.'[9] Alan Ashley, supervisor of studies in commerce, expressed similar thoughts in 1937: 'The object ... is ... to train men in the use of faculties, to give them a sound knowledge of economic theory in the widest sense, and to turn out graduates who can expect to apply themselves with success to the task of learning a business quickly, of becoming good citizens, and of living a full life.'[10]

The Toronto bachelor of commerce program has tried to maintain its liberal arts orientation by continuing to be a joint program in commerce and economics. Despite some strong views to the contrary, it still retains a liberal arts flavour rather than a professional management orientation.[11] Its objective is to give students an analytical and institutional background that enables them to assess the effect of changing market conditions on the plans of corporations or governments. The emphasis is on understanding the external environment of firms and on the provision of information to decision makers through accounting systems and through economic, financial, and marketing analysis. Although courses in organizational behaviour and a few management courses are available in the senior years, the course of study is not intended to provide an extensive grounding in business administration or management. It is not designed to develop within-the-firm managerial skills or to produce persons ready to assume general management responsibilities. At the University of Toronto, management education is primarily conducted in the graduate MBA or MMPA programs.

The first two years of baccalaureate studies are devoted to the study of the disciplines basic to commerce and economics – accounting, mathematics, and statistics – and to other arts and science subjects.[12] To fulfill a breadth requirement, students are expected to take a literature course and a humanities course, although an economic history course may be substituted for one of these. In total, at least four courses must be taken from outside the social sciences, although mathematics, statistics, and computer science courses are used to satisfy this requirement. In the third and fourth years, students may elect to concentrate on a commerce subject (accounting, finance, marketing, or organizational behaviour), undertake a more intensive study of economics, or choose a generalist program combining various areas. Students may obtain a specialist certification in economics, while also meeting the requirements for the degree of BCom., if they follow a prescribed regimen.

Graduates of the BCom. program, depending on the course of study they elect to follow, should be well prepared for graduate studies in accounting or economics,[13] to undertake further study to qualify for entry into the accounting or legal professions, or to take positions in business or government. Few graduates of the Toronto BCom. degree apparently enter MBA programs, because their undergraduate studies prepare an alternative career path for them. Some may wish to develop their specialization in areas such as finance or marketing by entering studies directed towards those concerns, rather than taking an MBA program, which is focused upon general management. The new Master of Management and Professional Accountancy degree does provide a specialist offering for those planning to enter accounting. There is a strong argument for specialists in finance, marketing, or operations management within a school of management to have a master's degree. The resurrection of the MCom. degree for this purpose would be one solution to the problem, since it is unusual to have a bachelor's degree such as the BCom. without a master's degree to which graduates in areas other than accounting may proceed.

The composition of students and staff in the undergraduate program changed markedly after 1971, when the Institute of Chartered Accountants of Ontario changed the requirements for certification as a chartered accountant to include a university degree roughly equivalent to a bachelor of commerce. Enrolment at Toronto increased markedly and a number of accounting courses were added. Currently, about half of the students enrolled in the program do so in order to meet the CA requirements. Most of the increased staff required to mount this expansion have been either part-time instructors from the accounting profession or full-time staff who have not gone through a research-oriented graduate program. Sufficient funding to meet this increased demand by hiring full-time staff who were graduates of doctoral programs was not made available by the university, even though the BCom. program generated a large cash flow. The provincial government gave the university more funding for each commerce student relative to other arts students.

The same BCom. program is offered on both the St George and Mississauga campuses of the University of Toronto and is available to part-time students through Woodsworth College. Recently the University of Toronto at Scarborough began offering a bachelor of business administration degree. The Scarborough program is 'high-quality pre-professional management education within the context of a liberal arts education for students interested in managerial careers.' It is a distinct program from that on the St George and Mississauga campuses and is administered separately. In 1998 the specialist program in economics at Scarborough was eliminated to allow the economics department there to focus on the integration of management studies into the study of economics in order to provide students with more marketable skills. There is also a major program in commerce and finance with the same entrance requirements as the bachelor of commerce program, which may be taken as part of the requirements for the BA or BSc. degree. The four-year major program in commerce must be combined with a major or specialist program in another area selected by the student; for example, political science, computer science, international relations, or a language. In a three-year program, a student may complete the degree requirement with only one major.

Commerce as Joint Programs of the Faculty of Arts and Science and the Rotman School of Management

In 1982 the department of political economy was dissolved and separate departments of economics and of political science were created. A task force was struck to recommend on the new administrative structure for the baccalaureate program and several proposals were adopted. The degree of bachelor of commerce continued to be awarded by the Faculty of Arts and Science and the students remained candidates in that faculty. The School of Management assumed full responsibility for teaching commerce courses, with the exceptions of public administration and managerial economics. The commerce teaching staff of the former department of political economy would, over time, become members of the School of Management.[14] Because the degree was a joint offering in commerce and economics, an administrative structure had to be designed that gave both disciplines a say in the overall structure. The position of chairman of the commerce program, later renamed director, who has been appointed by and reports to the deans of the two faculties, was created. That person was given responsibility for coordinating program content and students affairs.

In 1984 the chairman wrote a report on the state of the baccalaureate program that discussed the problem of the imbalance between the enrolment (three hundred a year admitted on the St George campus) and the available resources. Two possible solutions were suggested. The first entailed an increase in the budget for the St George campus offerings by roughly $240,000. This would have permitted a conversion of part-time to regular instructors and, where necessary, an upgrading of the quality of the permanent staff. The alternative was to reduce the size of the program. To implement the second option, a reduction of the intake on the St George campus from 300 to 150 students per year seemed appropriate.[15] No action was taken to implement in total, or in part, either of the proposed solutions.

A provostial review was announced in February 1988 and the committee's report proposed that the BCom. should be a joint offering by the School of Management and the Faculty of Arts and Science on the St George and Mississauga campuses. In addition, it suggested the program should receive resources sufficient to ensure an excellent program of instruction. The report noted that the second recommendation required a considerable increase in funding, but this course of action still has not been implemented.[16] BCom. students were jointly registered in the Faculty of Arts and Science and the School of Management beginning in 1992.[17] The regulations of the Faculty of Arts and Science are now applicable for matters relating to academic standards, while the School of Management is responsible for the staffing and teaching of commerce courses on the St George and Mississauga campuses. Following the practice of designating a course according to the name of the department that offers it, the commerce courses have been formally designated in the calendar as management (MGT) courses.

Has the liberal arts character of the baccalaureate degree been maintained? The incorporation of the teaching responsibilities into the School of Management has created a problem in maintaining the separate identity of similar upper-level commerce courses and MBA courses. When the same persons are teaching in the BCom. and MBA programs, the distinction between the BCom. as a liberal arts endeavour and the MBA as a professional management offering tends to disappear. It becomes convenient to teach the same courses to first-year MBA students and to upper-year commerce and finance students. The orientation of the BCom. program as a liberal arts program tends to be forgotten. Evolution may mean that the weaker species disappears – that management displaces commerce at the undergraduate level. This tendency may be offset if the academic staff know the history and original objectives of the programs in which they teach. Changes then could only come about after a review of the history and original objectives of the program and a full discussion of the consequences of the changes. A further complication in maintaining the original Birmingham influence has been a shift in the background of program administrators. During the first half of the century, the key persons – the two Ashleys, Mavor, Jackson, and Bladen – were all British university graduates. Recent deans – Tigert, Wolff, Arnold, and Halpern – have been graduates of American business school doctoral programs.

From Master of Commerce to Master of Business Administration

Up to 1950, sixty-two MCom. degrees had been conferred by the political economy department. During 1950 the university created the Institute of Business Administration to replace an Institute of Industrial Relations established in 1945, and it transferred the master of commerce program to this new entity.[18] The principal purpose of the Institute was to provide training for men and women who wished to prepare themselves for responsible performance in business and public-service careers. It operated within the School of Graduate Studies and was able to offer its facilities to graduate students of other departments who wished to diversify their programs by including subjects in administration. It also could authorize students to take courses in other departments as part of their studies of special fields related to administration.

The first director was Vincent Bladen (1950–3), professor of economics and the previous director of the Institute for Industrial Relations. Bladen left in 1953 to head the department of political economy, and he later became dean of the Faculty of Arts and Science. He was succeeded by T.C. Graham (1953–60). The Institute was staffed by Bladen by taking in three members of the former Institute, recruiting two persons from industry who were skilled in production management and administration, and bringing over three members of the political economy department to teach accounting, finance, economics, and marketing. The latter three returned to the department after a few years. Subsequently there were two acquisitions from the federal government, one from the accounting profession, one more from industry, one from another university, and two persons recruited directly on the completion of their doctoral studies.

When the Institute took over the master of commerce degree, the second year of studies was transformed into a business administration program, with candidates taking a required seminar on business policy and four courses from the following: corporation finance, advanced accounting, advertising and market research, production, industrial relations, and human relations in industry, or suitable courses in economics, political science, or sociology. The University of Toronto degree was criticized as a duplication of the University of Western Ontario's MBA program, which had been established in 1949. Bladen argued that there was room for more than one method of teaching business administration and, moreover, there were a large number of part-time students in Toronto who needed a local service. In 1960 the degree was changed from master of commerce to master of business administration and the name of the Institute was changed to the School of Business. Warren Main (1960–71) was the first and only director of the School of Business.

Three factors changed markedly the recruitment policy and research interests of the academic staff during the 1960s: in the 1950s the Institute's MBA program was directed primarily at part-time evening students, whereas in the 1960s the emphasis was placed on full-time students; a separate Centre for Industrial Relations was created in the School of Graduate Studies; and a doctoral program was inaugurated. With the shift towards a more academic orientation, the school began to recruit faculty directly from doctoral programs (principally from American universities) or to hire staff with established academic credentials. Several people left because they did not wish to be involved in the doctoral program. The three faculty members who had come from the Institute of Industrial Relations ceased to be full-time members by the end of the 1960s.

From School of Business to School of Management

In 1972 the university raised the status of several graduate professional divisions from schools, with a director as head, to that of a faculty, with a dean as head. The name of the School of Business was changed to Faculty of Management Studies. The choice of the name *Management Studies* was based on the growing trend to use *management*, not *administration* to better describe the program's focus and to reflect the fact that graduates of the Faculty were to be found in both the private and public sectors. The word *Studies* was added, following British precedents, to indicate that the academic staff engaged in research to *study* the practice of management. John Crispo was the first dean of the School of Management, and the subsequent deans were Max Clarkson (1975–80), Douglas Tigert (1980–5), John Sawyer (Acting Dean, 1985–6), Roger Wolff (1985–92), Hugh Arnold (1992–7), Paul Halpern (Interim Dean, 1997–8), and Roger Martin (1998–).[19]

The faculty now set their goal as establishing an outstanding postgraduate school by international standards. The educational philosophy has been based upon the proposition that there are three basic disciplines that must be mastered in order to perform well the general decision-making functions of a manager: quantitative methods, economics, and organizational behaviour. It was the feeling of the academic staff in the early 1970s that this discipline approach was essential to the isolation and enlargement of the body of knowledge common to the practice of management. In the 1980s, however, increasing emphasis was placed on the understanding of the total environment – economic, social, political, and international – and on the manager's role as a formulator of strategy.

Several significant factors affected staffing issues during the 1980s: an expansion of the Faculty's mission in 1983 to include an Executive MBA program; the adoption of responsibility for teaching commerce courses and the transfer of academic staff from the Faculty of Arts and Science to the Faculty of Management in 1982; and the creation of externally financed professorships. The increased emphasis upon educational offerings for middle managers (the Executive MBA and nondegree executive development programs) implied the necessity to have staff who could communicate and interact with mid-career executives, as well as teach MBA students who came directly from an undergraduate business degree program. The creation of externally financed professorships enabled the Faculty to recruit excellent academics from other universities or to provide conditions that enabled it to keep members of its current staff.

In 1986, the word 'Studies' was dropped from the Faculty's name, and during 1996 the formal designation was changed to the 'Joseph L. Rotman School of Management' in acknowledgment of a benefaction from Joseph and Sandra Rotman. Despite this change in title, the school retains its status as a faculty in the University of Toronto.

Evolution of the MBA Programs

In the 1950s the MCom. program had been primarily a program for part-time students. During the 1960–61 academic year, the number of full-time students in the two years of the MBA program only totalled about forty. Across the 1960s the emphasis changed and full-time MBA students were attracted, while the part-time program was reduced to a diploma in business administration, which became essentially the first year of the MBA program. Graduates of the diploma offering could, if their grades were sufficiently high, proceed to the second year of the full-time MBA.

From the early 1960s until the late 1970s, the first-year MBA students were divided into two streams. The first stream included those candidates who had a background in mathematics from their undergraduate studies — mainly graduates of engineering or science programs. Students in the second steam were given an introduction to mathematics, including some calculus, and a second course in operations research.

Through the 1970s the MBA continued to be a two-year offering, with the first year essentially a prerequisite year in which students received a grounding in the subjects that would normally be included in an undergraduate course of commerce studies. The second year was the true graduate program. During the 1980s this perception of the MBA program changed and it took on the characteristics of an American program, such as that offered at Wharton or Northwestern. The MBA program changed from being an extension of the BCom., one designed to produce accountants and analysts of the economic environment in which business and government operate, to an orientation that would produce managers. The two years of the MBA were made compulsory and very few exemptions were given for undergraduate work. Most incoming students had some business experience and this was taken into account during classroom sessions. Cases accordingly began to play a much larger role in the instructional process during the 1980s.

The core curriculum is now divided into three major components: the context of general management (economics, ethics, management skills development), functional area foundations (accounting, marketing, finance, organizational behaviour and human resource management, operations management, statistics, management information systems), and strategic management. In the first year, students are introduced to all three components. In the second year, students take a course in strategic management and nine electives.

The School of Management and the Faculty of Law offer a four-year joint program for those who wish to combine graduate education in management with the study of law. Graduates are awarded both the MBA and the LLB degrees.

In the 1970s the part-time MBA degree was reinstituted and the diploma was phased out. The curriculum for the part-time MBA differs only slightly from that for the full-time program. Since 1988, part-time MBA students may complete the schedule by evening classes across ten terms (fall, winter, and summer) over a period of forty months. This fast-track program enables students to stay together in a class or cohort for the first-year mandatory courses and the second-year strategic management course.

In 1983 an Executive MBA program, distinctive from the regular MBA and designed to take advantage of the fact that some students have middle-management experience, was begun. Executive MBA students attend for a full day on alternate Fridays and Saturdays and complete the schedule of studies in two years. The Executive MBA program represented the school's first financing of a degree program fully by tuition fees with no provincial funding. This allowed an increase in the number of academic staff, and the size of the various areas came closer to the critical mass needed for effective research and teaching. Initially, it was expected that the Executive MBA would fund six tenure-stream faculty positions. It also improved markedly the school's relations with the business community.

Master of Management and Professional Accounting

With the integration of the undergraduate commerce teaching staff for accounting into the Faculty of Management during 1982, this area began to play a more important role. Some of the staff who had taught only at the baccalaureate level now began to teach in the MBA program. More options were added, and in 1989 a schema leading to the

MBA degree was added for students wishing to acquire a deeper knowledge of accounting than would be obtained in the undergraduate curriculum. In part, this policy was a response to an increase in the requirements announced by the Institute of Chartered Accountants of Ontario for certification as a CA. The program covers seven terms, including five academic study terms and two co-op terms where students work in an accounting environment. Students with a suitable undergraduate background may have advanced standing and complete the program in four to six terms. The program is fully funded by tuition fees and most students have their tuition supported by the accountancy firms where they spend their work terms. The program was moved to the Mississauga campus of the University of Toronto in 1996 to give that campus a stronger presence in accountancy, and the designation of the degree was changed from an MBA to Master of Management and Professional Accounting (MMPA).

Doctor of Philosophy

Why should faculty members in a school of business do research, and why should schools of business have doctoral programs? Whitehead presents the following argument:

> [T]he proper function of a university is the imaginative acquisition of knowledge ... It can only be communicated by a faculty whose members themselves wear their learning with imagination. Do you want your teachers to be imaginative? Then encourage them to do research. Do you want your researchers to be imaginative? Then bring them into intellectual sympathy with the young at the most eager, imaginative period of life, when intellects are just entering upon their mature discipline. Make your researchers explain themselves to active minds, plastic with the world before them; make your young students crown their period of intellectual acquisition by some contact with minds gifted with experience of intellectual adventure. Education is discipline for the adventure of life; research is intellectual adventure; and the universities should be homes of adventure shared in common by young and old.[20]

In 1969 the Faculty of Management began admitting doctoral candidates into four areas: finance, marketing, organizational behaviour and human resource management, and business economics. In keeping with its research orientation, the degree is a PhD rather than a DBA. The program in business economics was not successful in attracting good students and ceased to admit new students in the late 1970s. A doctoral offering in operations management and a joint PhD program in finance and economics with the department of economics were added in the 1980s.

An aspect of the specialist versus generalist debate concerns the PhD program. It would expedite the progress towards the doctoral thesis if students were not required to obtain an MBA before proceeding to the doctorate. The specialist master's suggested above might be a more appropriate path to follow. The argument for the MBA is that the graduates of the doctoral program may be teaching MBA students and should therefore know the MBA program. Is a DBA program more appropriate than a research-oriented PhD for teachers of MBAs?

Relations with the Business Community

The MCom. and MBA programs in the 1950s and 1960s did not receive strong support from the university's administration and did not have a strong image in the business community. In an attempt to improve this situation, the 1971 search committee for a new dean looked for someone who had demonstrated a good relationship with the business community and was familiar with executive development initiatives. The recommendation of the search committee was, however, rejected by the president of the university, a decision that may have delayed the effective development of the school's relations with the business community by fifteen years.

In an attempt to improve relations with the business community, Dean Crispo did create in 1972 an advisory council of leading businessmen. Unfortunately, the council was too large and too diverse; it failed to function effectively and was allowed to disappear. Relations with the business community slowly improved in the 1980s when Dean Tigert began a corporate sponsors program that provided funds for summer research grants to junior academic staff in the tenure stream. During 1985 Dean Wolff created a Dean's Advisory Council: a small group of interested persons from the business community who meet regularly with the dean to advise on the business community's perception of the role of the faculty. The work of the advisory council has received strong support from two university presidents, George Connell and Robert Prichard.

Executive Development Programs

The Institute of Industrial Relations had begun in the 1940s a series of non-degree conference programs on industrial relations. The School of Business extended these in the 1950s to include business administration. In 1960 a weekly evening seminar on 'Management of the Enterprise' was begun and was quite popular. 'The Management Process' – a four-week course spread over four months designed to broaden the knowledge of managers – was started in the early 1970s. This represented the Faculty of Management's first major initiative in non-degree education for middle managers. More recent offerings have included Strategic Planning in Retailing, Organization Design and Redesign, Leadership and Change, Negotiating for Success, Strategic Marketing Management, and a variety of programs on derivative securities. The Faculty of Management developed a strong presence in *custom* programs designed for specific business or government organizations. Dean Tigert pointed out that 'companies are turning increasingly towards in-house programs' and 'universities cannot afford to ignore this key source of revenue.'[21] These programs involve members of the academic staff working in close partnership with client organizations in the design and delivery of executive programs exclusively for that client.

While the Executive MBA and executive development programs are important sources of revenue for the school, they do expose the school to 'businessman's risk.' The revenue from these programs is factored into the school's budget. Errors in forecasting enrolment can lead to significant shortfalls in revenue, and can be a source of budgetary problems. Bankruptcy becomes possible with trusteeship as an outcome.

The Mission and Vision of the Rotman School of Management

The provost of the university announced in September 1993 a process designed to formulate plans for each division within the institution for the period 1994–2000. The organizational mission, as it applies to professional education, was stated as follows:

> As a research university, the University of Toronto provides a strong base for professional education, both in established professional areas and in emerging areas that cross established professional and disciplinary lines.

> Nowhere is the translation of research strength into problem-solving
> capacity more apparent than in these professional areas.
>
> ... [T]he University of Toronto has the capacity to educate not only the
> professionals of tomorrow but also those who will educate professionals
> in the future. Given these strengths, it is appropriate that we play a lead-
> ership role in professional education in Canada.[22]

Thus, the bachelor of commerce, master of business administration,
and doctor of philosophy programs of the School of Management fit
into the university's mission.

In 1996 the Council of the School of Management adopted the following statement of its mission and its vision: 'Its mission is to provide
outstanding educational programs that enhance the effectiveness of
the participants and the competitiveness of their organizations in a
rapidly changing global environment and to foster management scholarship and professional practice of the highest quality. [Its] vision ... is
to be ... recognized by the business and academic communities as one
of the leading business schools in the world. It is to be a national
resource for business and a major contributor to enhancing Canada's
international competitiveness.'

The donation from Sandra and Joseph Rotman of $15 million to the
University of Toronto in December 1996 is the first step in achieving
the vision of the School of Management. The donation is to be matched
by the university from its endowment funds to create a $30 million
endowment fund in support of the school. The primary goal of this
fund is to attract and retain professors of the highest international cali-
bre by creating several endowed chairs. The funds are also to be used
to support programs and initiatives in entrepreneurship, globalization,
and technology, as well as graduate student fellowships and interdisciplinary projects. Previously, the Rotmans had made a donation of
$3 million as a contribution to the building of a new facility to house
the school: the Joseph L. Rotman Centre for Management. Dean
Wolff's creation of the Dean's Advisory Council was the seed from
which germinated the benefactions of the Rotmans. Joseph Rotman
was a graduate of the MCom. program, a part-time lecturer in the
School of Business (1964–6), and an original member of the Dean's
Advisory Council.

Recruitment of staff for a full-service school of management is a
complex problem. The diversity of programs requires a diversity of
academic staff. The school now contains individuals who are research-

minded, will add to the knowledge of management skills, and will work with doctoral students; people who will work closely with the business community, are familiar with management practices, and can develop cases for instructional purposes; and staff who are oriented towards professional accounting programs. The problems of recruiting and of developing tenure and promotion criteria that are fair to all members of such a staff have become complex tasks.

Moreover, in times of budget constraints and limited size of academic staff, it becomes increasingly difficult to give all programs the required amount of resources to maintain their current status. A balanced allocation of scarce resources among the undergraduate offerings, the PhD program, and the graduate programs becomes essential, but can be a source of conflict among administrators.

Summary

The University of Toronto, building on the diploma program begun in 1901, began the first four-year commerce and finance program in Canada leading to a bachelor's degree in 1909 and followed this with a bachelor of commerce program in 1920. These programs were joint specialist programs in commerce and economics based on the English model of the University of Birmingham, and were placed in a liberal arts environment that the University of Toronto still tries to retain by keeping the program rooted in the Faculty of Arts and Science. The desire of the business community for a more practical training in management techniques led to the creation in 1938 of the master of commerce, which became an MBA degree in 1960. Out of this has grown a full-service graduate business school: the Joseph L. Rotman School of Management. The Rotman School has a strong research base, with a PhD program and teaching staff designed to service various degree and executive programs. It also services the commerce half of the BCom. program in cooperation with the department of economics and is intended to give the degree its liberal arts flavour.

NOTES

1 This case study is based upon a mixture of documented history, personal recollections, and subjective impressions. It is restricted to programs on the St George campus and does not include the history of commerce pro-

grams on the Mississauga and Scarborough campuses of the University of Toronto, nor does it include business programs conducted by the Extension Division of the university or its successors: Woodsworth College and the School of Continuing Studies. An earlier version of the history of the degree programs is in J.A. Sawyer, 'Commerce and Management at the University of Toronto: A Brief History' in *ASAC Conference Proceedings: Business History* 17:24 (1996), 77–85. The author began his association with the BCom. program at the University of Toronto as an undergraduate in 1943 and joined the staff of what is now the Rotman School of Management in 1960.

2 This summary of the early history of the commerce programs is taken mainly from the detailed history in I.M. Drummond, *Political Economy at the University of Toronto: A History of the Department, 1888–1982* (Toronto: UTP, 1983). The reader may find it interesting to compare the origins of the University of Toronto commerce programs with those of Queen's University as described in chapter 3 of this volume.

3 S.M. Wickett, 'The University's Course in Commerce,' *Proceedings of the 41st Annual Convention of the Ontario Educational Association*, 1902, 279–83, outlined the program; quoted by P.A. Moreland, *A History of Business Education* (Toronto: Pitman Publishing, 1977), 152.

4 V.W. Bladen, 'The Role of the University,' *UTQ* 26 (1957), 483, 492. M. St.A. Woodside, 'The Value of the Humanities' and Sir Arnold Plant, 'Universities and the Making of Businessmen,' *UTQ* 26 (1957), 508–34, also make the case for liberal arts as a preparation for business. J.J. Clark and B.J. Opulente have written three volumes on the topic in the series *Thought Patterns*, published in New York by the St John's University Press: *Towards a Philosophy of Business Education* (1960), *Business and the Liberal Arts* (1962), and *Professional Education for Business* (1964).

5 The notion of the seven liberal arts appears to have originated with Martianus Minneus Felix Capella, about AD 400, at Carthage. In Capella's writing, Mercury gives his bride seven maidens, each one representing one of the seven liberal arts.

6 The *Encyclopedia Britannica* gives historical notes on these medieval universities.

7 C.T. Bissell, *The Strength of the University* (Toronto: UTP, 1968), 84.

8 *The Strength of the University*, 91 and 82.

9 Alfred North Whitehead, *The Aims of Education and Other Essays* (New York: Mentor Books, 1947; originally published by the Macmillan Company, 1929), 99, 101, italics added.

10 Letter from C.A. Ashley to H.A. Innis, head of the department of political economy, 2 November 1937; quoted by Drummond, *Political Economy*, 68.

11 An alternative approach to giving students both a liberal arts education and a business education is the one adopted by universities such as Harvard and Chicago, which offer only graduate education in business. Students are presumed to have obtained a liberal arts education in their undergraduate program. S.F. Teele and J.F. Chapman, 'Education for Business,' *UTQ* 26 (1957), 535–56, explain the Harvard approach.

12 In eighteenth-century Britain the teaching of economics had its roots in the teaching of two professors of moral philosophy at the University of Glasgow: Francis Hutcheson and Adam Smith. They lectured on jurisprudence and from the analysis of contracts came the necessity to deal with money and prices. British economics had, at that time, close association with law and philosophy and the notion of *natural price* became an economics concept.

13 Until the mid-1960s the BCom. program was in some respects a better preparation for graduate work in economics than was the Honours Economics and Political Science program. Students in the BCom. program received a good grounding in mathematics, statistics, and accounting. During this period nine Toronto BCom.'s went on to leading American universities to do a PhD in economics or finance and then returned to the University of Toronto to become professors of economics or finance.

14 Report of the FMS/C&F Task Force (19 April 1982).

15 The Commerce Programmes in the Faculty of Arts and Science of the University of Toronto: A Report by the Chairman (August 1984).

16 Provostial Review of the Commerce Programs: Report (April 1989).

17 Students in the commerce programs continue to register in one of the Arts and Science colleges: Erindale, Innis, New, St Michael's, Trinity, University, Victoria, or Woodsworth.

18 A fuller account of these developments is found in Vincent Bladen, *Bladen on Bladen: Memoirs of a Political Economist* (Toronto: Scarborough College in the University of Toronto, 1978), 108–9 and 122–4.

19 It may be of interest to note that four of the seven deans are BCom.'s (Crispo, Halpern, and Sawyer from the University of Toronto and Tigert from Queen's).

20 Whitehead, *The Aims of Education*, 101–2.

21 Douglas Tigert, 'The Changing Portfolio of Business Schools,' *Toronto Business Reports / 5* (Faculty of Management Studies, University of Toronto, 1985).

22 A draft of a provostial white paper, 'Planning for 2000,' was published in
    The Bulletin of the University of Toronto on 21 February 1994. (The quota-
    tions are from pages S3 and S12.) Following up on the provostial white
    paper, a document containing the plans for the various divisions of the uni-
    versity, including the Faculty of Management, was published on 2 October
    1995: 'Planning for 2000: Divisional "White Paper" Plans.'

5

From the Faculty of Administrative Studies to the Schulich School of Business: The Origin and Evolution of Professional Education for Managers at York University

JAMES GILLIES and COLIN DICKINSON

When Murray Ross became the first president of York University in 1959 he brought to higher education in Canada a philosophy somewhat different from that which historically prevailed in most of the nation. Rather than viewing the traditional British universities – Oxford and Cambridge – as the institutions to be emulated, Ross was convinced that in the latter half of the twentieth century Canada needed universities that were modelled on the great state institutions of the United States.[1] The characteristics of the latter were accessibility – many were, for years, essentially tuition-free – and public funding. Since the universities were financed by the taxpayers, it was an accepted proposition that they in turn had a responsibility to serve the community of which they were a part – and that responsibility was widely defined. It is not astonishing, therefore, that Murray Ross's vision for the new university included the development of professional schools, in those areas that the traditional universities had neglected, to meet the needs of the citizens of Ontario.

Background

By 1965, Ross was convinced that York had progressed to the point where the establishment of some type of education in administration was feasible. He was quite aware of the historical development and characteristics of business programs in Canada and was particularly cognizant of the pioneering program, based on the Harvard Business School experience, that had been developed at the University of Western Ontario. He also, because of his association with the University of

Toronto, was familiar with the undergraduate commerce and finance program offered by that institution, which produced many of the accountants in Canada. At the same time, he was following the upheaval taking place in business education in the United States and was convinced that the revolution occurring in the education of business people in that country should be brought, one way or another, to Canada, and that the conduit for doing so should be York.

In this view he was strongly supported by the board of governors of the university, a formidable group of leading Canadian business and professional people, under the chairmanship of Robert Winters, a former federal minister of Industry, Trade and Commerce. Metropolitan Toronto, with over a million people, was the seat of a provincial government, the location of most corporate head offices in Canada, the home of the largest trading exchange in the nation, and the centre of Canadian commerce, so the board was certain that the community could easily support a new, modern, contemporary business school.

Ross was very fortunate in having on his staff, as his special assistant, an imaginative young scholar, Dr Henry Best.[2] In order to move the project ahead, Best was commissioned (1) to prepare a formal paper on the feasibility of establishing a program at York and (2) to present some preliminary recommendations about the appropriate form of a program. Best soon concluded (given there were more than 150,000 people of college age, 30,000 public servants in the three levels of government, and an unknown but large executive population in the area served by York) that a large latent demand for educational opportunities in administration existed. Much influenced by the work being done in organization and management theory at the time, he believed there had emerged a body of knowledge about management that was applicable to almost any situation – that anyone who understood the fundamental principles of planning, staffing, organizing, directing, and controlling could apply them in any institutional setting. Consequently, Best recommended that York should establish, not a business school, but a faculty of administrative studies, with possibly six divisions or schools of administration – business, public, educational, health, social, and library.[3]

While Best's paper was not formally adopted, either by the senate or the board of governors of the university, it became the informal working document upon which plans for developing the program proceeded. It served this purpose well, because not only did it provide a firm assessment that there was a need for professional education that

York could meet, but by focusing on administration in general, rather than business per se, it went a long way in removing the vague feeling of unease that many academics, particularly those educated at Oxford and Cambridge, had about the propriety of offering professional business education within universities.

During his tenure as vice-president of the University of Toronto, Ross had contacted a Canadian, James Gillies, a professor and administrator in the School of Business at the University of California at Los Angeles, to see if he had any interest in coming to the University of Toronto to head the business program. Although for a number of reasons Gillies was uninterested in doing so, Ross kept in touch with him, and when the plans for the creation of the program at York began to firm up, in the spring of 1965, he once again contacted Gillies to see if he might come to talk to some of the people involved about starting a new professional program in business. Although he had no intention of leaving California, Gillies's interest was sufficiently piqued by Ross's enthusiasm that he agreed to visit Toronto, in March of 1965. During the trip, Gillies was deeply impressed by the commitment to business education of members of the board of governors, particularly the chair, Robert Winters, and of various members of the business community, and by the support of some (but by no means all) of the faculty members already at York for a new professional business school. Upon returning to California, Gillies proposed to Ross that he take a one-year leave of absence from UCLA to come to York to advise the university on the establishment of a school of business. Ross immediately accepted his offer, and on 1 July 1965 Gillies began his one-year stay in Toronto.

Creation of the York Faculty of Administrative Studies

Gillies's appointment, even though it was for only one year, basically set the long-term strategy for business education at York. He had been very active in the reforms of business education brought about by the Gordon/Howell report[4] and the largesse of the Ford Foundation. Consequently, he had strong views about the appropriate approach to business education. He was an advocate of the basic philosophy of American universities that post-secondary institutions should provide avenues for the upward social mobility of citizens, that there should be access for all who were qualified, and that universities, along with their historic functions of providing a place for the storehouse and dissemination of knowledge, the development of ideas, and the preservation of unimpaired freedom of discussion, were also the servants of the society that financed them. As such, his views on the role of the university, and by extension that of a business school, were very much in harmony with those of President Ross.

Gillies had no problem in accepting the general strategy of creating a faculty of administrative studies, as espoused in Best's document – indeed, he applauded the idea. He also believed that programs should be readily accessible to as many students as possible. This meant that they should be available to both full- and part-time students, that entrance should be possible at the start of any semester, and that there should be a full summer program. Moreover, he favoured concentrating on the development of graduate professional degree programs rather than on providing undergraduate work. He did not want to create, in any sense, an elitist program, other than in terms of the quality of the offerings and of the students. And he did not believe it would be wise to emulate (as Western had done) a program offered elsewhere.

These strategies were in tune with the financial realities associated with creating a new faculty at that time. In the 1960s funding of higher education in Ontario was directly linked to enrolment, and since a new school in a new university had no other sources of funding, if it was to have sufficient resources to offer a broad program, it had to have a large student body. Indeed, the informal motto under which Gillies began his work was simply, 'If you want to be good you have to be big.'

Given these parameters, Gillies's work for the year he was to be at York was quite clear. If the faculty was to open on schedule he had to do a variety of things within the university, within the general academic community, and within the business community.

(A) *Within the university.* Gillies had to persuade the senate and the board of governors of the university to enact legislation creating, with appropriate powers, a faculty of administrative studies; design curricula for the programs to be offered by the faculty; persuade the senate to adopt the curricula; persuade the existing faculty of the intellectual worthiness of education in administration; and persuade the university administrators to provide the financial support necessary for launching the initiatives.

Actually, he found completing these tasks was not difficult. He proposed that the new faculty be empowered to grant, through the Faculty of Graduate Studies, two degrees – a master of business administration and a master of public administration. To qualify for a degree, students would be required to complete a core curriculum of business subjects plus additional work in their chosen area of specialization and to participate in preparing a strategy study for an ongoing organization. All students, regardless of whether or not they were seeking an MBA or an MPA degree, would have to meet the same admission standards and complete the core courses. It was recommended that the programs be offered on both a full- and part-time basis and that students be able to begin at the commencement of the autumn, winter, or spring semesters.

The completion of the strategy study was included to meet the general university requirement that all students receiving a graduate degree must write a thesis. Doing so was neither appropriate nor feasible in a professional program, however. To fulfil the thesis requirement in the new faculty, under the direction of three faculty members (one of whom served as chair of the project) student groups of not more than eight, or less than six, had to select an ongoing organization and write a strategic study about that enterprise. Upon completion of the project, and before they received credit for the work, the students had to present their report to the organization. The project was designed to teach students to work in groups, to hone both their oral and written presentation skills, and, most important, to learn how to manage organizations successfully by integrating, in an overall study, the material they learned in core courses.

Although Gillies personally favoured offering only graduate programs in the faculty, the administrators and the general faculty of the university believed that there was an unfilled demand for undergraduate work in administration that York should try to meet. Consequently, Gillies proposed that the new faculty should offer a small, experimental, undergraduate program. He proposed that, instead of receiving direct admission to the Faculty of Administrative Studies, students should enrol in the Faculty of Arts, complete two years of general arts courses, and in the third year apply for admission to the Faculty of Administrative Studies. They would then take two years of general business courses and receive a bachelor of business administration degree. Admissions would be limited to one hundred students a year, for a total enrolment of two hundred.

During the spring of 1966, Gillies presented the plans for the new faculty, the proposed courses, and the admission requirements (which were the same as those published by the Faculty of Graduate Studies), plus the writing of the Graduate Admissions Test for Business, to the senate. They were approved without major dissent. In fact, the proposals were passed with the support of the dean of the Faculty of Graduate Studies, the dean of Arts and Science, and the principal of Glendon College. Gillies had little difficulty persuading the board of governors or the university's management to support the proposals – after all, they had initiated the idea of creating a business program. President Ross was a strong supporter of the new faculty and committed the necessary funding to meet Gillies's plan of accepting students in the autumn semester of the 1966–67 academic year.

(B) *Within the general academic community.* Gillies's most pressing task within the general academic community was to locate and hire a sufficient number of faculty members to allow the program to be launched in the autumn of 1966. He quickly learned that there was a more-or-less unwritten rule that Canadian business programs would not raid each other for staff. Obviously, this was a rule that he could not follow if the York initiative was to open on time. It was essential not only that the new faculty at York be well qualified academically but also that they be familiar with the Canadian economy and the business community. Consequently, he had to find scholars in Canada, and most of them, he assumed, would be in existing programs.

His assumption was wrong. There were, in fact, a large number of many well-qualified people – former faculty members at other business schools in Canada or the United States and outstanding executives working in the Toronto community, outside of academic institutions – who believed in the need for a new program in the area. From this group, supplemented by a number of faculty in existing institutions who wanted to become involved in the exciting task of creating a new faculty in Toronto, an extraordinarily competent number of potential faculty members was assembled. Most had their doctoral degrees and several had taught at major business schools.

There was, however, one difficulty in closing employment arrangements with prospective faculty members. No one was willing to come to an absolutely new, untested, unknown program without knowing who was going to be the dean of the faculty. Gillies was on a one-year leave from UCLA and it was well known that he planned to return to Los Angeles in May 1966. The problem was resolved when Gillies obtained an extension of his leave and decided to remain at York for one more year until the faculty was actually operating. Once his decision was made, the staffing needs for the first year were quickly completed.

(C) *Within the business community.* One of the reasons York's board of governors and administrators were confident a faculty of administrative studies could be established was the apparent strong support from the business community for a new business program in Toronto. Consequently, as plans for the creation of the faculty evolved, President Ross asked George Gardiner, a member of the board, to more or less provide leadership, from the board's point of view, for the project. It was a brilliant choice. Gardiner, a graduate of the Harvard Business School, who controlled a large number of business enterprises and was a very active and respected member of the Canadian business community, agreed to put together and chair a business advisory council. He invited the chair or chief executive officer of a leading firm in every major industry to be on the council, for which he had a few rules – no one could be a member who was not an owner, chief executive officer, or chair of a firm; no one could send a substitute to a meeting; and every member was expected to attend at least two of the three meetings a year. Basically, he assembled a 'who's who' of Canadian business enterprise to advise Gillies and to promote the new faculty. The group gave the new school something it could never receive in any other way – immediate legitimacy and credibility.

The faculty received an additional assist when the Canadian Imperial Bank of Commerce decided for its Canadian centennial project to create a unique scholarship program for business students coming to York. Under the program, fourteen graduates from universities across the country, one from each province and four at large, were selected to come to York for the first semester of their work. They then spent the second semester studying at Oxford and INSEAD, travelled across Canada meeting leading politicians, businessmen, and scholars during the summer, went to Harvard University in Cambridge, Massachusetts, for their third semester of formal work, and then returned for their final term, graduating with a York MBA. Not only was the program imaginative, exciting, and administered in inspired fashion by Donald Rickerd,[5] but it was well advertised throughout the nation. Indeed, there were posters announcing it, and application forms available, in every branch of the CIBC, as well as a continuing number of newspaper stories and TV comments as various winners of positions in the Centennial Fellowship Program, as it was known, were selected.

As a result of the CIBC program, and of the work in the community by the Council and by Gillies, who spoke to any and every group that would listen to him, plans for the establishment of a program in management education became quite well known. Indeed, when the establishment of the faculty was formally announced in February 1966 at a black-tie dinner for 250 Canadian executives, hosted by George Gardiner, there were few business leaders who had not heard, before a single student had taken a single course, about the business program at York.

By the spring of 1966 everything was in place for the opening of the new faculty of Administrative Studies – all the necessary university legislation was passed, a series of courses had been developed, a calendar had been prepared and circulated, and a faculty hired, ready to teach. While all evidence indicated that the target enrolment of fifty students for the first class in September 1966 would be reached, the new faculty members, many of whom initially met each other at the first meeting of the faculty council early in September, awaited the official registration day with considerable trepidation. They need not have worried. Instead of the forecasted fifty students, a total of three hundred and twenty-three were enrolled.

What were the essential components of the strategy for starting the faculty of Administrative Studies at York University that led it to become, within a few years, the largest graduate program in business education in Canada? The major ones were: (1) a total commitment on the part of the university's administration and the board to the creation of a professional school (regardless of the exact name) of management; (2) a university president who was highly aware and supportive of the changes occurring in business and public administration education in leading universities; (3) a president and board who sought out and hired someone to advise them on the creation of the faculty who had substantial experience as an administrator in a major program at a major university, as well as having a reputation as a scholar; (4) creation of a faculty of administrative studies with a program in business administration and public administration that gave the new enterprise distinction from other existing programs, thereby gaining support for its development from academics who otherwise might have been hostile; (5) emphasis on size, which because of economies of scale enabled the faculty to open with a critical mass of students and faculty members; (6) a sense of urgency in getting started that gave the program a momentum it would not have had if a longer time frame for development had been allowed; (7) limited resources, which dictated there could be no more than one year of planning and development before students had to be accepted; (8) the decision to meet the needs of all sectors of society by making offerings as accessible as possible to part- and full-time students; (9) strong support from a high-powered advisory council with a high-profile chair from the business community; and (10) a vision and absolute conviction that it was possible to build relatively rapidly an outstanding program in education for management in the metropolitan Toronto area.[6]

The last point is critical. Everyone connected with the establishment of the faculty – the board, the senate, the president, the chair of the advisory council, the dean, and newly appointed faculty members – were absolutely convinced that they were making educational history by creating a dynamic new program at York. As a result of this enthusiasm, everything was deemed to be possible and everyone worked with great eagerness and excitement to see that the vision for the future was turned into reality.

The Early Years of the Faculty, 1966–1972

Needless to say, the commencement of operations was marked by a number of problems. There was no building dedicated to the faculty's use and lectures were given in classrooms, wherever they could be found, at the new campus, which was constantly under construction. In spite of the great inconveniences, the spirit was strong and both faculty and students who taught or took the first classes remember the experiences as rewarding and exciting.

Applications for admission and enrolments grew rapidly – almost at a faster rate than the faculty could accommodate. However, while enrolment in the MPA degree program was high by Canadian standards – at one time the largest in the nation – the offering was dwarfed within the faculty by the growth of the MBA program. In order to lessen the imbalance and stimulate admission to the MPA – admittedly quite a different type of program in public administration than that offered at any other university in Canada – a number of initiatives were undertaken.

First, a strong advisory council was appointed, consisting of several federal and provincial deputy ministers plus two municipal government officials, chaired by Grant Glassco, who had recently headed a royal commission on the Canadian federal public service. Second, Malcolm Taylor joined the faculty as head of the MPA program. Taylor was former president of the Canadian Public Administration Association, founder and first editor of the Canadian Journal of Public Administration, former president of the University of Calgary and the University of Victoria, adviser to the federal government, provincial premiers, and royal commissions on health care, and one of the leading scholars in public administration in Canada.

Unfortunately, the public administration program never reached its intended potential. The program's advisory council did not play the same role in the development of the degree as did the business council for the MBA, primarily because the members (all professional public servants) were somewhat sceptical of the new approach to education for public administration – so much attention to administration and relatively little to traditional political science, sovereignty questions, and federal-provincial relations. Perhaps more important, most of them had some relatively close connection to existing programs at other universities. In addition, Mr Glassco passed away, and no one of his stature was found to lead the group.

In spite of the fact that the MPA program was relatively small compared to the MBA, there was never any thought that the original concept – that there was a body of knowledge about management that could be applied across all types of programs – should be abandoned. To the contrary, the management paradigm was strengthened with the addition of new programs. For example, in 1968 a program in arts administration was established exactly on the pattern of the MBA and MPA degrees.[7] Students were required to meet the general entrance requirements to the faculty, and to complete the first year common core of courses, a strategic study, and a year-long capstone management course. They took all their electives in the faculty of Fine Arts. Impetus for the creation of the program came from the fact that professional theatre, opera, ballet, and musical organizations throughout the nation were desperately in need of professional managers, with some knowledge of fine arts, to manage their activities.

In the early years, one of the most innovative developments, and well before its time, was the establishment of a joint MBA degree program with Université Laval in Québec City. Its purpose was to provide an opportunity for students from English Canada to learn French and more about French culture and the Québec business community, and for students from Québec to learn more about other parts of Canada by studying at York. At the same time, planning went forward for a program in law and business, which allowed students to complete a law degree and an MBA in four years, instead of the five required when the degrees were taken separately. When the program was inaugurated in 1973, it was the first of its kind in Canada.

The rapid growth of enrolment in the MBA and MPA programs, plus the introduction of the new programs, led to a constant need for more and more faculty members. The most important factor in assisting York, early in its history, to attract first-rate teachers and scholars was the availability of free funds for research. In the faculty's first year of operations, a division of research was established for the purpose of raising funds for research, disseminating research results, organizing research seminars, and generally encouraging all faculty to get involved in increasing knowledge in the areas where they were experts. The division started handsomely when a grant of $500,000 of free funds for research was obtained from the Ford Foundation in 1969, on the condition that the sum be matched within five years by the university. The importance of this money for the development of the faculty cannot be overestimated. While the grant was a vote of confidence in its future, it more specifically provided resources that enabled the dean, in a highly competitive hiring market, to offer potential candidates for positions research stipends, and summer appointments, as lucrative as they could obtain at other business schools on the continent.[8]

The regular educational and research programs were supplemented with the organization of a division of executive education, which offered a large number of one- and two-day seminars and, eventually, a two-week residence program. Designed as a profit centre, the division took some time to realize its potential, but it served an enormously valuable function in the early years by increasing awareness of the operations of the faculty throughout the nation.

During the start-up phase, 1966 to 1972, there was by and large little deviation from the strategies that underlay the founding of the faculty. Its obligation, as a unit of the university, to create and disseminate knowledge was more than met by the active research program and the rapid growth of the MBA, BBA, and other educational programs. The continuing commitment to answer the needs of the community was met by the establishment of the Arts Administration, Voluntary Sector, and Executive Development programs. Additional service to the community was provided by faculty members serving as directors of profit and not-for-profit organizations, advisers and members of royal commissions, and consultants to a host of organizations. The central thesis that there was a body of knowledge about management that could be applied to all types of organizations was intact and there was no indication that it should be changed. The faculty and administration had developed hand-in-hand with the growth of the operation with the appointment of outstanding support staff such as Air Commodore Leonard Birchall, Charmaine Courtis, and many others.

At the same time, certain ideas were abandoned and certain things were not done. Clearly no attempt was made to organize the faculty into separate schools of business, public administration, and so forth. The imbalance in enrolments made such an approach unfeasible. Moreover, no effort was made to organize the faculty into separate, independent departments with their own budgets; the prevailing philosophy was that the faculty was offering professional degrees and programs in management – not degrees of specialization in accounting, marketing, finance, and the other traditional areas of business or public administration.

During the early years, the administration and faculty at York were more inward-looking, in terms of their association with other academic institutions, than was probably wise. While there was awareness of the work of the Canadian Federation of Deans of Business and Administrative Studies, the orientation of the majority of the professors and the administration was to business schools in the United States. This was not unusual, since many of the faculty members and the dean, while Canadians, had spent a considerable amount of their academic career in institutions in that country. As a result, they had stronger connections south of the border than they had across the country. In addition, the University of Western Ontario's School of Business was generally considered a virtual clone of the Harvard Business School, and as such had not a great deal to offer to a new faculty that was not creating itself in the Harvard tradition. As a result, the faculty of Administrative Studies at York did not take as much advantage from the existing programs in Canada as it might have.

By 1972, after six years of existence, the York MBA attracted more students than any other such program in the nation; a PhD program was well under way; the executive development program was large and growing; the Division of Research was publishing reports from faculty members; and there was a complement of more than fifty full- and part-time faculty members teaching, consulting and researching. It was also a significant year for the faculty in that a new, larger building, designed specifically by and for the faculty, was opened.

During 1972, Murray Ross resigned as president of York, and Gillies resigned as dean of the faculty. Thus, a new dean had to be found, and eventually Dr Barry Richman, a Canadian educated at McGill and

Columbia, and a distinguished professor of management at UCLA, was appointed. A prolific writer, Richman had a strong academic reputation, based not only on his general writings about management, but particularly because of his research on management activities in China. Like Gillies, when Richman accepted the appointment, he took a leave of absence from UCLA so that he would have a chance to determine how much he enjoyed being a dean and being back in Canada.

It was a good thing he did, for he quickly found that he much preferred research and writing to the enormous amount of administration required of a dean in a new faculty at a rather young university. Moreover, he did not work well with the new president of York, David Slater. As a result, after only six months, he resigned and returned to his position at UCLA and his home in Malibu, California.[9] Given the circumstances and timing of Richman's leaving, an acting dean had to be appointed. Brian Dixon, a professor of marketing, who had been with the faculty since its inception, took over. A graduate of the University of Michigan, Professor Dixon was not interested in serving as dean over an extended period of time, and as a result of a search, Dr William Dimma was appointed to the position.

Bill Dimma had just been appointed executive vice-president of Union Carbide Canada when the faculty of Administrative Studies was launched. He had previously spent a year at Harvard Business School, but needed four or five course credits for an MBA degree. He was among the first students to join the part-time program at York, and upon receiving his degree, in 1969, decided to continue his studies, then considered changing his career to become an educator. He enrolled at Harvard in the spring of 1970 and graduated with a DBA, in June 1973. Immediately upon graduation, he returned to York as a member of the faculty. Given his rich business experience and recent academic training, he was a natural candidate for dean and was appointed to the position in February 1974. Two years later, he was offered the positions of president of Torstar Corporation and of Toronto Star Newspapers Limited. Having determined that, while he loved to teach, he was more interested in being an administrator in the private sector than in academe, he accepted the offer and resigned from the faculty in April 1976.[10]

Consolidation and Growth, 1972–1988

After having three deans in slightly over two years, the faculty was in need of stability in its leadership, and therefore particular attention was given to the search for yet another dean, in the hope of finding a candidate who was willing to make a long-term commitment to the position. Fortunately, such a person was found already serving within the faculty. Wallace Crowston came to York in July 1972, after receiving his PhD degree from the Massachusetts Institute of Technology, with specialization in information processing. His undergraduate degree was in applied science, but his interests were clearly in the application of computers and information processing to business. As such he was one of the pioneers in the field. Crowston was very popular with the faculty, and brought a collegial, somewhat laid-back management style to the position of dean. His great strength lay in understanding the needs of individual faculty members and in building strong linkages between the faculty and other parts of the university and the academic community. He maintained the advisory council, but was not as interested in strengthening contacts with the business community as he was in making certain that the faculty's educational programs were of very high quality, and that all professors were satisfied with their teaching and research situations.

This, change in emphasis did not mean that the faculty ceased its myriad activities and/or failed to add new endeavours. Under Crowston, the executive program to expand and enrolment in the MBA program continued to grow, the number of scholarships offered increased, some endowed professorships were acquired, new faculty members continued to be hired, and more and more elective courses were added to the curriculum. It was also during this time, under Crowston's leadership, that the Voluntary Sector Management program, the Max Bell Business-Government Studies, and the Entrepreneurial Studies programs were started. He also devoted a great deal of time and resources to the development of doctoral work, realizing that Canadian schools had to produce scholars and researchers to meet the growing need for faculty in universities. Crowston played an active role in the Canadian Federation of Deans of Management and Administrative Studies, serving as secretary-treasurer of the organization and Ontario representative for several years. In general, he worked more closely with administrative programs in other universities than had previous York deans.

During Crowston's period as dean, interest in management education throughout the world expanded exponentially. It is not astonishing, therefore, that he was very active with other deans in developing management programs, usually financed by the Canadian International Development Agency, in various countries. The special region of interest of the faculty of Administrative Studies was China, and during this period members of the faculty not only began developing and teaching courses in China for business people, but also became active in developing the education of Chinese teachers for Chinese programs. During Crowston's term as dean the first exchange programs outside of North America, for students in the faculty, were developed.

In 1984, Crowston, having served two terms as dean, decided to step down and return to his active career in teaching and research.[11] A search committee was struck to find a new dean, and the committee decided to look outside as well as inside the faculty for candidates and to consider – a major departure from the past – candidates from the business community. After an extensive search the committee recommended to the president that Allan Hockins be appointed. It was an interesting and controversial appointment. While Hockins did not have a PhD degree – his graduate work was limited to a master of arts from the University of Toronto – or any experience teaching in a business school or university, he did have a record of exemplary experience in both the public and private sectors. He was always interested in being a teacher, and through the years had maintained close relationships with many academics throughout the country. He was also extremely well known in the traditional Canadian government and business establishments. His educational philosophy was formed from universities more like Oxford than like the University of California, or any other American land-grant college.

Allan Hockins found the reality of university life, and administration, substantially different from what it is often assumed to be. Rather than having time to chat with students and discourse with faculty members, he found himself caught up in an endless round of university and faculty committee meetings, fund raising, and internal battles of an intensity that made corporate warfare seem like child's play. Moreover, coming entirely from the outside – he had never been a faculty member anywhere – he found it very difficult to understand and deal with the conflicting forces ever present in academic institutions. He did, however, bring to bear his experience with finance in smoothing out the budgetary processes within the faculty, streamlining, to some extent, the administration and developing the use of computers. In spite of an enormous commitment of time and energy, Hockins found that university administration was not how he wished to spend his time, and he resigned as dean and from the faculty in 1988 before completing his term.

The period 1972 to 1988 was basically one of consolidation and growth for the faculty. The fundamental concept of a faculty of administrative studies that could contain within its boundaries education for all types of administrative posts was retained and strengthened, the idea that there was a generic body of knowledge about management that could be learned through taking a core of courses was maintained, and the completion of a strategic study of an ongoing organization as a process for learning to work in groups and to hone personal skills was continued. Courses and programs were modified, added, and dropped; research programs were added and new fields of study were developed; but no radical changes in strategy were introduced. And yet, during that period, great changes took place in Canadian business. In 1966, when the first students were admitted to the faculty of Administrative Studies, Canadian business operated in an economy characterized by low levels of competition, mutually supporting relationships between business and government, substantial protection from international producers for most sectors of the economy, relatively conservative management, a tight-knit management community, a high proportion of foreign ownership, and a high degree of prosperity.

When Hockins completed his terms as dean in 1988, two decades later, the environment in which business operated was radically different. Increased globalization brought a higher level of competition in every sector, the mutually supporting relationships between business and government were less significant as international treaties limited what national governments could do, managers (whether they wanted to or not) were managing more aggressively, sector after sector of business was being literally transformed by information technology, the tight-knit relationship among management was disappearing as professionalism replaced cronyism and nepotism in the operation of enterprises, and the nation remained, through it all, relatively prosperous.[12]

The dramatic changes in business called for dramatic changes in the education for management. By the beginning of the 1990s, the challenge to business programs was no longer simply to produce traditionally educated managers; rather, it was to graduate a new type of professional manager – one who could compete in the global economy. In this new environment, graduates of business programs needed to know more about the culture and history of organizations, more about how to operate effectively when every producer in the world is a

TABLE 5.1
Schulich School of Business, number of faculty, selected years

	1966	1967	1968	1969	1970	1975	1985	1995
Full-time	13	30	32	42	36	54	62	71
Part-time	4	11	12	8	8	8	14	88
Total	17	41	44	50	44	62	76	159

TABLE 5.2
Schulich School of Business, enrolment by program, selected years

	1972	1973	1974	1975	1976	1977	1978	1979	1980	1981
PhD	2	2	1	8	8	13	13	18	11	11
BBA	169	217	195	180	214	226	244	283	255	230
MBA	799	897	941	1143	1175	1074	1154	1263	1160	1267

potential competitor, more about the various functional fields of business, more about the impact of computers and new technologies on business, and more about the appropriate role of business in society.[13]

One thing that the faculty no longer had to be concerned about was its legitimacy as a full-time member of the university community. By the early 1990s management education was totally accepted as an appropriate function for post-secondary institutions in Canada. In the faculty of Administrative Studies at York during 1966, there were 17 full- and part-time faculty members, 325 students, four non-academic employees, and no alumni. During 1996 the Schulich School of Business had 181 full- and part-time faculty members, over 2000 students, 90 non-academic employees, and more than 10,000 alumni. At York, providing education for managers, as at other major Canadian universities, was an unquestioned part of the university's mission.

In 1995 a major event in the faculty's history occurred. Seymour Schulich, chair and CEO of Franco-Nevada and Euro-Nevada Mining Corporations donated $15 million to the faculty. Upon receipt of the gift, the faculty became the Schulich School of Business.[14] While the Schulich gift, which was basically for the endowment of chairs and scholarships, did not have any particular strategic implications for the faculty, it has enabled the school, because of the increased resources, to implement its strategies in a more effective and efficient fashion.

Figure 5.1 Schulich School of Business, number of alumni, selected years

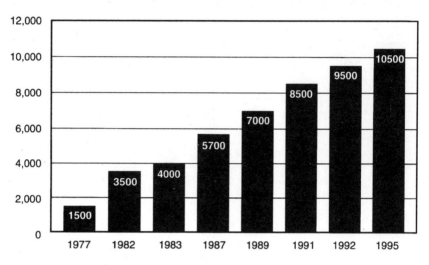

Summation

During the slightly more than three decades of its existence, many of the strategies upon which the York Faculty of Administrative Studies was founded have stayed in place. In 1996, as in 1966, the school is based on the belief that there is a body of knowledge about management and administration that is applicable to all types of organizations – public or private, for-profit or not-for-profit; that a publicly supported institution has an obligation to meet the needs, within rigorous academic standards, of the community it serves; that it must provide opportunities for education outside the academy in the most effective and user-friendly fashion possible; that it must be a place for the creation and dissemination of knowledge; that it must offer opportunities for the development of scholars in the field; and that it must always provide a forum for the free discussion of significant issues.

As the environment within which organizations operate in Canada has changed, and as the faculty has grown, these strategies have been modified and changed. As the millennium approaches, there is little doubt that, as a result of the increasing impacts of globalization and technology on business, new forms of funding, radically new methods of delivering information and teaching, and increasing competition among programs for students and faculty, even greater change will occur in the not-too-distant future in management education.

While one can be confident that the dean and faculty of the Schulich School of Business will create programs and strategies to deal with and benefit from these changes, it is highly unlikely that the strategic positioning of the school will change very much. Relevance, opportunity, service, and choice are the guiding principles upon which the school has been built, and they will probably be the ones that guide it into the future.

NOTES

1 Some of the state-supported universities in the United States are among the most eminent in that country, and some, e.g., the University of California and the University of Michigan, are ranked among the great universities in the world.
2 Dr Best later served as president of Laurentian University.
3 H.M. Best, 'The Establishment of Professional Faculties and Schools at York University' (unpub., 1965), quoted in L.T. Homer, *The Determination and Implementation of Purpose at New Graduate Schools of Administration* (Ann Arbor: University of Michigan, 1978).
4 Written by Robert Gordon, a member of the department of economics at the University of California at Berkeley, and James Howell of the Graduate School of Business at Stanford and funded by the Ford Foundation, this study, *Higher Education for Business* published in 1959, became the blueprint for major reform in business education in the United States. It recommended that: (1) students should complete a first degree in arts or science before commencing the study of business; (2) business programs should be two years in length and should lead to the awarding of a professional degree – a Master of Business Administration; (3) in the first year of the professional program students should be required to complete a course each in accounting, finance, marketing, personnel management, statistics or information systems, and business economics; (4) in the second year they should concentrate in an area of specialization plus complete a two-semester course in management; (5) the total program should consist of twenty semester courses, of which a minimum of twelve would be required of all students. The underlying philosophy upon which the proposed curriculum was based was that there is a discipline of management – manage-

ment theory – under which all knowledge about management can be subsumed.

5 Rickerd, a Rhodes Scholar and lawyer who was registrar of the university, joined the Faculty of Administrative Studies to teach business law. He eventually left academic life to become chief executive officer of the Max Bell Foundation, through which he had a profound influence on the evolution of many university programs in Canada.

6 Two or three years earlier McGill University undertook to revise its business program. A grant was secured and a small faculty was retained to plan a future program. In general the planning group opted to create an elitist program with great emphasis on organizational theory – somewhat like the developments that were taking place at that time at Carnegie-Mellon University in Pittsburgh. The proposed program was, therefore, to be small and very selective – the antithesis to the plan that Gillies proposed for York.

7 There is still some dispute as to where the first such program on the North American campus was established. UCLA claims the distinction, but Gillies believes the program at York was approved a month or two sooner. At any rate, there are now three major arts administration programs in North America – at UCLA, Yale, and York.

8 The Ford Foundation money was available to any faculty member with a substantial research project and a commitment to publish the research findings. It was not dedicated to one major investigation in any one field.

9 Richman, a Canadian, was able to obtain a visa to enter China at a time when such travel was banned for citizens of the United States. He took advantage of this situation, travelling extensively there and writing about his experiences. Tragically, shortly after his return to California, he suffered a serious heart attack and died in his early forties.

10 While Dimma did not stay long at the *Star*, he went on to have a distinguished career as a business executive, corporate director, and business commentator in the Canadian community. He retained his interest in York, serving on the board of governors, eventually as its chair.

11 Crowston soon found, however, that his real interests were in university administration. Consequently, a year after he left York he accepted an appointment as dean of the McGill Faculty of Management.

12 For a full discussion of these changes see James Gillies, 'The Emerging Revolution in Canadian Business Leadership,' in *Success: Canadian Leaders Prepare for the Next Century* (Toronto: Key Porter Books for the Schulich School of Business, 1996).

13 Dezso Horvath was appointed dean of the faculty of Administrative Studies in 1988. During the 1990s he led the school through many significant

changes including major curricula revisions, expansion of executive development education, strengthening of the undergraduate program, and, perhaps most significantly, creation of an international approach to business education. For a complete discussion of these developments see James Gillies, *From Local to National to International: The Evolution of Business Education at York University* (forthcoming).

14 Gillies, *From Local to National to International.*

6

The Evolution of Management Education in a Small Canadian University: The School of Business and Economics at Wilfrid Laurier University

ROBERT ELLIS and JOHN McCUTCHEON

This chapter has two parts. The first traces the evolution of the School of Business and Economics at Wilfrid Laurier University, while the second examines the nature of leadership processes within the school.[1]

1. The History of the School of Business and Economics

The evolution of management education at Wilfrid Laurier University is the story of a small department that prospered in the face of unique challenges and circumstances. The purposes of this research project were both descriptive and analytic: to chronicle the key changes and events in the school from its inception, and to discover and analyse the processes by which these changes came about. We should note some important limitations of the present research. Our focus is primarily on the role played by senior faculty and the deans in shaping the evolution of the school. We did not examine the role of staff and students in the school's development, but we recognize that their respective roles are of critical importance in the evolution of the school.

The changing role of business education at Canadian universities provides the context for interpreting change at Wilfrid Laurier. Early models of undergraduate business education had a liberal arts focus and emphasized the moral and intellectual skills that would transform students into 'gentlemen.'[2] Until the 1960s,[3] university-level business programs usually were directed towards training students primarily for accounting careers,[4] and had a clear vocational orientation.[5] Business courses were often housed in departments such as economics and political science, and were at times viewed with indifference by administrators.[6] Business departments were considered by many in the university community to lack academic respectability. Events in the 1960s released business schools from this dismal existence as enrolment almost tripled[7] and departments continually scrambled to meet student demand with new programs, courses, and faculty. Barbara Austin[8] makes the point that growth was not due to initiatives or innovations on the part of universities, but was driven by student interest. Business faculty were confronted with heavy teaching commitments and administrative responsibilities that left little time for research. In any case, few faculty were academically qualified and many of those with doctorates received their degrees in disciplines other than business.[9] The supply of doctoral graduates from foreign and Canadian business schools, while drastically short of demand, began to ease the shortage of qualified faculty at Canadian schools in the 1980s. Concurrently, there was an increasing commitment to academic research on the part of business faculty. By the late 1980s, it was evident that the legitimacy of business schools in the university environment was firmly established, thanks largely to efforts to enhance the quality and quantity of research.[10]

The history of the Wilfrid Laurier School of Business and Economics is discussed here in terms of eras that coincide with stages in its development. Information on the first period, Oral History (1925–60), is taken almost entirely from university calendars and documents in the university's archives. The information gathered from these sources was, for the most part, entirely unknown to current faculty and staff. The research method of oral history was used to capture the thoughts and feelings of faculty, staff, and administrators regarding the events and the leaders who helped shape the school over a thirty-year period. The oral history project at the school is described in detail elsewhere.[11]

Oral History Era, 1925–1960

The institution that became Wilfrid Laurier University was founded in 1911 and commenced operations in 1912 as the Evangelical Lutheran Seminary of Canada. This became the Waterloo College of Arts in 1924, offering post-secondary courses. The following year, the Lutheran Church, which controlled the institution, changed the name to Waterloo College, affiliated with the University of Western Ontario. The new institution soon began to offer honours programs in the arts. Students completed their first two years at Waterloo College, then transferred to the University of Western Ontario to complete their degree requirements.

The first eleven full-time faculty appointments at Waterloo College were made in 1925. Although no appointments were made in economics or business, Dr A.O. Potter, dean of Waterloo College and professor of history and French, taught Economics 020, 'Elements of Political Economy,' that first year. The following year, James H. Smyth was appointed as lecturer in economics. Professor Smyth held a bachelor of arts degree from Queen's University (1920) and qualified as a lawyer in 1923. Smyth's appointment to Waterloo College was full-time, but he also maintained a law practice in Kitchener. There were no adjunct business or economics faculty members at the time. The number of full-time faculty at Waterloo College peaked at seventeen in the 1930–31 academic year, and slowly declined to ten by 1937–38 as the effects of the Great Depression were felt (see table 6.1). The only business or economics course listed in calendars for the years 1926 through 1937 was Economics 020. The calendar description of this course includes elements that would now be included in business courses. This course was offered for students in the arts programs and there were no courses or programs in business.

Smyth left the college in 1937, and was replaced by Albert Moellman, who was appointed as professor in economics and business administration.[12] Moellman held a bachelor of arts degree from Saskatchewan and master of arts from McGill on appointment and soon after earned a doctorate from Marburg, Germany.[13] The 1938–39 calendar showed significant changes to business and economics programs, course offerings, and departmental organization. A department of business administration was formally created and transfer programs to the University of Western Ontario in business and secretarials were introduced.[14] These programs required the addition of Business 020, 'Introduction to Business Organization.' Courses in accounting for each transfer program were also added that year. Eight economics courses were required for an honours program that appeared in the calendar. No additional full-time or adjunct lecturers were appointed, so it is not evident who taught these courses.

The complement of full-time faculty at Waterloo College contracted during the Second World War to as few as eight, although there was

TABLE 6.1
Complement of full-time faculty

1925–26: (11,0,0,0)	1960–61: (32,1,3,3)
1926–27: (12,0,1,0)	1961–62: (41,4,4,3)
1927–28: (13,0,1,0)	1962–63: (55,7,4,1)
1928–29: (13,0,1,0)	1963–64: (64,7,5,0)
1929–30: (14,0,1,0)	1964–65: (77,6,7,0)
	1965–66: (88,7,7,0)
1930–31: (17,0,1,0)	1966–67: (103,8,6,0)
1931–32: (15,0,1,0)	1967–68: (142,12,6,0)
1932–33: (16,0,1,0)	1968–69: (178,16,7,0)
1933–34: (16,0,1,0)	1969–70: (169,16,7,0)
1934–35: (16,0,1,0)	
1935–36: (11,0,1,0)	1970–71: (168,13,7,0)
1936–37: (11,0,1,0)	1971–72: (197,11,8,0)
1937–38: (10,0,1,0)	1972–73: (147,10,8,0)
1938–39: (10,0,1,0)	1973–74: (154,13,9,0)
1939–40: (10,0,1,0)	1974–75: (162,15,9,0)
	1975–76: (184,23,14,0)
1940–41: (10,0,1,0)	1976–77: (198,27,13,0)
1941–42: (10,0,1,0)	1977–78: (209,30,13,0)
1942–43: (10,0,1,0)	1978–79: (224,36,13,0)
1943–44: (8,0,1,0)	1979–80: (220,35,17,0)
1944–45: (8,0,1,0)	
1945–46: (8,0,1,0)	1980–81: (223,38,16,0)
1946–47: (9,0,1,0)	1981–82: (234,44,17,0)
1947–48: (9,0,1,0)	1982–83: (238,47,18,0)
1948–49: (13,1,1,0)	1983–84: (239,49,17,0)
1949–50: (15,1,1,0)	1984–85: (242,49,17,0)
	1985–86: (256,54,16,0)
1950–51: n/a	1986–87: (266,54,18,0)
1951–52: (12,1,0,0)	1987–88: (274,58,17,0)
1952–53: n/a	1988–89: (280,59,17,0)
1953–54: (11,1,0,0)	1989–90: (306,64,22,0)
1954–55: (15,1,1,1)	
1955–56: (16,1,1,1)	1990–91: (305,61,21,0)
1956–57: (19,1,1,2)	1991–92: (316,64,20,0)
1957–58: (23,1,2,3)	1992–93: (327,64,22,0)
1958–59: (33,1,2,3)	1993–94: (320,62,22,0)
1959–60: (38,1,3,3)	1994–95: (320,66,21,0)

Key: 1934–35: (a,b,c,d)
   1934–35 indicates calendar issue
   a = full-time faculty at College/University
   b = full-time business
   c = full-time economics
   d = full-time secretarial science

always an appointment in economics and business administration (see table 6.1). Many faculty members also served as administrative officers. For example, R.C. McIvor, professor of economics and business administration, is listed in the 1946–47 calendar as the registrar, which would have reduced his time available for instruction. There was modest growth of full- and part-time faculty at the college during the immediate post-war years, but this was in arts, not business or economics. In 1948–49, the first 400-level business course, 'Introduction to Insurance, Estates, and Trusts,' appeared. This course was taught by a sessional faculty member with appropriate industry experience. This course and teaching arrangement still continues.

The number of full-time faculty in business and economics doubled to two in 1947 with the appointment of Herman O.J. Overgaard as assistant professor of economics and business administration. He was also the first appointment of a person with a business, rather than an economics or law, orientation. Overgaard was working for the Cockshutt Tractor Company in Brantford when he was approached by Dr Lloyd H. Schaus, dean of Waterloo College, whom Overgaard knew through the Lutheran Church. This was the start of Overgaard's long, distinguished career as a scholar, teacher, and administrator. On appointment, he held a bachelor of arts degree from Manitoba, but later completed a master of science and a doctorate in business at Columbia University. Dr Overgaard's accomplishments outside the university included election as president of the Administrative Sciences Association of Canada in 1974. He has been recognized by several academic organizations for his contributions to management education and international business.

As has been the case at many universities, courses in administration were not confined to the department of business administration. The department of secretarial science appeared for the first time in the 1954–55 calendar. A transfer program to Western had been offered since 1938–39, but this allowed the full complement of courses necessary to fulfill degree requirements to be offered on campus in Waterloo. The department offered eight courses that were patterned after 'Shorthand and Typewriting' and 'Office Practice.' These courses were part of a general arts program, with a secretarial-science option. There were three full-time members by 1957–58, including an associate professor, while business administration and economics still each had a sole member. The department was listed in calendars through 1961–62, when it was disbanded. Esther J. Brandon, who was an assistant professor in secretarial science, then joined the business department as a lecturer and thus became its first full-time female faculty member. She continued in the department through 1964–65 and also served from 1962 until 1972 as the dean of women and then the associate dean of students.

The middle of the 1950s marked the start of an extended era of great uncertainty and turbulence about the future of Waterloo College. In response to interest from local business, courses in engineering were first offered in 1957 by the Associated Faculties of Waterloo College. This organizational form was designed to attract full funding from the provincial government and was quasi-independent from Waterloo College. The Associated Faculties soon split completely from Waterloo College and formed the nucleus of the University of Waterloo, a separation that was very acrimonious and still dominates personal recollections from that era. Waterloo College received a new charter in 1960 that changed the name of the institution to Waterloo Lutheran University (WLU). The new university faced a very uncertain future as an underfunded, church-controlled institution operating in an environment where all other significant competitors were public institutions with far greater financial resources.

Emergence of the Business Department, 1960–1966

The decision was made to offer, commencing in the autumn of 1960, a full honours business program rather than just the first two years of a University of Western Ontario transfer program. Few, if any, students left the new program to complete their business degrees at Western. The first eight degrees (honours bachelor of arts in business administration) were conferred in May 1962. The size of the graduating class grew slowly through this period, with 29 business degrees granted in 1966 (see table 6.2). The students were predominantly male and admission standards were not demanding. In fact, the university had the notorious reputation of being 'last chance U.' But once admitted, students faced demanding standards that gave rise to the popular statement that 'WLU was easy to get into but hard to graduate from.' The business instructors faced an even bleaker situation, evidenced by a motion by the general faculty to offer admission to the program to any student admitted to the university. To ensure the survival of the institution, students were actively recruited by faculty visits to local and regional high schools.

TABLE 6.2
Business degrees 1962–67

Year	Men	Women
1962	8	0
1963	4	1
1964	14	2
1965	18	0
1966	29	0
1967	27	0

The full-time faculty complement grew in order to staff the extra courses required by the full degree (see table 6.1). Long-standing faculty who joined during this period included Glenn Carroll (1960), Basil Healey (1962), Paul Albright (1965), and Herbert Wedderburn (1966) in business; John Weir (1965) and Ralph Blackmore (1966) in economics; and staff member Maureen Kuske (1965). Herman Overgaard was actively involved in the recruiting process and was often the initial contact with WLU. An indication of the state of finances and mood of faculty at that time is illustrated by Blackmore's first day on campus. He was told by an arts faculty member, 'I hope you didn't give up a good job to come here – this place has no future.'

In 1965, the university was organized at the undergraduate level with all departments reporting to Dr L.H. Schaus, the long-serving dean of Waterloo University College, which was the undergraduate arm of WLU. The university grew rapidly and became administratively cumbersome. Business and economics were included in a department with sociology and political science, which may have been administratively convenient but was an unusual academic grouping. The business undergraduate program had grown to be the third largest in Ontario and some faculty held aspirations for the delivery of a graduate degree. As an interim measure, a department of business administration and economics was formed at the start of 1966, since the faculty felt their ambitions could be best met by the establishment of a semi-autonomous unit. A senate 'Committee on New Faculties, Schools, Institutes and Departments' was set up to deal with these and other issues.

In March 1966, Dr Herman Overgaard, as chair of the department, submitted a written proposal to the senate for the establishment of a School of Business and Economics (SBE). The rationale for this move included the following points: school status would add prestige to the university by improving its competitive position in business and economics; a school would facilitate recruitment of both faculty and students; most universities offering business used the structure of a separate school; a school including economics would be unique in Canada; and, finally, this was likely the only case of a department seeking special status at WLU. The structure of the proposed school included four departments: economics, accounting and finance, personnel and marketing, and management and international business. The proposal envisioned SBE being part of Waterloo University College rather than a free-standing entity. The senate approved the proposal, but did not deal with the issue of what title the head of SBE would hold.

The board of governors approved the concept on 11 April 1966 with the following motion: 'That the action of senate on March 14, 1966 be approved and that the proposed School of Business and Economics be established with four departments as of September 1, 1966 and that the school be headed by a Director until such time as graduate work is offered, and that the Director be responsible to the Dean of Waterloo University College. That Dr Herman O.J. Overgaard be offered the position of Director of the School of Business and Economics.'

Dr Overgaard was a visionary leader who was concerned with issues such as international business or development of a master's program long before they became popular with others. For the two decades after his appointment in 1947, he was either the appointed or de facto head of business at Waterloo College and WLU. In this period, the discipline of business not only grew but was strongly positioned for further development. After his retirement from Laurier, he received an award from the Academy of International Business in recognition of his life-long contributions to that field. He is remembered by staff for his graciousness and support.

The Early School Era, 1967–1974

Professor Glenn Carroll was appointed director of the new school 1 January 1967. The economics faculty had their own department, which allowed development along a path that was often quite different from that pursued by those concerned with business administration. It offered programs such as a cooperative option, a finance and accounting option, and an administration option that built on the unique structure of the school. In recent times there has been considerable cooperation in research and teaching. The business side of the school had a complex organizational structure, with eight full-time faculty organized into four departments that reported through the director. This structure also implied a philosophy of separation and specialization by discipline area that was new to the school. In reality, the structure was more apparent than real. As an example, the 1968–69 calendar showed four separate departments, but SBE Council minutes indicated that Paul Albright was the acting chair of business.[15] The formal structure does not feature in recollections from this era. When asked directly about the departmental structure, one participant said, 'Oh, we called ourselves anything we wanted.' In any case, this complex structure did not endure. In the 1969–70 calendar, the SBE structure included the departments of business administration, international business, and economics. In Carroll's last year as director, his title was changed to dean, with his status equal to other deans who reported to the vice-president, academic.

A significant innovation in this era was the creation of the High School Stock Market Game. This game evolved from an in-class, pen and paper stock market simulation created by Professor Ralph Blackmore. The potential of this simulation as a device to gain recognition among high school students for WLU was recognized, and the game was computerized in one of the very first uses of information technology at WLU. Funding for the operation of the game was gained through a partnership with the Toronto Stock Exchange. The game continues to operate and annually attracts several thousand contestants from across the country.

During Professor Carroll's term as director and dean, decision-making authority rested with faculty council, which included all full-time faculty members. Participants remember faculty meetings as long affairs that often continued informally at a club or restaurant. Attendance at faculty meetings was also very high. Collegial decision-making became embedded in the culture of SBE during that era and has been a prominent feature of the culture since then. Carroll brought remarkable interpersonal and communication skills to the position. One of his greatest achievements undoubtedly was recruiting. Many long-serving faculty members credit Carroll with their decision to come to WLU. Some of Carroll's former classmates or business acquaintances were directly recruited, while others recall his great charm during hiring interviews. At the conclusion of his term, there was no obvious internal candidate to succeed Professor Carroll and to provide the desired leadership for the school. Professor Carroll's contributions to the school as a teacher have become legendary within the university. His charisma, passion, and wit inspired generations of business students. In recognition of his remarkable teaching career, he won WLU's 'Outstanding Teacher Award' in 1986.

The new dean was Dr John R.G. Jenkins, who was hired from Northeastern University in Boston, where he was working while completing his doctorate at Harvard University. The new dean had considerable business experience and had taught marketing at the University of Toronto. Jenkins presided over SBE in a tumultuous era as the university's administrators decided whether to keep it a Lutheran institution and continue to receive provincial funding that covered operations at half the level of competing institutions and did not cover capital projects or to go 'provincial' and receive full funding, but at the perceived cost of the university's Lutheran heritage. The status quo was vigorously defended by many, including some in the SBE, but it was evident that WLU could not continue to compete for students and faculty. There would have been a major business school in the City of Waterloo, but it would likely have been at the University of Waterloo, while WLU would have atrophied if it had not become a public university with full funding.

It was clear during Jenkins's 1970–4 term in office that provincial funding would bring immediate benefits. Many faculty have mentioned that the likelihood of full provincial funding was a factor in their choice to come to WLU. It also allowed real progress towards the goal of a graduate program. The faculty had long desired a master of business administration (MBA) program, but little tangible progress had taken place. Faculty qualifications and university resources had been significant barriers, but the move to full funding made this goal possible. Jenkins's contribution was to provide leadership for the long task of putting together a proposal and starting it through the complex internal and external approval process. The president and vice-president, academic of the time, Frank Peters and Basil Healey, strongly supported the development of this initiative.

The groundwork was laid for another major project during Jenkins's deanship. It was obvious that co-operative education programs were highly successful at the University of Waterloo and at Jenkins's previous institution, Northeastern University, which featured the largest co-operative programs in Canada and the United States, respectively. Jenkins was highly supportive of Professor Robert Quinn's efforts to have a co-operative option in the business program. By the time Jenkins left office, the proposed program had been approved by business faculty and soon received final university approval. It should be noted that while both the MBA and co-operative programs were introduced after Jenkins's term ended, the foundations were laid while he was dean. The introductions of these two programs are often cited as being among the most significant events in the history of the business department.

A low point in Jenkins's term was the decision of the Canadian International Development Agency to terminate sponsorship of the international business program and of similar offerings at other universities. Dr Brant Bonner and Dr Herman Overgaard were the prime instigators of the program and had been heavily involved in its administration and instruction. The program was first offered in 1965–66 with a mandate to provide management training for business men and women and government officials from emerging nations. Students who were primarily from Asia and Africa came to WLU for a one-year program that culminated in a two-week European study tour. There was an opportunity for graduates of this program to stay on to earn a general arts degree. The program was innovative and forward looking, but did not have a substantial impact on other business students. International business program students did not attend classes with other WLU students and there is no evidence of curricular innovation resulting from the program. When the federal government removed funding, faculty and staff expertise in international business were not refocused into another format. It should be acknowledged that in the early 1970s, few faculty or students were interested in or recognized the importance of the international dimensions of business. Further, there were only a limited number of faculty members with international backgrounds or experience.

Jenkins believed that he had a strong mandate from WLU senior administration to institute change. Some of the goals he favoured, such as an increased emphasis on faculty research and publication, seemed revolutionary at the time and were not popular with many faculty members. Change is always difficult, and that is even more the case where the faculty expects a dean to be a manager rather than a leader or change agent. After his term was completed, Jenkins served on the faculty for a further eighteen years, making outstanding contributions to the school as a teacher and a scholar.

Growth and Consolidation, 1974–1995

Dr Max D. Stewart, an economist at the University of Alberta, was recruited to serve as the dean starting in 1974. He did not have significant administrative experience, but had taught at WLU during the 1950s and the 1960s. Many SBE faculty members were familiar with the new dean and he was aware of SBE culture and traditions. The university and the school were perched on the edge of a new era. The need for thrift, so necessary under the regime of a church-controlled institution, changed rapidly when WLU became a public institution. Funding per student increased by 100 per cent and there was also access to capital grants. The provincial funding system of that era operated on a per student basis that created an obvious incentive to increase the size of the institution. The business department and SBE were strong and offered a good base for growth. It became an implicit university policy to increase the size of the undergraduate business program and other SBE offerings.

The stage was set for Dean Stewart to preside over an era where growth was a constant. The total SBE faculty complement increased from twenty-four in his first year, 1974–75, to sixty-one in 1981–82, his final year as dean. This was an exciting period, when growth and innovation were the norm. The introduction, in 1975, of the co-operative option for undergraduate programs in business and economics significantly increased the attractiveness of WLU to potential students. Similarly, introduction of a part-time MBA program in 1976 filled a long-standing need of the local business community. Dean Stewart understood the implicit university strategy to increase the size of SBE and was determined that it would only occur if proper resources were forthcoming. This task was far from easy, as the university's administrators did not depart overnight from the long-standing heritage of frugality (described by one participant as 'on the thrifty side of cheap'). One tale of Stewart's tactics in the struggle for resources shows the determination that he brought to the task. For a period, he carried with him a long list of all the arts and science courses with enrolments of fewer than ten students. This would be brought out, shown, and commented upon at all suitable times. His tactics succeeded, for the faculty/student ratio did not change over the period he was dean, if allowance is made for the introduction of the MBA program. Dr Stewart was a forceful, hands-on manager who had a broad vision, yet paid far more attention to operational details than is usually the case with a dean. He had a prodigious capacity for work and was seen on campus at all hours of the day or night.

When Dr Stewart arrived in 1974, decision making was still primarily done by faculty on a collegial basis. Many policies and procedures dealing with programs, faculty, and other matters were also quite informal. The dean set about to alter the status quo. Rules and regulations governing academic programs were formalized and many aspects of faculty life became more regulated. Inevitably, growth brought about a distancing of faculty from everyday decision making.

Stewart recognized the significance of a large increase in the faculty complement. He was actively involved in the recruiting process and had lunch with many candidates. Some faculty members credit Dr Stewart's interest and involvement as a factor in their decision to come to Laurier. The new faculty slowly but inevitably changed the culture of the department through their interest in and commitment to research. Although most faculty accepted this transition as a desirable part of the academic maturing process, it was nevertheless a painful experience to some.

The business department structure changed quite dramatically during the Stewart era. By 1977, it was evident that the simple structure of a department headed by a chair would no longer suffice. A chair could offer administrative leadership, but the faculty members were becoming increasingly focused upon their functional areas. The department was becoming large and it was extremely difficult for a chair to administer a department of thirty faculty members with further growth expected. The title of 'chairman' did not seem to be of sufficient status given that the business department was far larger than any other on campus. A committee of three faculty members recommended that the department change to a matrix model with cells defined by program directors and area coordinators of functional areas. This recommendation was adopted, although there was some difficulty in getting the WLU administration to accept the title of associate dean for the head of the business department. This problem was resolved when the chairman of the business department, Professor Bill Curry, accompanied by the area coordinators, dropped in unannounced to see the president to emphasize the department's position.

As he was approached retirement, Stewart did not seek a third term, although he did serve as the acting vice-president, academic for the year after he left the deanship. Stewart left a school that was remarkably different than when he started. It was substantially larger, with a graduate program and a faculty who were increasingly interested in research. This was not accomplished without some pain. Some long-serving members felt that the quality of the working environment had eroded and that collegial decision making on academic issues had waned. The new dean was Dr J. Alex Murray, who came from the University of Windsor, where he had served as the acting dean of the business school. Murray's style was a sharp contrast to that of Stewart. The latter could be described as pursuing a vision largely articulated by his predecessor, while Dr Murray sought to create a new vision where the school would become increasingly linked to the business community, more global, and committed to a balance between research and teaching. Most significant was his desire to be fair and supportive of both departments and to encourage cooperation between the two. It should be noted that the combination of business and economics has been unsuccessful at other schools, given differences in size, power, and especially perspectives.

Dr Murray was described by a professor as an 'idea machine' who delegated administrative responsibilities so he could concentrate on innovation and change for the school. His approach was to run ideas past a small number of confidants. He would readily drop an idea if it did not meet with approval or he would make modifications in response to comments. This process continued with a steady expansion of the number of people who discussed and became committed to the proposal. By the time a proposal came to departmental meetings for approval, it was usually 'presold.' This technique was effective, since it prevented overt political defeats and also avoided mistakes.

Undergraduate program growth levelled out by the time Dr Murray became dean. Since then, undergraduate student enrolments have been essentially stable, although admission averages climbed significantly as the reputation and stature of the school grew. Nevertheless, the business faculty complement has increased by approximately fifteen members from an expansion of graduate studies and post-degree accounting programs. One of Murray's first accomplishments was guiding the creation of a full-time MBA program. This offering was designed initially to attract graduates of engineering and science programs, primarily from the University of Waterloo. More recently, it has been redesigned into Canada's first twelve-month MBA degree. Other advances during Murray's terms included the creation of various institutes, some of which were later restructured as their original objectives were met. The most successful of these has been the Laurier Institute, which has offered a variety of short programs to the business community and published numerous case studies. Murray also finally created an advisory group composed of a small group of highly influential business people. The need for such an advisory group had long been recognized, but its formation had frustrated earlier department leaders. The school also became more international with the establishment of various exchanges and curriculum enhancements. The trends of centralization of power and decreased involvement of faculty in decision making that had started under Stewart continued with Murray. In many respects, the department met with significant success during Murray's terms. Admission averages for the undergraduate program rose exceedingly high. Faculty research was widely published in professional and academic outlets. Graduates fared exceptionally well in the job market and on external professional exams. Murray's main contribution was to create an environment where such successes could occur.

This essay has been oriented towards the issues of leadership and administrative structure. It is also important to note that distinctive models of undergraduate and graduate business education evolved at Laurier. In chapter 11, Barry Boothman presents a general taxonomy for the categorization of Canadian undergraduate business programs based upon the stress placed on general education versus specialization and upon the weight of the business core curriculum in the first half versus the second half of a program. The WLU undergraduate degree is an outlier on this taxonomy owing to the relatively high non-business content and a design that places core business in the second and third years of baccalaureate studies. The unusual nature of the program evolved intentionally and is a matter of some pride to faculty who still use the term 'generalist' to describe the design and philosophy. This generalist philosophy has come under some criticism recently from those who believe it does not provide students with marketable skills. WLU has offered a part time MBA program since the late 1970s, but has only provided a full-time program since the late 1980s. The full-time MBA is a unique twelve-month program that is structured in integrative modules rather than traditional courses in the first term. This design is due to its relatively recent creation, which reflects contemporary curricular thought, and also the imperative to be innovative in order to compete with established programs.

2. Leadership Processes within the School

For the faculty participants in our study, leadership was a focal construct in their explanations of change and evolution of the school. Their descriptions of the leadership processes by which change came about were generally of longer term, more dynamic, and more complex than was anticipated at the outset of the study. We acknowledge that these descriptions are somewhat at variance with the dean-by-dean narrative earlier in this chapter. This incongruence highlights the nature of the leadership processes in the school. Attention is typically paid to the deans and their accomplishments, when in reality the processes are much more complex and involve many protagonists. Some of these leadership themes and processes that emerged from interviews with faculty are described below.

The role of the external environment. As noted by several participants, it appears that many of the critical events in the evolution of the school came about largely as a reflection of change in the external environment. This does not mean that individuals within the school did not play roles in facilitating these changes, but they could be viewed as taking advantage of opportunities or perhaps merely having hastened what was largely inevitable. Specifically, the forces that created the school of Business and Economics at WLU and led to its growth affected other Canadian universities in a similar fashion. The tremendous increase in student enrolments in business at WLU led to the hiring of many new faculty members and increasing power and status for the school both within the university and in the broader community, but this also occurred at other universities. If growth at WLU surpassed that of other Ontario and Canadian business schools, it could be attributed to the exceptionally strong economic and population growth over the last thirty years in the region surrounding the university. In this view, the school thrived because it was situated in an exceedingly prosperous area, thereby making it relatively easy to attract students, faculty, and resources.

As well, the University of Waterloo chose not to compete with WLU in the field of business and has always sent its students to WLU for business courses. Waterloo was helpful and supportive when the school created the co-operative education and full-time MBA programs. The relative proximity of WLU to the University of Western Ontario undoubtedly aided faculty recruitment. Several participants had come to WLU with their doctorates in progress, and the proximity to Western and their faculty advisers was highly influential in their decision to join. This same process occurred to a lesser extent for recruiting from Waterloo, York, and Toronto. While we do not wish to discount the role of individuals in the development of the school, it is clear that the environment encouraged and facilitated such development.

The role of senior university administration. It is also important to note that senior administrators at the university, especially the president and vice-presidents, shaped the development of the school. In 1971, the then-president signalled the shift from an institution primarily oriented towards teaching to one that emphasized a balance between teaching and research. This shift was resisted by many faculty members but has turned out to be a source of enduring strength to the school and university. As well, senior administrators either encouraged or discouraged various initiatives being undertaken by the school. The encouragement role is at variance with the popular vision of the unit's leaders battling the senior administration for resources. As one former president told us, 'You have to realize that these changes did not happen over a dead body. I was strongly supportive of the school growing.' The importance of the committed senior academic administration has been observed elsewhere.[16]

Individual versus collective leadership. The notion that groups of individuals working collectively can provide leadership seems at odds with our assumption that leadership is based on the ideas and actions of individuals. However, this was a common theme expressed by faculty when explaining how various stages in the evolution of the school were achieved. Faculty often had difficulty pinpointing one or two individuals who had primary responsibility for an initiative. Instead, they simply said that everyone had worked on it or that there was a team of people. This type of leadership may result from the unique nature of academic organizations, a collectivity of independent professionals of essentially equal status. Further, the long-term nature of the changes and projects allowed many individuals to become involved.

Leadership as a long-term, interactive process. We were astonished to discover how long standing some issues have been in the life of the school. Similarly, the critical changes that made the school what it is today involved many stages and were years in the making, which is consistent with the experience of other institutions.[17] For example, the creation of the MBA program is credited with helping to strengthen the status and image of the school. Active discussion regarding the importance of starting an MBA program are present in the minutes of meetings dating from 1966. Senior administrators embraced this idea in the early 1970s, as did a new dean. Discussions with government and other universities continued into the middle of the 1970s and the program commenced in 1976. It is worth noting that participants did not identify any major failures or setbacks in the history of the school. This long-term process may have been partially responsible for this phenomenon. Our naive assumptions about leadership were that individuals confronted discrete opportunities that arose in their environment and responded to those opportunities in a decisive and speedy fashion.

Successful leadership requires effective champions. In the case of some of the most successful initiatives associated with the development of the school, the dean typically had a faculty member who could champion the idea. It is clear that the initiative to create a co-operative education program arose from discussions between the dean and a senior professor, but the latter did virtually all of the negotiation and persuasion necessary for mobilizing faculty and administrative support for this educational innovation. Similarly, when the dean decided to launch a full-time MBA program in 1986, he did so in the face of considerable scepticism and opposition. The MBA directors whom he chose were not simply administrators but also champions of this cause with faculty, the business community, and potential students. It does not seem coincidental that most MBA directors were from the management and organizational behaviour area, and that they had the opportunity to put their lectures on negotiation, conflict, and persuasion into practice.

This strategy of having a champion do the 'down and dirty work' for a major initiative also had the benefit of shielding the dean from the conflicts and any long-term negative consequences that might ensue from them. It is noteworthy that almost without exception credit for major initiatives was attributed to the dean. Indeed, the administrators who reported to the dean were almost never mentioned by the participants in our study. Much of the activity and most of the accomplishments of these administrators are either invisible to faculty or forgotten by them over time. We were also struck by the longevity in office of the deans relative to the directors, department chairs, and associate deans, many of whom suffered an ignominious fate and left their positions embittered.

The leadership styles of successive administrators contrast sharply. Looking back over the history of the school, it is obvious that various administrators had sharply contrasting leadership styles. One view might be that as the school progressed through various stages, different leadership styles became appropriate and deans were chosen on that basis. For example, the co-operative education and MBA programs were started by a dean with an external focus, who was succeeded by a hands-on administrator who captured the resources to make these programs successful. We believe the process was considerably less rational. From our interviews with faculty and administrators, it seemed to us that the participants of the school still were often uncertain about the required qualifications and roles of these administrators. As a result, when a succession took place, one major criterion for the new administrator appears to have been, 'Different from the last person in terms of the things that irritated us.'

Leadership is not a focal construct for staff members. While faculty members discussed many different aspects of leadership and viewed it as important, staff members rarely mention this construct. It became apparent that staff members to date have not been a part of the academic initiatives and goals of the school. Our view that different leadership styles and actions somehow permeate to all levels of the organization is clearly naive.

Discussion and Conclusion

This chapter has chronicled the people and events that shaped the evolution of management education at Wilfrid Laurier University. Further, it has attempted to interpret those events from the perspective of leadership. We believe this chapter makes several important contributions to our knowledge about the history of management education in Canada. First, it provides a case study in the evolution of that subject at a small Canadian university. For Wilfrid Laurier University, it captures and records a history that was in danger of being lost. As well, it helps us to understand how change came about at Laurier. Future researchers may wish to compare the development of this faculty to that of other business schools in Canada.

We also believe that the Wilfrid Laurier school has been at the forefront of innovation in management education in Canada. Although there clearly are common forces that have shaped all business schools, the unique circumstances of Wilfrid Laurier led it to be a pioneer in co-operative education for business, in one-year MBA programs, and in international business education. 'Co-op' is widely viewed as one of the most successful innovations in education in Canada.

The sources of information for the history of management education at Wilfrid Laurier were both the written documents in the archives at Laurier and Western, and approximately seventy videotaped interviews with faculty, staff, and administrators. The deans and senior faculty figure prominently in these accounts of the events. What is given less emphasis in these interviews are discussions of broader contextual forces influencing developments. We chose to focus on the role and nature of leadership in understanding change at Wilfrid Laurier, both out of personal interest and because it is a focal construct in how individuals explain events in organizations.[18] The leadership themes that emerged from this project provide a number of interesting hypotheses about academic leadership that could be used to guide future research projects. We note that there would seem to be many future opportunities for exploring the role of other factors in influencing the development of business schools in Canada.

APPENDIX

Structure of units offering courses in business and economics*

1926†	Department of Political Economy (also referred to as Department of Economics)
1929	Department of Economic and Political Science
1938	Department of Business Administration
	Department of Economic and Political Science
1945	Department of Business Administration
	Department of Economics (Political Science courses still offered)
1946	Department of Business Administration
	Department of Economic and Political Science
1954	Department of Business Administration
	Department of Economic and Political Science
	Department of Secretarial Science
1959	Department of Business Administration, Economic and Political Science and Sociology
	Department of Secretarial Science
1962	Department of Business Administration, Economic and Political Science and Sociology (Secretarial Science included)
1965	Department of Business Administration, Economic and Political Science and Sociology (Secretarial Science no longer offered)‡
1966	Department of Business Administration and Economics
1967	School of Business and Economics created (1 September 1966) Departments include Accounting and Finance, Personnel and Marketing, Management and International Business Programs, and Economics
1969	School of Business and Economics Departments include Business Administration, International Business, and Economics
1973	School of Business and Economics Departments include Business Administration and Economics

* Separate faculties or schools did not exist before 1966.
† The year shown is the year that the new organization first appeared in the calendar. The actual change may have occurred up to a year earlier. The actual date, if known, is shown in brackets.
‡ Some documents refer to the Department of Economics and Business Administration, Political Science and Sociology.

NOTES

1 This study was supported by the Academic Development Fund, Wilfrid Laurier University. Order of authorship is alphabetical. We thank Heather Neil for her research assistance.

2 B.E.C. Boothman, 'Something Wicked This Way Comes: Orientations and Curricula of Undergraduate Business Programmes in Canada,' *ASAC Annual Conference Proceedings: Management Education* 11, part 10 (1990), 10.

3 Eric R. Gedajlovic, 'Undergraduate Business Programs in Canada: Where We Have Come from, Where We Are Now and Where We Should Be Heading,' *ASAC Annual Conference Proceedings: Management Education* 13, part 10 (1992), 22.

4 B. Sharma and L. Steier, 'Management Education and Development in Canada: Past, Present and Future,' *CJAS* 7 (1990), 2.

5 P.M. Maher, Business School Research: Academics Should Be Concerned, *CJAS* 7, (1990), 17.

6 Barbara Austin, 'ASAC: The Early Years of the Association, 1957–1972,' *ASAC Annual Conference Proceedings: Busines History* 15, part 14 (1994), 7.

7 Ibid., 6.

8 Ibid.

9 Maher, 'Business School Research,' 17.

10 Ibid., 16.

11 R.J. Ellis and J.C. McCutcheon, 'Understanding Leadership Processes in a Business School through Oral History,' *ASAC Annual Conference Proceedings: Business History* 17, part 24 (1996), 39–56.

12 Smyth continued his association with Waterloo College until the 1960s in the capacity of university solicitor.

13 Waterloo College calendars indicate that Moellman received his doctorate from Marburg (University). It is likely that the doctorate was actually conferred by Phillips University, Marburg, Germany. WLU currently has an exchange program with this institution.

14 Departments were created when courses in that discipline were added. In early years, departments did not always have full-time faculty members.

15 Wilfrid Laurier University Archives, Minutes, School of Business Administration and Economics, 13 September 1968.

16 J. Zolner, 'Moving the Academic Graveyard: The Dynamics of Curricular Change,' *Selections* 12: 2 (1996), 1–10.

17 Ibid.

18 J.R. Meindl, S.B. Ehrlich, and J.M. Dukerich, 'The Romance of Leadership,' *ASQ* 30 (1985), 78–102.

7

Development by Design: A History of the Faculty of Management at the University of Calgary, 1967–1991

VERNON JONES and GEORGE S. LANE

The Faculty of Management at the University of Calgary (initially known as the Faculty of Business) formally came into existence on 1 July 1967. During the period from 1967 to 1991 the faculty was committed to creating a strong professional school, as evidenced by its focus on management practice, close links to the business community, and curriculum development in accordance with the accreditation standards of the AACSB (American Assembly of Collegiate Schools of Business). The evolution and growth of the faculty followed from a series of initiatives involving both the academic and business communities as well as the Government of Alberta. This chapter describes the evolution of the faculty, emphasizing significant events and its history of 'development by design.'

Beginnings[1]

The origin of the University of Calgary can be traced to 1945, when the Calgary Normal School became the southern extension of the University of Alberta's Faculty of Education. Soon thereafter, Calgarians began pressuring the provincial government to expand university course offerings in Calgary. The first year of the University of Alberta bachelor of commerce program was offered in Calgary in the autumn of 1953. Those who successfully completed the first year were then able to transfer automatically to the University of Alberta, in Edmonton, for the balance of the program. In 1961, the second year was added to Calgary's offerings. During 1966, after some strife and many representations, the University of Alberta, Calgary (UAC) became an autonomous institution, the University of Calgary. A year later, partly as a result of pressure from the community, the commerce program gained faculty status.

Before becoming a faculty, the bachelor of commerce program offered by the Faculty of Arts and Science involved basically an economics and accounting curriculum. The 1967–68 University of Calgary *Undergraduate Calendar* describes three course sequences in the BCom. program, each requiring twenty full courses to be taken over four years. All sequences required six full courses in economics. The dean of the Faculty of Arts and Science at an academic planning meeting, 7 December 1966, observed that 'the present commerce programme within the Faculty of Arts and Science is in its second year; that it is an academically respectable programme, but that there are some indications that it is not meeting the needs of students – many are transferring out.'[2] He thought it expedient to establish commerce as an independent entity.

At the meeting of the General Faculty Council held 11 May 1967, a motion to designate commerce as a faculty cited 'five points' as to why that status should be given:

(1) the initial acceptance of this programme will depend upon the status given the administrative unit;
(2) it will make it competitive with Edmonton for students;
(3) it will aid greatly in relationships with the community, particularly in seeking their support of the programme;
(4) the Board [of Governors] has already indicated that they would prefer Faculty status;
(5) and as professional schools are a characteristic of the twentieth century development of higher education, the University should capitalize on this and the blending of such programmes with liberal education.

After considerable debate over the question of 'faculty' versus 'school,' the lack of any provision for base funding, the desires of the community and the board of governors, and the impact on other academic units, the motion favouring the establishment of the faculty passed by a margin of one vote.[3]

Foundations

The founding dean of the faculty was a Canadian, Dr James M.A. Robinson, who had served as the executive secretary of the American

Assembly of Collegiate Schools of Business (AACSB) while completing his doctorate at Ohio State University. Robinson had been a contributor on behalf of the AACSB to the seminal Ford Foundation (Gordon and Howell)[4] and Carnegie Foundation (Pierson)[5] reports. With his AACSB experience and as the dean of a new faculty, Robinson was in a unique position to shape its destiny.

Dean Robinson tells the story of how on his second day on the job someone arrived at his door with a loaded file cabinet. 'What's that?' he asked. 'Your two hundred and some students,' was the reply. It was July and Robinson had no staff, no space, and little budget. Somehow classes had to be organized by September for first-, second-, and third-year students. Fortunately, he was able to tap the always supportive Calgary business community to find part-time instructors who were willing to take up the task.[6]

Robinson understood the evolving nature of business education in the United States through his association with the AACSB and his familiarity with the Ford Foundation and Carnegie reports. He defined four objectives for the new business school:

1 to develop conceptual understanding – the capacity to perceive the whole of an idea – in business and administration;
2 to provide a foundation for the development of professional competence and the ability to analyse and synthesize;
3 to provide a logical approach to decision making and to recognize, anticipate, and solve problems;
4 and to impel the development of organizational skill, skill in interpersonal relationships, and skill in communication.

Robinson felt that teaching was the principal function of the faculty, but that instruction should be founded upon a tradition of scholarship that encouraged new ideas and knowledge. Since business could not be isolated from the social, cultural, and physical environment, it was imperative that individuals have an understanding of the humanities, physical sciences, and social sciences. Accordingly, the business school would seek to provide a solid base of liberal education consistent with that of other professional faculties, strive to provide adequate breadth in its own curriculum, and maintain a continuing interaction with other disciplines.[7]

Robinson undertook a number of important initiatives. First, he adopted a program-based form of organization and avoided the departmental form found in many discipline-oriented faculties. Second, he developed a curriculum in which professional business courses were taught in the later years following an arts and science base. This idea would become formalized later in the faculty's 'two-plus-two' bachelor of commerce program. Third, it was established as a professional school, which limited specialization and placed the business school in a generalist context. Finally, he implemented a program that was mainly consistent with AACSB standards, thus laying the groundwork for subsequent AACSB accreditation.

Robinson's contributions to the faculty were immense. He was able to avoid the struggles at many American schools to extricate themselves from a vocational model of business education and intended to set the faculty firmly on the path to professional education, for which he had a strong vision along the lines of a law or medical school, founded on the liberal arts but focused on managerial practice. However, his problems were also legion. The faculty had been established without a base operating grant. As enrolments rose in the business school its faculty was constantly fighting the other university faculties and departments for an equitable reallocation of university funds. The chronic under-funding meant that the faculty's financial resources were very restricted, and plagued its development for years. An undated submission of the faculty, entitled 'Budget Complications of the Development of the Faculty,' noted that for the academic year 1967–68 it generated through tuition fees and provincial grants a total of $1,327,480, but the net operating expenditures were limited to $62,200 or 4.7 per cent of the funds generated. The approved budget for the following year, while larger, was expected to appropriate only 7.2 per cent of funds generated. The faculty went on to request 'a substantially larger portion of the funds it generates.'[8] In April 1972, a protest was again made about the budget allocation, concluding with the statement, 'In view of the circumstances, it is recommended that the University of Calgary reconsider the merits of having a Faculty of Business.'[9] Throughout this period, the faculty experienced significant growth in enrolment (see table 7.1) but inadequate financial support.

A New Direction

Robinson retired from the deanship on 30 June 1972. He had accomplished much towards establishing the faculty as a professional school,

TABLE 7.1
Growth in the size of the student body in the Faculty of Business (4-year bachelor of commerce)

Year	Full-time	Part-time	Annual total	Increase (%)
1966	276	5	281	–
1967	330	30	360	28
1968	473	44	517	44
1969	569	48	617	19
1970	702	54	756	23
1971	724	80	804	6
1972	792	117	909	13
1973	930	206	1136	25

Source: University of Calgary Faculty of Business annual report, 31 March 1974

but its future was insecure. Dr Ed Sugars served as acting dean from 1972 to 1973, and applied for the deanship emphasizing a continuing strong focus on management practice. However, the university opted to appoint Dr Stephen Peitchinis from the department of economics. A prominent academic economist, Dr Peitchinis was well regarded on campus and was thought to be able to represent the interests of the faculty quite effectively. He was to serve as dean for a two-year period until 1975.

Dean Peitchinis first concentrated on overcoming the faculty's difficulties with the university, especially with the approval of a master's degree. During the previous two years, the faculty had unsuccessfully attempted the introduction of an MBA program, but had been unable to prepare a proposal acceptable to the Faculty of Graduate Studies. 'Prior to April 1, 1973, the Faculty of Business had submitted two proposals detailing a graduate programme in Business Administration, but they were returned by the Committee of the Faculty of Graduate Studies Council with instructions to re-examine, re-structure, re-write and then re-submit. The academic staff of the faculty were discouraged and seemed to believe that someone, somewhere was determined to obstruct the introduction of such a programme. The mood of the academic staff was one of disillusionment and disgust with what they believed to be unfair treatment.'[10]

Dean Peitchinis supported a graduate program positioned differently from the traditional MBA towards a 'Management Studies' orientation. The new degree was introduced as a master of management studies (MMS). The MMS had the advantage that it did not exactly duplicate the already existing MBA at the University of Alberta (thus accelerating university and government approval) and it included, significantly, provision for a concentration in 'Small Business and Entrepreneurship.'[11] The approval of the MMS signalled the arrival of graduate education in the Faculty of Management. At the same time, the undergraduate program was reorganized around two specialized core areas: accounting and organization management. Students wishing to pursue finance, management science, or marketing could do so with the organization management specialization.

Dean Peitchinis also established a business advisory council, later known as the Management Advisory Council (MAC). This initiative proved to be one of the most important in the development of the faculty. Originally consisting of ten business leaders from Calgary, the MAC would play a critical role in influencing the university and provincial government towards a supportive role for management education. At the same time, a smaller advisory committee for the accounting program was also established.

In the spring of 1975 Dean Peitchinis resigned his position and returned to the economics department. He had made significant accomplishments in his short term of office, but with his strong academic and research interests he had found himself often in conflict with faculty members and with the senior administration of the university.[12]

Building the Infrastructure

Dr George Lane was appointed acting dean for the 1975–76 academic year and, subsequently, dean for the years from 1976 to1981. Dr Lane had recently joined the university from Sir George Williams University in Montréal (after 1970, Concordia). A native Albertan, Lane held a bachelor of commerce degree from the University of Alberta and was a certified management accountant. He also held an MA and a doctorate in business from the University of Washington. He had been the founding chair of the School of Business at the Saskatchewan Technical Institute and a consultant to the vice-president of Sir George Williams University. These experiences had resulted in his becoming familiar with the Ford and Carnegie reports, the AACSB accreditation standards, and the literature on professional schools.

Lane had discovered upon his arrival at the University of Calgary that there was an ongoing debate about whether the bachelor of commerce program should be organized by the professional programs offered, or by the several disciplines, such as marketing, within the programs common with those of the Faculty of Arts and Science. Further, this debate was taking place within the context of the larger question of 'What is a university?' The choice for the faculty became quite clear. Life would be easier (and probably resources more forthcoming) if it followed the discipline model in the arts and science tradition. In the words of the university, 'Educate, don't train.' The voice of the business community was equally clear. It expected graduates that not only knew things, but knew how to do things. Employers wanted graduates with knowledge, skills, and professional attitudes. Lane sought advice from Don Mills, a professor of sociology at the university who had co-authored a book on professionalization.[13] Whether managers should be viewed as professionals or not was not altogether clear. What was clear was that members of a profession are practitioners. It seemed reasonable to conclude therefore that the faculty should strive to be viewed as a professional school whose graduates would be practitioners – who in the course of time would come to be regarded as professionals.

Dean Lane had some immediate problems as well. These included a lack of appropriate physical facilities, an inadequate operating budget, inadequate salary scales, and a lack of status within the university environment.[14] The University of Calgary's Faculty of Business was not the only business school facing these difficulties. Dr Max von Zur-Muehlen, coordinator of research and special projects at the Institutional and Public Finance Branch of Statistics Canada, as well as an experienced observer of the management education scene in Canada, noted:

The fact that business schools have 'arrived' is not reflected in the internal funding of universities. The schools still receive less of the cake than they should, based on enrolment figures. Part of the reason is the traditional feeling among professors and administrators that business and management studies are not wholly academic and therefore not deserving of the same encouragement as academic fields. Changes come largely from the division of new funds and universities have seen little of these in recent years. With more students seeking admission to commerce programs, business schools may find themselves caught in a squeeze – quality or quantity. Student-teacher ratios in business schools are already woefully behind those for universities as a whole (31 for business schools versus 13.5 for all disciplines in 1974–75).[15]

By the middle of the 1970s the faculty was growing rapidly. In 1975, it had 28.6 full-time equivalent faculty members and the third largest number of course enrollees on campus, accounting for approximately 10 per cent of the total enrolment of the university.[16] In von Zur-Muehlen's terms, it seemed clear that if the Faculty of Business was to avoid a 'quality or quantity' squeeze it would have to get a handle first on the 'quantity' issue, and plan for 'quality' second. Accordingly, the faculty members began to consider whether enrolment in the undergraduate program should be limited.

At about this same time, the University of Calgary introduced a new concept in undergraduate education called the 'University College.' The idea was that students would spend either one or two years obtaining a more general/liberal education in the University College before making a commitment to a specific program. This fit well with the faculty's plan that students should qualify for admission and be accepted only after some period of post-secondary studies. Accordingly, the faculty opted for the 'two-plus-two' program, that is, two qualifying years in University College or a community college and two years within the Faculty of Business completing the Bachelor of Commerce. A quota on admission was established at 330 qualified students entering the third year. The first two years were qualifying, the third year (after admission) was a core management program and the fourth year was for specialization or 'concentration' in a specific field. The program thus kept its strong liberal arts commitment, combined with a general management emphasis with limited specialization. This positioned the Bachelor of Commerce for a successful application for AACSB accreditation. Exceptions were made for accounting students qualifying for the Canadian Institute of Chartered Accountants.

On the quality side, the faculty embarked on a strategic planning exercise culminating in a 'Statement of Goals and Objectives' approved by the faculty council in 1976 (see exhibit 1). The most significant result of this exercise was that the faculty returned to the concept of a 'professional' school as originally described by Dean Robinson. The statement of goals was written in an attempt to encourage a sense of community within the faculty.

EXHIBIT 1
Faculty of Business *Statement of Goals and Objectives*, 1976

We, the Faculty of Business, shall strive to become:

1 A truly 'professional school,' recognized and treated as such by other parts of the university and by the community at large.
2 A faculty with a reputation for excellence which will in turn enhance the reputation of the university as a whole.
3 A faculty that provides an outstanding working-learning environment for faculty members, students and support staff alike.
4 A faculty that is able to attract and to hold outstanding faculty members who have, or are able and willing to acquire, at least a national reputation.
5 A faculty where scholarly and professional activities of a high quality are encouraged, supported, expected and rewarded.
6 A faculty that attracts and selects excellent students and relevant programmes.
7 A faculty that is regarded as a major contributor and a 'good citizen' within the university community.
8 A faculty that is regarded as a major contributor and a 'good citizen' within the community at large.
9 A faculty that is vital; a faculty that recognizes the dynamics of its environments and the changing needs of its publics.

A four-point strategy was adopted as follows:

- Professional orientation as characterized by an emphasis upon interpretation and application of theory to practice
- School of management focus as opposed to a school of business focus. We view this focus as employing not a de-emphasis of the functional areas, but rather the addition of non-business environmental considerations to the studies in each function area.
- Emphasis upon broad management education with limited functional specialization at the undergraduate level. Emphasis upon broad management education with limited functional specialization and/or limited environmental specialization at the graduate level.
- Assume a position of leadership in graduate education in this province.[17]

The faculty was also facing some pressure to departmentalize along the lines of traditional disciplines: accounting, finance, marketing, and so on. However, in 1975, full departmentalization was rejected in favour of emphasis on programs. Area groups were organized along discipline lines, but they did not have budgetary authority or responsi-

bility for appointment, tenure, and promotion. The faculty also began
to conceive of its mission more broadly than as serving business and
started to emphasize different environments: entrepreneurship and
small business, large business, international business, and public institutions. During 1978 the formal title of the business school changed
to the Faculty of Management to reflect this broader, professional orientation.

While the organizational structure and name were changed, the
Business Advisory Council also renamed itself the Management Advisory Council (MAC). In conjunction with the Calgary Chamber of
Commerce, MAC commissioned Foster Research to prepare a study
entitled 'Requirements for Post Graduate Management Programs at
the University of Calgary.'[18] The president of Foster Research, Gordon
Pierce, had a long-time connection with the faculty. He had taught at
the University of Western Ontario in the 1950s and part-time at the
University of Calgary in 1966–7. He had served as the first chairman of
the Business Advisory Council, but now assigned himself the role of
project manager and proceeded to seek out the best information and
expertise he could find on the development of business schools.

The Foster report, completed in January 1979, confirmed the need to
significantly expand the full-time master's program and executive
development courses as quickly as planning, staffing, and funding
would permit. It recognized the faculty's need for a 'properly designed
and equipped building' of approximately 150,000 square feet. It recommended filing with the Government of Alberta a letter of intent con-
cerning a PhD program to begin no earlier than 1984 and outlined a
number of ways (financial and non-financial) that the business community could assist the Faculty of Management. The recommendations
of the Foster report were strongly endorsed by the Calgary Chamber of
Commerce.[19]

When W.A. Cochrane became president of the university in 1974, he
began a series of evaluation reviews by presidential task forces. After
completing reviews of several other faculties the president decided to
initiate a review of the Faculty of Business. The task force, chaired by
Professor D. Gillmor of the Faculty of Environmental Design, reported
in May 1979, some five months after the Foster report.[20]

The Gillmor report was highly critical about the status of the business school. The committee was concerned that the growth had been
too rapid and that there were problems with teaching quality and
program administration. Over the summer and autumn, a detailed

response to the report was prepared.[21] The Gillmor report and the faculty response were then reviewed by yet another committee, chaired by Dr L. Bruton of the Faculty of Engineering. This committee was to draft recommendations for the university's General Faculties Council.

The Bruton committee concluded that the critical tone of the presidential task force (Gillmor) report was justified but noted also that the current administration had inherited many of the problems and had implemented improvements. 'The Faculty of Management,' stated the Bruton report, 'is feeling many of the stresses of rapid growth, suffering too many changes in educational philosophy and poor understanding of its problems by the University community.'[22] The recommendations of the Gillmor report endorsed by Bruton included the following:

- the faculty should move in the direction of the pragmatic model of business education
- the faculty should give first priority to building and maintaining a high quality undergraduate offering
- the faculty should revise its merit system to give higher priority to teaching accomplishment
- the Vice-President (Services) should give high priority to providing contiguous space for the faculty.[23]

Significantly, however, the Bruton committee rejected several of the Gillmor recommendations, including one that would effectively remove the possibility of a new building for the business program in the foreseeable future.

The spring of 1980 found the faculty in a dilemma. On one hand, it was clear from the Foster report that the business community wanted it to grow rapidly, especially at the graduate level and with executive programs. On the other hand, the message of the university was that 'there was still prevalent a growth mentality that required to be curbed.'[24] Indeed there was an apparent sentiment within the university that it might be detrimental if the faculty were permitted to grow in accordance with the demands of students and employers. Some thought that a large business school would adversely alter the institution's fundamental character. 'The debate may well be sharper at the University of Calgary than anywhere else in the country. We have a booming economy and a diversifying business community that clearly wants a bigger and better Faculty of Management; they're faced with a small but ambitious faculty slapping quotas on Bachelor of Commerce enrolments because it hasn't the resources to do otherwise, and an overall university situation of declining enrolments and funding.'[25] Robert Willson, a prominent Calgary businessman and, later, chairman of the board of governors commented, '[T]he average Faculty of Management is hard-pressed to demonstrate its academic purity to the average university administration and, simultaneously, its relevance to the community. The faculty has to do a balancing act, as a result, and suffers from real ambivalence.'[26]

Nevertheless, the further development of the faculty seemed inevitable. In June of 1980, Dr Peter Krueger, vice-president, academic offered to carry forward a proposal for 'base-funding' to the Policy and Planning Committee of the university and, if that were approved, to forward it to the government of Alberta. By July, 'A Proposal for the Enhancement of the Faculty of Management' was prepared that requested incremental base funding to be spread over the following five years.[27] The Management Advisory Council, led by chairman Walt Dingle, enthusiastically endorsed the proposal, pledged to 'materially aid' in the process of enhancement, and agreed to undertake some direct approaches to both the university administration and government leaders in the hope of obtaining positive responses to the enhancement initiative.

For a number of years Dean Lane and members of the Management Advisory Council had held informal discussions about the possibility of a building to house the Faculty of Management. This was of particular interest to Ralph Scurfield, a member of MAC and the president of the NuWest Group, a prominent Calgary house builder and land developer. Scurfield had at one time attended the fourteen-week Advanced Management Program at the Harvard Business School and believed strongly in the value of graduate business and executive education. He also believed that the future of the Faculty of Management could be leveraged with the construction of a building. With its own facility, the other things, including budgets, programs, status, and salary scales would follow. Years later, MAC Chairman Walter Dingle would refer to an important 'meeting at the Ranchman's Club,' with Ralph Scurfield, university president Norman Wagner, and a number of senior Calgary business people.

On 9 March 1981, University of Calgary president Norman Wagner announced that Scurfield had decided to donate $4 million on behalf of himself and his family and $4 million on behalf of the NuWest Group.

These funds were to be matched by the Government of Alberta for a total of $16 million, which could be employed for the construction of a home for the Faculty of Management and its graduate programs. At the same time, Scurfield challenged the rest of the business community in Calgary and southern Alberta to contribute to providing for the development of the Faculty of Management. Mr Klaus Springer, chairman of the board of Carma Developers, immediately pledged $400,000 to establish the Carma Chair.

George Lane retired as dean in 1981. Through his focus on a practitioner orientation, Lane had secured the faculty's future as a professional school. Moreover, his extensive work with the Management Advisory Council and the Calgary Chamber of Commerce, resulting in the Scurfield Hall donation, would be pivotal for the future development of the faculty.

'It's Time for Growth'

On 1 July 1981, Dr P. Michael Maher became the new dean. Maher held a degree in engineering from the University of Saskatchewan and had worked as a research and development engineer with Du Pont of Canada. After completing an MBA from Western Ontario and a PhD from Northwestern, he had served as research director with the Faculty of Business at the University of Alberta and, most recently, as dean of the College of Commerce at the University of Saskatchewan. Noted for his enthusiasm and entrepreneurial attitude, Maher sought to join forces with the business community to give the faculty a profile that would compare favourably with North America's most outstanding business schools. 'It's time for growth,' Maher observed, recognizing some important fundamentals were now coming into place.[28] Maher was to serve four consecutive terms as dean (1981–99).

Maher's plans included the establishment of endowed chairs, the formation of strategic research themes, and the introduction of a full-time MBA program, as well as executive development courses. He proposed to send faculty 'downtown' to share their academic knowledge and learn the needs of the business community. His most immediate challenges were the need to develop the MBA as a 'flagship' program and to attract and keep 'high profile faculty.'[29] Maher's intent was to develop a 'full service' business school with the following priorities:

- to establish fund raising and to create an endowment fund

- to secure base funding for a full-time MBA program
- to establish executive programs
- to ensure the academic quality of both the bachelor of commerce program and MBA (through AACSB accreditation)
- to supervise the design and construction of a state-of-the-art business school facility, Scurfield Hall

Maher needed to move quickly to capture the momentum of the Scurfield Hall donation and his own appointment. By March 1982 he had developed an ambitious plan to guide future developments. A comprehensive proposal, 'Academic Program Directions for the Faculty of Management,' called for a rapid pace of growth and, in particular, a radical expansion of the MBA program. Controversy immediately erupted over the potential dislocation of other units on campus, the ability of the faculty actually to meet these targets, and the lack of PhD qualified instructors. Nevertheless, after considerable debate the university's General Faculties Council voted to endorse the scheme.[30] An aggressive development plan was now in place. Maher's activities extended well beyond the internal environment of the university. He encouraged the establishment of a provincial task force on management. This group included representatives of the government, the private sector, and management schools and was chaired by the deputy minister of advanced education, D.E. Berghofer. Reporting in February 1984 to the Honourable Dick Johnston, minister of advanced education and the Honourable Hugh Planche, minister of economic development, the task force offered a blueprint for government support of management education – including strategic direction and funding mechanisms.[31]

Maher also moved quickly to establish new sources of funds. The first of these initiatives was the Associates Fund. This was an annual drive whereby individuals could become associates of the faculty with a donation of $1000 per annum. Associates were invited to participate in periodic special events, usually involving distinguished speakers. Initially, in 1984, fifty-two associates were enrolled. The first priority for these funds was to support student competition teams organized and led by Dr Bob Schulz. One of the faculty's most dynamic and colourful professors, 'Dr Bob,' as he was known by students, had personally financed student travel and accommodation to Queen's University to enter the Intercollegiate Business Competitions. The Associates' Fund was immediately put to use to defray Schulz's expenses with stern warnings that personal use of funds was not to be repeated. Not deterred in the slightest, Schulz went on to coach the teams for many years, achieving a string of successes at Queen's, Concordia, and elsewhere. Indeed, for many years, it seemed the school's reputation was based primarily on the performance of Dr Bob's teams. The Associates Fund was used for other important causes, particularly to support student events, the Career Development Office, and a distinguished lecture series.[32] Crucially, however, the Associates' Fund provided Dean Maher with important experience and seed money for the planning of a major fund-raising initiative known as the Future Fund campaign.

Unlike the Associates program, the Future Fund was to be an endowment campaign, linked to the Scurfield donation. Dean Maher, along with the university president, Dr Norman Wagner, and Mr Walter Dingle, a retired Imperial Oil executive and chair of the Management Advisory Council, developed a strategic campaign to approach several regional and national corporations. The campaign was chaired by Mr Hal Wyatt, vice-chair of the board of the Royal Bank of Canada, and had a financial objective of $4.8 million to be matched by the Government of Alberta.[33] In spite of difficult economic times in Alberta associated with the declining energy prices and real estate values of the early 1980s, the campaign was very successful, with more than $5 million in donations and pledges by 1985. By 1988, when it ended, the Future Fund endowment had exceeded $12 million.[34] An important element of the campaign was the 'naming of rooms' in the new building. A corporation or individual donation would be recognized with the appropriate signage, and the room would be known as the 'Esso Theatre,' the 'Alberta Energy Company' case room, or the 'Dingle' conference room. The recognition of corporations and business leaders was intended to reflect the alliance between the university and the business community. The campaign also established theme areas for the development of teaching and research. These included tourism, entrepreneurship, technology management, international business, financial services, and energy management.

In 1981 the master of management studies (MMS) program had been renamed the MBA program but was still offered on a part-time basis only. An important element of Ralph Scurfield's vision was a development of graduate and executive programs. Since its inception the faculty had struggled with inadequate base funding and, owing to provincial funding restraint in the early 1980s, the operating expenses

Figure 7.1 Faculty of Management expenditure information

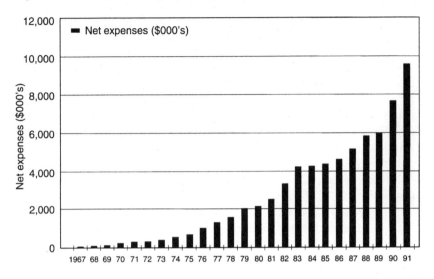

Source: University of Calgary Fact Books, 1996, 1995, 1994, 1989, 1985, 1982, 1978, 1975, 1972

Note: Net expense data are as of 31 March.

remained level from 1983 through 1986 (see figure 7.1). The funding of a full-time daytime MBA program envisioned in the 1982 'Academic Directions' document became the critical requirement for increasing the base operating budget and enabling the delivery of substantial graduate programs. The Management Advisory Council, according to Maher, played the crucial role behind the scenes. Liaising effectively with both the university's administrators and the provincial government and drawing on the Berghofer report, MAC argued that the funding for a full-time MBA program was the last important criterion if the new building, Scurfield Hall, was to be a success. With new facilities and a growing endowment fund, the base funding was needed to enable the faculty to recruit and develop the best possible academic staff. After many representations, the government approved funding for a full-time MBA program commencing in 1986, as well as enhancement funding for the BCom. program.[35] A significant element of the MBA expansion was the commitment to support programs in entrepreneurship and new ventures. As a result of this and other support to the New Venture Group, the Faculty of Management, led by Professors Ed McMullan, Wayne Long, and Jim Graham, developed unique capabilities in teaching and research in entrepreneurship. The New Venture program generated significant economic spinoffs and job creation in the Calgary area.[36] Moreover, this program would eventually propel the formation of the 'Enterprise MBA' program, which was designed to help students establish and develop new ventures.

Concurrent with the development of the MBA proposal, the faculty in 1983 also moved aggressively into executive development. The major challenge at first was to develop capable but inexperienced faculty members to a level where they could teach and provide assistance to practising managers and executives. Using his considerable experience both at the University of Western Ontario and in the business world, executive programs director Mike Fuller invited senior business people in Calgary to 'go back to school.' Each faculty member would design a class, assign pre-reading including a case study, and conduct a 75-minute class for the assembled business executives. Following intensive debriefing, the faculty member would then develop another class and experience a second critique. Within a year a team of confident and capable instructors were able to launch a four-week residential executive development program at the Chateau Lake Louise. Years later, the EDP was merged with the Banff School of Advanced Management, but the training sessions remained. Every Friday morning at 7:30 a.m., year after year, the 'Friday Morning at the faculty' sessions showcased faculty talent and renewed community linkages.

Since the establishment of the faculty in 1967, successive deans and at least a few faculty had been committed to seeking AACSB accreditation at the appropriate time. Robinson, as a former AACSB executive secretary, and Dean Lane in particular were well versed in the literature on management education and committed to AACSB standards. Maher, however, was initially reluctant about the accreditation process. While he was an active member of AACSB, he was concerned about the ability of the Faculty of Management to qualify for accreditation and whether the effort might be divisive internally. It would be preferable to support and be accredited by a Canadian agency if one existed. American accreditation was not seen as desirable by some faculty members, while others saw it as unnecessary in Canada and unduly restrictive for future development.

An accreditation team was formed including Dean Maher as well as former dean George Lane and associate dean (academic) Vern Jones. They concluded that there were several important reasons in favour of accreditation. The most obvious was that the rival school at the University of Alberta in Edmonton was already accredited. Unless there was AACSB accreditation at Calgary, the University of Alberta would be seen as the premier business school and would be more readily able to attract government funding or business community support, as well as to recruit and retain top-flight American-educated faculty. A second reason was that the AACSB accreditation provided a level of quality assurance for both the BCom. and MBA programs. The BCom. program since its inception had been developed following the AACSB accreditation guidelines, as was the new full-time MBA. The best possible way to signal quality and to ensure it continued to evolve appropriately was a commitment to accreditation. A third reason was that the business community and Management Advisory Council were strongly behind AACSB accreditation. Many American-based firms distinguished between higher- and lower-quality business schools simply on the basis of whether they were accredited or not. The strong Alberta link to the energy industry and to American business made AACSB accreditation more critical than in other Canadian provinces. A fourth reason, finally, was that the administrators of the faculty were keen to take advantage of a performance review conducted by an outside professional organization. The Gillmor report of the late 1970s had been highly critical of the faculty. Would it not be better, some suggested, to have those reviews conducted by an independent outside agency whereby deans of accredited schools passed judgment rather than internal, and potentially less knowledgeable, committees? An external professional review, even if American-based, seemed a far preferable alternative. In the autumn of 1984, the faculty submitted a self-study plan.[37] After some further revisions, the bachelor of commerce program with its 'two plus two' format, along with the balance between liberal and professional education, passed the accreditation test. With new facilities nearing completion and improved funding for a full-time MBA program on the way, the AACSB visitation team made a positive recommendation, and the Faculty of Management's programs were accredited in 1985. The University of Calgary joined the University of Alberta as one of only two AACSB accredited schools in Canada at the time.

Part of Ralph Scurfield's vision for the Faculty of Management was that the facility constructed to house its operations should be state of the art. It was not to be just another university building, but one specifically designed for a full-service graduate program in business. A building committee toured a number of business schools across North America, giving consideration to such matters as classroom design, library, computer facilities, student areas, faculty offerings, open space, and a myriad details. Construction started in 1984 on an eight-acre site located on one corner of the campus.

Scurfield Hall was officially opened on 7 April 1986. Not only was it functional, but it was architecturally unique, absorbing natural light from windows on exterior walls and a common area (the NuWest Common) that rose three floors to a skylight extending the full length of the building. Its many features included a trading post from the Toronto Stock Exchange. More than 130 individuals and corporations, who had contributed to the Future Fund in amounts from $5000 to $500,000, were recognized in the building.[38] Tragically, Ralph Scurfield had died in a skiing accident just months before the opening. He was represented at the opening by Mrs Sonia Scurfield and the Scurfield family.

A New Strategic Plan

By the mid-1980s, the faculty members could look forward to the completion of Scurfield Hall and a new process was established for developing a revised mission, strategic objectives, and a long-term plan. Central to this effort was to create a strong sense of identity as 'The Management School of Western Canada.' A draft development plan tabled on 16 August 1981, followed by a faculty retreat, established the following new direction: 'The mission of the Faculty of Management at the University of Calgary is to contribute, at an internationally recognized standard, to the effectiveness of management practice in Western Canada and beyond.'

There was a widespread belief that the University of Calgary could position itself as a major Canadian business school focused upon 'management practice.' The major rival schools in western Canada, the University of Alberta and the University of British Columbia, had established reputations with a strong academic research focus. The University of Calgary, newly accredited, and with close ties to the business community, would focus on the practice of management. Dean Maher declared that 'while other business faculties focus on issues of interest to their fellow academics, the Faculty of Management at the

EXHIBIT 2
Faculty of Management development plan for the years 1986–1995

Mission

The mission of the Faculty of Management at the University of Calgary is to contribute, at an internationally recognized standard, to the effectiveness of management practice in Western Canada and beyond.

Strategic Objectives

Eleven strategic objectives to foster excellence in teaching, research and service have emerged as an output of the faculty retreat of September, 1985, and various discussions by faculty of the Draft Development Plan.

1. To put ourselves in a position where we can effectively compete for (and have the advantage of choice); and retain doctorally qualified faculty members, through competitive salaries and other incentives.
2. To secure a financial position comparable to that of the better schools of management on this continent.
3. To have additional facilities constructed to accommodate, among other initiatives, an expanded Bachelor of Commerce program, a management research centre, and an expanded Executive Development program.
4. To maintain and enhance the accredited status of our BCom. and MBA programs.
5. To initiate and develop a doctoral program of reasonable size and strong reputation.
6. To internationalize our teaching, scholarship and service.
7. To incorporate entrepreneurship (as well as stewardship) in our teaching scholarship and service.
8. To devise and develop the capacity to respond to new teaching research and service initiatives as well as opportunities for expanding present programs.
9. To enhance our relationship with other parts of the university and in turn further their understanding of us.
10. To develop a strong 'sense of community' of the faculty.
11. To firmly establish our identify as 'The Management School of Western Canada.'

University of Calgary will focus on matters of interest to practicing managers and the business community.' There were several strategic objectives identified in the development plan of 1986 (see exhibit 2).[39] Perhaps most important was the goal of putting the faculty in a stronger position to recruit and retain doctorally qualified faculty through competitive salaries and other incentives. Other emergent objectives included expansion of the bachelor of commerce program, establishment of a PhD program, construction of additional facilities, and defining a stronger sense of community within the faculty. The plan also included a strong commitment to maintain and enhance AACSB

Figure 7.2 University of Calgary degrees awarded in management

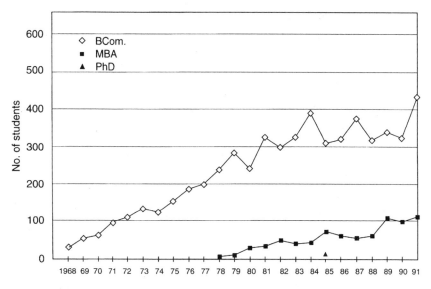

Source: University of Calgary Fact Books, 1996–97, 1991–92, 1986–87, 1981–82 and 1977–78

Notes: Reliable BCom. data for 1966 and 1967 was not available. Each year includes spring and fall convocation information.

accreditation for the BCom. and MBA programs. The faculty was confident in its future and looked forward to continuing rapid development. Dean Maher was renewed for a second term commencing 1 July 1986.

From the establishment of the faculty in 1967 until 1979 the enrolment in the bachelor of commerce program had grown at a steady pace. However, with the introduction of an admission quota of 330 students in 1977, a limit had been placed on further expansion. From 1979 to 1991, the quota was maintained and although the number of degrees varied somewhat through this period, the number of graduates in 1991 was almost exactly the same as in 1981 (see figure 7.2).

Throughout the 1980s the pressures to expand the BCom. program steadily mounted. While in 1978 and 1979 the faculty could only just meet the quota of 330 students, by the late 1980s the number of applicants far exceeded the space available, to the extent that the minimum grade-point average required for admission was close to 3.0 (a B average). Many applicants were turned away, causing back-up problems in other faculties and departments. Moreover, many students, along with their parents, believed in an entitlement to an accessible bachelor of commerce program. The improving quality of the BCom., the new facilities in Scurfield Hall, the success of Dr Bob Schulz's student competition teams, the high pass rate of students on the Uniform Final Exam set by the Canadian Institute of Chartered Accountants, AACSB accreditation, and a visible and proactive dean all combined to make the bachelor of commerce a highly attractive degree. The word 'access' became widely recognized as the critical funding/enrolment issue for the faculty and the university at large.

In January 1989, the faculty proposed a significant expansion of the program.[40] Approved in 1990, the BCom. expansion, when it was fully implemented, provided an additional $3.9 million in operating funds as well as significant capital grants and a fourth floor for the south side of Scurfield Hall. The expansion also provided for an additional complex of classrooms in the adjacent new Professional Faculties Building. A new concentration in tourism was added, supported by the faculty's first 'co-op' program. The admission quota was raised from 330 students to 510, including 60 tourism students. Critically, the bachelor of commerce expansion proposal included a statement of intent by the faculty to bring forward a scheme for a doctoral program. This proposal, five years in the planning stages, was initially resisted by the government because it duplicated the program at the University of Alberta. The faculty now argued that recruiting the best professors to support the BCom. expansion could not be successful without a doctoral program.[41]

By 1991, the expanded BCom. was in place, a new fourth floor of Scurfield Hall was open, and the faculty was nearing completion of a major recruiting effort. From a full-time faculty equivalent (FTE) complement of approximately 70 before the introduction of the new MBA program in 1986, the faculty had grown to an FTE of 134 in 1991 (see figure 7.3). Most of the recruiting effort concentrated on younger colleagues with a strong potential for research. Along with the approval of the PhD program in 1990, a new generation of faculty promised a much stronger orientation towards research.

Through the 1980s Dean Maher continued his efforts to raise funds from the private sector. Particularly notable was the campaign to establish a chair and a program in insurance and risk management. A cam-

Figure 7.3   Faculty of Management full-time equivalent academic staff

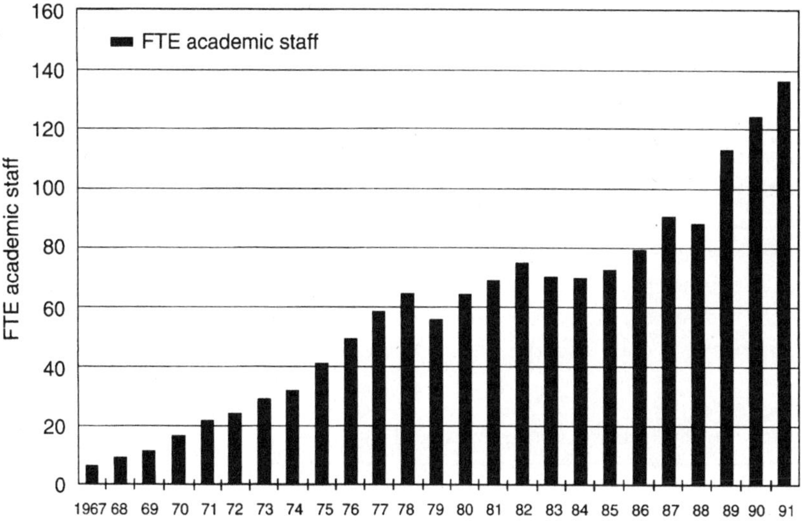

Source: University of Calgary Fact Books, 1996, 1995, 1994, 1989, 1985, 1982, 1978, 1975, 1972.

Notes: FTE academic staff are as 31 December.

paign led by the dean and Mr Tony Thibaudeau and the insurance industry leaders raised over $800,000 to support an endowment. These funds were double matched by the Province of Alberta, and by 1991 the total endowment came to $2.4 million. The first students were admitted to the program in the fall of 1991.[42]

Dean Maher's directive in 1981, 'It's time for growth,' had been fulfilled. The faculty was now entering a new period with significantly different challenges. As a full-service business school, with 'bricks and mortar,' an adequate operating budget, and a full complement of programs, the faculty's objectives for the next five to ten years were more ambiguous. The Management Advisory Council, led by strategy chair Don Heasman, was concerned that the current, more academically qualified, students might lack leadership abilities and 'street smarts.' MAC wanted to see a more aggressive, competitive school. Dean Maher expressed concern about the future, challenging academics to greater relevance in research in an article published in the *Canadian*

Journal of Administrative Sciences.[43] At the same time, a new generation of faculty were emphasizing research and scholarship, new instructional methods, keeping pace with technology and greater diversity among faculty and students. The AACSB-sponsored study *Management Education and Development* by Porter and McKibbin stated that 'more diversity of mission (but not of quality) is vital' for university-based management education and that 'soft skills,' lifelong learning, and globalization were to be some of the new challenges.[44] Clearly, the position of the Management Advisory Council, as well as the faculty, was that it was time for movement towards a position of leadership in management education and research. Another extensive planning process involving the MAC and the faculty established 'Leadership in a Changing World' as a new mission (see exhibit 3).[45]

EXHIBIT 3
Mission of the Faculty of Management, 1991

Leadership in a Changing World

The mission of the Faculty of Management at the University of Calgary is to be internationally recognized as a leader in management education and research. Our goals are:

• to instill in our students qualities of leadership and knowledge of the practice of management
• to be a leading contributor to the advancement of management practice through applied research
• to recruit and develop outstanding faculty who are committed to teaching and scholarship and who are recognized for the significance of their work
• to be a leader in planning and the development of facilities for management education supported by state-of-the-art information technology

---

An emphasis on attracting and retaining faculty, as well as developing facilities, was consistent with the 1980s. However, words like 'changing world,' 'developing leadership skills,' 'scholarship,' and 'research,' as well as 'information technology,' heralded a substantial change to a more complex environment. Significantly, however, the mission of the faculty was still focused on the 'practice of management' and founded upon a 'dynamic relationship with our community.' On his appointment to a third term as dean, Maher stated, 'It's vital that we don't sit back and relax now that we've been successful in reaching many of our earlier goals. During 1990, the faculty worked with the long-range planning subcommittee of the Management Advisory Council to develop a new mission statement and a plan of strategic objectives to take the faculty into the twenty-first century.'[46]

Epilogue

The post-1991 era presented greater challenges for Calgary's Faculty of Management than had been anticipated. Most significantly, owing to fiscal restraint, a downsizing of the university's operating grant from the provincial government by approximately 20 per cent over a three-year period was to arrest the growth in the faculty's operating expenses and FTE academic staff. Nevertheless, in spite of a forced reduction in the size of the academic staff and the operating budget, enrolments were maintained and both the expanded BCom. and the PhD programs were successfully implemented. But in 1991 the faculty was placed under 'continuing review' by AACSB because of the deployment of PhD qualified faculty across all programs and concerns about the research output. However, with some adjustments, and a strong affirmation to support research in the new strategic plan, the faculty was successfully re-accredited in 1992.

There were also some important new developments. Research productivity, as measured by journal publications and successful grant applications, substantially increased, thereby fulfilling commitments to the AACSB and improving the general reputation for scholarship.[47] The full-time MBA program was completely redesigned to focus on enterprise development, including an integrated modular teaching format and a 'clinic' where students were assigned to work with emerging and successful venture development firms. This fulfilled a long-time promise to developing entrepreneurial education in the MBA program. A full-cost recovery Executive MBA program was introduced jointly with the Faculty of Business at the University of Alberta in 1995, and an MBA in Poland was initiated in cooperation with the Warsaw School of Economics. A bachelor of hotel and resort management program was introduced in cooperation with the Southern Alberta Institute of Technology. The faculty increasingly emphasized partnerships, private sources of funding, and a need to focus on strategic advantages in a more competitive marketplace for management education.

Twenty-five years after its establishment in 1967, the Faculty of Management had made significant progress and clearly ranked among the major teaching and research business schools in Canada. Not only was the faculty 'full service' in the sense of offering a complete array of management programs, it had an outstanding building, a dynamic new academic staff, and state-of-the-art technology. Moreover, it had developed unique expertise in strategic areas including new-venture development, tourism, insurance and risk management, and energy management. Nevertheless, the important constants remained. These included a professional program based on a liberal education, adherence to quality, especially the standards of AACSB, a supportive relationship with the business community, and a commitment to planning or 'development by design.' Ralph Scurfield's vision when he donated funding for the building in 1981 had, for the moment, been fulfilled.

> It is our hope that this gift will be the seed from which a school of excellence will grow. Obviously the provision of physical facilities will not do that. It will require an increased number of highly qualified professors and it will require able and dedicated students. It is our hope that the business community in Calgary and Southern Alberta will consider joining us in our mutual goal to build one of the top business schools in North America.[48]

APPENDIX

University of Calgary Faculty of Management chronology, 1945–1991

1945	The Calgary Normal School becomes the southern extension of the University of Alberta's Faculty of Education.
1953	The first year of the bachelor of commerce degree is introduced at Calgary. Students transfer to the University of Alberta for completion of program.
1957	The Calgary branch of the University of Alberta becomes the University of Alberta, Calgary (UAC).
1961	The second year of the BCom. is introduced; students transfer to the University of Alberta for final two years.
1966	An autonomous University of Calgary comes into existence on 1 July.
1967	General Faculty Council at the University of Calgary approves the establishment of a Faculty of Commerce (later Business) by a margin of one vote. Dr James M.A. Robinson appointed as the first dean of the

Faculty of Business. GFC approves the faculty's Statement of Objectives and new four-year curriculum for the BCom.

1972 Dr Edmund Sugars is appointed acting dean.

1973 Dr Stephen B. Peitchinis is appointed dean.

1974 A Business Advisory Council is established. The undergraduate program is reorganized around two core areas: accounting and organization management.

1975 Master of Management Studies (MMS) is introduced as a part-time program. Dr George S. Lane is appointed acting dean (appointed dean in 1976). Faculty is restructured on a program and area basis. Offices of Research and Publications, and Alumni and Community Relations are established.

1976 Statement of Goals and Objectives is approved by Faculty of Business Council.

1977 The bachelor of commerce program is converted to the 'two plus two format' (two years qualifying before admission to the faculty); a quota is introduced, limiting the intake at third year to 330 students. A 'Management & Society' minor program is introduced to serve students of other faculties. The Management Resource Centre and Career Development Office are established.

1978 Name of faculty is changed to Faculty of Management.

1979 Calgary Chamber of Commerce and the Management Advisory Council present a study, 'Requirements for Postgraduate Management Programs at the University of Calgary,' by Foster Research (Foster report). Report of the presidential task force to review the Faculty of Management (the Gillmor report). A student team coached by Dr Bob Schulz is entered in the Intercollegiate Business Competition at Queen's University, initiating the faculty's active involvement in student competitions. The faculty is admitted to partnership in the Banff School of Advanced Management (BSAM).

1981 President Norman Wagner announces that Mr Ralph Scurfield and his family have donated $4 million and NuWest Development another $4 million for the construction of a new building for the Faculty of Management (to be matched by the provincial government). Mr Klaus Springer, chairman of the board of Carma Developers pledges $400,000 to establish the Carma Chair in Business. The MMS designation is changed to MBA. First special-case PhD student is admitted. Dr P. Michael Maher is appointed dean of the Faculty of Management.

1982 Alberta Energy Corporation establishes the AEC Summer Fellowship program to assist with the recruiting and retention of superior teachers and researchers.

1983   The faculty's first executive development program is launched at Chateau Lake Louise.

1984   Associates program is formed, with 52 members.

1984   Future Fund campaign is launched, with target of $4.8 million to provide support to be matched by the provincial government. Donors are to be recognized in Scurfield Hall.

1985   Faculty receives accreditation for BCom. and MBA programs from American Assembly of Collegiate Schools of Business (AACSB). Petroleum Land Management program established, with financial support from the Canadian Association of Petroleum Land Management and oil and gas companies. New Venture program established focusing on entrepreneurship and venture development.

1986   Faculty of Management Council approves a new Development Plan, emphasizing a focus on 'management practice.' A 'full-time day-time' MBA program is established with provincial funding. Scurfield Hall is officially opened on 7 April by the Honourable Dave Russell, minister of advanced education. Dr P. Michael Maher is reappointed to a second term as dean.

1988   The Future Fund endowment exceeds $12 million.

1990   BCom. expansion is approved, raising the quota from 330 students a year to 510; a new concentration in tourism is to be introduced; a PhD program is approved. As part of the expansion, funding is provided by the Government of Alberta to add a fourth floor to the south-west side of Scurfield Hall.

1991   Endowment of $2.4 million is established to support a chair in insurance and risk management. Major recruiting effort is undertaken to expand the faculty to 100 full-time positions. A new mission and strategic plan are adopted emphasizing leadership, the practice of management, and applied research. Dr P. Michael Maher is reappointed to a third term as dean

---

NOTES

1 Adapted from T.J. Black, 'The History of the Faculty of Management,' May 1978 (unpublished internal document).

2 *Minutes*, Academic Planning Committee #8, 7 December 1966.

3 *Minutes*, 12th meeting of General Faculty Council, 11 May 1967.

4 R.A. Gordon and J.E. Howell, *Higher Education for Business* (New York: Columbia University Press, 1959).
5 F.C. Pierson, *The Education of American Businessmen* (New York: McGraw-Hill, 1959).
6 Interview with Dr James Robinson, 19 February 1997.
7 *Minutes*, 18th meeting of General Faculty Council, 14 December 1967.
8 *The Budgeting Needs of the Faculty of Business*, table IV, p. 10 (undated).
9 Memo from Dean J. Robinson to Mr J.A. Hamilton, Controller, 18 April 1972.
10 *1973–74 Annual Report*, Faculty of Business, 7.
11 Meeting with Dr W. Long, 25 June 1997.
12 Stephen Cook, 'Deans Falling by U of C Wayside,' *The Albertan*, 10 April 1975.
13 H.M. Vollmer and D.L. Mills, eds, *Professionalization* (Englewood Cliffs, NJ: Prentice-Hall, 1966).
14 George Lane, 'From the Dean,' *Network*, June, 1981.
15 *Financial Times*, 25 October 1976.
16 *Faculty of Management AACSB Self Study Report* 1, 31 July 1984.
17 *The Business Faculty, Statement of Goals and Objectives*, 5 March 1976.
18 Foster Research, *Requirements for Postgraduate Management Programs at the University of Calgary*, January 1979.
19 *Minutes*, Calgary chamber of commerce.
20 D. Gillmor et al., *Report of the Presidential Task Force to Review the Faculty of Management*, May 1979.
21 *Response to the Report of the Presidential Task Force to Review the Faculty of Management*, November 1979.
22 L. Bruton et al., *Presidential Drafting Committee: Faculty of Management*, 11 January 1980, 2–3.
23 Ibid., 4–5.
24 *Minutes*, 190th meeting of the Executive Committee of General Faculties Council, 29 January 1980.
25 Penny Williams, 'Bargaining for a Super Business School: Does the One Hand Know What the Other Is Doing?' *Calgary*, June 1979, 29.
26 Ibid., 30.
27 *A Proposal for the Enhancement of the Faculty of Management*, 15 July 1980.
28 J. Miller, 'Management Dean Sees Challenges Ahead,' *Network*, December 1981.
29 Ibid.
30 *Minutes*, 225th meeting of GFC, 25 March 1982, item 225.4.1.
31 D.E. Berghofer, *Management Education and Executive Development in Alberta: Report of the Management Education Task Force*, 24 February 1984.

32 S. Hamer, ed., *The Associates: Partners in Management Education* [U. of Calgary], Fall 1990.

33 *The Future Fund, Invest in Tomorrow's Managers Today,* Autumn 1984.

34 *The Future Fund, A Report to Donors,* 1988.

35 *Proposal for a Full-time, Day-time MBA Program.*

36 J.L. Chrisman, *Economic Benefits Provided to the Province of Alberta by the Faculty of the University of Calgary,* University of Calgary, September 1994, 28–29.

37 *AACSB Self-Study Report,* 1984.

38 J. Ramsay, 'Scurfield Hall ... Not Just Another Pretty Space,' *Network,* June 1986, pp. 2, 3.

39 *Faculty of Management Development Plan (1986–1998);* approved by Faculty of Management Council.

40 *Proposal for the Expansion of the Bachelor of Commerce Program,* January 1989.

41 Ibid., 2.

42 D. Damov, 'A Dream Coming True,' *Network,* October, 1991, 36–9.

43 P.M. Maher, 'Business School Research: Academics Should Be Concerned,' *CJAS* 7 (1990), 16–20.

44 L.W. Porter and Lawrence E. McKibbin, *Management Education and Development: Drift or Thrust into the 21st Century?* (New York: McGraw-Hill, 1988), 314–31.

45 *Faculty of Management Strategic Plan,* 1991.

46 'Congratulations, Mike!' *Network,* October 1991.

47 M. Munro, *Research Round-Up,* 27 November 1995.

48 A. Gupta and E Mayes, 'An Evening with the Scurfields,' *Network,* January 1981, p. 5.

8

Business Studies at Saint Mary's University: Progress with a Human Touch

HAROLD J. OGDEN and CATHY DRISCOLL

Saint Mary's University, in Halifax, Nova Scotia, is rooted in the historical traditions and teachings of the de La Salle Brothers, the Irish Christian Brothers, and, more recently, the Jesuit order. A tradition of Christian social concern has influenced the university's relationship with the local community over the years. This chapter traces the evolution of commerce studies at Saint Mary's University, describing it in both the context of its historical traditions and the development of business schools elsewhere in the country.[1]

History of Saint Mary's University

Originally, in 1802, the mission of the founder, Reverend Edmund Burke, was to offer the Irish Catholics of Halifax a chance to attend college or the seminary.[2] In the early nineteenth century, legal restrictions prohibited any school from receiving provincial government support unless it was founded by the Church of England.[3] These legal restrictions, along with financial pressures, prevented Saint Mary's from opening until 1818, when it was established as a school for boys.

A mission of giving the underprivileged a chance at education has permeated much of the history of Saint Mary's. The university's history has also been characterized by a lack of means and a campaign for wider recognition and academic stature. For most of the nineteenth century Saint Mary's College was financially supported and administered by the Catholic Archdiocese of Halifax. The college / high school changed sites four times during these years. Difficulties in being able to afford suitable professors prevented any real development of the school until the middle of the century. College-level courses were first taught in 1840,[4] and the college and high school were formally separated in 1852, when degree-conferring status was made permanent.[5] Further financial pressures forced the university to close from 1881 to 1903. Although Saint Mary's was able to reopen in 1903, a lack of funding forced it to resort to extreme lengths to reduce costs. The college had to let many of the laymen go, and as Shook has pointed out, in 1905 Mr Charles, the president, 'had himself to prepare lectures in commerce for which he prepared himself by enrolling simultaneously in an evening course given elsewhere in the city.'[6]

Under the direction of the Irish Christian Brothers, Saint Mary's worked hard at establishing a reputation as a university college. '[The college] had always been "embedded in a high school" and had received little recognition from established universities.'[7] In 1940, the Irish Christian Brothers withdrew, and the Jesuits took over the administration of the university. Money donated from the estate of Patrick Power, a prosperous Haligonian businessman, helped alleviate some of the funding problems. The university moved from Quinpool Road to its present location on Robie Street, with the construction of the McNally Building beginning in 1951.[8] The college finally gained university status in 1952, and in 1963 the Saint Mary's high school was phased out.[9]

The Beginnings of Commerce Studies

One of Saint Mary's first commerce faculty members, Gerrard Jackman,[10] reflected at the time on the events of the past century and noted that 'it was not really until the turn of the century that the transaction of business was moving from the simple state to the highly complicated mechanism of our day.' Jackman pointed out that some of these changes included the use of economics in everyday life, and the recognition that banking, advertising, and law had roles to play in the conduct of business. According to Jackman, 'the niche of the university trained man can only be an ever-increasingly important one.'

Table 8.1 shows the timing of a number of events in the development of business studies at Saint Mary's. The university began offering commercial courses after its reopening in 1903. The 1907 calendar listed courses in the business skills of bookkeeping, spelling and penmanship, business English, shorthand, and typewriting. Later, in 1917, a higher level commercial diploma was offered that incorporated similar courses.

TABLE 8.1

Chronology of events in the development of business studies at Saint Mary's

1907	Earliest calendar found included a list of commercial courses
1917	Higher-level commercial diploma offered
1933	First commerce diploma courses offered
1936	First bachelor of commerce graduates, including Harold Beazley
1940	Jesuits take over from the Irish Christian Brothers
1945	Commerce diploma dropped
1946	Faculty of Commerce formed
1952	Saint Mary's College changed to Saint Mary's University
1960	Business administration area formed
1968	Women admitted to the university
1970	Saint Mary's becomes a public university
1972	Harold Beazley's term as dean ended
1974	MBA program started
1978	The department of business administration reorganized into departments of separate functional areas
1990	EMBA program started
1993	Faculty of Commerce adopts the name of Frank H. Sobey

The first of what might be considered modern business studies took the form of an economics course, 'The Relation of Economics to Other Subjects,' that was first offered in 1923 as part of a series of social-sciences subjects to be taken in the bachelor of arts degree program. During the following ten years, several other economics courses were introduced as the discipline developed in the social sciences. Economics departments at other universities and colleges often developed as a separate faculty, independent of the business studies area.[11] At Saint Mary's, however, economics was closely associated with commerce as soon as the Department of Commerce was formed and has remained so since becoming a department in the Faculty of Commerce when that faculty was formed in 1946.[12]

The first Saint Mary's commerce courses, as such, were offered in 1933 as part of a diploma program that included courses in accountancy, economics, commercial geography, political science, and commercial law, as well as languages and humanities. A year later, the diploma program was expanded into a bachelor of commerce degree program. During 1937, Mr Harold Beazley completed one of the first three commerce degrees granted by Saint Mary's, winning two medals for academic achievement. That autumn, he was hired as a faculty member and head of the commerce department, a position he held in one form or another for most of his professional life.

The influence of the Jesuits can be seen through the early years of the program. The Jesuit quest has been for a general, humanistic education open to everyone. According to LaFarge, 'The Jesuit believes that the four years of college should primarily be not in order to acquire a given number of isolated facts, not merely to obtain vocational skills as a preparation for a lucrative position in later life. His program is the fitting of man for life by a distinctive cultural foundation of intelligence, self-expression, observation, and reasoning power.'[13] The academic calendars of the time go beyond simply listing courses and programs to stress the need and expectation for the moral and physical development of students. Courses such as 'Economics in Society' and 'The Relation of Economics to Other Subjects' reflect how the humanistic tradition influenced the curriculum during this period.

The issue of rigour versus relevance has been argued in business programs for many years. Jones and McLean[14] have recognized that even at the time of their early development, business schools tended to organize themselves along a vocational/theory dimension and have cited examples of extreme positions. Saint Mary's appeared to take a position in the middle, but tended towards the vocational. Initially, commerce studies at Saint Mary's were designed 'for students who desire the advantage of a higher education but who look forward to commerce as a professional career.'[15] The emphasis on religious, moral, and physical development suggested a broad liberal education approach. The curriculum, however, tended to focus on the skills and tools needed in business. Emphasis was give to topics such as accounting, tax, and finance. The 1937 curriculum included five courses in economics, four in accounting, and one each in business math, business organization, political science, and the history of money. In 1945, as standards continued to rise, the commerce diploma was no longer offered. All students were now enroled in the bachelor of commerce program.

A Broader Perspective

When business schools in North America underwent major changes in the 1960s, Saint Mary's was no exception. Many business programs were criticized for being too vocational and, on the recommendations of the Ford and Carnegie Foundation reports of 1959, which proposed 'a better balance between a liberal and vocational emphasis in business education,' many schools attempted to broaden their curricula.[16] A change in the orientation of commerce studies at Saint Mary's is apparent in the calendars of the time. For example, the 1956 calendar stated that 'a broad technical training [was] of paramount significance in the field of competitive business.' By 1961, however, there was no mention of technical training and the curriculum had broadened considerably. During 1960 the business administration area was formed, offering courses in marketing, finance, production, human relations, and policy. Other courses in the faculty included five in accounting and eight in economics. These, by 1970, had increased to twenty-three courses in business administration, ten in accounting, and seventeen in economics.

Some, however, have noted a less positive result of these reports. For example, Locke observed how the 'scientizing' of management studies was becoming the new paradigm.[17] Behrman and Levin pointed out that, after these reports were published, there was a sudden growth in the influence of behavioural science, statistics, and applied mathematics in the area of business studies.[18] In the business administration area at Saint Mary's a more scientific orientation could be seen in such new courses as linear and dynamic programming, organizational behaviour with an emphasis on behavioural science, and marketing research, which stressed scientific measurement. The program structure also changed over this period. Beginning in 1957, students were given the opportunity to declare a major field of study in either accounting or economics. By 1963, all students were required to declare a major field in either accounting, economics, or the newly offered area of business administration.

Saint Mary's reputation for a high-quality undergraduate commerce program grew during this period. Several factors contributed to this trend, including the university's development of an accounting program and a number of innovative new courses in the area of business administration. In 1955, a marketing course based on case analysis was added through the economics department. During the 1960s, 'Business and Its Environment,' which examined social issues, was offered.[19] As early as 1964, management instruction included a computer simulation game running on what was the first electronic, digital computer in Atlantic Canada.

During the 1950s the faculty began to serve broader markets, introducing evening and part-time courses. An evening division was created to provide upgrading for teachers with degrees; in the area of business studies a number of commerce courses were offered.[20] Part-time studies expanded in the 1960s with initiatives such as the Canadian Industrial Management program, which was successful from the start, attracting personnel from the military, government, and larger companies in the area.[21]

Periods of Growth

The number and size of institutions of higher learning, and business schools in particular, grew considerably from the 1960s to the 1980s in North America. The number of students who graduated from the St Mary's commerce program increased more than tenfold across this period. There were two periods of rapid growth in enrolments at Saint Mary's and its business programs. One was during the late 1960s and early 1970s, the other in the middle-to-late 1980s. In the first period, the number of business-school degrees awarded increased by more than five times, while total degrees from the university jumped more than threefold. It was observed that 'Saint Mary's had the largest full-time increase of any university in the Atlantic provinces for each of the last four years.'[22] Growth during this period could have been even greater but for a general shortage of qualified faculty at the time.[23] This was a period of growth in other ways for Saint Mary's as well. Women were first admitted to Saint Mary's as full-time students in 1968, but few at first studied commerce. In 1970, Saint Mary's became a public university with a senate and a board of governors. According to academic vice-president Hugh Gillis, the change in 1970 from a private to a public institution required Saint Mary's to move beyond its historic traditions and purpose, as 'the change in status from a private to a public institution has meant an inevitable change in the stakeholders with which the university is involved and, implicitly, in the responses which the university should make to the needs and aspirations of these stakeholders.'[24] In 1973, Saint Mary's was one of the first universities in Canada to allow mature admission, whereby work experience and community involvement would be considered for admission in lieu of a high school diploma.[25] The construction of the Loyola Building, the Patrick Power Library, and residence buildings began to accommodate the growth in enrolment.

In the second upturn, during the 1980s, school officials credited enrolment increases to poorer economic times during which students would choose a local university to save money.[26] The physical education complex, named 'The Tower,' was built around this time, freeing teaching room in the McNally building.

Overall, the rate of increase in the number of business degrees awarded has exceeded the overall rate of growth in the school. The number of commerce degrees as a proportion of the total number of degrees awarded has stabilized between 30 and 35 per cent. This is well above the average in North America of 13 per cent.[27] According to Sam Jopling, a former dean,[28] the growth of commerce studies at the university may be attributable to several factors. First, the relatively small, cohesive faculty may have resulted in more of a tendency to accept commerce as a legitimate area of study and not limit its growth. Also, much of the growth may be credited to the first dean, Harold Beazley, whose outstanding leadership resulted in a well-recognized accounting program and a solid reputation in business studies in general.

Leadership

One figure stands out in the leadership of the Saint Mary's business studies. Harold G. (Babe) Beazley dedicated most of his life to the institution. As well as being Saint Mary's first commerce graduate, Beazley became the first head of the commerce department and, later, dean of the faculty. In a testimonial in 1990, one year after Beazley's death, David Hope credited him with building the accounting program at Saint Mary's. Paul Cormier, a former student and colleague of Beazley over the years, said that 'there would not be any commerce faculty at all if it weren't for him.'[29] Under his leadership, the first separate faculty of business in Atlantic Canada was developed. He was a founding member of the Association of Deans of Canadian Schools of Business and was active in the American Assembly of Collegiate Schools of Business.

Personally, Beazley was described as pleasant, friendly, likeable, and unassuming, with a tremendous devotion and loyalty to Saint Mary's. He was observed to have provided vision and continuity of leadership during his tenure, having earned the confidence of the faculty and senate as well as the Jesuit fathers, which included the university's presidents.[30] Initially, Beasley developed the accounting program. During the late 1960s and early 1970s, the faculty grew and the course offerings were broadened by Beazley to include much of what is seen in the calendar of today.[31] His contribution to this growth was characterized by hiring good people, convincing them that Saint Mary's could be the best, encouraging them to do their best, and supporting new initia-

TABLE 8.2
Leadership of the Saint Mary's Faculty of Commerce

Harold Beazley	
Head of dept.	1936–40
Dean	1953–72
Dennis Connelly	1972–76
Sam Jopling	1976–83
Frederick C. Miner	1983–88
Colin Dodds	1988–92
Paul Dixon (acting)	1992–94
A. Scott Carson	1994–96
Paul Dixon	1996–

tives. Harold Beazley was awarded an honorary DLitt. degree and was appointed dean emeritus at the end of his term. When he retired from full-time teaching in 1981, he was appointed professor emeritus.[32] After 49 years of service to Saint Mary's, including several more years of part-time teaching, he officially retired in 1985. The subsequent leadership of the faculty is outlined in table 8.2.

Reorganization

Commerce became a faculty at St Mary's in 1946 with two departments, accounting and economics. The business administration area was added to the accounting department in 1960. With the surge in interest in business studies during the late 1960s and early 1970s, courses were added and faculty hired. However, the department became too large to manage efficiently, as it grew to nineteen faculty members and fifty-two courses across different areas. For several years, various restructuring proposals were examined, and in 1978 the entire faculty was reorganized into the five departments that exist today: accounting, economics, management, marketing, and finance and management science (the last two were combined because of their small size and common quantitative orientation).

MBA Program

The demand for graduate management education also grew throughout the 1960s and 1970s. While Saint Mary's received provincial approval to offer an MBA degree in 1968,[33] it began to supply the degree only in

1974, after the program's development during Dennis Connelly's term as dean. Initially, a proposal was examined to offer the program jointly with Dalhousie, but a final agreement was never made and Saint Mary's started its own initiative.[34] In the program, there were two general options a student could take. If interested in general management, a candidate might pursue a general program of study or, alternatively, specialize in one of several functional areas. The first sixteen MBA degrees were awarded in 1976; in 1996, Saint Mary's awarded ninety-five degrees. Originally, the Saint Mary's MBA was directed towards science, engineering, and liberal arts students who wanted to complement their education with a business degree. By 1996, however, approximately 35 per cent of the students had business undergraduate degrees. The Saint Mary's MBA tends to cater to local demand, with 50 per cent of the students completing their degree on a part-time basis.

In the mid-1980s, North American MBA programs were criticized for producing technical specialists rather than the leaders needed by business.[35] Many business schools in North America have overhauled their traditional MBA offerings. The emphasis has moved to people-oriented skills, management under uncertainty, and conflict management, with a shift away from traditional numbers-oriented, discipline-based programs.[36] However, some schools have been more hesitant to change.[37] Saint Mary's, along with other schools, has placed increased emphasis on the study of strategic management as an integrated approach to studying business.

As MBA degrees increasingly became 'commodities,' schools have tried to differentiate by specialization or manner of delivery.[38] A focus on senior management is one way to differentiate. Efforts to offer education to senior managers are not new. Silver,[39] for example, has reported on weekend MBA programs for executives. In 1953, Saint Mary's was a sponsor of the Atlantic Summer School for Advanced Business Administration. While not a graduate-level course, this five-week program, sponsored jointly by twelve Atlantic universities, was provided for senior executives.

Since this time, executive MBA programs, wherein senior business people are given the chance to earn their degrees by studying on a concentrated schedule, have grown in popularity. The Saint Mary's EMBA was launched during 1990 under the direction of Hermann Schwind. Meeting Fridays and Saturdays on alternate weeks, students completed four courses in each of the four semesters in the program. The first EMBA class of twenty-three graduated in 1992. Since then, annual enrolment has ranged from seventeen to twenty-four candidates. With such small numbers, the students enjoy close personal contact with the professors, and instructors are able to tailor material to their needs and expectations.

Rationalization

While attracting considerable attention in the press recently, the idea of combining universities in the Atlantic provinces has been around for a long while. Governments and policy makers have long been concerned about inefficiencies in the system of higher education and have proposed various solutions over the years. The earliest effort in this direction was in 1876, when the provincial government formed the University of Halifax, which consisted of an affiliation of a number of extant institutions of higher learning.[40] This effort did not last long, because the government stopped making university grants, and Saint Mary's closed in 1881 for twenty-two years. In 1921, the Carnegie Foundation offered a million dollars to federate Atlantic Canada's colleges with Dalhousie.[41] The offer was never accepted by the parties involved.

The Catholic church recognized a need to amalgamate the universities as well. In 1963, it asked Laurence Shook to analyse Catholic education in Halifax. He recommended a federation of the Catholic institutions in Halifax to form the University of Halifax. A number of issues were examined, but a resolution was not found.[42] Rationalization of university faculties and services was again examined during 1979, when Saint Mary's sponsored a forum on the future of smaller universities.[43] In 1992, in a context of severe government cutbacks, the provincial government stepped up efforts in this direction through the Nova Scotia Council on Higher Education. The strength of business programs at Saint Mary's was recognized at the end of this round of efforts during the spring of 1996, when the provincial government presented a plan for higher education in Nova Scotia.[44] In this plan, the university would assume a 'leadership role' in business education in the province, which would include the construction of a new building for the faculty and the establishment of a PhD program.

Other Recent Developments

In 1993, the business school was renamed the 'Frank H. Sobey Faculty of Commerce' in honour of a prominent Nova Scotia food retailer and developer. An advisory board made up of twenty-one leading business professionals throughout Canada was created in 1994 to advise the dean. Concentrations in global studies and entrepreneurship have been added to deal with the changing needs of today's students. Newly developed programs have been introduced at the MBA level, including an accounting 'co-op' program and specialist programs in human resource management / industrial relations, small business and entrepreneurship, and fiscal and financial studies.

Conclusion

Saint Mary's University has grown from a small, combined high school / college to a leading public university in Atlantic Canada. Today, it   has the largest business faculty in Atlantic Canada with over sixty full-time professors. Business studies have played, and will continue to play, an important part in the growth and development of the university. The development of commerce studies resulted both from changing demands and forces in business education and the institution's Catholic history. Although the university has had autonomy from archdiocesan control since 1970, the Jesuits continued to have both a direct and indirect influence on administration and the overall culture of the school. The last Jesuit faculty member, for example, retired only in 1996 and the new university chaplain is a member of the Jesuit order.

The area of business studies has developed in much the same way as have many business schools in the country. What seems to set the faculty apart is a humanistic approach. This was acknowledged in the university's 1983 submission to the Nova Scotia commission on post-secondary education. 'In our commerce program, for example, the intention is not to graduate an accountant or marketing analyst so narrowly trained that he or she cannot reflect sensibly on larger issues of social importance, but instead to root professional expertise in a broad humanistic context.' Also, a tradition of outreach to the local community through the development of continuing education and part-time programs and a focus on non-traditional students illustrates the concern with providing educational opportunities to everyone. Finally, there is a closeness of faculty to the students that is not found in some schools. To quote Dr Ken Ozmon, the current president of the university, 'There is a tradition at Saint Mary's of small classes and professors who know each student by name; it is a small university and we intend to maintain that quality of education.'[45]

NOTES

1 The authors wish to thank Wendy Bullerwell and Heather Thompson, both of Saint Mary's University, for their assistance. The research for this paper was supported with a Saint Mary's Senate Research Grant.
2 L.K. Shook, *Catholic Post-Secondary Education in English-Speaking Canada: A History* (Toronto: UTP, 1971).
3 'Forty years service: AMDG,' *Saint Mary's Times* 10:4 (February 1981), 1.
4 Shook, *Catholic Post-Secondary Education.*
5 *Saint Mary's University Factbook, 1994–1995.*
6 Shook, *Catholic Post-Secondary Education,* 64.
7 Ibid., 66.
8 'Saint Mary's Celebrates 30 years at the Gorsebrook Campus,' *Saint Mary's Times* 11:2 (October 1981), 1.
9 Shook, *Catholic Post-Secondary Education.*
10 Gerrard J. Jackman, 'Why Commerce?' *The Collegian,* Halifax, Saint Mary's College, Graduation number, 1934.
11 R.R. Locke, *Management and Higher Education since 1940: The Influence of America and Japan on West Germany, Great Britain and France* (Cambridge: Cambridge University Press, 1989).
12 Saint Mary's College, *Calendar, 1946.*
13 J. LaFarge, *The Jesuits in Modern Times* (New York: American Press, 1928), 92.
14 D.G.B. Jones and P.A. McLean, 'Ahead of the Class – The Founding of Commerce at Queen's,' in B. Austin, ed., *ASAC Proceedings: Business History* 16:15 (1985), 79–85.
15 Saint Mary's College, *Calendar, 1940.*
16 B. Sharma and L. Steier, 'Management Education and Development in Canada: Past, Present and Future,' *CJAS* 7 (1990), 1–10.
17 Locke, *Management and Higher Education.*
18 J.N. Behrman and R.I. Levin, 'Are Business Schools Doing Their Job?' *HBR* 59 (January–February 1984), 140.
19 V. Baydar, former faculty member, interview, 2 May 1997.
20 K. Cleary (1997), secretary to the senate, interview, 1 May 1997.
21 Dennis Connelly, former dean of commerce, interview, 1 May 1997.
22 'What Makes Saint Mary's Run?' *Saint Mary's Times* 1:1 (March 1972), 1.
23 Connelly interview, 1 May 1997.
24 H. Gillis, 'Maroon and White,' *Saint Mary's Times* (October 1973), 7.
25 J. Sharpe, director of continuing education, interview, 24 April 1997.
26 'Enrolment Up Again,' *Saint Mary's Times* 15:1 (October 1985), 3.
27 Locke, *Management and Higher Education,* 161.

28 Sam Jopling, former dean of commerce, interview, 30 April 1997.
29 P. Cormier, former faculty member, interview, 8 May 1997.
30 Cormier interview, 24 April 1998.
31 Ibid.
32 K.L. Ozmon, 'Memorandum to All Faculty and Staff Re: Dr. Harold Beazley – Funeral Arrangements,' 23 October 1989.
33 Cleary interview, 1 May 1977.
34 Connelly, 1 May 1997.
35 Behrman and Levin, 'Are Business Schools,' 142.
36 S. Leith, J. Kovacheff, and C. Price, 'Re-engineering the MBA in Canada,' *CBR* 2:2 (1994), 32–5.
37 M.J. Cudd, J. King, and B. O'Hara, 'Assessment of the Nature and Status of the MBA Restructuring Trend,' *JEB*, September–October 1995, 44–8.
38 R. Wild, 'The Business School in a Busy World,' *MD* 33:9 (1995), 17–23.
39 G. Silver, 'Starting a Weekend MBA for Executives Program,' *CNV*, Autumn 1976, 13–15.
40 Shook, *Catholic Post-Secondary Education*, 62.
41 *Saint Mary's University Factbook, 1994–1995.*
42 Shook, *Catholic Post-Secondary Education*, 100.
43 'Forum on the Smaller University,' *Saint Mary's Times* 9:2 (October 1979), 3.
44 'Saint Mary's Wins Doctoral Program in Business,' *Chronicle-Herald* (Halifax), 5 April 1996, A2.
45 'Increase in Enrolment at Saint Mary's,' *Saint Mary's Times* 14:2 (October 1984), 1.

9

Tracking History and Strategy at Memorial's Faculty of Business

ROBERT W. SEXTY and GINA PECORE

The history of business/management education at Memorial University of Newfoundland is described and analysed here utilizing a tracking methodology and the strategy concept. A description of an organization's past should not only outline historical events, but also provide an analysis of those events. In order to accomplish the first of these objectives, this chapter describes the history by utilizing a 'tracking' method,[1] and explains this historical record by analysing it in terms of Mintzberg's definition of strategy as 'a pattern in a stream of decisions'[2] and his reference to the process as one of 'crafting strategy.'[3]

The Tracking Methodology

The 'tracking' methodology was developed by Mintzberg and his colleagues in a research project at McGill University between 1971 and 1984. The strategies of eleven diverse organizations were tracked over several decades, and the results were published in several sources. In the published studies, the steps involved in tracking are described as follows:

1 Data are collected and chronological lists and graphs are developed of the most important events or streams of actions for each organization. Examples of events include new product introductions, numbers of stores or branches, size of fleets, and profits. Related trends and events in the environment are recorded, as are available figures on performance.
2 The lists and graphs are examined to deduce the patterns in streams of decisions or actions referred to as strategies.

3 If feasible, graphical representations of the strategies are developed to identify whether there are distinct periods in their development, for example, periods of flux, major changes, or leaders. By analysing changes in all the strategies inferred, major turning points in the history of the organization are identified.

4 Interviews and in-depth reports are used to study key points of change in an organization's strategic history and to identify the underlying causes of the major changes. This step is a shift from the rather systematic analysis of tangible data to a more probing investigation of softer data.

5 The findings are studied to develop conclusions about the process of strategy formulation. The research team meets to analyse the data, focus on a set of major conceptual issues, and draw theoretical conclusions from the results.[4]

The published results of the research project did not include application of the methodology to educational institutions, although McGill University is mentioned as one of the organizations studied. There is no mention of a faculty or school of business having been a research subject. This paper will concentrate on steps 1 through 2. Universities, by their nature, usually document events through reports prepared by committees, task forces, faculties, and governance bodies. Thus, some of the material for step 4 is likely already available, but has not been incorporated into this paper. Some tentative conclusions are developed in this paper about strategy at Memorial's Faculty of Business, but they are based on the more systemic analysis of steps 1–2 rather than the in-depth investigation through steps 3, 4, and 5.

Types of Strategies

The McGill research project involving the tracking of strategies in various organizations was anchored in Mintzberg's three types of strategies as illustrated in figure 9.1. He makes a distinction between deliberate, unrealized, and emergent strategies. Deliberate strategies are realized as intended, while unrealized strategies are not realized as intended, and emergent strategies are realized in the absence of or despite intentions.[5] Thus, a realized strategy can be brought about deliberately or as a response to an evolving situation.

Mintzberg's views on planning are widely known and have recently

Figure 9.1 Types of strategies

received considerable attention.[6] It is not possible to summarize these views here, but some main points of his thinking will assist in understanding the history of strategy at Memorial's Faculty of Business. Mintzberg is concerned with the overemphasis and reliance on formal planning, which he believes is limiting and lacks vision. Though planning may stimulate actions, it is also likely to paralyse an organization in the status quo. He states that there are ways to create strategy other than by formal planning: visionary leadership that articulates the future; and learning organizations where leaders unleash the firm's dynamic capabilities. It is the tracking methodology and Mintzberg's views about strategy making that we have chosen to examine the history of the Memorial business faculty.

Memorial's Faculty of Business Administration

Commerce, or accounting, courses were initially taught at Memorial during the early 1950s, but the first candidates who received the degree of bachelor of commerce did not graduate until 1957. For the purpose of this study, that will be the initial year for a chronicle of the faculty. This section attempts to capture the stream of actions in the organization through graphic representations. The actions are presented in four categories: infrastructure, academic program development (or curriculum), enrolment, and performance indicators. Each will be elaborated upon.

Infrastructure

This category of actions will summarize the organizational arrangements existing in the organization over time. The actions identified are presented in figure 9.2 and include leadership, organizational status, number of faculty, physical accommodations, establishment of auxiliary units, and support staff. Some of these items require further explanation.

The unit experienced frequent changes in leadership during the years 1957 to 1975, but since then has had four directors/deans in twenty years (figure 9.2a). The unit evolved from a department within the Faculty of Arts to a separate faculty in 1981 (figure 9.2b) and has remained non-departmentalized since then. The faculty appointments include only tenure and tenure-track appointments (figure 9.2c), and exclude contractual and part-time appointments. The unit was housed in the Arts/Administration Building until 1974, and then experienced several moves until occupying its own building in 1979 which was expanded in 1987 (figure 9.2d). A fund-raising campaign to finance the furnishing of the renovated and expanded building was undertaken in 1987–88 and supported by forty-six local and national corporations.

Several auxiliary units have been established since 1973, beginning with the introduction of the Co-operative Education unit to the most recent in 1994, the Centre for International Business Studies (figure 9.2e). Between 1957 and 1975 support staff was modest, but increased substantially as programs and numbers of faculty increased (figure 9.2f, staff for auxiliary units not included except for co-operative education). The addition of specialized staff over the years is interesting to note: 1979, executive assistant to the dean; 1987, computer specialist with second staff added in 1991; 1988, media production technician; 1990, graphic artist; and 1995, information officer.

Academic Program Development

In figure 9.3, aspects of academic or curriculum development are presented. Figure 9.3a identifies the stream of actions that have occurred in the development of the business administration program. Major actions occurred in 1967 with the revision of the program's orientation from commerce or accounting to business administration, and in 1973 with the establishment of the first mandatory business undergraduate co-operative education program in Canada. This action was significant and has been a feature of Memorial's business faculty ever since. Figure 9.3b identifies some of the curricular innovations. Memorial was one of earliest Canadian business programs to introduce courses in business communications, 1971; business ethics, 1975 and 1978;

Figure 9.2 Infastructure

(a) Leadership – Heads/Directors/Deans

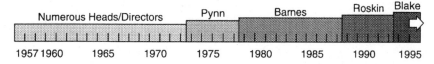

(b) Unit status in university

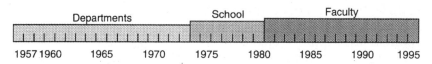

(c) Faculty appointments

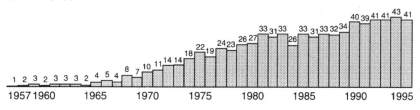

(d) Physical accommodations

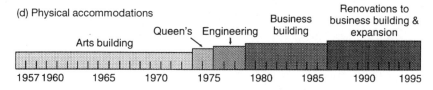

(e) Auxiliary units

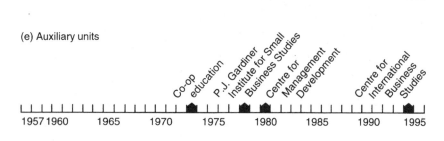

(f) Support staff

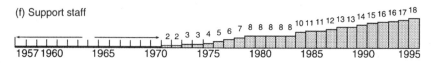

Figure 9.3 Academic program development

(a) Program development

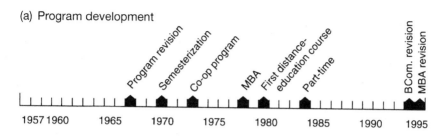

(b) Selected course innovation

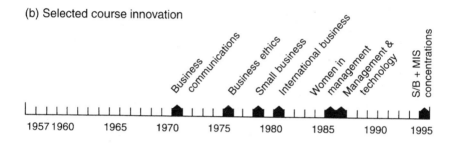

small business, 1978; international business, 1981; women in management, 1986; and management and technology, 1987.

Enrolment

In the operation of any educational institution, enrolments are important data. Figure 9.4 presents in graphic form enrolments in the undergraduate and graduate programs. Also significant are the proportions of full- versus part-time attendance. The enrolment drop in 1984 occurred as a result of the institution of grade 12 in Newfoundland schools.

Performance Indicators

The fourth category of actions attempts to measure the performance of the organization in various ways, including numbers of graduates, Associates Program revenues, operating expenditures, outreach initiatives, student competition wins, recognition awards, and research grants. Undergraduate and graduate degrees awarded are portrayed

Figure 9.4 Enrolment

(a) Undergraduate (full-time)

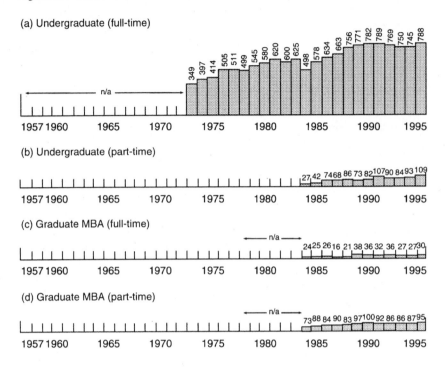

(b) Undergraduate (part-time)

(c) Graduate MBA (full-time)

(d) Graduate MBA (part-time)

in figures 9.5a and 9.5b. The number of BCom. degrees awarded has increased substantially. Data on operating expenditures (figure 9.5c) are only available at this time for the years since 1984. In the decade since then, expenditures have more than doubled. Several significant outreach initiatives are presented in figure 5d: the establishment of the Advisory Board and an Associates Program (1984), participation in student competitions, and an international program at Memorial's campus in the United Kingdom. One activity, corporate contributions, is presented in figure 9.5e.

Memorial's involvement in case and essay competitions is presented in figure 9.5f, where the total of first-, second-, and third-place winnings are charted. The availability of scholarships to students is another indication of performance, but data were not available. The placement of students in the co-operative program would have been another good performance indication, but again data were not available.

Figure 9.5 Performance indicators

(a) Undergraduate degree (BCom.)

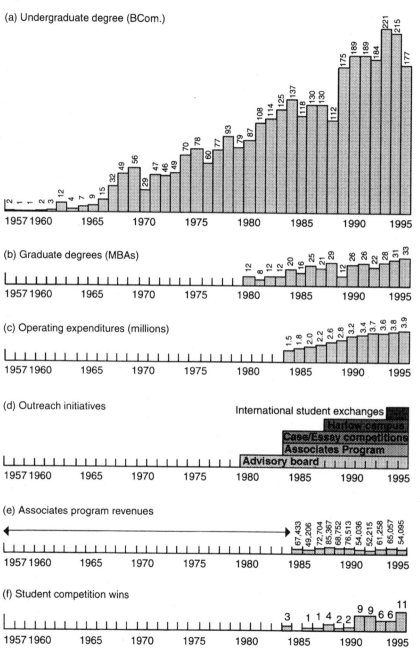

(b) Graduate degrees (MBAs)

(c) Operating expenditures (millions)

(d) Outreach initiatives

International student exchanges

Harlow campus

Case/Essay competitions

Associates Program

Advisory board

(e) Associates program revenues

(f) Student competition wins

Figure 9.5 (concluded)

(g) Recognition awards

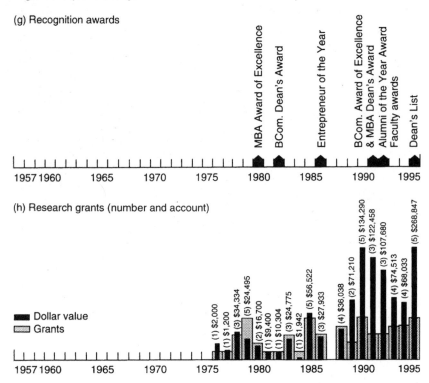

(h) Research grants (number and account)

Initiatives to recognize faculty, students, the business community, and alumni were started primarily in the 1980s and 1990s (figure 9.5g). One indication of faculty member research activities is portrayed in figure 9.5h, where the number and total amounts of research grants received are recorded. One faculty research performance indicator omitted is the scholarly activities and publishing record of faculty members. Insufficient information existed to compile these data in a reliable manner.

Limitations to Data and Approach

There are two limitations to the data and approach used here: the data is incomplete and, given the dry character of the descriptive statistics, there is an absence of qualitative insights. Some limitations to the data presented in figures 9.2 through 9.5 should be acknowledged. Despite the records maintained by the university, gaps existed in the data or they were not readily retrievable. Approaches to recording actions changed over time, making consistency in presentation difficult. Various types of data were maintained by academic year, while others were by calendar or fiscal years. Some information was obtained by interviews and on occasion it was not possible to verify facts and dates mentioned. The authors made an effort to present data as accurately as possible.

The data that has been presented is quantitative, and the history of a business faculty certainly would be enhanced if accompanied by stories or incidents gathered from oral history. There are several stories that have become legendary at Memorial's Faculty of Business, and in this context they serve to illustrate how the numerical presentation of this faculty's history could be enhanced by the consideration of oral history. The following, as organized by categories found in this paper, are examples of the faculty's most well-known stories.

Leadership. The leadership provided by an organization's director or dean influences its progress.

- In the 1980s, the director of the School of Business single-handedly converted the status of the organization from school to faculty. There was no input requested from, or consultation conducted with, any faculty members.
- Directors or deans of Memorial's Faculty of Business Administration have shown individual preferences for support faculty and have shaped the long-term structure of the support staff group. One introduced the position of research assistant, another the position of graphic artist, and most recently an information officer was added to the faculty.
- The limited influence of some of our deans and directors has, at times, been publicly demonstrated. In one instance, at the departure dinner for one dean, the dean of another faculty said in a videotaped message, 'Your Dean had six major battles with the Administration, and lost them all!'

Faculty turnover. With faculty turnover a problem, the recruitment of faculty was always a priority with directors and deans. These issues can be particularly difficult problems for universities that are geographically isolated from major metropolitan centres. Memorial's Faculty of

Business Administration, therefore, has had its share of 'characters.'

- One faculty member held another full-time university teaching position at an American university while employed at Memorial.
- Another held a teaching position and a full-time job in the business community.
- As support for his appointment renewal, one colleague presented over 1000 pages of materials, most of which were transparency overheads.
- Many faculty members author books, but one had a unique approach. He requested copies of all textbooks in his area. They were torn up and filed by topic, and the files later became the source of materials for this own books.
- In any faculty group, some never write any books, but spend a lot of time talking about it. The most noteworthy example at Memorial was a colleague who for decades was writing a book on 'love.' No one had the courage to ask how the topic related to business or management.

Physical accommodations. Physical accommodations played a role in the development of business education at Memorial. The faculty had about a twenty-year journey to the present location in its own building.

- In the early days, the business professors were located in the Arts and Administration Building across from the departments of religious studies and philosophy. One professor of religion was pleased when a stock-market ticker tape was installed; he became a frequent reader. It was never established whether he did better or worse than the business professors at investing.
- From the Arts Building, the faculty moved to the Theology College, situated on the edge of campus. The influence of religion was not obvious on professors or students even though a chapel existed.
- The penultimate move was to scattered quarters in the newly constructed Engineering Building. The original proposal had most business professors accommodated in windowless rooms. Faculty members made it clear to the director that this was unsatisfactory and sent him back to renegotiate. Needless to say, there never has been a 'closeness' between the two faculties.

These stories add another dimension to the numerical data that this essay is based on. One story that Mintzberg would appreciate was the secretary in the earlier times of the faculty who practised fortune telling on a 'Ouija' board. The personal fortunes, or misfortunes, of faculty members were predicted, but not those of the faculty itself. It was a missed opportunity, for what better way was there to provide a vision of the future and to create strategy? The stories presented illustrate the possibilities for enhancing a numerical presentation. Perhaps at some future time the faculty's history will be enhanced by a more detailed collection of oral histories.

Observations regarding Possible Historical Strategic Periods

The actions portrayed in figures 9.2 through 9.5 represent organizational growth. Enrolments and the numbers of faculty members grew through the 1980s. The establishment of several auxiliary units represented a form of organizational diversification. No new program initiatives indicating growth in existing programs were undertaken in the 1980s. The budget multiplied 2.5 times between 1984 and 1994. However, further examination of these actions, along with background materials and experiences, indicates that the enacted strategy was one of constrained growth. There are two main factors that contributed to this constraint: a limit on undergraduate enrolment initiated in 1981, and a shortage of faculty.

Enrolment in the co-operative undergraduate program was limited to approximately two hundred students and was accomplished by increasing admission qualifications and by imposing an informal entrance limit. Limits were also placed on the course availability for non-business students. A non-cooperative program was not introduced even though considerable demand existed, but a part-time program introduced in 1984 was used by a relatively small number of candidates to obtain the bachelor's degree. These actions resulted in a levelling off of enrolment in the late 1980s. Although full-time undergraduate enrolment plateaued around 1988, the numbers of degrees awarded did not. One explanation for this is that completion rates were higher because of the more academically qualified students entering the program. Enrolment and degrees awarded in the MBA program have been relatively stable. This may be explained by the limited market potential of the program.

Academic staffing levelled at about 33 to 34 instructors between 1981 and 1989, and about 40 since 1990. The faculty has never been fully staffed with tenured, terminally qualified personnel, and during the past ten years approximately 30 to 40 per cent of total course section offerings have been staffed with non-tenure and non-tenure-track instructors, most without doctoral qualifications. Academic staff turn-over has been a continuing problem, and one estimate in 1988 was that over 100 individuals who had been hired to tenure-track positions in the previous two decades had not been retained.

The fifteen-year period between 1971 and 1985 was characterized by major actions that established the local reputation of the Memorial business faculty. The co-operative program was introduced and faculty members were progressive in the introduction of new courses. The establishment of a small business institute and management develop-ment unit represented advanced thinking. At the end of the period, several actions began that have served the faculty well, for example, participation in case and essay competitions, and the Associates Program.

Concluding Comments

The actions described in the previous pages can be related to the types of strategies identified by Mintzberg. On the one hand, there was little evidence of a deliberate strategy having been formulated for the Fac-ulty of Business Administration at Memorial, except for the limits on enrolment. A realized strategy appears to have emerged as the faculty responded to an evolving situation largely influenced by a shortage of resources.

The tracking of actions illustrated in this paper demonstrates that the faculty had many achievements during the 1957 to 1995 period. Reliance on emergent strategies to form the basis of realized strategies may appear to have been satisfactory, but there are two difficulties with this assertion. First, it assumes that the past performance is all that the faculty was capable of achieving, or that it should have achieved. In other words, more reliance on deliberate strategies may have accomplished more.

Second, reliance on emergent strategies may not be satisfactory in the future. The faculty has been confronted by an even more turbulent environment in the latter half of the 1990s. Competition will increase for students, especially graduate students, as they will be offered an increasing selection of private, executive, and distance programs.

Enrolment may even decline, a situation that has not been experienced in the past. The shortage of qualified academic staff may limit enrolments and the development of new programs. Also, faculty turnover now represents a greater difficulty because replacements may not be possible with hiring freezes. Continuing and increasing reliance on non-tenure-track appointments may weaken the capability to mount innovative courses and programs. As such, the faculty may not adequately respond to program development for the future. The undergraduate program revision in 1995 involved incremental changes, with few innovations in content or delivery approaches. An even greater challenge exists with the MBA program, as the 1995 revision may have failed to take adequately into account the changes in the graduate-education marketplace and its new demands for curriculum content and delivery mechanisms.

It appears that, while reliance on emergent strategies in the past has been acceptable, future dependence may leave the faculty vulnerable. Given this historical account of the faculty's actions and strategies, the administrators of Canadian business schools would be well advised to contemplate some form of strategic analysis in an effort to accomplish the changes that are necessary to meet the demands of the management/business education environment in the next century.

NOTES

1 H. Mintzberg and J. Waters, 'Tracking Strategy in an Entrepreneurial Firm, *AMJ* 25 (1982), 465–99. H. Mintzberg, W.D. Taylor, and J. Waters, 'Tracking Strategies in the Birthplace of Canadian Tycoons,' *CJAS* 1 (1984), 1–27; H. Mintzberg, 'Crafting Strategy,' *HBR* 65 (July–August 1987), 66–75.
2 H. Mintzberg, 'Patterns in Strategy Formation,' *MS* 24 (1978), 934–48.
3 Mintzberg, 'Crafting Strategy.'
4 Mintzberg and Waters, 'Tracking Strategy,' 466–7; Mintzberg, 'Crafting Strategy,' 75.
5 Mintzberg, 'Patterns in Strategy Formation.'
6 H. Mintzberg, 'The Fall and Rise of Strategic Planning,' *HBR* 72 (January–February 1994) 107–14; H. Mintzberg, *The Rise and Fall of Strategic Planning* (New York: Free Press, 1994).

10

The Administrative Sciences Association of Canada, 1957–1999

BARBARA AUSTIN

The Administrative Sciences Association of Canada (ASAC) is the national association of Canadian university management professors. ASAC has promoted, and evolved with, the development of management education as an academic discipline in Canada. Currently, ASAC is structured to emphasize the activities of its functional divisions, similar to its American counterpart the Academy of Management (AoM), although the processes that evolved at ASAC, since its inception in 1957, are different in several ways. ASAC has included the functional areas of marketing, finance, and information systems and, until 1978, accounting, which the Academy has not. ASAC is bilingual and tries to balance regional representation on its executive. The evolution of ASAC into an academic association took almost thirty years, since it was dependent upon the gradual professionalization of Canadian management faculties, a process that ASAC, in turn, influenced. By the late 1980s, the legitimacy of business schools in Canadian universities was firmly established, thanks largely to efforts to enhance the quality and quantity of research.[1] ASAC, an institution with a repertoire of highly developed processes and entrenched shared beliefs, supported by faculty from across Canada, contributed to the general rise in research standards in Canada.

The Canadian business school deans sequentially created two associations – after several name changes, the Administrative Sciences Association of Canada and the Canadian Federation of Business School Deans (CFBSD) – to spread their concerns nationally. While the leadership of these two associations changed regularly, their early conception of professionalism, shaped initially by a handful of deans, eventually spread through the Canadian management education system, although some faculties reflect these professional values much more than do others.

This study began with the request of the ASAC executive, to the author, to write the association's history. No conditions were set. The association's archives, held at UQAM, were made available. The document collection, beginning with the association's formation in 1957, includes the minutes of the general and the executive meetings, an extensive collection of correspondence and monographs, and copies of the *Proceedings* and newsletters. All past-presidents were invited to describe the issues and activities during their watch, and many were interviewed. Some respondents sent supporting documents from their personal files. As well, prominent deans were invited to comment and were interviewed, again when possible. The sources represent both intentions recorded at the time and the participants' later reflections and include the opinions of academics from across Canada.

The history is described here in three phases, each period reflecting different 'rules of the game.'[2] In Phase I (1957–71), a handful of deans, a powerful sponsoring elite, created ASAC as a collective to promote their professional perspective of business education. A reconfiguration in Phase II (Gaining Legitimacy as a learned society, 1972–85) was necessary when the deans turned ASAC over to the professoriate, who, with their assistance, sought equity with other Canadian academic associations in the Learned Societies of Canada. Together, ASAC and the deans successfully campaigned for recognition from government funding agencies. This gained, in Phase III (1986–97) ASAC left the Learneds to become an independent academic association with its separate conference and journal. Free from the organizational constraints of the Learned Societies, ASAC further developed its services to management professors. When the International Federation of Scholarly Associations of Management (IFSAM) was formed, in 1990, ASAC was a founding member. Through IFSAM, ASAC is linked to a global network of management professors.

Phase I. The Deans' Professional Project, 1957–1971

ASAC was initiated by the deans of business schools from leading Canadian universities in order to create an institution to coordinate their individual efforts in improving business education. In 1954, a preliminary meeting on the formation of an association for university commerce-school professors was held after the Learned Societies of

Canada conference involving Dean Tom McLeod (College of Commerce, University of Saskatchewan), Dean Earle MacPhee (School of Commerce, University of British Columbia), Prof. John Weldon (Department of Economics and Political Science, McGill University), Prof. Jean-Jacques St. Pierre (École des Hautes Études Commerciales, University of Montréal), and Dean B.A. Lindberg (School of Commerce, University of Alberta). They sought to raise their individual status, in part, by raising the average quality of the profession nationally in order to obtain recognition and resources.

In 1957, the deans formed the Association of Canadian Schools of Commerce and Business Administration (ACSCBA), meeting at the same time as the annual conference in June of the Learned Societies of Canada. The original mission of the association was 'the promotion and improvement of higher education in the various fields of commerce and business administration,'[3] and to be a forum for scholarly research at meetings held with, but not as a member of, the Learned Societies. The Learneds is an umbrella organization that coordinates the annual meetings of dozens of academic groups in the humanities and social sciences at a selected university. The ACSCBA modelled itself after the Canadian Economists Association, the closest reference group in the Learneds, because business subjects were often taught in economics departments before separate commerce departments or faculties were created. The ACSCBA could not meet the Learneds' requirement that an association be sustained by individual memberships, because of a lack of faculty interest in paying membership dues. The deans authorized the institutional membership fees, attended the conference regularly, and filled almost all executive positions.

Beginning in 1959, the deans (chairs/directors) of faculties (schools/departments) of commerce also held meetings before the ACSCBA conference. This was expedient because of the shortage of travel funds, and because most deans had some teaching duties and were interested in attending sessions at the Learneds. These meetings turned the association away from its original concept of promoting research towards being a club for deans to discuss their immediate administrative problems. At the conference itself, which some faculty also attended, a minimal academic program of a half-dozen papers, solicited by the executive, usually on the subject of curricula, was presented.

As well as the economists' association, the Canadian deans admired, and when possible were mindful of, the American decanal association the Assembly of Collegiate Schools of Business (AACSB). ASAC tried to be both types of institutions, academic and decanal, but could do neither as well as it might have liked. The Academy of Management (AoM) originally was not an organizational model. It began in 1936 as a group of around twenty members who met over the Christmas holiday to discuss papers, quite separately from the AACSB.[4] In 1957, when the Canadian association was formed, the AoM had about fifty members and was run on the basis of personal friendship.

Conditions in Canadian business schools did not support academic research. In 1957, only 11.8 per cent of business professors had doctorates, compared to the Canadian average of 41.7 per cent for all faculties, and they were slightly younger and had lower salaries than the system average.[5] Business faculties were overburdened by large classes, heavy teaching loads, and administrative demands, without the support of an infrastructure of graduate assistants. The courses were primarily in accounting, with perhaps production and marketing, driven by requirements determined outside academe. Within their universities, business schools faced indifference and underfunding, and often were not accepted as an academic discipline. The pressing concerns were determining curricula, setting standards, and finding faculty, not academic research. Enrolments tripled in the 1960s, as students used university degrees, not in the liberal arts tradition of disinterested knowledge, but to find jobs.[6] The ACSCBA tried improve these conditions, but not by dealing directly with issues of pay, benefits, and security. Conditions would improve by redefining the work, by delineating the knowledge base, of the profession.[7]

The deans who developed the large Canadian schools of management, and who supported the activities of the ACSCBA, often sought the role models for creating their programs from American universities. Queen's was influenced by the University of Chicago and the Harvard Business School;[8] the University of Western Ontario by Harvard;[9] McGill by Wharton;[10] and the University of British Columbia by a combination of ideas from Stanford, Chicago, Wharton, and Harvard.[11] There were exceptions. The École des Hautes Études Commerciales (HÉC), Montréal, followed the template of HÉC, Paris,[12] and the University of Toronto chose the University of Birmingham as its prototype.[13]

For many years, the majority of Canadian business school professors with doctorates had earned their degrees at American universities. They drew on those experiences when making choices for their schools, and for the ACSCBA. Thus, while the organization of the

ACSCBA reflected Canadian conditions, the institutional role models guiding its members' actions often were taken from successful business schools in the United States. The ACSCBA was a totally volunteer organization, with an executive spread across the country, and met very infrequently. The shared values learned in American schools provided a common bond.

The deans of larger and more professional schools, especially Queen's and UBC, while involved in improving their own schools, tried to enhance national standards through the ACSCBA.[14] They also sought parity with professional schools – law, medicine, architecture – at their own universities.[15] In smaller schools, most faculty members were hired only to teach course content, often accounting. By socializing with the directors of the smaller schools, the deans from the major universities tried to improve the practices of all schools, and, by making them more alike, enhance the general level of professionalism in the field.

The deans, synonymous with the ACSCBA, saw their priority as gaining government funding to develop qualified faculty to feed the huge demand for business programs. The twenty-eight members at the third annual meeting in 1959, held at the home of the host, Dean McLeod, at the University of Saskatchewan, passed the motion 'Be it resolved that this Association recommends to the Presidents of all Canadian universities that they give urgent and serious consideration to the need for a PhD programme in business education,'[16] that is, to 'set about producing the producers.'[17] This motion not only addressed the crisis in faculty qualifications, but would eventually create a common socialization process, because 'the professional school or the university spawn a subculture of their own, to which relatively large numbers of apprentices are exposed.'[18] Within the decade, doctoral studies were launched at Western, UBC and Queen's.[19] Another policy recommendation of the 1959 ACSCBA meeting, intended to encourage research, reflected the very basic needs for materials and information. 'The Association will exchange, among its members, information regarding sources and kinds of library materials and other facilities helpful for research and teaching.'[20]

If the crushing demand by students for business education was not enough to deal with in 1959, the paradigm of what business education should be shifted radically. The stinging criticisms of American business schools levelled by the Ford[21] and Carnegie Foundation[22] reports, the call for a 'great transformation'[23] in management education, goaded the American AACSB into initiating sweeping changes in U.S. business programs. The reports marked a watershed, demarcating management education from commerce. Until 1959, external professional bodies, particularly of accountants and bankers, had a major role in setting curricula. Management issues were largely unexplored. Both reports criticized commerce programs for their narrow, vocationally-minded programs, and lax standards. Business research was termed not scholarly and inclined to use anecdotal methods. Frank Pierson, the author of the Carnegie Foundation report urged business schools to improve the standards of faculty and emphasized the role of rigorous research methodologies in achieving this end.[24] In 1959, only a few American business schools such as Stanford, Case Western, MIT, and the Carnegie Institute of Technology did research on management, but soon research on the new paradigm spread through the AACSB schools. The two reports expressed the belief that research could create an internally generated knowledge base, developed by professors in their studies of praxis, to aid in teaching. Business schools now encompassed two kinds of knowledge, one externally, the other internally derived. 'One is functional (knowledge of Accounting, Marketing, etc.), and the other is general (ability to decide, to lead, to work with and within groups, to assimilate new ideas, etc.).'[25] Management knowledge was not determined by an external governing body as found in law, medicine, and accounting, but grew through the efforts of the academic societies at their refereed conferences and in their journals.

The research orientation also influenced some of the traditional subjects. 'Some auxiliary management functions, like Accounting, Marketing and Finance, which had previously been based exclusively on the job, became objects of rational study in colleges and universities. These auxiliaries were not necessarily studied with the aid of science. Much of what people learned was normative (i.e., best practice), but academics employed scientific conceptions, drawn especially from economics and statistics, in their research and teaching in order to make these functional auxiliaries more managerially coherent and useful.'[26] The lack of research output was not limited to commerce faculties. Claude Bissell, a former president of the University of Toronto, commented that during the 1950s the 'Canadian academic tradition was amateur and genteel; if you did not expose yourself in print, you were in a strong position to comment freely and sharply on those who did.'[27]

In Canada, the infrastructure to deal with the criticisms needed another decade of groundwork. The reports, which explicated what the knowledge base should be and set in motion strategies for research and teaching, were discussed by a panel at the 1960 ACSCBA conference and in a commissioned report of the implications for Canadian business schools at the 1961 conference. At the 1965 conference, especially fractious debates on the nature of business education were played out before the association. The thrust of the change was to make business education, particularly at the graduate level, education in general management, rather than a specialization. Under the Ford proposal, endorsed by the AACSB, to be accredited programs had to consist of a core program with a limited amount of specialization. The MBA was defined as a professional degree in management. The old idea of business schools, at least at the graduate level, being a training ground for specialists in accounting, production, and marketing was challenged. It was argued by the proponents of the changes that there was a sufficiently developed body of knowledge about management to create a discipline of study.

Bringing such a major change into the curriculum of many schools was not easy. Business school programs, primarily undergraduate, served the professional associations of the accountants and bankers. Only a few American schools did research on management, yet this was the direction in which all business education was moving. In Canada, three deans, Philip White (UBC), Jack Wettlaufer (Western), and James Gillies (York), led the drive in the executive meetings for making this change in focus in Canada. Participants in the ACSCBA meetings, in the 1960s, recall frequent, heated arguments. The furious debates indicate the organization had reached a point where standardization had become the central issue, implying that 'a measure of cognitive commonality has already been achieved within each conflicting group.'[28] The effect of these debates was the gradual emergence of a professional view of management education in the large Canadian universities. Because of the ACSCBA, the deans from the big schools were in contact with the directors and department chairs and with faculty, who were normally remote from academic influences and did not feel much pressure to change. Even if the professional values espoused lacked meaning to the directors of some of the smaller schools, the meetings still provided new models for developing programs.

In these early years, the ACSCBA could not mount a blind-refereed academic program. The few papers presented at the conference were invited because research in management was minimal. In 1963, the

ACSCBA changed its name to the simpler Association of Canadian Schools of Business (ACSB).

The ACSB responded to the challenge of the Ford and Carnegie reports by seeking research funding. Access to government funding was blocked because without individual memberships the association could not qualify for membership in the Social Science Research Council (SSRC). Consequently, the ACSB sought private assistance from Seagram's Bronfman Foundation. From 1965 to 1978, the Bronfmans' generous funding of ACSB's executive meetings, MBA and doctoral fellowships, and faculty research grants narrowed the divide between business school standards and acceptable levels of academic performance as evaluated by government funding agencies.

The main focus for management faculties was not research, however, but on trying to find the faculty and resources to deal with the huge number of students. Five PhDs in administration were graduated in Canada in the 1960s. This had little influence upon existing practices owing to an explosion in demand for business education. The enrolments at Canadian universities nearly tripled during the 1960s. In Ontario alone, to Queen's, Toronto, Ottawa, Western, and McMaster – all of which had commerce faculties or departments – were added the University of Waterloo (1957), Royal Military College (1957), Waterloo Lutheran, now Wilfrid Laurier University (1959), York University (1959), Carleton (1959), Laurentian (1960), Windsor (1963), Trent (1963), Brock (1964), Guelph (1964), and Lakehead (1965). The University of Toronto created two satellite campuses, Scarborough (1965) and Erindale (1967). All of the new universities either offered business programs from the beginning, as was the case at Laurentian, or introduced them in response to student demand, as at Brock.

The deans, led by Philip White, formed their own association, the Canadian Federation of Deans of Management and Administrative Sciences (CFDMAS), in 1969, in order to work for parity with the decanal associations of other faculties.[29] They felt that the development of business schools had reached the point where faculty could operate their own affairs as a learned society. The deans began meeting in the autumn, mostly in conjunction with the annual meeting of the Association of Universities and Colleges of Canada (AUCC). They admired the AACSB model, but as yet could not meet its high standards. While many Canadian management faculties paid for membership in the AACSB in order to receive its guidelines, only a few Canadian faculties earned accreditation from the AACSB by demonstrating the high standards of its program.[30] Deans delegated faculty to promote the ACSB; Dean White of UBC, for example, instructed Larry Moore, later an ACSB president, to become involved.[31]

Decoupled from the deans and their agenda of administration problems, the faculty members of the ACSB could return to the association's original mission of encouraging research. Beginning with the 1969 conference, the program expanded research presentations to thirty-four papers, from seven the year before, although the papers continued to be solicited rather than blind-refereed. Dean John Mundie (Manitoba), president of the ACSB, and the only dean remaining on the ACSB executive, was determined that the 1970 ACSB conference at the University of Manitoba would be conducted as an academic conference, although the Learned Societies of Canada continued to refuse the ACSB membership. The precedent was established of selecting the conference chair from the host university. From over forty presentation submissions, twenty-two were selected. For the first time, a final copy of each paper was due before the conference. The papers represented a range of functional disciplines, but were not divided into divisions. Management education was a popular topic. In 1972, the ACSB changed its name, for the third time, to the Canadian Association of Administrative Sciences (CAAS).

Phase II. Gaining Legitimacy as a Learned Society, 1973–1985

Early in 1972, while still receiving some financial support from the deans, CAAS initiated individual memberships, enabling it to become a member of the Learned Societies. In addition, membership in the Social Science Research Council, a granting body for federal research monies, was essential in order that management professors be eligible for research funding. CAAS's membership in the SSRC was difficult to arrange, 'as other members of the SSRC did not consider business professors to be quite respectable academically.'[32] Robert Crandall (Queen's) became an ex-officio member of the SSRC, lobbied for CAAS's membership, and put forward the names of CAAS members for various SSRC committees. In 1973, CAAS was admitted as a full member. While providing some travel grants, however, membership did not result in SSRC funding for management research proposals. Attending SSRC meetings while president of CAAS in 1974–5, Crandall 'came away convinced it was largely a waste of taxpayers' money used to support a self-serving academic establishment.'[33]

The CAAS president, Roger Miller (Sherbrooke), proposed using the divisional structure developed by the Academy of Management. The Academy's first large-scale meeting, in 1969, initiated ten divisions, switched the meeting time to August, and included tourist literature in the call for papers, thereby encouraging members to travel with their families. Miller energetically travelled to campuses across Canada, promoting a new vision of CAAS, which included starting a journal. CAAS would borrow the divisional aspect of the Academy, and be 'no different from American societies' except on subject matter, with CAAS encouraging 'empirical studies along discipline lines using the Canadian context as a source of information.'[34] Research on Canadian issues was little understood in American associations and not readily accepted by U.S. journals.

To successfully compete in their universities, Canadian management professors needed to practise credible research methods, to indicate both their personal merit and the collective credibility of their faculty. By collectively espousing the institutional beliefs of academe, which many management faculties could not in fact meet, the professors were able to get badly needed resources that enabled them to come closer to the professional standards. CAAS was important to management faculties in their negotiations with universities and government agencies to obtain resources to help them meet academe's institutional norms.

Initially, however, CAAS had great difficulty in attracting both dues-paying members and quality papers for presentation at its annual conference. 'For years Canadian business scholars had been decrying the lack of a Canadian forum of scholars in which to present their research. However, for the first several years, the cost of belonging to such a forum, together with the perceived greater prestige of forums in the United States, discouraged many professors from joining and participating. In retrospect, this was surprising since the spirit of Canadian nationalism was running very high at the time.'[35]

The sixteenth annual conference, in 1972, held with the Learneds at McGill, was organized for the first time by functional disciplines, shifting the emphasis of the conference to divisional activities. The number of papers in the five divisions reflected the extent of research activity: organizational behaviour (10 papers); finance and managerial economics (8); marketing (7); accounting information systems (5); management science (4), with additional sessions on business policy (a panel discussion), business and government (2 papers), careers (2), and management education (1). The deans indicated they would be looking for

CAAS papers in their annual reviews. If credentialled knowledge is 'an opportunity for income,'[36] and hence a source of power, the deans needed an external peer-managed mechanism for determining credentials. A Canadian association encompassing all the functional subjects, helped the deans in determining the market value (merit) of an individual's 'knowledge.' Ironically, the deans could coerce CAAS into becoming an academic institution after they turned it over to faculty.

During 1973, 70 papers were presented, up from 26 in 1972. For the first time, the conference program was planned by the divisions, reflecting the increased number of disciplines (codified knowledge systems) in management programs. Peer interaction within the divisions often created rigorous standards. The largest founding division was organizational behaviour, followed by marketing, finance and managerial economics, management science, and accounting information systems. The *Proceedings*, published since 1957, changed from one volume printed by Queen's after the conference to microfiche, in 1975, again sent out after the conference. In 1977, the marketing division published a print copy of its proceedings before the conference, which had the effect of reducing the time spent, literally, reading the papers, leaving more time for discussion. In 1978, the marketing division started a blind-review process, requiring submissions at an earlier date. Accounting/MIS followed suit. The CAAS executive then published the proceedings of the other three divisions and instituted a policy of blind-refereeing for all divisions. A policy was established that the *Proceedings* be published in a separate number for each division, edited by the program chair, collectively forming a volume, with a standard cover and presentation. Divisional best-paper awards were gradually introduced. Three new divisions were admitted, reflecting the expansion of management programs: policy, 1978; production and operations management, 1979; and international business, 1981. The 1978 conference, held at the University of Western Ontario, featured developments in management education, with Dean Bud Johnson (Western) speaking on 'Teaching and Researching Business Management: The Western System,' while in counterpoint Jean-Marie Toulouse (HÉC) and Henry Mintzberg (McGill) spoke on 'A New Approach: The Joint PhD Program in Administration' they had initiated at the four Montréal universities.

The *Bulletin*, the association's newsletter, was published twice yearly. Membership directories were regularly issued, and a placement service organized at the conference. In 1977, the association changed its name for the fourth time, from CAAS to the Administrative Sciences Association of Canada (ASAC).

The standards defined by the Ford and Carnegie reports began trickling down from the larger universities to the isolated faculties in smaller schools. The annual conference became the forum for developing the professional models followed in many American schools. While ASAC was started by the faculties of large universities, it was not carried forward by them. In the long term, it was sustained by the medium-size schools.[37] Faculty in big universities generally had little interest in ASAC and sent their research findings to international conferences, competing directly with professors in the U.S. schools.

The separate organization of the deans had developed a number of projects. The Economic Council of Canada (ECC) increasingly was interested in 'Management' and collaborated with the deans in joint endeavours. From 1978, there were quarterly Federation of Deans executive meetings and many more committee meetings in Ottawa in conjunction with the ECC. The deans also developed working contacts with a number of national organizations, federal departments, and agencies. In 1979, the Federation of Deans drafted a new constitution, taking the name the Canadian Federation of Deans of Management and Administrative Studies (CFDMAS), and established a permanent secretariat in Ottawa as 'an instrument of policy formulation at the national level.'[38] Through press statements and subsequent media coverage the Federation of Deans became known as the representative agency for Canadian management schools. The reorganization also enabled the Federation of Deans to function as a legal entity and as a learned society, a help in obtaining funding.

Critical statistical and interpretive material was provided by Max von Zur-Muehlen, who had decided that management education was an important strategic initiative. He gained leave from Statistics Canada to work under the direction of the Economic Council of Canada and prepared several publications that demonstrated that business schools were not appropriately treated in the Canadian university system.[39] Max Clarkson, dean of the University of Toronto Faculty of Management Studies, was chosen as the first chair of the CFDMAS. The team of the two Maxes was a 'powerhouse in terms of making things happen.'[40]

In 1977, a new funding agency, the Social Sciences and Humanities Research Council of Canada (SSHRC) was formed, offering an opportunity for funding business education and research that membership in the Social Science Research Council had failed to provide. Both the faculty and decanal associations had stabilized and could galvanize to present their problems to the SSHRC. The deans, in the spring of 1978, conducted a three-day strategy conference at Banff to discuss ways to improve management education and research in the context of the changing social, political, and economic environment in Canada.

Max Clarkson summed up the depressing if not desperate situation:

> The major impetus for the expansion of university management educa-
> tion has come from the students themselves. Since the early 1970s
> increasing numbers of students have directed their attention to profes-
> sional subjects, in order to provide themselves with comparative advan-
> tages on the labour market, where employment opportunities to general
> arts and science graduates have apparently diminished ... But the rapid
> growth of enrolment at schools of management in recent years has
> imposed a severe strain on faculties, as the parent universities have been
> unable or unwilling to reallocate resources to this area of growth. Conse-
> quently student/faculty ratios have become badly distorted. In 1978
> about 12 per cent of all university students in Canada were enrolled in
> schools of management and business administration, but less than 5 per
> cent of all faculty were teaching in these areas, and only 3 to 4 per cent of
> the universities' budgets were allocated to these activities. This imbal-
> ance is the crux of the problem. Management education and research at
> Canadian universities have been, and still are, underfunded and the out-
> put of management schools, in terms of graduates, will continue to lag
> way behind the United States by any measure of comparison ... The situ-
> ation has become even more serious now that total university enrolment
> is leveling off or declining and provincial support for post-secondary
> education is being reduced across Canada. This makes it extremely diffi-
> cult for universities, whose budgets are declining in real terms, to reallo-
> cate to growth sectors, even if they consider such reallocation necessary.
> The prospect, therefore, is for more of the same.[41]

Clarkson and several decanal colleagues were received by the first president of SSHRC, on his first day in office, 'to initiate negotiations for more equity in the allocation of research and PhD support funds.'[42] SSHRC responded by establishing the Consultative Group on Management Education to define the nature, and survey the state, of management research and graduate education in Canada. Allan Blair, president of ASAC, served as an associate member of the consultative group, giving faculty, through ASAC involvement, input distinct from that of the deans. Stanley Shapiro (McGill) coordinated the drafting of the report. In Ottawa, James Gillies, a senior policy adviser to the prime minister, promoted the idea of an agency to funnel research funds to management faculties. Shortly before his departure from office, Prime Minister Clark endorsed the idea.

To acquaint government and the private sector with the problems management faculties were facing, and to hear their reaction, the CFDMAS and ASAC jointly sponsored a conference, 'Managing in the 1980s: The Crisis in Management Education and Research,' held in Toronto during October 1979. The conference was based on the premise that 'Canada's management capability has obviously not kept pace with the events and pressures of the 1970s ... How will we manage as leaders in management education, to make sure that students in our programs will learn what they need to learn in order to manage effectively in the 1980s?'[43] The conference delegates studied several briefs prepared by the consultative group. Dean Laurent Picard (McGill) summarized the group's report recommending that management education and research be designated a national concern and as such be the recipient of a strategic grant of $3 million a year to evaluate and fund research proposals from management school faculty members.[44]

During September 1980, the CFDMAS and ASAC held a second joint conference in Toronto, 'Managing in the 1980s, Themes for Management Research,' to identify the key research topics to be accorded priority for funding from the SSHRC Strategic Grants program, and to advise on how the program should be managed. With a few exceptions, the entire ASAC executive, as well as the division and program chairs, were present and participated. The report of the conference identified six criteria for choosing research priorities, selected strategic areas for research, suggested guidelines for managing the Strategic Grants program, and explored the establishment of an ASAC journal funded by SSHRC.[45] Following the conference, the ASAC Committee on Strategic Grants mailed a questionnaire, 'Proposals for Areas of Research in the National Concern.' The replies affirmed the findings of the CFDMAS report.

By 1980, these efforts had resulted in support from SSHRC for a doctoral fellowship program, methodology seminars, and faculty research grants. Workshops were held every year, from 1981 to 1987, organized by ASAC and the deans, to address themes on functional business subjects and to promote interdisciplinary discussions. In 1982, following a widespread letter-writing campaign orchestrated by the president, Robert Sexty, ASAC received SSHRC funding to support a journal, the *Canadian Journal of Administrative Sciences (CJAS)*. The editor, Ronald Burke (York), published the first issue in 1984.

The Federation of Deans had involved strong representation from the private sector in the 1979 conference 'Managing in the 1980s,' which created sound working relationships. Initial contacts with the Business Council on National Issues was established and relationships developed with other business organizations such as the Canadian Chamber of Commerce, the Canadian Manufacturers' Association, and the Canadian Federation of Independent Businesses. These activities helped to develop the Canadian Chamber of Commerce of Business Management Education Task Force. At its 1983 annual meeting the chamber passed a number of motions in support of management education. Subsequently, two past chairs of the Federation of Deans, John Gordon and Michael Maher, served as members of the chamber's board. Dean Maher (Calgary), representing the CFDMAS, also approached the Canadian International Development Agency (CIDA) and created an international management program using the skills of Canadian professors.

With the SSHRC programs, and ASAC's part in shaping them, 'ASAC became a free-standing player, a force in government discussions, and in negotiations with the Canadian Federation of Deans.'[46] ASAC president Allan Blair, reporting the new developments in the relationships between ASAC, the SSFC, and SSHRC to the executive, commented: 'It seems that our opinions are now taken into account by the two groups and that new directions taken are much more in line with our thinking than they used to be.'[47] Conference themes were designed to pass around the information about the SSHRC funding developments in business research, including the grant application and publication process, and about educational standards.

By 1986, ASAC defined itself as a creator of 'communication instruments ... through the granting of awards, managing research and travel grants (when available), as well as maintaining close relationships with business or government institutions who have some interest in our activities – SSHRC, SSFC, CAAA, the Secretary of State, the Federation of Deans, as well as business institutions like publishers.'[48] By promoting institutional values, ASAC's legitimacy was recognized by its organizational field.[49]

Phase III. A Scholarly Professional Institution, 1986–1995

By the mid-1980s, with its credentials affirmed by government agencies in the form of grants, and the annual conference a flourishing concern, ASAC found membership in the Learneds constraining. ASAC left the Learneds in 1986, ostensibly for financial reasons, because the membership fee provided little of value that ASAC could not provide on its own. Behind the move was the fact that ASAC had developed a membership base and standards allowing it to stand alone through its divisions as a smaller version of the Learneds, thereby supplanting the need for contact with other disciplines encompassed by the Learneds. The relationships with the CFDMAS and SSHRC were more beneficial. On its own, ASAC could continue to model itself on the more rigorous standards used by the American management and marketing societies, rather than the more relaxed happenings of the Learneds. Socialization at the conference could be intensified with dinners and receptions, while the 'Publishers' Exhibit' focused on business issues.

The first independent conference, held at Whistler, BC, in 1986, was very successful. The ASAC executive decided to continue the practice, although the deans strongly requested that ASAC return to meeting with the Learneds.[50] New divisions were created: women in management, organizational theory, 1991; human resources, management education, 1992; entrepreneurship, 1993; and tourism, business history, 1995. Even after the formation of the human resources division, organizational behaviour continued as the largest division, followed by marketing, policy, finance, information systems, human resources, and international business.

At the Academy of Management, an acceptance rate of one-third of papers submitted is enforced across all divisions. Rigid conformity to the Academy model is not workable with ASAC's multiplicity of disciplines and small national population base. As a result, ASAC faces a problem of assuring both the quality of papers and attendance at the conferences. At ASAC, the executive recommends an acceptance percentage, but in fact it is left to the program chair to exercise selectivity. In 1994, the overall acceptance rate was 50 per cent, with the larger divisions having the lowest rate (policy 24 per cent, marketing 36 per cent) while entrepreneurship and operations management had a much higher acceptance rate. Throughout its history ASAC has had the problem of Canadian academics sending their better papers to international conferences.[51]

In 1979, the majority of members of the accounting/MIS division did not renew their ASAC memberships. In 1976, the Canadian Academic Accounting Association (CAAA) had been incorporated to improve the standards of accounting education and research, not only of academics, but of practitioners, government and business accountants, as well. In 1978, the CAAA took over the organization of the accounting/MIS division's program within ASAC. The following year it organized a separate conference at the Learneds, immediately after the ASAC conference, drawing funding from industry corporate sponsors. The much reduced division was renamed 'information systems' in 1980 to reflect the change in focus. By 1981, the CAAA had over five hundred members and published a quarterly newsletter. In scheduling its conference just after ASAC, the CAAA expected that its members could continue to attend ASAC sessions. When ASAC left the Learneds in 1986, interaction with the accountants was severed, although beginning in 1996 they held sessions in the same location as, but before, the ASAC conference. This arrangement has allowed accounting professors to stay on and attend the ASAC conference, but has not resulted in united action by the two organizations' executives.

After 1986, running an independent conference greatly increased the work of the executive, and the expenses of the association. New features were added to the conference. The duration was extended from two to two-and-a-half days in 1985. In 1986, the membership list was computerized. That year, at Whistler, a 'Fun Run' was initiated, which became an annual event. A doctoral consortium was begun in 1989. A best dissertation award, and a best student conference paper award, encouraged student participation. In 1992, for example, more than seventy doctoral students participated. The divisions organized distinguished speaker sessions, sometimes jointly, for supportive audiences. Survival kits for executive members, and program chairs, helped to clarify tasks.

The *Canadian Journal of Administrative Sciences*, published under the editorship of Ron Burke (York), 1984–7, Jean-Claude Chebat (HÉC) 1988–90, Vishwanath V. Baba (Concordia), 1991–6, and Abolhassan Jalilvand (Concordia), 1996–9, continued to improve the quality of submissions and the review and editorial processes, and developed respected area editors. The editorial board reflected the regional, cultural, and disciplinary diversity of the ASAC membership. Jean Pasquero (UQAM), the book review editor, introduced innovative features such as comparative reviews of textbooks for the Canadian market. A multidisciplinary panel annually selected the 'best paper,' which appeared in the journal. In 1992, the journal was indexed to the indices compiled by the Institute of Scientific Information (ISI), including *Current Contents*, the ISI source index, and the ISI *Citation Index*, giving *CJAS* authors worldwide visibility.

Participation in ASAC levelled off, with only a quarter of Canadian management faculty taking membership, although the association is an umbrella group for all academic functions, except accounting. This affected grants from SSHRC, which are based on membership. ASAC reached the limits of its available financing. Expenses were increasing – especially those associated with membership in IFSAM, the international management association, CJAS, executive travel, and the conference *Proceedings*. Positing that membership was linked to attendance at the annual conference, the executive held conferences in locations that would draw participants: Whistler, 1990; Niagara Falls, 1991; Québec City, 1992; Lake Louise, 1993; and Halifax, 1994. The locales did act as a draw, although the east- and west-coast conferences created travel cost barriers for members near the other seaboards. The proliferation of international conferences, with acceptance standards lower than those of ASAC, created added competition. The establishment of a permanent secretariat, which might help expand ASAC's scope beyond the details of the annual conference, was considered too expensive. Two executive positions were abolished in 1995 to reduce the administrative and travel costs. The deans and faculty of the largest Canadian universities generally did not attend the conference, although they sent their doctoral students to experience the process. The absence of the leading Canadian researchers gave ASAC a national, rather than possibly an international, conference status. By 1999 the ASAC executive realized it had a major problem. The number of members and the number of participants at the annual conference had been declining since 1993. The Saint John conference attracted many PhD students but few experienced researchers. The executive hoped the joint conference of ASAC and IFSAM in Montréal in July 2000 would interest members enough to return to the association.

ASAC left interaction with government agencies to the deans, who financed a permanent secretariat in Ottawa to collect and distribute information, and act as a government lobby. In the 1980s, the CFDMAS, with the support of the Canadian International Development Agency

(CIDA) launched several global multimillion-dollar international management development and research networks in Africa, China, Latin America, South-East Asia, and India. During 1989, there was an attempt by a half-dozen of the larger management schools, calling themselves the 'lead schools,' to take the CIDA contract in China out of the hands of the CFDMAS and put it into their own. In response, Deans Colin Dodds (Saint Mary's) and Michael Maher (Calgary) led in the formation of a Canadian Consortium of Management Schools (CCMS), initially with thirty management faculties as members. The CCMS explained to CIDA that their membership was open, not elite, representing the majority of Canadian management professors. The government decided in favour of the CCMS. The CFDMAS members voted to cease their international project role and, in the 1990s, shifted their focus to domestic issues – particularly building stronger links with the Canadian business schools through an associates program. In 1995, the title of the association was changed to the Canadian Federation of Business School Deans (CFBSD), and it now emphasizes quality management education and the professional development of business school administrators. The CFBSD collects and monitors data on business faculty salaries, enrolments, graduates, and operational costs and fees at its members' institutions. Its publications strengthen Canadian management education and its global contacts.

The establishment of the CCMS was a defensive move against elitism. In 1999, there are two decanal organizations in Canada. Dean Michael Maher, a dynamic member of both organizations, feels 'it is possible that the Federation (CFBSD) and the Consortium (CCMS) could merge and we once again could have a strong organization working together.'[52]

In the 1990s, the ASAC executive defined the association's role as being 'to run the Annual Conference and *CJAS*,' and its mission 'to encourage and reinforce achievements of Canadians in Administrative Sciences.'[53] ASAC was a founding member of the International Federation of Scholarly Associations of Management (IFSAM), formed in 1990 as the international umbrella organization of national management societies, which includes associations in the United States, France, Germany, Britain, and Japan. Through IFSAM, ASAC is involved in the globalization of management knowledge. ASAC is thus oriented to international developments in management education and interacts less than it did with other academic disciplines in Canada.

Discussion and Implications

ASAC's mimicry, first of the Canadian Learned Societies, then of the American Academy of Management, was played out in three phases. Oliver[54] has described a range of possible strategies that organizations use to respond to the institutional process: acquiesce; compromise; avoid; defy; manipulate. ASAC, in different phases, used three of these strategies: in Phase I, manipulate; in Phase II, compromise; and in Phase III, acquiesce. The choice of strategy was connected to the prevailing type of leadership. Scott[55] has examined the social location of groups who build organizations to determine whether leadership is a bottom-up or top-down process. The phases in the institutionalization of ASAC show three scenarios in the strategy/leadership relationship: Phase I was top-down; in Phase II complimentary strategies originated at both the top and bottom; and Phase III was bottom up, from the divisions.

In Phase I, the deans of the large universities collectively used their top-down position on the executive to manipulate[56] management education in Canada through the socialization of all deans, chairs, and directors, the influential constituents. Meeting with the Learneds freed the deans/executive from making conference arrangements and put them in contact with other decanal groups. The critical issue was to shape the values and criteria necessary to enact the institutional norms of management education defined in 1959 by the Ford and Carnegie reports. The processes to enact these norms within ASAC had to await the further development of a supportive infrastructure within the individual university management faculties. Having hammered out the institutional values in the fractious debates in the 1960s, the deans created their own organization, the CFDMAS, in order to gain parity with other decanal associations and with the other professional faculties at their individual universities.

The deans maintained close ties with ASAC, guiding it though Phase II, encouraging a strategy of compromise.[57] Through cooperation, ASAC and the deans placated and accommodated the state funding agencies to win legitimacy in the organizational field for the institutional norms they had determined in Phase I. This period of 'Extending Legitimacy' was 'intense and proactive as management [in this case the deans and ASAC] attempts to win the confidence and support of wary potential constituents.'[58] Funding helped faculty to develop professionally, but in addition, the recognition by government agencies of management education as a profession had the broader implication of state recognition.[59] Many deans, through their annual reviews of faculty activities, and control of travel grants, gave participation at the annual conference of ASAC increased status with Canadian faculty. Ironically, the same year, 1973, that ASAC was finally accepted for membership in the Learneds, it adopted a divisional structure similar to that of the American Academy of Management. It was present in the Learneds, but its structure reflected an external and international configuration that increased its legitimacy by imitating new practices in its organizational field.[60] The change was proposed and communicated by Roger Miller, but it was not questioned. ASAC fell into divisional activity easily because many Canadians presented papers at American conferences and divisions were 'taken for granted' as the way things were done.[61]

By the mid-1980s, the role of management faculties in universities had normalized. They were usually accepted as equals by other faculties. ASAC left the Learneds to better develop its mission of promoting research. The deans generally, but especially those from the large universities, withdrew from active involvement. ASAC, in Phase III, became the venue for the presentation of research, especially on Canadian topics, and an opportunity for faculty from across Canada to socialize, a purpose served by a strategy of acquiescence.[62] Canadian universities produced enough PhDs to supply most staffing requirements. The scholarly activity of evaluating and disseminating research was generated by the divisions. The executive was absorbed with arrangements for the annual conference. ASAC had a more restricted view of its social role in the organizational field than it did in Phase II, seeing a limited number of operations and actions as possible.

With legitimacy in the organizational field gained, an organization's standardized components can be loosely coupled.[63] The increasing differentiation in the functional areas of business schools was reflected in ASAC. The loose coupling and bottom-up process permitted the 'codification of a new area ... the articulation of a sub-paradigm,'[64] providing an opportunity for new scholarship to emerge, the purpose of the organization. Ashforth and Gibbs[65] have described this situation as one of 'Maintaining Legitimacy': where, having 'adjudged the organization credible, constituents tend to relax their vigilance and content themselves with evidence of ongoing performance vis-a-vis their interests and with periodic assurances of "business-as-usual."' In the United States, management and marketing have separate associations;

in Canada, the very loosely coupled structure of ASAC facilitates the requirements of these diverse groups, and the addition of new ones. ASAC had reached a point where its strategy/structure was similar to that of the leading American associations, the Academy of Management and the Academy of Marketing Science, given the difference that it operated in a national market with one-tenth of the U.S. population. It refined its role to focus on being the national association for Canadian management research.

When ASAC's activities were normalized in the mid-1980s, the deans and faculty of many of the major schools largely withdrew their participation. The Canadian Federation of Business School Deans was absorbed for a decade in global projects. The large central Ontario management faculties (Toronto, York, Queen's, and Western) have been unwilling to host the conference, a possible threat to ASAC's continued legitimacy. ASAC does not appear to meet the expectations of all Canadian constituents. By the mid-1990s it had expanded to eighteen divisions to try and serve different research interests. Ginzel, Kramer, and Sutton[66] describe this type of situation as a dual problem of both informational and strategic complexity. The institution serves diverse audiences with more heterogenous expectations and motives. '[A]s the number of interested parties increases, so does the difficulty in constructing a single, coherent account that will satisfy all members of the audience.'[67]

While there is an inherent irony in the fact that ASAC was created by the large universities to further their advancement as internationally recognized institutions, and then abandoned by them when their aim was achieved, this should not detract from the excellent job ASAC has performed in the critical roles of communicating standards and of guarding academic freedom for individual Canadian faculty members. 'Pushed to the limit "academic freedom" ... may be explicit freedom from administrators, even from peers in other disciplines, but it is not implicit freedom from colleagues in other universities ... No force matches that of the implicit and explicit influences of professional affiliation.'[68] ASAC is the most immediate instrument for Canadian professors in management faculties to demonstrate professional judgment in their particular function, and to gain credibility in order to take their place in the traditional collegial model of consensus building in their university. Faculty participation in ASAC can help build a commonly accepted ideology, and provide evaluators with a standard to determine merit. The divisions create Canada-wide collegial support groups more easily than is possible in the larger international associations. ASAC is the most accessible conference for Canadians, a place to meet a wide range of professors and refresh professional judgment, and where a new consensus can be developed, or at least discussed, creating professional influences and alliances that may prove more important than the values of the home institution. It functions as an essential interconnection among the functional specialties, and between management faculties, both in Canada and internationally.

In 1999 the possibility that ASAC can continue as a national forum for business research is less certain. Few senior business-school academics in the big ten and second-tier Canadian universities attend the ASAC conference or become members, although the participation by the doctoral students and junior faculty of these schools helps initiate this group into the processes of academic research. More seriously, in the late 1990s, Canadian business schools have felt the need to prove they meet international standards and international standards mean international conferences. Previously, management faculties, with the exception of the big ten, focused on local or regional markets. After 1990, enrolments in Canadian business schools declined and competition between schools increased. Still, a study published in 1994[69] found that most Canadian business faculties opposed accreditation with the American Assembly of Collegiate Schools of Business. Some rejected the idea that an American agency might be qualified to judge Canadian programs, while others viewed the cost of application and membership as excessive. UBC had been a member in the 1970s, but in 1994 only the management faculties of the two Alberta universities, Calgary and Alberta, were AACSB members.

In the late 1990s, just as Canadian firms felt intensified pressure by global competitors, so Canadian management faculties felt that AACSB accreditation helped establish their legitimacy relative to their Canadian and international competitors. In 1997 two business faculties in Québec, Laval and Concordia, gained accreditation. Both institutions' efforts were overshadowed by universities with long-time international reputations that conferred presumed superiority on the business faculties, Laval by the HÉC and Concordia by its Montréal neighbour, McGill. By obtaining accreditation when their rivals did not do so, Laval and Concordia could draw attention to the high standards of their programs and faculty research both to aid in recruiting students to their programs and to impress potential employers of their graduates. Recently business faculties at two big universities, Queen's and the University of Toronto, went through the evaluation scrutiny and were accredited in 1998 and 1999 respectively. The University of Manitoba was also admitted in 1999, while more Canadian business faculties are in the accreditation process. Anecdotal reports of faculties preparing to enter the process include universities from across Canada. This accelerating trend by larger business schools to meet international standards, to draw away from the smaller, regional institutions, and to see their competitors as international will be a challenge for ASAC.

APPENDIX

Association presidents and conference locations

---

* = Dean or director of faculty or school

1957–62: Association of Canadian Schools of Commerce and Business Administration (ACSCBA)

1	1957	T.H. McLeod,* Saskatchewan	1957	University of Ottawa
2	1957–8	W.J. McDougall,* Carleton	1958	University of Alberta
3	1958–9	W.A. Thompson,* Western	1959	University of Saskatchewan
4	1959–60	Clement Lockquell,* Laval	1960	Queen's University
5	1960–1	L.G. Macpherson,* Queen's	1961	Sir George Williams
6	1961–2	John Sawatsky,* Toronto	1962	McMaster University
7	1962–3	Ralph Harris,* Manitoba	1963	Université Laval
8	1963–4	D.E. Armstrong,* McGill	1964	Prince of Wales, PEI

1963–72: Association of Canadian Schools of Business / Association Canadienne des Écoles de Commerce (ACSB)

9	1964–5	G.N. Perry,* UBC	1965	University of British Columbia
10	1965–6	John Wettlaufer,* Western	1966	Université de Sherbrooke
11	1966–7	Roger Charbonneau,* HÉC	1967	Carleton University
12	1967–8	Lloyd Barber,* Saskatchewan	1968	University of Calgary
13	1968–9	Gunther Brink,* Sir George	1969	York University
14	1969–70	John Mundie,* Manitoba	1970	University of Manitoba
15	1970–1	John Mundie,* Manitoba	1971	Memorial University
16	1971–2	Roger Miller, Sherbrooke	1972	McGill University

1972–7: Canadian Association of Administrative Sciences/Association Canadienne des Sciences Administratives (CAAS)

17	1972–3	Vance Mitchell,* UBC	1973	Queen's University

1	1973–4	Herman Overgaard, Waterloo Lutheran	1974	University of Western Ontario
2	1974–5	Robert Crandall, Queen's	1975	University of Alberta
3	1975–6	Michael McCarrey, Ottawa	1976	Université Laval
4	1976–7	Larry Moore, UBC	1977	University of New Brunswick

1977: Administrative Sciences Association of Canada / L'Association des Sciences Administratives du Canada (ASAC)

5	1977–8	Dawson Brewer, York University	1978	University of Western Ontario
6	1978–9	Glen Mumey, Alberta	1979	University of Saskatchewan
7	1979–80	Allan Blair, Science Council of Canada	1980	Montréal (UQAM)
8	1980–1	J. Brent Ritchie, Calgary	1981	Dalhousie University
9	1981–2	Robert Sexty, Memorial	1982	University of Ottawa
10	1982–3	André Théoret, Sherbrooke	1983	University of British Columbia
11	1983–4	Roger Hall, Manitoba	1984	University of Guelph
12	1984–5	J. Ronald Collins, Guelph	1985	Université de Montréal
13	1985–6	Michel Laroche, Concordia	1986	Whistler (Simon Fraser)
14	1986–7	William Wedley, Simon Fraser	1987	University of Toronto
15	1987–8	Robert House, Toronto	1988	Halifax (Saint Mary's)
16	1988–9	Hermann Schwind, Saint Mary's	1989	Montréal (McGill)
17	1989–90	Hamid Etemad, McGill	1990	Whistler (Simon Fraser)
18	1990–1	Udayan Rege, Brock	1991	Niagara Falls (Brock)
19	1991–2	Steven McShane, Simon Fraser	1992	Québec City (Laval)
20	1992–3	André Petit, Sherbrooke	1993	Lake Louise (Calgary)
21	1993–4	Gary Moore, Calgary	1994	Halifax (Dalhousie)
22	1994–5	Tony Schellinck, Dalhousie	1995	Windsor (Windsor)
23	1995–6	Andy Andiappan, Windsor	1996	Montréal (HÉC)
24	1996–7	Alain Gosselin, HÉC	1997	St John's (Memorial)
25	1997–8	Lessey Sooklal, Memorial	1998	Saskatoon (Saskatchewan)
23	1998–9	Lou Hammond Ketilson, Saskatchewan (Saskatoon)	1999	Saint John (UNB Saint John)
24	1999–2000	Gregory Irving, UNBSJ	2000	Montréal (UQAM)

Note: As the first unwieldly name indicates, the association was a group of schools, not of individuals. The name adopted in 1963 is shorter, and bilingual, but its acronym is different in English and French, and unpronounceable in both. The third try reflects the popularity of the term 'administrative sciences' in the 1970s, but again, the acronym is different in the two languages. Finally, in 1977, the name ASAC was adopted, producing the same acronym in both languages in a form that can be pronounced without sounding like alphabet soup. To confuse things a bit more, ASAC dates its founding to 1973, when it was admitted to the Canadian Learned Societies and was named CAAS. In 1973, the annual conference numbering was reset to one again, ignoring the continuity of the association since 1957. Until 1985, the conference was held at a university chosen by the Learneds. Beginning in 1986, ASAC chose its own conference location, a hotel near the host university.

NOTES

1 P.M. Maher, 'Business School Research: Academics Should Be Concerned,' *CJAS* 7 (1990), 16–20.
2 D.C. North, *Institutions, Institutional Change and Economic Performance* (Cambridge: Cambridge University Press, 1990).
3 ACSCBA Constitution, June 1957.
4 C.D. Wrege, 'The Inception, Early Struggles, and Growth of the Academy of Management,' in D.A. Wren, ed., *Papers Dedicated to the Development of Modern Management* (Norman, Okla.: Academy of Management, 1985), 78–88.
5 M. von Zur-Muehlen, *University Management Education and Research in Canada* (Ottawa: Statistics Canada, 1979), 21
6 M.B.E. Clarkson, 'The Alien MBA,' *CBR* 6:1 (Spring 1979), 24.
7 W.R. Scott, *Institutions and Organizations* (London: Sage, 1995).
8 See chapter 3, 'Daub and Buchan. 'Business Education at Queen's 1889–1988.'
9 D. Sanders, ed., *Learning to Lead* (London: University of Western Ontario, 1993).
10 S. Shapiro, interview, June 1993.
11 P. White, interview, June 1993.
12 See chapter 2, 'The Founding of the École des Hautes Études Commerciales de Montréal.' See also Harvey, *Histoire de l'École des Hautes Études Commerciales de Montréal, Tome 1: 1887–1926* (Montréal: Québec/Amérique–Presses HÉC, 1994).
13 See chapter 4, 'From Commerce to Management: The Evolution of Business Education at the University of Toronto.'
14 R. Crandall, personal communication, 23 June 1993; White interview, 1993.
15 White interview, 1993.

16 ACSCBA, minutes of first annual meeting, 7 June 1957.
17 M.S. Larson, *The Rise of Professionalism: A Sociological Analysis* (London: University of Chicago Press, 1977), 71.
18 Larson, *The Rise of Professionalism*, 45.
19 The deans of the largest business schools, supporters of the resolution, acted on it. The senate at Western responded to the challenge and started the first PhD program in business in Canada, in 1961. In 1969, the University of Toronto PhD program began, with specializations in finance, marketing, organizational behaviour, and business economics. The same year, UBC started a PhD in administration, with specialization in finance, marketing, and organizational behaviour.
20 ACSCBA, minutes of third annual meeting, June 1959.
21 R.A. Gordon and J.E. Howell, *Higher Education for Business* (New York: Columbia University Press, 1959).
22 F. Pierson, *The Education of American Businessmen* (Toronto: McGraw-Hill, 1959).
23 K. Polanyi, *The Great Transformation* (Boston: Beacon Press, 1964).
24 Pierson, *The Education of American Businessmen.*
25 R.R. Locke, *Management and Higher Education since 1940: The Influence of America and Japan on West Germany, Great Britain and France* (Cambridge: Cambridge University Press, 1989), 217.
26 Locke, *Management and Higher Education*, 70.
27 C. Bissell, *Halfway Up Parnassus: A Personal Account of the University of Toronto, 1932–1971* (Toronto: UTP, 1974), 71.
28 Larson, *The Rise of Professionalism*, 42.
29 White interview, June 1993.
30 By 1999, seven Canadian management faculties had AACSB accreditation: Alberta, Calgary, Concordia, Laval, Manitoba, Queen's, and Toronto.
31 L. Moore, interview, June 1993.
32 J. Mundie, interview, June 1993.
33 Crandall, 1993.
34 R. Miller, 'A Proposal for CAAS Mission Statement,' CAAS executive committee meeting, January 1972.
35 Crandall, 1993.
36 M. Weber, *Economy and Society* (London: University of California Press, 1978), 304.
37 This tendency has been noted by several observers, including Robert Crandall (Queen's) and John Mundie (Manitoba), former ASAC presidents, and is supported by the membership lists and by counts of participation by university at the conferences.

38 Clarkson, 'The Alien MBA,' 22.

39 M. von Zur-Muehlen, *Business Education and Faculty of Canadian Universities* (Ottawa: Economic Council of Canada, 1971); *Guide to Business Education Programs at Canadian Universities* (Ottawa: monograph, November 1976).

40 M. Maher, personal communication, 8 June 1977.

41 Clarkson, 'The Alien MBA,' 22–3.

42 M. Clarkson, personal communication, 8 June 1997.

43 Consultative Group, *Consultative Group on Research and Graduate Education in Business Management and Administrative Studies Report* (Ottawa: CFDMAS, December 1979), 13.

44 Consultative Group, *University Management Education and Research: A Developing Crisis* (Ottawa: CFDMAS, April 1980).

45 CFDMAS, *Report of the National Conference Managing in the 1980s: Choosing Themes for Management Research* (Ottawa: CFDMAS, February 1981).

46 R. Sexty, personal communication, 1993.

47 ASAC executive committee meeting minutes, March 1980.

48 ASAC *Bulletin* (Spring 1986).

49 For discussions on legitimization, see J.A.C. Baum and C. Oliver, 'International Linkages and Organizational Mortality,' *ASQ* 36 (1991), 187–218; J.W. Meyer and W.R. Scott, *Organizational Environments: Ritual and Rationality* (Beverly Hills, CA: Sage, 1983); and J. Pfeffer and C.R. Salancik, *The External Control of Organizations* (New York: Harper & Row, 1978).

50 ASAC executive committee minutes, 1 November 1986.

51 ASAC *Bulletin* (Fall 1995).

52 M. Maher, personal communication, 9 June 1997.

53 ASAC executive committee meeting minutes, 27 February 1993.

54 C. Oliver, 'Strategic Responses to Institutional Processes,' *AMR* 16 (1991), 145–79.

55 Scott, *Institutions and Organizations*.

56 Oliver, 'Strategic Responses,' 157–9.

57 Ibid., 153–4.

58 B. Ashforth and B. Gibbs, 'The Double-edge of Organizational Legitimization,' *OS* 1 (1990), 177–94.

59 K.M. Macdonald, *The Sociology of the Professions* (London: Sage, 1995), 68.

60 J.S. Meyer and B. Rowan, 'Institutionalized Organizations: Formal Structure as Myth and Ceremony,' *AJS* 83 (1977), 340–63.

61 See P.L. Berger and T. Luckmann, *The Social Construction of Reality* (New York: Doubleday, 1966), 57, on this phenomenon.

62 Oliver, 'Strategic Responses,' 152–3.

63 J.W. Meyer and B. Rowan, chapter 2 in W.W. Powell and P.J. DiMaggio, eds,

The New Institutionalism in Organizational Analysis (Chicago: University of Chicago Press, 1991), 14.

64 Larson, *The Rise of Professionalism*, 43.

65 Ashforth and Gibbs, 'The Double-edge of Organizational Legitimization,' 183.

66 L.E. Ginzel, R.M. Kramer, and R.I. Sutton, 'Organizational Impression Management as a Reciprocal Influence Process,' in L.L. Cummings and B.W. Staw, eds, *Research in Organizational Behavior* 15 (Greenwich, Conn.: JAI Press, 1993), 227–66.

67 Ibid., 254.

68 C. Hardy, A. Langley, H. Mintzberg, and J. Rose, 'Strategy Formation in the University Setting,' in J.S. Bess, ed., *College and University Organization: Insights from the Behavioral Sciences* (New York: New York University Press, 1984), 169–210.

69 D.F. Coleman, P.C. Wright, and J.M. Tolliver, 'American Style Accreditation and Its Application in Canada: Perceptions of Utility,' *CJAS* 11:2 (1994), 194–8.

11

Canadian Management Education at the Millennium[1]

BARRY E.C. BOOTHMAN

Who – what power named the name that drove your fate? –
what hidden brain could divine your future,
steer that word to the mark,
to the bride of spears,
  the whirlpool churning armies,
    Oh for all the world a Helen!

Agamemnon

Many things I can command the Mirror to reveal, ... and to some I can show what they desire to see. But the Mirror will also show things unbidden, and those are often stranger and more profitable than things which we wish to behold ...

J.R.R. Tolkien, *The Fellowship of the Ring*

In key ways the second half of the twentieth century was *la belle époque* for Canadian management education. The enrolment in business programs more than doubled each decade until the 1970s and even then continued to grow at a strong pace. Faculties of administration had accounted for less than 3 per cent of full-time enrolment at the baccalaureate level before 1950. By 1991 every Canadian university had constructed undergraduate business programs, propelling an increase in this share to 13 per cent of full-time, and 17 per cent of part-time, students. Between 1961 and 1991 the number of MBA programs quintupled, while the enrolment expanded tenfold. Doctoral-level offerings in business had not been established thirty years previously, but by 1991 fifteen universities serviced more than 450 candidates, a group that represented about 2 per cent of Canadian PhD students.[2] This growth unfolded not just as a response to strong demand for individuals knowledgeable about business, but from the efforts of dedicated personnel at many institutions.

Despite these accomplishments the term 'fin-de-siècle' has come into vogue among many business academics, a phrase which refers to a sense of ending and the germination of a new environmental reality. This attitude has emerged not from millenarian speculation but from a recognition that the field has entered an era of maturity. Management always has been distinctive within a university context, since faculty members not only carry out teaching and research but are widely expected to demonstrate relevance in those endeavours, that is, to facilitate the improvement of enterprises in the public and private sectors. Since the late 1970s, however, many scholars and practitioners have claimed that North American business schools have failed to meet social needs, have fostered undesirable attitudes, or have ignored important issues. The focus of the criticisms has been the curricula of business programs, since these actuate the perceptions of different schools about the appropriate patterns of student learning and career preparation. The millennium thus offers a convenient, if quite artificial, time for a reappraisal. Historical periods are rather like people in one respect. They can be assessed at the end for achievements, values, and limitations.

This essay looks back to survey various factors that have moulded the state of the art and peers forward to consider the issues that will reconfigure current practices in the proximate future. It examines the nature of Canadian management education in three acts. The first probes the changing environmental conditions which confront Canadian business schools and the concerns that many observers have raised about contemporary practices. The second extends the analysis by appraising the orientations and the content of business programs, while the third section considers several of the contradictory forces that are propelling the further evolution of the field.

1. Fin-de-Siècle

Business faculties experienced heightened demand for their services during the latter half of the twentieth century as students sought career-oriented disciplines with direct employment opportunities. Growth rates varied among programs in different regions, with the most rapid increases occurring in Québec and western Canada. Because administration had been declared as a major by 27 per cent of undergraduates in the United States, there still appeared to be considerable room for expansion in Canada, even though American enrolment marginally declined after 1982. But enrolment in Canadian baccalaureate programs actually peaked at 13 per cent of the full-time student population during 1991, and the number of business undergraduates has since dropped by 5 per cent, while the population of graduate candidates has increased slightly.[3] Tendencies have differed from institution to institution, with some retaining stable patterns while others have experienced sharp declines. Owing to prolonged recession, the reorganization of economic sectors, and corporate downsizing, the Canadian demand for business majors has reached saturation in many areas. There are needs for individuals to staff entry-level positions or to supply specialized skills, but a degree no longer represents (if it ever did) a guaranteed vehicle for career success.

The expansion and replacement of faculty generated an annual need for approximately one hundred new appointments from 1971 until 1989, when hiring precipitously collapsed. A significant proportion of the personnel who were hired during the 1960s or 1970s are approaching retirement. The aging of this population was expected to trigger a new wave of recruitment, but during the 1990s numerous schools postponed staffing plans or hired less-qualified individuals. Reductions in operating grants compelled many faculties to cut support services, not replace retirees or eliminate sessional lecturers, thereby decreasing their flexibility and sometimes weakening the quality of program delivery. At the time of writing, the administrations for several of the largest universities had announced their intentions to launch extensive recruiting efforts with the coming of the new century in order to renew their professorate capabilities, but budgetary restrictions still hamper the ability of many other institutions even to consider the possibility of new staff who may provide innovative approaches. This problem has been compounded by the tendency of doctoral candidates in business administration to train in narrow specialities, not an interdisciplinary locus that can abet effective teaching or flexibility in program staffing. Garnering support for research also became more problematic during the 1990s as governments slashed the monies for funding agencies and universities. Sixty-eight proposals in administrative studies received more than $2.4 million from the SSHRC in 1992. By 1995 only 29 proposals worth $1.4 million were approved, and most observers have expected this source of funding to become insignificant within a decade.[4] Moreover, the salaries and support services that Canadian business faculty have received in comparison to their American counterparts have steadily deteriorated. Estimated by one analyst as a reduction of more than 40 per cent since the early 1980s exclusive of exchange-rate shifts or escalations in taxation rates, this condition has compelled many of the best scholars to relocate to the United States and the private sector.[5]

From its inception, management as an academic field has attracted criticism from practitioners and scholars. This has been a function of the very nature of professional education, since a compromise must be struck among the competing requirements of teaching, research, and service to the university and business communities – a reconciliation that can be difficult given the diverse and often unique circumstances of different organizations.[6] To a greater degree than other disciplines, there are alternative pedagogical approaches and a broad range of topics which should be covered. Accordingly, no single model or theory has guided program design and within alternative orientations there have been variations derived from distinct institutional goals, teaching styles, or patterns of course sequencing.

A tidal wave of criticism aimed at business schools arose in North America around 1979 and has continued relatively unabated to this day. In part, this phenomenon reflected disillusionment about the effectiveness of management education, since the competitive status of many American or Canadian firms eroded dramatically after the 1950s. Clearly, some observers felt, business schools must be to blame as the progenitors of a new professional management paradigm and they must be disseminating poor tools or concepts. For some commentators, problems associated with the shift towards greater academic rigour in management subjects raised questions about institutional policies, while for others the very expansion of business programs was an unfavourable development that undermined the traditional role of post-secondary education. The major critics have included journalists, practitioners, and academics and their concerns have been well known to management educators. Numerous surveys therefore reappraised the status of the field of business administration, of which the most famous has been a 1988 monograph, *Management Education and Development: Drift or Thrust into the 21st Century?* by Lyman Porter (University of California, Irvine) and Lawrence McKibben (University of Oklahoma). While this analysis and other works were carefully supported with empirical evidence, the overwhelming majority of the critics have relied upon impressionistic data. A few have been revanchist, seeking a return to an earlier tradition or treating administrative studies as a scapegoat for social problems, but most writers have advanced thoughtful reappraisals. Virtually all have recognized that some issues are not unique to management education, but are problems that afflict universities qua social institutions.

One consequence resulting from the adoption of a discipline-based orientation in management education after 1960 has been characterized as a 'new vocationalism.' This trend resulted from population growth, which saturated job markets and triggered competition for marketable skills as well as a college degree. The expansion of management programs unfolded in tandem with increases in the enrolment for job-related studies such as law, engineering, and dentistry. In response to student demand, business schools elaborated career-track offerings between functional disciplines and then specialized streams within disciplines. Some reviewers have claimed that these practices weakened the autonomy enjoyed by universities from business or government influence. Others have linked it to changes in policies that eliminated the priority traditionally given to the liberal arts. Historians David Bercuson, Robert Bothwell, and Jack Granatstein have noted in a delightfully caustic review that every Canadian university eviscerated regulations that compelled educational breadth and thereby created a 'supermarket curriculum.' Most departments now offer streams of specialized learning, and '[a]ll these programs are based upon the assumption that students should have the freedom to choose. But why should they have such freedom? Few first-year students have the knowledge or experience to choose the sort of program that would give them a solid foundation of essential knowledge. Like kids in a candy store they will usually grab at the brightest baubles – or the easiest courses ... Such a system does not offer freedom, it gives license. Some students may choose wisely, but society no longer can afford to gamble on the wisdom of nineteen-year-olds.'[7] Within business schools the trend toward greater specialization has been repeatedly condemned for spawning a generation of technocratic analysts who may be highly knowledgeable about functions like accounting and finance but know little else about the world where they must survive.[8]

Contemporary business curricula have been condemned by academics and practitioners for a litany of perceived sins. Various authors have claimed that instructors focus upon problem solving, not problem definition, or that the most popular theories reinforce risk-averse attitudes by identifying solutions in terms of short-term financial or market-share criteria rather than innovation and the long-term construction of competitive advantage. The key to business success, Robert Hayes and William Abernathy noted in a heavily cited article, is 'to create value where none existed before. Such determination, such striving to excel, requires leaders – not just controllers, market analysts, and portfolio managers.'[9] Three issues have tended to attract the most criticism. For nearly forty years, as part of the shift towards an academic paradigm, business schools have given much greater emphases to subjects requiring quantitative analytical techniques versus the 'soft' aspects of administration, such as organizational behaviour or human resource management. Second, the communications skills, especially written, of business graduates have been described as woeful and deteriorating. Many faculties also are alleged to provide weak coverage of integrative or general subjects like production and service management, international business, the environmental framework of business, and entrepreneurship.[10]

Numerous critics have portrayed business schools as isolated and conservative, reluctant to alter their practices despite well-publicized calls for modifications. Lyman Porter and Lawrence McKibben declared that success had bred complacency and a propensity to imitate, not innovate. Business faculties, who had always insisted that companies carry out strategic planning, often did not practise what they taught. 'Relatively little planning for anything beyond next semester's classroom schedule ... really takes place in a great many schools,' they noted. 'Inertia of tradition, inadequacy of marginal resources ... and especially lack of incentive systems with which to reward change in academia all combine to inhibit strategic planning.'[11] Despite widespread demands for revisions, 'nothing much has changed,' one Canadian review observed in 1990. 'The occasional "integrative" course has been added to the first or last year of the program; the odd course in ethics has been grafted into the program; the old "business-and-society" or "business-and-the-changing-environment" course has been resurrected ... and many schools have initiated curriculum reviews. But for most schools, it's still pretty much business as usual.'[12]

Faculties of management always have been encouraged to ensure that teaching and research are applicable to business situations. The development of coherent theory was anticipated as a logical step in the development of a professional discipline but, despite the ascendancy of the academic paradigm, it remains widely assumed by many practitioners and scholars that a practical dimension should be retained to keep studies relevant and aid people other than just those concerned with the advancement of knowledge. The transformation of business schools after 1960, however, triggered widespread complaints about the loss of this element at many institutions, about an intellectual isolation by researchers who were predominantly concerned with fulfilling their responsibilities to one constituency – the academic community.[13] Henry Mintzberg of McGill's Faculty of Management, a major writer in the field of strategic management, argued that a doctoral degree has represented a license to teach business in universities, but the schools 'do not generally hire people capable of teaching true managerial skills ... The PhD is a research degree, and in good part it attracts introverts, people who want to bury themselves in a library under a stack of data.' As a consequence, different specialities in business administration became dominated by '"number crunchers" and "behavioral scientists" who strut around like high priests seeking to ensure a degree of "scientific" rigor in research sufficient to detach researchers from the very organizations they are supposed to understand.'[14] One review portrayed academic faculty members as individuals 'who had never succeeded in business, but who could tinker, both mathematically and behaviourally (and often on irrelevant databases) with significant problems and who often deluded themselves and others into believing that they had actually found a solution.' Rather, they 'applied their new sciences to unreal problems' and in their research ran 'from the responsible, risk-taking, externally-focused, multidimensional, and high achievement area of corporate life toward a more sheltered risk-free existence.'[15]

Not surprisingly, this phenomenon has been linked to a gap between the research conducted by business-school faculty and that sought by managers. Much of the early writing about management principles was done by or for practitioners who coped with the difficulties experienced by specific companies. However, contemporary scholars have been critiqued for insularity, for dealing with narrow research topics versus general management themes. The recruitment of personnel from disciplines like psychology and sociology fulfilled a key goal, an upgrading of academic standards, but the introduction of so many faculty (often without training in basic management theory) tended to fragment the field. Joseph McGuire noted during 1982 that academics seemed to be 'less interested in the substance of management theory' and more with the internal validity of research than they had been thirty years earlier, with few new 'elegant' or 'sophisticated' hypotheses being proffered. Richard Whiteley similarly observed that 'much research in management studies seems to be *ad hoc* and opportunistic in its selection of problems and approaches, with little coordination of tasks or outcomes.' Harold Koontz, a prominent scholar in general management, was blunter and argued that a fragmentation of management research had emerged from narrow academic perceptions of specialties. The outcome had been 'a jungle of confusing thought, theory and advice to practicing managers.'[16] 'The simple fact is that there is far too little cutting edge research on management issues going on in Canadian business schools,' Roger Smith, Alberta's former business dean, declared. This problem was compounded by the tendency of scholarship in management, as in other disciplines, occasionally to be swept up by fashions and fads of short duration. 'New techniques in management practice, often touted as a "sure-fire" means to success, result in an outpouring of literature and examination,' Michael Maher of Calgary legitimately pointed out. 'Such techniques often fall by the wayside as new methods are introduced and these are subjected to scrutiny.'[17]

The issue emerged because academics and managers have perceived research questions and define relevance in different ways. The incentive systems at most Canadian universities have not rewarded efforts to apply research findings in business settings and usually have depreciated consulting-based studies that advance 'ready-to-use-knowledge.' Concerned with gaining tenure and promotion, or with establishing credibility in their chosen areas, business scholars have been moulded by the review processes conducted by their colleagues and academic journals. These have favoured demonstrated emphases upon research methodologies and the articulation of concepts or theories that supposedly will illustrate originality. People or companies are not studied as particular cases but as instances that permit investigators to establish or disconfirm generalizations about organizations. Researchers try to isolate and reduce the influence of extraneous factors from data collection in order to gain warrantable statements about different relations. Time, in the form of pressing decisions, may not be an influence since appraisals can be reserved until evidence accumulates. Practitioners, in contrast, perceive themselves as clients who have issues which must be resolved within discrete time frames. Working within organizations, they approach problems holistically and qualitatively, concerned about the symbolism or implementation problems associated with different solutions.[18]

The different areas of management studies now have well-established bodies of knowledge, scholarly journals, and lines of inquiry. If less-innovative models or concepts have emerged over the last two decades, it probably reflects a transition from the heady days of initial investigation and theory development to the more mundane obligations of theory verification. Nonetheless, mounting frustration among practitioners about the type of research carried out at business schools has been evident, particularly in the larger American market. Some business leaders have lobbied for a reconfiguration of the priorities given to teaching and research, and a few have even recommended that faculty focus overwhelmingly on the former.[19] A growing number of business organizations have organized a range of educational and developmental activities in-house or have employed private consultants. In Europe and Japan, on-the-job training historically has been a preferred model for management education, and business representatives occasionally have suggested that this approach might be applied in North America to a greater degree.

Various observers also have been bedevilled by the tendency of many instructors at Canadian business schools to disseminate uncritically models that were developed to explain American phenomena. Because the size of the textbook market limits the economic viability of distinctively Canadian monographs, faculty necessarily use American monographs or 'Canadianized' versions of those materials. However, many of the theories dominating subjects like strategic management and finance have been based upon the behaviour of 'Fortune 500' enterprises that are characterized by massive economies of scale and scope, extensive internationalization, cutting-edge technology, or a diversification of ownership. The appropriateness of the findings to Canadian conditions can be dubious, since large parts of the economy are characterized by regionally organized markets, public-sector regulation, trailing-edge technologies, and the control of major companies by families or entrepreneurs. Thus, students and practitioners regularly complain that business faculty give grossly inadequate attention to the actual organizational traits and environmental framework of 'Canadian' capitalism.

Across North America there also has been concern about the values and attitudes of management students. The business media have tended to portray business studies, especially those leading to an MBA degree, as a vehicle to social prosperity. Magazines like *Business Week* and *Canadian Business* annually rank different schools, creating lively debates about which are supposedly the best. Such exercises are fraught with methodological problems and the surveys reflect sampling biases or subjective views of the faculty reputations rather than any measurement of objective criteria.[20] However, the articles have reinforced popular beliefs that business education is a prerequisite for career success Thus, it is not surprising that the primary motivation cited by candidates who enter the programs has tended to be the desire to secure good employment after graduation, not necessarily an interest in the subject itself.[21] Business majors, while they rarely have clear pictures of what jobs actually may be available, uniformly expect companies to offer interesting assignments, supportive superiors, and a balanced lifestyle that will allow them later to establish their own prosperous firms.[22] MBAs frequently have been singled out by practitioners as an uncaring, immature elite who have unrealistic career expectations – the Sherman McCoys of the next generation.

Surveys have documented beliefs among executives that business students are weak in communications or interpersonal skills, or leadership capabilities like 'vision' and 'willingness to take calculated risks.' Business-school graduates are often described as overly focused on quantitative and short-run technical issues or unprepared to take broad, long-range perspectives. Ironically, commentators have concurrently described them as unduly careerist, lacking loyalty, and wanting to assume decision-making responsibilities too quickly.[23] All observers have noted that some values can be traced to social norms, the media, or other cultural factors and that major variations can be found among students located in different countries. One study, for example, characterized English Canadian students as emphasizing personal and materialistic issues with a pragmatic self-oriented perspective, whereas students in France tended to be more negative about corporate conduct and gave greater value to spiritual or social concerns.[24] Survey data in the United States have mapped a widespread concurrence among human-resource directors that business graduates have high work motivation and analytical skills; but, unlike business-school deans or faculty, only 15 per cent of the directors have described business students as well prepared for their first jobs. When questioned, corporate respondents tend to raise a laundry list of areas where management students lack proper knowledge: the social or political environment, entrepreneurship, international business, ethics, and an understanding of how the business world really operates.[25]

The suggestions advanced to correct these perceived deficiencies have been highly consistent. While some entail slight modifications of current policies, others require the fundamental reconfiguration of institutional operations. The recommendations usually encompass an interrelated set of initiatives: expand the breadth of liberal arts obligations; augment the courses that integrate functional activities with offerings on production, the business environment, and ethics; adjust the current proportions of quantitative vis-à-vis qualitative courses; add topics like technological literacy and communications skills; give greater stress to entrepreneurial and strategic thinking; encourage leadership and stewardship rather than management; internationalize the curriculum; and develop programs that will facilitate life-long learning.

All of the commentaries need to be treated with circumspection, since the authors sometimes overstate their assertions about supposed deficiencies and rarely distinguish between institutions. Corporate executives always have given contradictory signals about the appropriate dimensions of management education, as one influential study noted in 1959: 'Business itself is pulled in two directions. It feels increasingly the need for educated men who have the breadth, perspective, and flexibility of mind to cope with a business environment that grows in complexity and changes with bewildering rapidity. Yet it also feels the pressure for more and better trained specialists who can master the technical problems that have been spawned by the technological and organizational revolution of the twentieth century. Thus business looks to the colleges to give it generalists and specialists, if possible embodied in the same person.'[26]

Surveys have indicated that chief executive officers favour the recruitment of generalists who have demonstrated competence in languages, international business, or human resource management. The personnel directors who actually conduct hiring, in contrast, have tended to select individuals with specialized technical skills. Regardless of the veracity of criticisms advanced by some practitioners against management education, most business students have recognized the criteria that many firms have employed in praxis and the market differentials that may be received by accomplished technocrats or MBAs. The signals sent by business have been similarly mixed on other issues. Surveys, such as one by the Corporate Higher Education

Forum task force, found that Canadian companies have given verbal, not necessarily tangible, support to questions like the internationalization of management or the hiring of women and minorities at the senior executive level.[27] In any event, there are limits to what an educational program can accomplish, and the list of adjustments desired by different observers has been so extensive that several years of additional studies would be necessary.

Some critiques of management education have been unfair in several ways. Although business schools must provide graduates who can meet the current and future needs of companies, this does not mean conforming to short-term objectives espoused by corporate representatives or supplying neatly packaged ideas. Within the broader mission of their institutions, management faculty should be expected to prepare individuals for the complex roles they must play as citizens and to contribute to their social development by advancing the boundaries of knowledge. The trend towards specialization within the field should be recognized as part of a fundamental pattern of institutional development. As reviewed in the first chapter of this volume, Canadian universities during the twentieth century began with an orientation that emphasized the classics or liberal arts and then evolved in the direction of increasingly sophisticated training in the professions, the physical or social sciences, and the humanities. The notion that an emphasis should be given just to teaching, moreover, is a forced dichotomy. There are productive academics who perform poorly in the classroom, just as there are excellent teachers who are weak researchers. Superior faculties balance teaching and research, since post-secondary education, by its very nature, should seek not merely to transmit information but to supply original, thought-provoking materials.[28]

Some of the weaknesses can be traced to a more fundamental problem – the deterioration of primary and secondary schooling across North America. During the past thirty years, the learning experience at those levels has been successively fragmented by waves of ideological reforms aimed at developing individuals who can think creatively. Proposals from reformers for child-centred or process-oriented education generated a series of well-intentioned, but sometimes ill-conceived, initiatives that eliminated standardized testing and deleted history, geography, and language skills from the mandatory curricula. Lobbying from interest groups concurrently spawned a series of efforts to foster learning via 'de-streaming' or 'de-coursing,' while other initiatives positioned a range of symbolic or politically correct topics into programs at the cost of less time for traditional subjects. The most recent fad has been for 'learning outcomes' or 'results-based' education, which supposedly will enhance the abilities of individuals to cope with the conditions resulting from rapid technological and social change. Students under this regime are not expected to master specific skills or subject content, but to display 'complex role performances' that theoretically will link classroom sessions with real-life situations. The successive revisions of elementary and secondary schooling have allowed positive gains like individualized instruction or a diversification of teaching techniques, but university instructors usually can point to unintended consequences: systemic grade inflation, encouragement of mediocrity versus excellence, poor learning habits, and weakening performance in mathematics, the sciences, or languages. Indeed, the decline in numerical and grammatical scores on scholastic aptitude tests became so marked after 1980 that to mask the trend a rolling average (rather than a fixed standard) was adopted. Despite all of the social experiments, it has been estimated that one million Canadians will have graduated from secondary schools during the 1990s functionally illiterate. Many more have a tenuous knowledge about basic subjects – including mathematics, geography, or even the history of their own country.[29] Not only is it dubious whether management education represents the agent to rectify these deficiencies, the problems have unfortunately become so entrenched that remedial efforts by universities come too little, too late for many students.

Clearly there are widespread beliefs that fundamental problems have emerged, but because the criticisms often rely upon impressionistic evidence it may be asked whether the perceived gaps can be documented. Accordingly, the next section considers the programs offered by Canadian universities with an analysis that proceeds through two stages. The generic orientations of curriculum design at the baccalaureate and graduate levels will be considered, then the dimensions of the mandatory component of the programs will be summarized descriptively. The findings from this review subsequently can be employed as a basis for identifying directions for change.

2. The State of the Art

Curriculum design represents the key strategic issue that must be handled in a university. The development of educational programs requires an identification of the types of knowledge or skills that should be delivered, the determination of appropriate sequences of instruction, and the prioritization of topic areas. These choices, when aggregated, constitute intellectual frameworks that define how learning will unfold and illustrate how faculties perceive their fields. Curricula also provide valuable diagnostic indicators about the goals that different schools deem important. As Richard Hofstadter and Stewart Handy noted forty-five years ago in a magisterial survey of American higher education: 'A college curriculum is significant chiefly for two things: it reveals the educated community's conception of what knowledge is most worth transmitting to the cream of its youth, and it reveals what kind of mind and character an education is expected to produce. The curriculum is a barometer by which we may measure the cultural pressures that operate upon the school.'[30] The orientation and content of curricula mould budgetary, hiring, and pedagogical decisions. Thus, although program design should be guided by academic criteria, the choices can be significantly influenced by the competitive status of institutions – their ability to attract students and qualified instructors, to secure resources, or to garner aid from external interests.

Questions of strategy and policy are, by definition, wicked problems. Strategy may be characterized as the patterns of decisions, goals, and initiatives by which executives define the mission of an organization, what business or businesses the enterprise is in, and the future dimensions of its endeavours. Policy represents the plans, procedures, and guidelines which are established to realize those expectations.[31] The successful formation and implementation of organizational strategies require managers to match activities with resource capabilities and to adjust activities to environmental threats or opportunities. They also must shape administrative structures and internal processes to ensure commitment by the individuals who are designated to carry out the organizational goals. Strategic choice thus constitutes the normative function of executive leadership, a task with complex options that can be hard to identify and with choices that must be reached despite incomplete data or uncertainty about the outcomes. Once made, those decisions cannot be easily reversed, since resources are allocated in ways that condition an enterprise's distinctive competencies and competitive advantages as well as the synergy or interrelationships among its operations. The delineation of strategies and structures over time mould the beliefs of those who have influence, thereby creating parameters upon future choices or setting off waves of lesser decisions that alter functional activities.[32]

The task of curriculum development can prove invidious because different educational approaches cannot easily be documented as superior or inferior. Most faculty members conscientiously try to enhance their own course offerings, but decision making about the general curriculum of a program frequently is supply driven, a function of the interests and values of specific instructors or the ability to recruit qualified personnel. Additions or deletions of subjects may prove controversial because of their impact on the 'turf' of existing departments. Choices must be made about the technology or modes of learning: lectures, seminars, case discussions, projects, teleconferencing. Program design also has to take into account the views of non-management departments. Many business faculties have limited discretion for making changes at the undergraduate level because university-wide enrolment patterns and resource allocations may be affected, but at the graduate level numerous business schools operate as quasi-autonomous units. Instructors also must agree about how education should condition the self-actualization of students. Individuals might be propelled towards becoming generalists, experts in a field, or pragmatic problem-solvers. As noted in the first essay of this volume, among business schools this issue has taken the form of repetitious debates about whether functional specialization versus generalism should be encouraged. Finally, the expectations of students or employers and the probable responses of rival institutions must be considered. A congruence about this set of issues must be achieved despite the concerns that individuals will raise about the impact of alterations upon their teaching and research obligations. Not surprisingly, although business schools formally reappraise their curricula every five to seven years, adjustments tend to occur incrementally rather than from systemic reorganization. Faculty members rarely attempt to survey the population of North American programs and instead consider 'comparable' institutions or seek out models from well-recognized schools. Inertia and group-think, not innovative change, thus can dominate the choice process, and proposals may succeed only if there are clear priorities or if the support of key individuals can be mobilized. Perhaps it is not surprising, therefore, that at a few institutions the general policies of 1999 are not significantly different from those of 1979 or even 1969.

For any organization various modes of behaviour theoretically might be pursued. In practice, issues such as competitive strategy, administrative structure, or technology of supply restrict the range of viable options. Variety may be limited by fashions and fads as admin-

istrators imitate other enterprises or enthusiastically embrace new topics and concepts that seemingly address the concerns of relevant
stakeholders. Organizations qua organizations hence adopt behavioural orientations that are characterized by configurations of strategies, infrastructure, and schema of shared beliefs. These may emerge
as frameworks that have been prescribed by managers a priori or as
patterns that result from the ad hoc conduct of organizational members. Nonetheless, the essence of a behavioural configuration is the
idea that systemic modes of conduct tend to be created by interdepen-
dent relations among the factors that are crucial for strategic effectiveness. Each configuration has an enduring theme with its own logic,
integrity, and evolutionary momentum.[33] If the fundamental imperatives change, marginal shifts can prove insufficient and a transformation into a new configuration must occur. Gestalts of systemic
behaviour are easily documented for academic institutions. At the
level of the overall university, a pattern of degrees and facilities will be
elaborated. Some become full-service research-oriented entities, while
others tend to engage in selective activities or emphasize teaching and
community-service functions.[34] Departments or faculties normally
elaborate programs that both conform with the broad organizational
mission and meet the perceived needs of relevant stakeholders. The
content or treatment of subjects may vary among instructors, but program configurations fall into logical patterns because of academic
norms about the 'common body of knowledge,' the flexibility conferred by the duration of studies, and the appropriate pedagogical
tools.

The Orientation of Baccalaureate Programs

As observed in the first chapter of this volume, alternate concepts
moulded the development of management education. These have been
characterized in the literature on post-secondary education as generalist versus specialist, qualitative versus quantitative, pragmatic versus
theoretical, practitioner versus research-oriented. The terms have over-
lapped, have been vague, and often are used in deprecatory ways.
Undergraduate programs traditionally have varied according to two
dimensions. Faculties have placed different emphases upon high
versus low breadth of education, that is, they have diverged about
whether students should be required to secure advanced learning in
subjects other than business administration. American colleges, for

instance, have periodically shifted between the priorities given to the liberal arts or vocational training.[35] The growth of industrial enterprises during the period of 1920 to 1960 stimulated the demand for managers, and business offerings at many universities in the United States were configured to enhance functional skills for entry-level positions in specific industries. While leading schools like Harvard remained centred upon the preparation of graduate students for general management, at numerous institutions the emphasis upon pragmatic vocational training became so advanced that it was difficult to determine whether faculty members were teachers or businessmen.[36] In response, a growing proportion of educators sought a reorientation that would ensure that management was treated as a profession analogous to law or medicine. Abetted by reports commissioned by the Ford and Carnegie Foundations and by initiatives from the American Assembly of Collegiate Schools of Business (AACSB), many business faculties sought a more balanced treatment, with advanced courses in the arts or sciences as well as management. Since 1970, as the complexity and technical sophistication of administrative offerings have expanded further, a drift towards vocational training has re-emerged.

Institutional practices also have differed according to the timing of management offerings. Some universities pace courses across the entire length of studies, while others weight them towards the latter half of programs. The former approach facilitates a concentration in an area of interest, while the latter presumes that specialization should not occur until students acquire intellectual maturity. When the dimensions of educational breadth and programmatic timing are combined, the product is a categorization schema of four gestalts as shown in table 11.1. Each, in the purest of forms, has represented an approach that can be distinguished by mission, the treatment of business versus non-business courses, and the degree of permissible specialization.

'Liberals' have been undergraduate programs offered by faculties that have retained the assumptions of early-twentieth-century management education: universities should supply a background in the liberal arts and treat subjects like business administration as ancillary to that mission. Most of the Canadian schools before the 1960s conformed to this orientation and, like the mission of their institutions, were concerned with providing a general education for young gentlemen. This orientation continues to typify the basic design of the bachelor of commerce program at the University of Toronto, which has not been systemically revised since 1968 and which retains a heavy

TABLE 11.1
Configurations of baccalaureate business programs

	High emphasis upon breadth of education	Low emphasis upon breadth of education
Business courses taken across undergraduate studies	**Liberals** *Mission:* Undergraduate education supplies a broad background, especially in the arts, to develop well-rounded persons. Studies of 'practical' subjects are limited. *Business courses:* From Years 1 to 3 or 4 and often supplied by non-business faculties; multidisciplinary focus. *Core curricula:* Selective (often less than 12 explicit 'business' courses), truncated, with key business functions not covered or just available as electives. Heavy weight given to economics, the humanities, or social sciences. *Non-management electives:* Extensive criteria (10 courses or more) during studies, stipulations for advanced learning in non-business areas. *Specialization:* Severe restrictions placed upon business electives. Formal concentrations do not occur in sub-areas of business but majors with other disciplines are encouraged.	**Analysers** *Mission:* Undergraduate education is geared to the development of technical expertise necessary for career entry positions. *Business Courses:* From Years 1 to 4 and supplied by business faculties; emphases upon business functions. *Core curricula:* Broad (10 to 14 business courses), but schools make requirements according to areas of sub-specialization. Normally weighted towards quantitative areas, but sometimes extensive qualitative offerings. *Non-management electives:* Nominal criteria (0–4 courses) occur in Years 1 and 2, and then limited options unless related to commerce. *Specialization:* Students quickly focus upon business and take numerous business electives (7 or more) with a formal concentration. Policies may require specialization in sub-areas.

TABLE 11.1 (concluded)

	High emphasis upon Breadth of education	Low emphasis upon Breadth of education
Business courses taken primarily in the second half of degree studies	**Generalists** *Mission:* Undergraduate education provides a background about different subjects, but should enable students to secure, concurrently, a grounding in a spectrum of management activities. *Business courses:* Spread over Years 1 to 4 and given by business faculties; Program entry during Year 1, but bulk of business core after Year 2. *Core curricula:* Extensive (14 business courses or more), aimed at capturing the breadth of concerns addressed by managers. *Non-management electives:* Extensive (8 courses or more), but spread throughout the length of studies. *Specialization:* Restrictions placed upon ability to take business electives during Years 3 and 4. Concentrations in sub-areas not encouraged, but may be taken informally.	**Professionals** *Mission:* Undergraduates secure a foundation in the arts and sciences for intellectual maturity and then may learn about management skills and practices. *Business courses:* Weighted into Years 3 and 4, sometimes with the 'formal' entry into a program delayed, although some courses may be taken in Years 1 and 2. *Core curricula:* Extensive (14 business courses or more), aimed at capturing the the breadth of concerns addressed by managers. *Non-management electives:* Extensive (8 courses or more), but occur mainly during 'pre-management' years. *Specialization:* Students take various business electives (4 to 7), but program policies, or the duration of 'official' business studies, restrain the ability to garner intense specialization in sub-areas.

emphasis upon economics vis-à-vis business. At Trent and Winnipeg, administrators have stressed liberal arts education as the institutional mission. This also was the initial orientation of some of the programs founded during the 1960s since these new faculties could supply only a limited range of courses. Liberal programs have emphasized moral and intellectual development, not vocational training, by supplying a grounding in the humanities. Students have been propelled towards multidisciplinary perspectives since the regulatory guidelines stipulate extensive courses in non-management subjects. Approximately one-third to a maximum of one-half of undergraduate studies are devoted to commerce – usually defined as economics, accounting, and finance. Other aspects of business administration may be elective or dealt with as a function of student interest or faculty availability.

As corporate practices became more sophisticated, most schools broadened their curricula by adding courses in production, marketing, organizational behaviour, and business policy. During the 1950s business academics came to perceive the liberalization of management offerings as a superior method for ensuring intellectual breadth vis-à-vis courses in the humanities and social sciences. To accomplish this objective, tenure-track positions were offered to specialists in psychology, sociology, history, and law. The appointments were expected to ensure that students received an integration of liberal and vocational issues. Historical or political topics, for instance, could be addressed in courses dealing with business and the environment, while ethical problems could be examined in marketing seminars. These initiatives expanded the mandatory component of business curricula, reconfiguring numerous programs towards a 'Generalist' orientation that provided a comprehensive foundation in the activities of management but still required extensive non-business electives.

Two additional configurations have emerged since 1960. 'Professionals' are programs explicitly modelled after the recommendations of the Ford and Carnegie Foundation reports. Both surveys claimed insufficient attention had been given to non-business subjects beyond the first year of baccalaureate education and complained about an unreasonable expansion of mandatory business courses. The reports advanced detailed but similar proposals for a curriculum consisting of three elements: a general education covering different areas of course work that represented approximately 50 per cent of studies, another 30 to 40 per cent geared to high-quality analytical courses in administration, and the balance as a limited concentration in a subspecialty of management (preferably with half of that component in a complementary non-business subject). Professional programs accomplish this schema by designating non-management courses during the first half of baccalaureate studies and then stipulating a set of required business courses during the third year. Course sequencing often is enforced by delaying the official entry of candidates into business programs until the conclusion of the first or second years.

Concurrent shifts in the values of undergraduate students created additional pressures for career-oriented programs. Since most Canadian schools initially adopted Liberal or Generalist orientations, the faculties avoided the controversy over industry-specific courses that occurred in United States. However, the growth of Canadian programs after 1960 coincided with a relaxation of institutional regulations enforcing educational breadth and with the introduction of policies that facilitated disciplinary specialization. The confluence of these forces allowed a drift towards an 'Analyser' orientation. In practical terms, this configuration has been distinguished by policies that stress vocational training in a business function. The goal is accomplished by slashing the criteria for learning in non-management subjects and positioning mandatory business courses into the first half of undergraduate studies. The latter half of a program then can be devoted to an area of concentration. In addition, after the mandatory courses have been completed, specialization can be intensified by varying course requirements among different concentration areas. The programs usually have stressed accounting, finance, and marketing since these subjects represent the primary markets for undergraduates, but many now have offerings in international business, human resource management, information systems, or organizational behaviour.

The orientations of undergraduate programs can be gauged by descriptive measures such as the number and sequencing of core courses, the minimum and maximum number of 'business' electives (which exclude obligations in economics, mathematics, and computer science), and the criteria for non-management courses. Table 11.2 summarizes the policies guiding the population of sixty-two business degree programs available from fifty-three Canadian universities during 1999.[37] Since the late 1970s, all of the undergraduate degrees that required five years or ten terms of full-time study have been shortened. Most of the schools that supplied three-year programs have extended the duration of studies to four years, although some have retained shorter 'pass' degrees as options for marginal candidates or

TABLE 11.2
Undergraduate business curricula, 1998–1999

| | | | Number of programs that stipulate | | | |
	Total core size	Business core courses	Non-management core courses	Minimum non-mgmt. electives	Minimum business electives	Maximum business electives
0–2 courses	–	–	14	17	11	1
3–5 courses	–	1	28	12	17	1
6–8 courses	1	1	19	14	22	17
9–11 courses	–	–	–	13	10	17
12–14 courses	7	20	1	4	2	14
15–17 courses	5	22	–	1	–	5
18–20 courses	13	11	–	1	–	5
21–3 courses	24	6	–	–	–	2
24–6 courses	7	1	–	–	–	–
27 courses or more	5	–	–	–	–	–
Total	62	62	62	62	62	62

Note: A course has been defined as a 'single-term' or 13-week offering with approximately three hours of class time per week. 'Full-year' or 'quarter-courses' have been treated respectively as two or one-half courses. The data in this and subsequent tables do not include course or seminar obligations that are not given credit weight in degree programs.

students preparing for careers in professions like law. Universities in Québec have not followed this trend, since students attend CEGEP institutions after high school and take courses in mathematics and social sciences during this equivalent of the first year of baccalaureate studies. Four-fifths of the four-year programs are forty single-term courses in length. Eight universities require the completion of forty-two or more courses, with the highest parameters set by the University of British Columbia, the University of New Brunswick at Fredericton, and the University of Victoria.

Canadian programs that have followed a Liberal orientation have stipulated eighteen mandatory courses or fewer. Offerings supplied by humanities or social-science faculties, rather than schools of management, constitute a large portion of these obligations. The mandatory or 'core' component ranges from nineteen to twenty-four courses for programs conforming to a Generalist perspective. These schema typically have augmented the number of required courses so that students will receive a comprehensive grounding in various aspects of management. Expansion of the core curricula has been treated by many business schools as a trade-off for policies that have blocked concentrations or restricted the number of advanced electives that may be taken, but the size of the core has varied among the programs that are configured towards an Analyser orientation. While most programs fall within a range of fifteen to nineteen courses, several require more than twenty-five. The former tend to alter requirements for students who pursue different concentrations and candidates sometimes have nominal obligations for courses outside of their areas of specialty. The latter retain curricula that are sequenced across the length of baccalaureate studies. Programs with a Professional configuration usually have between sixteen and twenty mandatory courses, frequently with one course in each management topic. Students cannot achieve intensive specialization, since the mandatory business courses occur after 'pre-management' years and concentrations are not permitted until the final year of studies, if at all.

Each approach has dealt distinctively with non-management electives – optional courses in areas not directly related to management. These are defined by policies sketched in university calendars, rules that vary from ambiguous procedures to detailed compendia of courses and sequencing patterns. Analyser programs typically have nominal obligations, often as low as zero to four courses. Candidates complete one or two courses in the arts or sciences during their first or second year of studies and may later choose to take several electives. Whether the offerings truly are 'non-business' in character can be arguable, since numerous universities permit the obligations to be fulfilled by electives in computer science, mathematics, or economics. Programs conforming to the Generalist or Professional configurations tend to stipulate a minimum of five to ten non-management courses exclusive of core requirements and have imposed sharp limits upon the definition of 'non-management' subjects. The schools otherwise have left the selection of electives to students, but a minority have demanded the completion of a coherent group of upper-level electives outside of business or economics, that is, significant learning in another discipline. Generalist and Professional programs have varied with respect to the sequencing of those obligations, with the former distributing non-management electives across the time frame of studies and the latter tending to weight the requirements into the first half.

Canadian universities have always given give lip service to the notion of educational breadth, but institutional regulations have been relaxed to the point where they are often meaningless. Approximately two-thirds of Canadian programs define a minimum number of non-business courses and then allow candidates (subject to review by the business faculties or university registrars) to decide how those criteria will be met. As shown in table 11.2, forty-three of the sixty-two programs during 1998 have permitted students to take eight courses or fewer in subjects not related to management. In more than half of the programs, candidates can secure business degrees even though fewer than four introductory-level courses in the arts or sciences might have been completed.

Twenty-nine schools have allowed concentrations and eleven make specialization mandatory. Within the parameters set by another eight schools, concentrations may be pursued informally. The number of institutions allowing formal specializations are as follows: accounting, 26; management, 25; marketing, 27; finance, 23; human resource management, 21; management information systems or computer science, 20; management science, 13; and economics, 12. A small minority allow concentrations in other topics. A minimum of four to six courses tend to constitute a concentration. Most programs do not have well-defined restrictions for electives in sub-areas, but about half require a minimum of two upper-level courses in other sub-areas. Thus, in real terms, six to eight electives may be taken in a sub-area. The exceptions to this practice are the schools that stress accounting and allow more electives since many students wish to join professional associations after graduation.

Figure 11.1 illustrates the approximate orientation of the Canadian baccalaureate programs during the 1998–99 academic year. Schools located away from the intersection of the axes closely follow the attributes of an orientation, while those near the axes share traits from other configurations. On the horizontal axis, institutional emphasis is gauged by the proportion of studies devoted to courses in business administration. In practice, transitions towards Analyser or Professional orientations become very evident if business courses exceed 50 per cent of baccalaureate studies. The position of each program has been determined by combining the number of mandatory business courses and an average of the minimum and maximum management electives. Because institutional practices vary, courses in the humanities, mathematics, and social sciences (including economics) have been necessarily categorized as 'non-business,' even if those offerings are in the core curricula or are delivered by instructors within a business school. For the faculties that allow concentrations or advanced learning in economics or other business-related disciplines, the level of specialization thus might be understated. On the vertical axis, segmentation has been made by the timing of mandatory 'business' courses. Schools near the top of the axis (such as Windsor and Manitoba) have weighted the core curricula into the first half of baccalaureate studies, while those near the bottom (like Western and Alberta) have positioned it during the second half. As can be seen in figure 11.1, despite some outliers most faculties conform (especially in Ontario, Québec, and Atlantic Canada) to the Analyser profile. Indeed, most of the institutions that had alternative curriculum orientations in 1985 (such as Winnipeg, the University of New Brunswick, or York) have been reconfigured towards this orientation.

The Orientation of Graduate Programs

Baccalaureate education has been perceived as pre-professional, since it deals with students seeking career entry positions. Regardless of the orientation, all undergraduate programs seek to inculcate intellectual maturity and a repertoire of tools or ways of understanding. Given this foundation of learning, graduate management education accordingly focuses upon techniques of qualitative or quantitative analysis, but the line of approach varies among faculties. Master's programs in the arts

Figure 11.1 Orientations of undergraduate programs, 1998–1999

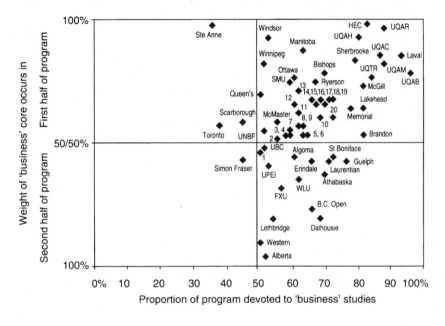

1. Trinity Western; 2. University of Northern British Columbia; 3. Brock; 4. York;
5. Calgary; 6. Waterloo; 7. Hearst; 8. Victoria; 9. Concordia; 10. Trent;
11. University College of Cape Breton; 12. Acadia; 13. Mount Saint Vincent;
14. Carleton; 15. Mount Allison; 16. Regina; 17. UNBSJ; 18. Saskatchewan;
19. Moncton; 20. Nipissing

and sciences draw upon populations of students who have demonstrated superior talent at the undergraduate level. Candidates for those
degrees pursue more intensive studies and research in their areas of
specialization. Professional programs deal principally with knowledge
dissemination and skill development for individual careers. Not only
have many candidates not received baccalaureate training in business,
but current or prospective managers pursuing part-time studies represent a key segment of the student population and greater emphasis
therefore must be given to general management topics. Master's studies in the arts and sciences also represent an intermediate stage from
which the best may advance to doctoral programs; but the MBA is a

terminal degree, one not intended to prepare individuals for doctoral-level work.

Graduate programs can be differentiated on two dimensions: pedagogical structure and breadth of coverage. Studies may be carried out exclusively via course work or by a mix of courses and empirical investigation. The latter stresses an intensive pursuit of knowledge and research within a field, while the former channels academic specialization around the issues addressed by individual courses. Second, programs can supply a comprehensive coverage of topics or a short simple acquaintance. The combination of those dimensions produces a classification schema of four orientations analogous to, but distinctive from, baccalaureate education: Fundamentalists, Analysers, Traditionals, and Bridgers. Table 11.3 outlines their respective traits and the orientations of Canadian business schools are segmented in table 11.4.

'Fundamentalist' programs supply a background about management for individuals who wish to upgrade their knowledge through a year of full-time study of a set of functional courses. This configuration typifies graduate diploma offerings in business and some executive MBA degrees that have been shorter or less sophisticated than the main programs supplied by the same institutions. 'Analyser' programs have two years of course work with a broad core curriculum and set of electives, occasionally allowing some specialization by students in a sub-area of business. As has occurred at the undergraduate level, this configuration tends to stress accounting, finance, and marketing but a few institutions have extensive offerings in qualitative areas like personnel or international business. 'Traditional' programs follow the historical role of graduate education and orient studies around a thesis or project. These schema entail a year of full-time study and presume the necessary prerequisites were earned at the baccalaureate level. 'Bridgers' are programs that supply a grounding in business but augment it with coverage of another discipline. Numerous interdisciplinary schema in the arts and sciences fit this orientation, and among professional programs joint MBA/LLB degrees (which take four years to complete) are the most frequent manifestation.

Because their publication preceded the introduction of MBA degrees by most Canadian universities, the Ford and Carnegie Foundation reports had a major impact on graduate management education. Numerous business schools initially established programs according to the guidelines of the faculties of graduate studies at their institutions and were heavily weighted with courses about research methods and

TABLE 11.3
Configurations of graduate business programs

	Emphasis upon basic treatment of management	Emphasis upon extensive treatment of management
Graduate education consists solely of business courses	**Fundamentalists** *Mission*: Graduate business education should provide a grounding in the functional areas of management. Terminal degree. *Business courses*: During Years 1 and 2, no courses taken other than those directly related to management. *Core curricula*: Selective (less than 8 'business' courses), truncated, with some functions not covered. *Specialization*: Constraints placed upon availability of business electives. Formal concentrations do not occur.	**Analysers** *Mission*: Graduate business education should provide an understanding of the varied aspects of management and the acquisition of expertise in an area of interest. Terminal degree. *Business courses*: Across Years 1 and 2, with few, if any, electives outside of management. *Core curricula*: Broad (9 to 12 'business' courses) core to provide a grounding in management. *Specialization*: After Year 1, candidates are encouraged to develop a concentration in a sub-topic.
Graduate education includes non-business or research components	**Traditionals** *Mission*: Graduate education should enhance an understanding of management, but should employ a research orientation that may later be applied at a sophisticated level in the private sector. Intermediate degree. *Business courses*: Weighted in Year 1 (if any) or front of Year 2. Empirical research is an important and large component. *Core curricula*: Year 1 (if any) consists of core courses, and two or three core offerings in Year 2. *Specialization*: Thesis or major project research, not courses, as a means of achieving depth.	**Bridgers** *Mission*: Graduate education should establish background knowledge about management, but should broaden student orientations by cross-disciplinary or cross-cultural applications. Joint or supplementary degree. *Business courses*: Weighted across program. Courses in another discipline often constitute a major component of studies. *Core Curricula*: Year 1 devoted to business core, non-business core courses in Years 2 and 3. *Specialization*: Electives encompass non-business areas, not just courses in business functions.

TABLE 11.4
Orientations of Canadian MBA programs, 1998–1999

Fundamentalists	Analysers
Secondary programs: Graduate diploma in administration; some executive MBA degrees	*Primary programs:* Alberta, Athabaska, Calgary, Concordia, Dalhousie, Guelph, HÉC, Laurentian, Laval, McGill, McMaster, Manitoba, Memorial, Moncton, Ottawa, Queen's, Regina, SMU, Saskatchewan, SFU, Sherbrooke, Toronto, UBC, UNBF, UNBSJ, UQAB, UQAM, Victoria, Western, Windsor, WLU, York

Traditionals	Bridgers
Primary programs: Carleton	*Primary programs:* Joint MBA-LLB degrees, MBA-Health Science degrees
Secondary programs: Alberta, Laval, Saskatchewan, SFU, UQAM	*Secondary programs:* York International MBA, exchange programs

requirements for empirical research; but after 1970 the recommendations of the Foundation reports were quickly adopted. If gauged by
institutional policies, most Canadian programs closely fit the Analyser
configuration during 1999 (see table 11.4). In the past, Lakehead has
approximated the Fundamentalist archetype by supplying a schema of
ten courses (the equivalent of the first year of studies), while a few
institutions offered a graduate diploma as an intermediate step
towards an MBA. The Carleton program continues to pursue a Traditional orientation with a year of work entailing courses in an area of
specialty and an empirical research endeavour. Candidates who have
not studied business must complete a group of remedial courses before
entry. The number of universities requiring an empirical thesis and
courses in research methods has steadily declined since the 1970s,
although some institutions have retained the original approach, either
as an optional process for securing an MBA or as criteria for a degree
like an MSc.

A graduate degree in business typically has entailed the completion
of twenty courses across two years of full-time studies, although students who have taken management at the baccalaureate level may seek
a reduction in those obligations. Despite widespread perceptions that
the duration of programs has been reduced across the past decade, half
of the Canadian universities retain this guideline and another quarter

TABLE 11.5
Graduate business curricula, 1998–1999

	Number of programs which stipulate				
	Duration of studies in number of courses	Size of business core	Size of non-business core	Total core courses	Total elective courses
0–0.5 courses	–	–	8	–	3
1–2 courses	–	–	25	–	1
3–4 courses	–	–	–	–	4
5–6 courses	–	–	–	–	9
7–8 courses	–	2	–	2	5
9–10 courses	1	8	–	5	9
11–12 courses	–	9	–	6	1
13–14 courses	–	6	–	8	1
15–16 courses	1	6	–	8	–
17–18 courses	6	2	–	3	–
19–20 courses	15	–	–	1	–
21–2 courses	8	–	–	–	–
23 or more courses	2	–	–	–	–
Total	33	33	33	33	33

have extended the requirements. As shown in table 11.5, eight institutions ask for the completion of fewer than nineteen courses, but only three schools have attempted to deliver a full-time schedule of studies in less than fifteen months. New obligations (such as human resource management and management information systems) have been added in response to student or practitioner demands, but faculties normally have chosen not to eliminate other required courses or to decrease options – thereby extending the duration of studies. This policy may have enhanced the perceived legitimacy of the more recently created faculties versus schools with well-established reputations. Most programs have eleven to fourteen core courses, but twelve stipulate more than fifteen, seriously restricting the number of possible electives.

Following the recommendations of the Foundation reports, the required component of graduate programs has been uniform for all students and is taken in a rigid sequence. However, several programs have mandatory and 'optional core' components that allow limited variations according to student skills or interest. For students who already hold a baccalaureate degree in management, business schools tend to limit the ability to gain advanced standing in core subjects.

Most, if not all, schools insist that candidates take certain subjects that may be in the core curriculum (like strategic management, business-government relations, or international business) regardless of undergraduate performance. Major variations tend to be outcomes of programmatic orientations. The core entails fewer than five courses for Traditional programs, since background knowledge about business from baccalaureate education is presumed. Carleton's management faculty, for example, has defined the core as a set of courses in research methods and an area of specialty. As schema trying to cover two or more disciplines, Bridger programs expand the number of mandatory courses at the expense of electives. York's International MBA, for instance, requires eight courses in addition to the functional and general management courses taken by students in the business school's flagship program.

Graduate business programs tend to have six to eight elective courses but the choices often are not free. A third of the institutions limit candidates to four or five courses in a sub-area of business. Another third have regulations stipulating a division of optional courses among functional areas or a selection from specific groups of electives. Consequently, the prospects for detailed specialization in a sub-area of business usually are modest unless an MBA is taken as a second business degree. Only fifteen programs stipulate research projects as part of the degree criteria and the practices vary significantly among institutions. Some ask for individual research endeavours, while others require group work. Six of the faculties with a compulsory project give it a single course weighting, and the remainder treat the effort as equivalent to two courses. When taken as electives, projects tend to be given a weight of two or three courses and projects rarely have been accorded a weight higher than two courses if a thesis option is available. Eight schools permit academically superior candidates to develop a thesis that tests extant theories or surveys management practices. The thesis normally is treated as equivalent to three or four courses, a weighting that is somewhat less than that accorded in the arts and sciences.

A majority of the schools that have revised their MBA offerings since 1992 have borrowed concepts originally developed for executive development programs. Term courses at several institutions have been broken up into modules that vary from four to eight weeks in length. In a few cases, established courses have merely been divided and the segments repositioned to different points in the curricula; in others, new subjects or pedagogical approaches (like internships or videoconferences) have been added. The reorganized curricula typically are advertised as 'results-oriented' and involving an integrated and applied learning process. Several business schools also have attempted to reduce the duration of studies, claiming professional managers are reluctant to put their careers on hold for two years or bear the dual responsibilities of full-time employment and part-time studies. Like similar initiatives undertaken in the United States and Europe, these experiments have been intended to differentiate MBA programs from undergraduate offerings at the same universities and to ameliorate some of the perceived deficiencies of management education outlined in this essay. It is too soon to appraise the effectiveness of the innovations, but the reviews vary, with praise for some efforts and complaints about poor organization, fragmented learning, and a 'dumb-down' of the MBA degree at others.

The 'Core' of Management Curricula

If Canadian business schools have adopted analogous orientations towards management education, do they also concur on the content that should be taught? Recommendations from the Foundation reports, and the accreditation processes of the AACSB, have provided guidance for curricula decision making in the United States. The Assembly was organized to provide consistent standards because of uniquely American conditions: hundreds of colleges, a mix of private- and public-sector ownership, and quality differences among state regulatory agencies to the extent that some were not 'judged adequate to forestall or stop educational chicanery.'[38] Even among institutions that have not been accredited by the AACSB, the guidelines are widely perceived as desirable goals about the importance and weight that should be accorded to different subjects.[39] There has never been a national agency in Canada and even the federation of business school deans has declined to issue policies for curriculum content. Most Canadian faculties have opposed accreditation with the AACSB. Some have rejected the very notion that an American agency might be qualified to judge Canadian programs, while others have viewed the costs of application and membership as excessive.[40] Since Canadian governments have followed British practice, with autonomous universities created by royal or provincial charter, consistency in program content should theoretically be attainable. In fact, topic coverage has been diverse and has been a function of idiosyncratic curriculum development at different institutions.

Diversity in curricular content does not necessarily mean inadequate education. It can build upon distinctive competencies, permit the introduction of innovative topics, or allow the testing of new techniques. In their 1988 study, Porter and McKibben castigated American faculties for replicating 'model' programs with a 'cookie cutter mentality.' University administrators, they suggested, seemed to be afraid of doing anything that would differentiate business schools and weaken the perceived legitimacy of their programs or graduates, a problem that may have been stimulated by the acceptance of AACSB standards. 'The desire to be like others, or least not very different, is not an exciting way to advance the cause of management education.'[41] Different faculties will have dissimilar populations of students, alternative career paths of graduates, or distinctive service obligations owing to the nature of local economies. But excessive diversity can have deleterious qualitative implications. Students compelled to study near home may attend programs that leave them deficient relative to individuals educated in other locations, a condition that may be compounded by the strengths and weaknesses of the personnel at specific universities.

Given the absence of another set of widely accepted standards, Canadian practices may be gauged by the recommendations of the Foundation reports and the AACSB. These were intended to ensure that students mastered a standard curriculum that encompassed five subject areas. This foundation was expected to entail at least ten courses, or one-quarter of baccalaureate work and a minimum of two semesters at the master's level. Although the criteria have been criticized by some administrators as restrictive, the AACSB has never argued that the 'common body of knowledge' must be covered in particular ways. Considerable flexibility has been shown during its accreditation processes for variations in the sequencing or proportion of time devoted to different subject areas, since schools have different objectives and resources. The key questions have been whether important areas have been covered comprehensively, and whether faculties have used integrative mechanisms to highlight issues relevant to general management.[42] Because several topic zones overlap, segmentation can be difficult and the transition towards integrative courses at the master's level makes content analysis difficult unless course syllabi are examined carefully. Table 11.6 summarizes the minimum number of core courses in different subjects that are stipulated by Canadian undergraduate programs, while table 11.7 outlines the criteria for master's offerings.

TABLE 11.6
Undergraduate core requirements, 1998–1999

	Minimum number of term courses stipulated by programs						
	0.0	1.0	2.0	3.0	4.0 or more	Total	Core optional
Quantitative areas							
Accounting	0	3	38	13	7	62	3
Economics	2	5	29	16	10	62	1
Finance	8	25	22	7	0	62	2
Mathematics	21	17	20	3	1	62	0
Management Science/ Statistics/Data Analysis	5	13	30	13	1	62	0
Production or Operations Management	21	33	8	0	0	62	1
Qualitative areas							
Business Environment	33	22	5	1	1	62	6
Entrepreneurship	57	5	0	0	0	62	2
Human Resource Management	38	24	0	0	0	62	2
Industrial Relations	48	14	0	0	0	62	2
Integrative	59	2	1	0	0	62	2
International Business	56	6	0	0	0	62	5
Introduction to Business	42	18	2	0	0	62	1
Introduction to Computers/ Software	31	28	3	0	0	62	3
Introduction to Management	40	20	2	0	0	62	0
Law	28	33	1	0	0	62	1
Management Information Systems	27	30	5	0	0	62	2
Marketing	6	31	23	0	2	62	1
Organizational Behaviour/ Theory	2	31	26	2	1	62	1
Strategic Management	6	34	14	5	3	62	1
Communications	33	22	5	1	1	62	0
Languages	36	10	11	4	1	62	0

The Foundation reports asked for a minimum of a year's study of accounting, quantitative methods, and management information systems (MIS) including computer applications. Most Canadian universities equal or significantly exceed those guidelines at the baccalaureate level. Thirty-eight programs require two term courses in accounting and twenty actually stipulate three courses or more. Thirty demand

TABLE 11.7
MBA Core requirements, 1998–1999

	Minimum number of courses stipulated by programs						
	0.0	0.5	1.0	1.5–2.0	3.0 or more	Total	Core optional
Quantitative areas							
Accounting/Control	2	–	10	19	2	33	0
Economics	9	7	10	7	–	33	0
Finance	5	1	19	8	–	33	1
Management Science	5	4	15	9	–	33	0
Production/Operations Management	11	4	16	1	1	33	1
Qualitative areas							
Business Environment	19	11	3	–	–	33	0
Entrepreneurship	31	2	–	–	–	33	1
Human Resource Management	16	3	13	1	–	33	0
Industrial Relations	28	3	2	–	–	33	0
Integrative	27	–	1	2	3	33	0
International Business	24	4	3	2	–	33	1
Introduction to Business	31	1	1	–	–	33	0
Law	30	3	–	–	–	33	0
Management Information Systems	8	5	19	1	–	33	0
Marketing	4	1	24	4	–	33	1
Organizational Behaviour/ Theory	4	2	18	6	3	33	2
Strategic Management	2	1	16	11	3	33	0
Communications	28	–	4	1	–	33	0
Research Methods	24	1	7	1	–	33	0
Project/Major paper	18	–	6	6	3	33	2

two courses in quantitative methods (other than pure mathematics), while fourteen require three courses or more. Twenty-three programs require the completion of two term courses in computer science and MIS. The criteria for computer applications vary significantly among schools, with some stipulating introductory courses for software or computers during the first year of studies, while others require offerings in MIS at more senior levels. If measured by university policies, only ten programs clearly ask for courses in each aspect, but most of the schools with two courses appear to review the different elements despite the supposed content outlined in calendar descriptions. An analogous pattern has occurred at the graduate level, but the demands for quantitative materials have not been as intensive. Twenty-two of thirty-three programs stipulate more than one course in accounting and control systems. However, nine ask for less than a term course in statistics and fifteen ask for the equivalent of one course. Nearly two-thirds of the master's programs stipulate at least one course in MIS.

AACSB guidelines call for a minimum of a full year's study of production, marketing, and finance. Thirty-one undergraduate programs require a single course in marketing, while twenty-three stipulate two courses. For finance, twenty-five stipulate one course while twenty-two require two; but eight programs have not included finance in the core curriculum. Forty-one programs mandate at least one course in production or operations management, but twenty-one do not have any compulsory obligations. At the master's level, twenty-eight of thirty-three programs ask for one or more courses on marketing, twenty-seven stipulate at least one course on finance, and eighteen require the equivalent of one course on production. Several of the graduate programs, which have not created functional courses for these topics, handle the materials in integrative courses.

A more problematic case has been the recommendation for two term courses at the junior or senior levels in the areas of organizational theory, organizational behaviour, and interpersonal communications (not to be confused with courses that teach written or verbal communications skills). Forty years after the publication of the Foundation reports, half of the Canadian undergraduate programs still do not meet that basic goal. The exceptions include not only small schools or those located in geographically isolated areas, but programs like those offered by McGill, Ottawa, Western, Toronto, and British Columbia. Some institutions skirt the goal by supplying an introductory course to business or management during the first year of studies, a tactic that is inconsistent with the guidelines, since sufficient depth of knowledge cannot be delivered. Several of the universities that require a single course try to present aspects of organizational theory within full-year courses on strategy. Nonetheless, mandatory coverage of the 'soft' side of management within the core curricula of Canadian programs often has been surprisingly weak. Twenty-four universities have baccalaureate requirements for human resource management but thirty-eight have not included the subject. Only fourteen require a course dealing with labour relations. At the graduate level, a majority of the programs stipulate one course in organizational behaviour, while approximately a third have higher obligations. Slightly fewer than half of the programs require a term course in human resource management and almost all have deleted industrial relations from the core.

AACSB guidelines stipulate a minimum of a year's study of the legal and economic environments of organizations, along with appraisals of social and political influences. It is in this area that Canadian undergraduate programs always have been woefully deficient vis-à-vis their American counterparts. Although most have elective offerings, only half of the schools stipulate a term course in business law. Twenty-nine require courses on the business environment, but these encompass numerous approaches like business and society, public administration, business history, and (occasionally) business ethics. The record is similarly weak at the master's level, with only two programs requiring a term course on the business environment; none have obligations for law. Eleven programs have limited the coverage to six-week modules that deal with business and the environment and three have modules on business law.

The fifth area recommended by Gordon and Howell and the AACSB has been a minimum of a year's study of administrative processes at the senior level, that is, integrative analyses and strategy appraisals for an entire enterprise. A third of the Canadian undergraduate programs meet those suggestions, with two courses or more in strategic management, but thirty-four stipulate one term course. Surprisingly, six undergraduate programs do not have a mandatory course, although three of those cases are accounted for by the University of Toronto and its satellite campi at Erindale and Scarborough. Several universities, such as Queen's and Western, always have stipulated a full-year course in strategy, but since the 1980s the number of schools employing two courses or a full-year offering has decreased markedly. At the graduate level, almost all programs stipulate at least one term course and the balance is accounted for by integrative courses.

The AACSB recently has sought to add international business and entrepreneurship for a new subject area. Canadian business deans have given verbal support to enhanced coverage but the topics remain elective, if available at all. Only six undergraduate and nine graduate schools have placed international business in the core, and similar problems emerge in terms of the attention given to other contemporary issues. For example, there has been a consensus about the need to train managers who can cope with diversity and change, but fewer than a fifth of the Canadian programs even offer electives. These usually are given at the master's level and the courses encompass subjects such as cross-cultural management, women in management, or changing managerial roles.[43] Despite the publicity that business associations and the media have given for the management of innovation and technology, the subject rarely can be found even as an elective at Canadian business schools.

Like the courses supplied by faculties of management, the policies governing non-business subjects have significant variability. Economics has been handled in alternative ways at the baccalaureate level. Twenty-nine programs stipulate two courses in economics. For half of this group, the requirement is fulfilled by introductory courses during the first year of studies; the other half demand courses in micro-economics and macro-economics during the second or third years. Twenty-six schools require three courses or more, usually with advanced work at the junior or senior levels in economics. Those criteria often represent a legacy from earlier iterations of commerce curricula that were dominated by economics departments. Some schools have retained the obligations because the faculty wish to give strong emphases to finance and accounting, while in geographically peripheral areas an emphasis upon economics can be linked to the local supply of instructors. In contrast, only seventeen of thirty-three MBA programs require a single term course in economics. Nine faculties have deleted economics from the core curriculum. Although several cover the subject during integrative courses, others have made the successful completion of undergraduate economics courses a prerequisite for program entry.

At the baccalaureate level, twenty-four schools stipulate two or more courses in pure mathematics (normally calculus and algebra), which are taken during the first year of studies. Seventeen stipulate one course and, very surprisingly, twenty-one have no obligations. Several of the institutions with low requirements are oriented towards the liberal arts and have not stressed quantitative subjects, while others have emphasized applied courses in management science, data analysis, or operations research. The schools with the weakest obligations for mathematics usually are located in peripheral geographic regions, and the regulations probably reflect student capabilities and difficulties in securing qualified instructors. Although most baccalaureate programs mandate advanced secondary schooling in English or French as a prerequisite for entry, only twenty-six have university-level obligations and those are limited to introductory courses in literature or essay writing. Most Canadian universities have eliminated language proficiency tests, even though the examinations can detect candidates who lack the most rudimentary capabilities in grammar and spelling. Twenty-nine undergraduate programs require courses in communications, offerings that tend to stress verbal, rather than written, skills. At the MBA level, most schools have not included mathematics, languages, or communications in the core. It has been widely presumed that the subjects either are inappropriate for graduate studies or should have been mastered previously. However, many MBA programs have elaborated not-for-credit seminars covering these areas that must be taken before classes formally begin.

This snapshot provides a static portrait, but several longitudinal changes can be gauged by comparing the 1999 data against earlier surveys.[44] For instance, there has been a modest reduction in undergraduate and MBA obligations for statistics since the late 1980s. Economics has been dramatically reduced as a component of graduate curricula during the past decade, but has marginally increased as part of baccalaureate studies. The most widespread addition has been MIS, a logical development given the importance of personal computing and electronic media. Canada has retained a predominantly service-based economy for several generations, a condition that accounts for the incremental deletion of labour relations from the core. Although courses in human resource management sometimes have replaced those deletions, a majority of schools still do not accept the subject as a key component. Few Canadian undergraduate programs in 1985 had offerings aimed at enhancing communications skills but, trying to address the concerns of practitioners, many now have mandatory courses.

3. What Is to Be Done?

The preceding section reviewed the patterns associated with contemporary management education in Canada. The case histories presented in this volume also highlight the concerns with program design that have unfolded from the experiences of different schools. Since each faculty confronts a distinctive environment and must fulfill broader institutional goals, future developments will unfold on an organization-specific basis. Students at different universities, through choices of electives and instructors, also may be able to compensate for curricular tendencies or deficiencies in programmatic content. Contemporary

334   Barry E.C. Boothman

Figure 11.2 The forces driving Canadian business schools, 1999

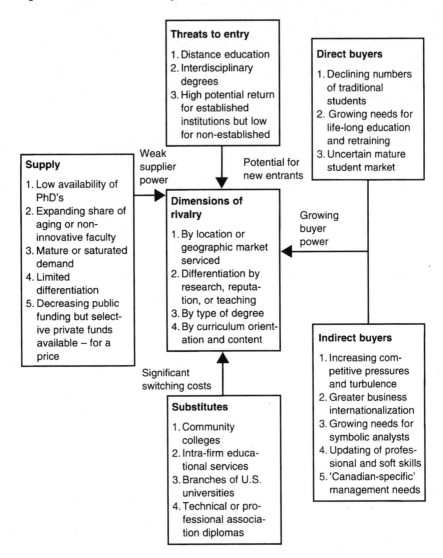

practices have not just been moulded by the traits of different institutions but are products of education as a form of economic activity, since universities must compete for resources and garner users by servicing identifiable markets, providing desirable services, and differentiating themselves from other enterprises. Since the nineteenth century, business schools have been influenced by the expectations of different interests and by infusions of capital from the private and public sectors. It is logical, therefore, to consider how their activities may alter in the foreseeable future.

Confronting a New Reality

In his classic work, *Competitive Strategy*, Harvard's Michael Porter advanced a framework for appraising strategic conduct in different industries. Although the model normally is used for the analysis of profit-oriented sectors, it may be easily employed with not-for-profit activities as shown in figure 11.2. Competition among Canadian business schools has been conditioned by several forces: the bargaining power of buyers, the availability and performance of substitutes, the potential for new entrants, and the bargaining power of suppliers.[45] Although they cannot be properly categorized as clients or customers, students and companies respectively constitute the direct and indirect buyers of their services. These interests historically have retained limited bargaining power, since the number of available faculty has been low relative to the demand for management education. Hiring by Canadian universities dropped during the late 1970s as weakening demand and cutbacks in public funds compelled rationalization of services, especially in the humanities and social sciences. Although enrolment also declined for American business schools after 1980, faculty vacancy rates of 15 per cent or higher prevailed among their Canadian counterparts for another decade. With extensive consulting or employment offerings in the public and private sectors, the exit barriers for good researchers were also low. Management faculties in Canada thus remained able to define their programs in a semi-autonomous manner. Most focused upon local or regional markets with limited direct competition even in metropolitan areas.[46] This situation has altered since 1990 as enrolment in Canadian programs has followed the American trend, a pattern that has yet not been reversed. Mergers, corporate downsizing, and industrial rationalization have reduced the demand for new employees in many industries or in traditional functions like accounting and marketing. At the same time, corporate needs for educated personnel have expanded in new ways, with requirements for individuals capable of handling international operations, competitive turbulence, changes in Canadian markets, or new information systems.

In theory, a variety of substitutes have always existed for university education about business administration: community colleges, intra-firm training, consultants, and diploma offerings from professional associations. These have represented discrete segments because of high switching costs or difficulties in estimating the relationship between expenses and performance. Community colleges, for instance, are vocationally oriented and draw upon populations of candidates who may not qualify for university, whereas corporate training is aimed at upgrading personnel with materials appropriate for the needs of individual firms. In the larger and more competitive American market, there are unmistakable signs that the traditional barriers between educational mechanisms are eroding rapidly. Non-university providers now are accepted modes of delivery, in activities that range from vocationally oriented workshops to university-level executive programs. Distance education has become more economic with new modes of delivery and may prove effective for handling many of the technical issues that business schools have emphasized since the 1960s. Perceived deficiencies in university offerings concurrently have led companies such as Alcan to develop their own degree programs for human resource management, competitive strategy, or business-government relations. Various multinational enterprises have developed alliances with educational institutes in other countries to supply programs that will meet their needs. Entry into educational services requires heavy investments in infrastructure and personnel that decrease the potential return for new entrants, but once the sunk costs have been incurred, long-term gains can result as firms 'grow their own' managers through a mix of on-the-job practice and in-house training. Similar executive development efforts have been launched in central Canada, and it appears to be only a question of time before such initiatives cut into the demand for university services.[47]

The overwhelming majority of management faculty members in Canada were hired during the era of growth between 1960 and 1990. Not only do the business schools have an aging population, but owing to cutbacks in government funding, many have limited prospects for attracting excellent scholars. For individuals with valued expertise, the exit barriers remain low. Only anecdotal evidence is available on faculty turnover, but it suggests that at weaker institutions many of those

Figure 11.3 Current versus ideal skill levels of business faculties

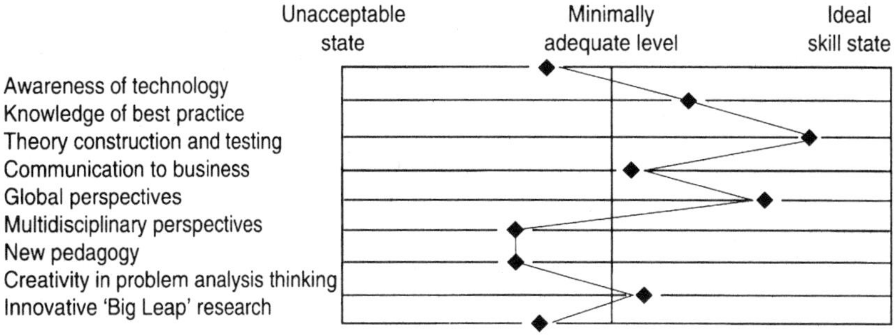

Source: Report of the AACSB Faculty Leadership Task Force, 1995–1996
(St Louis, 1996), 6.

who can go, will. This trend is most visible in areas like finance and management information systems, where excellent PhD graduates may earn considerably more from private firms or can negotiate superior packages from foreign universities. Because the current faculty also inculcated the beliefs that accompanied the period of expansion, the actual (rather than rhetorical) capacity for innovative changes in curricular design may prove constrained at some institutions. This issue was recently highlighted in a task force report for the AACSB that related the perceived discrepancies between business school policies and practitioner expectations to faculty skill deficits. Using the qualitative ranking shown in figure 11.3, the task force has argued that management faculty do well in theory construction or testing and often know which functional practices have been effective in the private sector. However, substantive weaknesses remain in areas like multidisciplinary approaches, new pedagogies, technological awareness, or novel research.

Canadian universities have always varied in status – a 'Big Ten' of research-intensive organizations (like Toronto and British Columbia) and the rest predominantly teaching-oriented. Shifting patterns of public- and private-sector funding are formalizing a tiered system, regardless of the desires of politicians or academics. American state universities (such as Ohio, Michigan, or Illinois) charge tuition or service fees that range from 70 to 85 per cent higher than Canadian levels. American public universities receive one-third more income per student, predominantly in the form of state appropriations and research funding from the federal government.[48] A shrinking elite of Canadian institutions can mobilize resources to sustain quality teaching and research, although the status of several rests on historic reputation. A middle group supplies good programs and research from individual scholars. The remainder deliver teaching or consulting services for local markets, but lack either the resources or personnel for sustained research.

The financial difficulties have been tackled in several ways. Trying to attract more students, business faculties now send out recruiters to secondary schools in markets that have supplied other institutions or have expanded the geographic scope of operations. Queen's business school privatized its flagship MBA program and began delivery of courses coast-to-coast for much higher tuition fees. Western also has delivered MBA instruction via video-conferencing and, at the time of writing, McGill planned a privatization of its graduate program. But this option is not viable for most faculties and the size of the distance-education market remains uncertain. In the wake of partial deregulation of tuition fees by several provincial governments, a second option has been to raise rates towards the benchmark level of American state universities and to charge differential fees for professional disciplines vis-à-vis the humanities or social sciences. This course of action, however, may conflict with public policy objectives such as accessibility to university education, and there are, of course, no guarantees that the revenues will actually trickle down to professional faculties. The tuition levels that any university can charge inevitably will be conditioned by the quality and perceived reputations of specific programs, a development that again will institutionalize a tiered system.

Many business faculties have tried to offset budget reductions by soliciting funds from private firms – a practice that has included sponsorship of buildings, classrooms, cafeterias, and even course syllabi. Although they have benefited from the services supplied by universities, Canadian firms historically have been miserly in supporting post-secondary education relative to their American counterparts, and contributions understandably tend to go to the better institutions. For example, it took the former president of the University of New Brunswick two years of full-time effort to garner corporate donations totalling $30 million, while the University of Toronto has approximately $900 million in endowments and Harvard more than US$11 billion. Since even the University of Toronto has reported difficulties in mobilizing the resources that permit the recruitment of 'world class' faculty, the capabilities of weaker organizations are questionable.[49] In any event, external funding may prove a Faustian pact that many faculty members will not accept despite the short-term gains. Having contributed significant monies, donors logically may demand to oversee the allocation of funds or to influence the activities of the recipients. Certainly, as the relationship between supply and demand alters further, students and companies will demand greater roles – pushing for improvements of program quality, enhanced services, or emphases upon applicable knowledge and teaching.

Old Problems, New Destinies

Several observations may be raised to conclude this review dealing with the state of Canadian management education.

1. *If gauged by the curricular policies of Canadian universities, there has been an evolution towards a single educational orientation at the baccalaureate and master's levels since 1980.* When the sixty-two undergraduate and thirty-three graduate programs are surveyed superficially, there appears to be a diverse group of orientations. The calendars and glossy brochures issued by each faculty claim students will receive a differentiated education. Variations occur owing to pedagogical techniques, the unique capabilities of personnel, and the availability of support services. But the more important issues are whether the level of diversity is *apparent* rather than real, and whether universities and private-sector firms have encouraged different orientations. Because business faculties belong to universities with different missions, or have student populations with disparate goals and career paths, the long-term development of management education requires a diversity of approaches. The rhetoric of administrators notwithstanding, programmatic structure has been characterized by replication and conformity. Many faculties have conscientiously strived to improve their offerings, but to a greater degree than in the United States, there appears to be a reluctance to incur the costs associated with developing alternative schema.

The spread of the Analyser orientation has been predicated upon student desires for career success through functional specialization. A pertinent question is whether or not that has been true. Reliable Canadian data are not available, but the topic has attracted considerable research in the United States. The experiences of different types of graduates indicate that entry into the work force initially is shaped by their chosen fields during baccalaureate studies. Recruiters screen applicants for grade-point average, work attitudes, extracurricular activities and, especially, academic specialty. For entry-level positions that often need technical skills, liberal arts graduates have tended to face fewer prospective openings and lower salaries than career-oriented majors. Accounting and business students, while faring better than individuals from the liberal arts or social sciences, have not had as much success gaining well-paid jobs as those who have majored in engineering or computer science.[50] Liberally educated graduates as a group, once they have secured private-sector employment, tend to perform at least as effectively as those who have taken career-oriented studies. Even at entry-level positions liberal arts majors perform comparably because their breadth of knowledge frequently compensates for weaknesses in functional skills. Longitudinal studies have not found a relationship between managerial salary and undergraduate major. Instead, higher earnings tend to be correlated with attendance at an institution with a strong reputation, intellectual self-confidence, and a personal drive for achievement. At the senior levels of companies, where analytical skills and creativity are crucial, no single field of study has predominated and in some areas BAs have proved more successful in their career development than have MBAs.[51] The available research suggests cognitive competence in technical functions has a marginal influence on career progress. Instead, administrative or general executive skills (such as the capacity to think conceptually, to integrate information, and to communicate) become more important as individuals ascend through corporate hierarchies. Successful management at the upper levels of companies also requires skills in handling social and environmental issues, a competence that can be abetted by a knowledge of non-business subjects.

2. *Canadian business schools must acknowledge and give strong institutional backing to the principle of educational breadth simply because of its long-term value to career executives.* Surveys of senior managers regularly indicate that an expansion of educational breadth will be favourably received, but the evolution of Canadian programs may leave observers less sanguine about a change in that direction. Adoption of the Analyser orientation fits well with faculty members' concerns for career success by allowing them to establish professional legitimacy through research and course delivery in distinctive sub-areas. It is also difficult to avoid the impression that many instructors, having been narrowly educated in their specialties, do not appreciate interdisciplinary learning. But not only have employment markets become saturated with business graduates, community colleges and distance education increasingly will supply the sorts of technical training for

which university faculties have become known. Functional skills depreciate as service technologies or industrial conditions change, whereas cognitive and behavioural capabilities increase in importance during a career.

Universities are more than mere vocational institutes. They retain a wide range of resources in different departments and cross-disciplinary options that most programs have not fully tapped. Business students not only should be encouraged to seek out alternative sources of ideas, but should be propelled to maximize their learning experiences. There is considerable room for management faculties to build strong competitive positions by developing educational orientations other than those of the prevailing wisdom. These include combined program streams with social science or arts departments (other than the usual joint degrees with economics or computer science) or management courses tailored for students in professions like forestry or education. Ironically, secure niches could be established by some faculties if they moved away from the practice of supplying full-service Analyser programs (which cover most business functions) to selective operations providing excellent undergraduate training in areas like MIS, marketing, or international business – but retaining strong breadth requirements. To ensure quality control at the baccalaureate level, students should take a *prescribed* set of non-business courses and then a significant group of advanced electives in a non-business major. Indeed, in a era of budgetary restraint, management faculties can easily accomplish a reconfiguration by reducing the business component of undergraduate studies. At the master's level, the goal can be enhanced by liberalizing the curricula further or co-opting non-management faculty to deliver breadth-enhancing modules.[52] For instance, business history has been an MBA course at the Harvard Business School since 1927, but not even one Canadian faculty has introduced a similar offering.

3. *The diverse patterns of core requirements substantiate most of the complaints that have been raised about poor coverage for different subjects and the failure to address these gaps represents a serious risk for individual faculties.* Major improvements have been made in the depth and quality of curricula since 1960, yet business schools cannot be all things to all people. Certain types of learning are life-long endeavours that require postdegree executive education, not several years of university studies. There are limits to the quantity of courses that can be designated as mandatory. Nonetheless, it is difficult to believe the claims of some institutions that students have 'majored' in business by taking numer-

ous courses in accounting and economics, but not a package that encompasses finance, law, MIS, and strategy. The pedigree of a business education must remain suspect if the curriculum has not required university-level courses in mathematics or languages. Forty years after the publication of the Foundation reports, many schools still handle qualitative topics poorly, with minimal obligations for studies in organizational behaviour or human resource management. A consensus has long prevailed among Canadian deans of business administration that greater emphasis must be placed upon the environment of business because of industrial reorganization, rapid technological change, interdependence between markets, and assertive lobbying by interest groups.[53] The rationales should be self-evident for the mandatory inclusion of both international business and business-society courses. Even though the subjects have been widely adopted elsewhere, coverage in Canada remains the exception rather than the rule.

Several aspects of future developments can be perceived by examining the curricular revisions undertaken by American universities since 1985. The most visible shift has been a declining status for finance, accounting, and other quantitative subjects. Although finance and accounting majors at most business schools still outnumber the students who specialize in other areas, there has been a trend away from quantitative areas and towards marketing, manufacturing, and management information systems. This development has been partially a function of decreased hiring from financial service firms and ethical scandals during the 1980s, but it has also reflected new priorities. A 1994 study by the University of Southern California indicated that students who secured the highest mathematical scores on GMAT examinations (which are used for the assessment of MBA applicants) were consistently the same people who had the lowest scores on management aptitude tests. Concurrently in Britain, the Council for Management Education and Development identified nine future areas of knowledge and skills needed for competent management. Contrary to expectations, the emphasis was almost exclusively upon non-technical issues such as personal skills, information management, the environment of management, managing people and resources, or client/customer relations. Numerous observers have viewed the reports as further evidence that mathematical expertise is largely irrelevant to good management.[54]

American schools have responded with a series of initiatives, in particular with much greater emphasis upon 'soft' skills: management, people, interpersonal relations, or leadership. In 1985 the AACSB announced a ten-year project for the development of leadership courses. Harvard concurrently launched electives dealing with the management of family-owned enterprises and company politics. The business faculty at the University of Chicago, known since the 1960s for an emphasis upon quantitative subjects, created a 'Leadership Exploration and Development' program. By 1997 the institution's catalogue gave far more coverage to that component than to mathematical subjects. One survey has indicated that in operations management and quantitative methods the pedagogy has become less mathematical and more managerial, giving greater stress to service firms, quality, and competitive strategy. The locus of analysis appears to be moving away from technique and towards application and interpretation. MIT in 1988 launched a master's degree in management and marketing (MMM) that combined courses from engineering and business, an initiative that has been replicated by Carnegie Mellon, Northwestern, and Stanford.[55]

A second type of initiative has entailed a greater role for international business issues. New York University, Columbia, and Harvard launched major initiatives to 'globalize' their curricula, while others like Case Western created research institutes or teaching facilities abroad. The University of Chicago became the first large institution to offer a specialized degree, the International Master of Business Administration. Smaller schools moved quickly in the same direction and by the early 1990s international business had replaced finance or computers as the most popular subject in American graduate programs. The number of courses proliferated, with options in multinational strategy, international law, and organization. Stanford currently has more than eighteen separate courses, offering the most comprehensive schema. Brochures from American graduate schools typically stress this reorientation. The University of Pittsburgh proclaims that its business curriculum 'provides a global management perspective in every phase of the program,' while the University of North Carolina has incorporated 'the international realities of business into every aspect of the program to assure that students are poised to compete in a global environment.' The expansion has been so rapid that since 1991 there has been a serious shortage of qualified faculty in the United States. Substantive efforts to develop programs that will provide training for international business have been conducted by several Canadian universities such as Saint Mary's, York, and Simon

Fraser. For most others, public rhetoric notwithstanding, it remains business as usual with new options or internationalization of the curriculum a function of individual faculty interest rather than coherent organizational policy.[56]

Two other subjects have garnered considerable attention in the United States. The number of universities teaching entrepreneurship grew from 10 to 340 between 1967 and 1987 and, in response to student desires to learn about risk-taking rather than administration, has since spread to the point where most graduate programs have an entrepreneurship stream. The scale of the change was indicated by a 1993 survey of UCLA's MBA graduates, which found that more than a fifth had gone into start-up firms and companies with fewer than two hundred employees. A decade earlier, few, if any, took that career path.[57] Courses in business ethics can be traced back to a 1916 offering by the Harvard Business School, but before the late 1980s the subject never attracted widespread interest. Most faculties considered it theoretical, impossible to teach, or a function of individual conscience. Financial scandals and concerns about the values of executives, however, have led to expanded treatment of ethics at major American institutions. The tendency has been to appraise ethical issues as a component of existing courses, not as a separate subject, but the present level of coverage is more extensive than ever.[58]

In Canada, despite corporate sponsorship, entrepreneurship never has garnered strong support at most universities. Indeed, since 1995 the number of active entrepreneurial centres has declined. Many of the relevant journals are not well regarded by academic peer-review processes, and courses have often been handled by less research-oriented faculty, thereby weakening the professional legitimacy of the subject. Although ethics has been added to the curriculum by a few Canadian universities, most have lacked interest or have not been willing to reallocate scarce resources.

4. *Meeting the needs of students and business will require more than the simple addition or reduction of different topics; it will entail the long-term modification of pedagogical practices and new forms of program delivery.* The revision of business curricula alone will not offset criticisms of existing practices or ensure adaptation to new environmental conditions. Rather, it will be necessary to develop new ways of presenting materials. None of the probable approaches are entirely new, but each runs contrary to the gestalt of the last thirty years. Since the publica-

tion of the Foundation reports, business programs have been organized with single, separate subjects. Students have been taught to break problems into separate components and then analyse them through functional techniques. The risk of this orientation has been long recognized: a tendency by individuals to let functional criteria (costs, profitability, market share) drive an enterprise's mission and not the reverse. Students instead should deal with a company as a complete entity, recognizing the interrelationships between functions and assessing the trade-offs between them that are associated with organizational actions. The primary integrative mechanism has been a course in strategic management taken during the final year of baccalaureate or master's studies. By the late 1980s a consensus emerged among the administrators of American business schools that a single course could never communicate a holistic perspective effectively. Faculties initially responded by elaborating interdisciplinary courses and fieldwork obligations that compelled students to look at subjects holistically. The most substantive initiative was a new model first elaborated by Wharton that replaced single-subject teaching in the MBA curriculum with broad integrative courses and cross-disciplinary research projects.[59]

This schema provoked considerable discussion and has propelled revisions of MBA programs at numerous institutions. McMaster University and the University of New Brunswick, for example, reordered their courses into smaller components, replacing twenty term courses with forty modules, while the Schulich School of Business at York University broke up several courses and worked on strengthening integrative features across the curriculum. The most extensive revision was undertaken by the University of British Columbia, which reorganized its MBA program into five integrative courses, a set of specialized modules, and a major practicum. The experiments, if successful, may propel a pedagogical transformation, but building an integrative approach will prove daunting even at the best universities. A reconfiguration of this sort entails faculty retraining, teamwork, and extensive collaboration, as well as a willingness to make explicit trade-offs between functional and interdisciplinary materials. Consequently, although discussions have been conducted at several institutions, similar action has not unfolded at the baccalaureate level. Moreover, the effectiveness of the MBA revisions has varied between institutions and the examples of 'model' schools have sometimes been imitated by other faculties without proper consideration of the fit with organizational capabilities.

Numerous commentaries have focused upon technology as a factor that will transform university teaching from the lecture or seminar formats. New forms of media have provided real-time communications, enabling teachers and students to interact over long distances as if they were in the same room. Video-conferencing, which Queen's and Western have employed for the delivery of MBA courses, has represented the most utilized medium. Also heavily promoted has been the Internet, which supposedly can supply courses time-tabled and taught like those at a university: work at a predetermined pace, regular contact with instructors, deadlines, and examinations. But suggestions that a major transformation in teaching techniques may quickly unfold should be received sceptically; indeed, alternative services have long been traits of various institutions. Even during its formative years the business school at Queen's offered correspondence courses, while Athabaska University and British Columbia's Open Learning Agency have specialized in distance education. The University of South Carolina has provided an MBA-by-TV since the late 1970s, but most similar initiatives, including a commuter train MBA by Adelphi University, failed to gain a significant clientele. Then and now, the alternative services meet the needs of non-traditional learners who cannot physically attend university campi, but the size of that market has never been accurately gauged.

One common misconception has been a belief that 'real-time' technologies represent cost-efficient mechanisms for servicing large numbers of candidates. In fact, these services are very resource-intensive. Video-conferencing currently is the most expensive instructional medium, while Internet courses require infrastructure support, software development, and a massive expansion in the hours that faculty must devote to student contact and guidance. Anecdotal evidence suggests that video-conferencing for MBA programs has had mixed outcomes, whereas student performance on correspondence courses remains quite effective. Internet courses have a potential for the delivery of introductory topics or specialized materials for professional accreditation, where much of the learning can be handled through student exercises and frequent tests. Their value for qualitative, complex, and unstructured subjects has yet to be demonstrated. The long-term trade-offs also have not been considered in any depth. Will employers truly place a similar value upon a degree earned through video-conferencing or the Internet as they would for one earned on campus? What will be the impact upon learning from the formalized and impersonal atmosphere of distance education versus the spontaneous interaction that occurs in a classroom? The new technologies may make it possible to service new groups of students, but it remains unclear how they will affect existing operations or how most business schools will mobilize sufficient resources for their utilization.[60]

Two other types of strategic choices have represented more tangible adjustments. In the United States, there has been a growing tendency to create customized programs that meet the needs of specific firms or industries. After four decades of program delivery through functional courses, companies have sought integrative kinds of academic education that are tailored for their problems. Before 1960 American colleges supplied industry-specific courses: meat-packing production, mine technology, and the like. The new offerings, in contrast, are temporary and are disbanded after helping the clients deal with practical issues. Programs are built around integrative themes: organizational restructuring, crisis management, or management of research-intensive organizations. A second American initiative has entailed the revision of business-school missions from full-service provision to niche marketing. The business faculty at Case Western University, for example, has reconfigured its activities around not-for-profit management, while other faculties have emphasized health care, agribusiness, or sports management. Despite concerns from some academics about excessive specialization, this pattern appears to be spreading as different schools construct distinctive competencies that will provide them with stable markets and professional legitimacy.

5. *Fundamental organizational change at Canadian business schools, not incremental tinkering with existing practices, will be an essential concomitant of renewal.* Educators will recognize that the preceding issues are hardly new, but if educational innovations are to occur, it will be predominantly through business schools, although universities and companies may provide valuable support. Redirecting strategy in a university context is difficult. Each management faculty conducts a heterogeneous set of activities and must satisfy demands from numerous stakeholders with very limited resources. Moreover, universities are organized as professional bureaucracies that carry out complex but repetitive assignments. Quality control is enforced first by hiring individuals who have established the requisite expertise or professional norms through doctoral training and then by various forms of

peer evaluation, leading to the categorization of instructors on the basis of expertise and their assignment to specific courses. Faculty members tend to control their own jobs, often work independently of their colleagues, and therefore are likely to regard demands for greater coordination of professorial activities or for alterations of course content as unqualified interference with the areas placed under their professional jurisdiction. In addition, most universities have decentralized administrative structures and limited mechanisms for guiding faculty conduct outside of tenure or promotion procedures. This framework can make strategic planning and the elaboration of coherent patterns of activity problematic.[61] It also is a curious paradox that the schools which provide fine executive development programs have rarely instituted similar efforts for enhancing the capabilities of faculty members.

Some of the likely changes in the organizational arrangements of business schools will not be appreciated by many instructors. Professional bureaucracies organized by business function operate mechanistically and are best suited to simple stable environments. For nearly forty years, business schools in North America have advised executives to construct 'organic' structures with divisions or 'strategic business units' that can more readily cope with environmental complexity and turbulence. In a similar vein, they have portrayed extensive teamwork, re-engineering, and continuous improvement, or regular monitoring, as indices of good management. It is, therefore, somewhat ironic that many business schools do *not* practise what they preach and tend to rely upon administrative arrangements that have been abandoned by the enterprises hiring their graduates. Numerous American faculties have begun to emulate corporate practices by reorganizing into service units like international business, agribusiness, or the management of technology. Concurrently, task forces and informal mechanisms have been elaborated to reduce hierarchies and break down the disciplinary barriers that exist between faculty. The revised MBA programs similarly require new approaches, since studies are organized as integrated modules with distinctive learning techniques. The courses entail committed teamwork by instructors, the development of a coherent action plan, repetitive consultation with colleagues and students, and collaboration to ensure consistency. Professorial autonomy must be constrained, since modifications intended to suit private goals can compromise program delivery, a policy that many faculty members will oppose as a constraint upon innovation or spontaneous experimentation. For successful programs, however, this may represent the instructional trend of the future, a corporate rather than individualistic approach.[62]

The new environmental conditions and the need to redefine organizational missions could not come at a worse time for Canadian business schools. With cutbacks in government funding and aging or shrinking faculty, many lack the resources for substantive action. Strategic change does not necessarily lead to constructive development. With schools asked to do more with less, if organizational missions are not elaborated carefully, there is a risk of de-motivation, bureaucratization, and a downward spiral of activities.[63] Extremely wicked policy dilemmas now confront management educators with choices that cannot be long delayed. The most forward-looking schools have recognized the problems of substantive change and have begun a process of renewal. As with all things, each faculty will respond according to its capabilities. Fortune's tides will take some to new vistas and destinies, while others will rest on wilting laurels as the business and academic worlds pass them by.

NOTES

1 Earlier iterations of this essay were presented at conferences of the Administrative Sciences Association of Canada and the Atlantic Schools of Business. Valuable critiques and suggestions were made by Sandford Borins, Daniel Coleman, Jocelyn Desroches, Paul Dixon, Robert Sexty, Ronald Storey, and James Tolliver. The author, of course, remains solely responsible for the line of argument and any errors of fact.

2 Statistics Canada, *University Enrolments and Degrees* (Cat. 81-204), and *Education in Canada* (Cat. 81-211). See also table 1.1 of chapter 1 in this volume.

3 Statistics Canada, *Education in Canada: Advance Statistics* (Cat. 81-204), April 1998.

4 Author's estimates from data published by the SSHRC in its *Annual Report, 1991–1992* and *Statement of Disbursements for 1995–1996*. This data does not include doctoral candidate support or monies issued under the strategic grants initiatives.

5 R. Smith, 'The State of Management Education and Research in Canada: One Perspective on Progress and Problems,' *CJAS* 7 (1990), 12–13.

6 There are numerous articles and monographs on the nature, and early criti-

cisms, of business education, but among the more useful are L.S. Lyon, *Education for Business* (Chicago: University of Chicago Press, 1931); B. Haynes and H. Jackson, *A History of Business Education in the United States* (Cincinnati: South-Western, 1935); E.G. Krnepper, *A History of Business Education in the United States* (Ann Arbor: Edward Brothers, 1941); and A.L. Pickett, *Collegiate Schools of Business in American Education* (Cincinnati: South-Western, 1945). A valuable bibliography can be found in P.S. Hugstad, *The Business School in the 1980s: Liberalism versus Vocationalism* (New York: Praeger, 1983), 121–46.

7 D.J. Bercuson, R. Bothwell, and J.L. Granatstein, *The Great Brain Robbery: Canada's Universities on the Road to Ruin* (Toronto: McClelland and Stewart, 1984), 73. See also the papers in W.A. Nelson and C. Gaffield, eds, *Universities in Crisis: A Medieval Institution in the Twenty-First Century* (Montréal: Institute for Research on Public Policy, 1986).

8 G. Bickerstaffe, 'Crisis of Confidence in the Business Schools,' *IM* 36 (August 1981), 87–9. W.A. Dymsza, 'The Education and Development of Managers for Future Decades,' *JIBS* 13 (1982), 9–18. D.L. Joyal, *Trends and Developments in Business Administration Programs* (New York: Praeger, 1982).

9 R.H. Hayes and W. Abernathy, 'Managing Our Way to Economic Decline,' *HBR* 58 (1980), 77. See also C. Meek, W. Woodworth, and W. Dyer, Jr, *Managing by the Numbers* (Don Mills, Ont.: Addison-Wesley, 1988).

10 J.C. Mason, 'Business Schools: Striving to Meet Customer Demand,' *MR* 79 (1992), 10–14. 'A Job for Life: A Survey of Management Education,' *The Economist*, 2 March 1991, S3–26. 'Universities: Towers of Babble,' *The Economist*, 7 January 1994, 72–4. 'Reengineering the MBA,' *Fortune*, 24 January 1994, 38–45. 'What's Killing the Business Deans of America?' *Fortune*, 8 August 1994, 64–8.

11 L.M. Porter and L.E. McKibben, *Management Education and Development: Drift or Thrust into the 21st Century?* (New York: McGraw-Hill, 1988), 310.

12 L. Van Esch, K. Melenchuk, and J. Sagebien, 'To B. or Not to B.? The B. Schools Under Attack – Again?' *CJAS* 7 (1990), 22.

13 J.B. McGuire, 'Management and Research Methodology,' *JOM* 12 (1986), 5–18. W.W. Williams, 'Institutional Propensities to Publish in Academic Journals of Business Administration,' *QRE* 27 (1987), 77–94. B.M. Oviatt and W.D. Miller, 'Irrelevance, Intransigence, and Business Professors,' *AME* 3 (1989), 294–312. P.M. Maher, 'Business School Research: Academics Should Be Concerned,' *CJAS* 7 (1990), 16–20.

14 H. Mintzberg, *Mintzberg on Management: Inside Our Strange World of Organizations* (New York: Free Press, 1989), 85, 79.

15 J. Behrman and R.I. Levin, 'Are Business Schools Doing Their Job?' *HBR* 59 (January–February 1984), 144–5.

16 J.W. McGuire, 'Management Theory: Retreat to the Academy,' *BH* 25 (July–August 1982), 31–7. R. Whiteley, 'The Fragmented State of Management Studies: Reasons and Consequences,' *JBS* 21 (1984), 331–47. R. Whiteley, 'The Scientific Status of Managerial Research as a Practically-Oriented Social Science,' *JMS* 21 (1984), 369–90. H. Koontz, 'The Management Theory Jungle Revisited,' *AMR* 5 (1980), 175–87.

17 Smith, 'The State of Management Research,' 12. Maher, 'Business School Research,' 18–19.

18 G. Morgan, 'Paradigms, Metaphors and Puzzle Solving in Organizational Theory,' *ASQ* 25 (1980), 605–22. W. Bennis, 'Using Our Knowledge of Organizational Behavior: The Improbable Task,' in J.W. Lorsch, ed., *Handbook of Organizational Behavior* (Englewood Cliffs, NJ: Prentice-Hall, 1987), 29–49.

19 For example, see S. Smith, *Report of the Commission of Inquiry on Canadian University Education* (Ottawa: AUCC, 1991). This study, although aimed at universities in general, puts forward many of the arguments that have been aimed at management education.

20 J.D. Hunger and T.L. Wheelen, *An Assessment of Undergraduate Business Education in the United States* (Charlottesville, Va.: McIntire School of Commerce Foundation, 1980), 2–19.

21 E. Arbuckle, 'The M.B.A. Today – A U.S. Perspective,' in *Touche Ross Report on Business Education* (New York: Touche Ross, 1984), 25. Porter and McKibben, *Management Education and Development*, 99–103.

22 J.E. Slater, 'The Humanities and Business Leaders,' in *Touche Ross on Business Education*, 39–42. R. Hodgson, 'Destiny or Disappointment: Which Will It Be?' *BQ* 53 (Spring, 1989), 5–8.

23 Behrman and Levin, 'Are Business Schools Doing Their Jobs?' 142–7. E. Cheit, 'Business Schools and Their Critics,' *CMR* 27 (1985), 43–62. P.S. Hugstad, *The Business School in the 1980s*, 84–92.

24 S.A. Ahmed and J. Jabaes, 'Comparative Study of Job Values of Business Students in France and English Canada,' *CJAS* 9 (1988), 51–9.

25 K. Fleet, 'Why Have British Business Schools Failed?' *Touche Ross Report on Business Education*, 5–9. Porter and McKibben, *Management Education and Development*, 101–18.

26 R.A. Gordon and J.E. Howell, *Higher Education for Business* (New York: Columbia University Press, 1959), 5.

27 Corporate Higher Education Forum, *Going Global: Meeting the Need for International Business Expertise in Canada* (Montréal: Corporate Higher Education Forum, 1988), 2.

28 L.R. Gomez-Mejia and D.B. Balkin, 'Determinants of Faculty Pay: An Agency Theory Perspective,' *AMJ* 35 (1994), 921–55.

29 R.M. Stamp, *The Schools of Ontario, 1876–1976* (Toronto: UTP, 1982), 216–24. P.C. Emberley and W.R. Newell, *Bankrupt Education: The Decline of Liberal Education in Canada* (Toronto: UTP, 1994), 15–70. Similar difficulties in the United States were traced by different authors including C. Finn, 'Education That Works: Making the Schools Compete,' *HBR* 62 (September–October 1987), 63–8, and T.P. Rohlen, 'Why Japanese Education Works,' *HBR* 62 (September–October 1987), 42–5.

30 R. Hofstadter and S. Handy, *The Development and Scope of Higher Education in the United States* (New York: Columbia University Press, 1952), 11.

31 K.R Andrews, *The Concept of Corporate Strategy,* 2nd ed. (Homewood, Ill.: Richard D. Irwin, 1971), 18.

32 H.W.J. Rittel and M.M. Webber, 'Dilemmas in a General Theory of Planning,' *PS* 4 (1973), 155–69. An excellent discussion of the issues can be found in J.B. Quinn, *Strategies for Change: Logical Incrementalism* (Homewood, Ill.: Richard D. Irwin, 1980).

33 D. Miller, 'The Genesis of Configuration,' *AMR* 12 (1986), 686–701. H. Mintzberg and J.A. Waters, 'Of Strategies, Deliberate and Emergent,' *SMJ* 6 (1985), 257–72. A reality check on the logic of organizational configurations is H. Mintzberg, 'Beyond Configuration: Forces and Forms in Effective Organizations,' in H. Mintzberg, ed., *Mintzberg on Management: Inside Our Strange World of Organizations* (New York: Free Press, 1989), 252–300.

34 C. Hardy, A. Langley, H. Mintzberg, and J. Rose, 'Strategy Formation in the University Setting,' in J.L. Bess, ed., *Colleges and University Organization: Insights from the Behavioral Sciences* (New York: New York University Press, 1984), 169–210.

35 Hugstad, *The Business School in the 1980s,* 1–11. Gordon and Howell, *Higher Education for Business,* 5.

36 C.J. Kiernan, 'The Rise of the Collegiate School of Business,' in B. Opulente, ed., *Thought Patterns: Towards a Philosophy of Business Education* (New York: St John's University, 1960), 3–11. F. Pierson, *The Education of American Businessmen* (New York: McGraw-Hill, 1959), 36–41.

37 The data relate to the primary degree offerings from each university (bachelor of administrative affairs, bachelor of business administration, bachelor of commerce, bachelor of management, or bachelor of accounting). Numerous universities offer distinctive secondary degrees and diplomas that   have not been included. For the purposes of analytical consistency, the four-year or honours programs supplied by universities, were used for the data set except for most Québec universities where attendance at CEGEP institutions has replaced the first year of baccalaureate studies.

38 H. Orlans, *Private Accreditation and Public Eligibility* (Lexington, Mass.: Lexington Books, 1975), 7.

39 The most sustained analysis of contemporary curricula has been Porter and McKibben, *Management Education and Development*, 67–87. The study was commissioned by the AACSB and, not surprisingly, shared many of its goals and values. Various papers dealing with specific aspects of management education have reached similar conclusions, but also have documented less than universal acceptance of AACSB standards: D.L. Joyal, *Trends and Developments in Business Administration Programs* (New York: Praeger, 1982); L.C. Nehrt, 'The Internationalization of the Curriculum,' *JIBS* 18 (1987), 83–90; J. Thanopoulos and I.R. Vernon, 'International Business Education in the AACSB Schools,' *JIBS* 16 (1987), 5–25; P.H. Etemad and P. Berman, 'The Challenge of Rigor and Relevance in Management Education and Development,' *ASAC Proceedings, Management Education and Development* 11, part 10 (1990), 61–72; B.L. Kedia and T.B. Cornwell, 'Mission Based Strategies for Internationalizing U.S. Business Schools, *JTIB* 5 (1994), 11–29.

40 D.F. Coleman, P.C. Wright, and J.M. Tolliver, 'American-Style Accreditation and Its Application in Canada: Perceptions of Utility,' *CJAS* 11 (1994), 194–8.

41 Porter and McKibben, *Management Education and Development*, 314–15.

42 American Assembly of Collegiate Schools of Business, *Accreditation Council Policies, Procedures and Standards* (St Louis: AACSB, 1986).

43 E.J. Mighty, 'The Responsiveness of Management Education to Workplace Diversity,' in A. LaPointe and G. Gorman, eds, *ASAC Proceedings: Management Education*, 16, part 10 (1995), (Montréal: Hautes Études Commerciales), 39–50.

44 B.E.C. Boothman, 'Something Wicked This Way Comes: Orientations and Curricula of Undergraduate Business Programs in Canada,' in L. Steier, ed., *ASAC Proceedings, Management Education* 11 part 10 (1990), (Vancouver: Simon Fraser University), 9–21; and 'The Contours of Graduate Business Programs in Canada,' *Proceedings, Twenty-First Atlantic Schools of Business Conference* (Halifax: St Mary's University, 1991), 445–54. The surveys for 1985 and 1989–91 covered most, but not all, of the Canadian programs.

45 M.E. Porter, *Competitive Strategy: Techniques for Analyzing Industries and Competitors* (New York: Free Press, 1980), 3–33. The Porter framework has been applied by Oviatt and Miller to explain the insularity of business schools. See 'Irrelevance, Intransigence and Business Professors,' 305–7. The authors misused the model by regarding the business professorate

(rather than institutions or groups of institutions) as the unit of analysis and by treating functional disciplines as segments.

46 The best illustration of this phenomenon has been Metropolitan Toronto. The Faculty of Administrative Studies (now the Schulich School of Business) at York University has focused upon graduate offerings and the baccalaureate degree often has been perceived as a 'poor cousin' staffed with junior-level instructors. The University of Toronto's bachelor of commerce degree predominantly comprises courses in economics, finance, and accounting. In the view of this writer, the Faculty of Management, while providing a good graduate program, appears to have been less responsive to local market demand for a strong baccalaureate offering. Ryerson's faculty complement has been composed largely of MBAs rather than PhDs and has taken an avowedly vocational thrust. Many young Torontonians, therefore, have taken their education in business at other institutions.

47 'A Job for Life,' S16–20.

48 D. Bercuson, R. Bothwell, and J.L. Granatstein, *Petrified Campus: The Crisis in Canada's Universities* (Toronto: Random House, 1997), 33–4.

49 Toronto *Star*, 23 March 1998.

50 These results have been mapped with good consistency in *Recruiting Trends*, an annual survey published by the placement services department of Michigan State University. Now dated, but still informative, studies have included A.S. Bisconti, *Who Will Succeed? College Graduates as Business Executives* (Bethlehem, Pa.: College Placement Council Foundation, 1980); D.G. Winter, D.C McClelland, and A.J. Stewart, *A New Case for the Liberal Arts: Assessing Institutional Goals and Student Development* (San Francisco: Jossey-Bass, 1980); and A.W. Vandemeer and M.D. Lyons, 'Professional Fields and the Liberal Arts, 1958–1978,' *ER* 60 (1979), 197–201. Less systematic but more recent data are presented in the *Chronicle of Higher Education* and the *Journal of Business Education*.

51 R.E. Beck, *Career Patterns: The Liberal Arts Major in Bell System Management* (Washington: Association of American Colleges, 1981); S.T. Burns, *From Student to Broker: Observations from the Chase Bank* (Washington: Association of American Colleges, 1983); A. Howard, *College Experience and Managerial Performance* (New York: American Telephone and Telegraph, 1984); R.G. Schaeffer and A.R. Janger, *Who Is Top Management?* (New York: Conference Board, 1982); M. Useem and J. Karabel, *Pathways to Top Corporate Management* (Boston: Boston University, Center for Applied Social Science, 1985).

52 See R.B. Smith, 'The Liberal Arts and the Art of Management,' and D.W. Butler, 'The Humanities and the M.B.A.,' in J. Johnston et al., eds, *Educating Managers* (San Francisco: Jossey-Bass, 1986), 21–33, 143–69.

53 See CFDMAS, 'Report of the National Conference Managing in the 1980's: Choosing Themes for Management Research,' 2 February 1981. The research agenda endorsed by Canadian deans of management attracted considerable American interest since it was reprinted in the *SMR* 53 (Winter 1982), 68–9.

54 D. Hornby and R. Thomas, 'Towards a Better Standard of Management,' *PM* 21 (1989), 52–5. 'Management Material,' *CA Magazine* 127 (December 1994), 9. C.A. Daniel, *The MBA: The First Century* (London: Associated University Presses, 1998), 276, 280.

55 D. Greising, 'Chicago's B-School Goes Touchy-Feely,' *BW* 27 November 1989, 140. R.L. Carraway and J.R. Freeland, 'MBA Training in Operations Management and Operations Methods,' *Interfaces* 19 (July–August 1989), 75–88. J.C. Mason, 'Business Schools: Striving to Meet Customer Demand,' *MR* 81 (September 1992), 10–14. 'Move Over MBAs: Here Come MMMs,' *Fortune*, 18 January 1990, 16.

56 T.S. Chan, 'Developing International Managers,' *JMD* 12 (1994), 38–46. Daniel, *The MBA* 268. See also S.T. Cavusgil, *Internationalizing Business Education: Meeting the Challenge* (East Lansing: Michigan State University, 1993).

57 *New York Times*, 24 March 1987. L.H. Cusimir, 'Entrepreneurship and MBA Degrees: How Well Do They Know Each Other,' *JSBM* 26 (July 1988), 71–4. C. Oliver, 'Intrapreneurship and Entrepreneurship Amongst MBA Graduates,' *MD* 29 (1991), 8–11. A. Wallenstein, 'Can You Teach Entrepreneurship?' *BW*, 27 October 1993, 139–43.

58 T.W. Mulligan, 'The Two Cultures in Business Education,' *AMR* 12 (1987), 593–9. M.S. Lane, 'Ethics in Education: A Comparative Study,' *JBE* 8 (1989), 943–9. D.L. McCabe, 'The Effects of Professional Education on Values and the Resolution of Ethical Dilemmas: Business School vs. Law School Graduates,' *JBE* 13 (1994), 693–700.

59 H.J. Leavitt, 'Educating Our MBAs: On Teaching What We Haven't Taught,' *Calif. MR* 31 (Spring, 1989), 38–50. 'Wharton Business School: A New MBA,' *The Economist*, 14 December 1991, 71–4.

60 This paragraph draws upon interviews with representatives of Queen's, Western, and Athabaska who summarized their faculties' experiences. I also appreciate the insights provided by Dr Donald Dixon of the Open University of the Netherlands about the resource implications associated with Internet education. The Open University services more than 20,000 students worldwide, most of whom could not physically attend a university.

61 H. Mintzberg, *The Structuring of Organizations* (Englewood Cliffs, NJ: Prentice-Hall, 1979), 352–8. H. Rosovsky, *The University: An Owner's Manual* (New York: W.W. Norton, 1990), 248–57, 262–73.

62 A balanced and thoughtful commentary can be found in J. Harvey and A. Langley, 'Applying Quality Principles in Business Schools: Potential and Limitations,' *CJAS* 12 (1995), 128–43.

63 For a penetrating analysis of this phenomenon, see A.G. Bedeian and A.A. Armenakis, 'The Cesspool Syndrome: How Dreck Rises to the Top of Declining Organizations,' *AME* 12 (February 1998), 58–63.

Contributors

BARBARA AUSTIN is a professor in the Faculty of Business, Brock University. Her publications have examined issues in business strategy, organizational theory, and business history.

BARRY E.C. BOOTHMAN is an associate professor in the Faculty of Administration, the University of New Brunswick at Fredericton. His research is concerned with the historical development of the 'visible hand' of professional management in the Canadian public and private sectors.

P. BRUCE BUCHAN is Professor Emeritus in the School of Business at Queen's University. He is researching a history of the East India Company from a strategic management perspective.

MERVIN DAUB is a professor in the School of Business at Queen's University. His publications have addressed subjects in the fields of economic forecasting, energy policy, and business history.

COLIN DICKINSON has master's degrees in business administration and political science. He is employed in corporate banking with the Bank of Nova Scotia, Toronto.

CATHY DRISCOLL is an assistant professor in the Faculty of Commerce at Saint Mary's University. Her research is concerned with social issues in business and multi-stakeholder collaboration.

ROBERT ELLIS is Director of the MBA program and Associate Dean of Business (Human Resources and Research) of the School of Business and Economics at Wilfrid Laurier University. His research interests span leadership and management education.

JAMES GILLIES is Professor Emeritus of Policy, and the former Director of the Max Bell Business-Government Studies Program in the Schulich School of Business at York University. He has been the founding dean of the Faculty of Administrative Studies and a vice-president at York University, a member of Parliament for the constituency of Don Valley in Toronto, a policy adviser for the Progressive Conservative Party of Canada, and the chair of the Economic Council of Ontario. A director of more than thirty-five corporations, he also has served on the boards of numerous not-for-profit organizations. A prolific author, he has written more than 150 articles and has authored or contributed to more than a dozen books including *When Business Fails* (1981), *Facing Reality: Consultation, Consensus and Making Economic Policy for the 21st Century* (1986), and *Boardroom Renaissance: Power Morality and Performance in the Modern Corporation* (1991).

PIERRE HARVEY is Professor Emeritus and a special consultant to the Director of the École des Hautes Études Commerciales de Montréal. His fields of interest have been the economics of labour and Québec's economic development. He has contributed to several public enquiries, including the Picard Commission which investigated labour disputes in the ports of the St Lawrence River valley, and he has been involved with diverse international projects. He is author of *Histoire de l'École des Hautes Études Commerciales de Montréal, Tome 1: 1887–1926* (1994), *Histoire de la profession d'expert-comptable au Québec, 1880–1990* (1996), and *Histoire de l'École des Hautes Études Commerciales de Montréal, Tome 2* (1998).

VERNON JONES is Professor and Associate Dean (External) of the Faculty of Management at the University of Calgary, and the former Executive Director of the Banff School of Advanced Management. His research interests are in the areas of management education and Canadian business.

GEORGE S. LANE is Professor Emeritus and former Dean of the Faculty of Management at the University of Calgary. He has conducted research and served as a consultant in the area of management education.

JOHN McCUTCHEON is a member of the Accounting area in the School of Business and Economics at Wilfrid Laurier University. His research interests span financial accounting and accounting ethics.

HAROLD OGDEN is an assistant professor in the Faculty of Commerce at Saint Mary's University. His research has focused upon consumer and industrial buyer behaviour.

GINA PECORE is a communications officer with the Faculty of Business at the Memorial University of Newfoundland.

JOHN A. SAWYER is Professor Emeritus of the Joseph L. Rotman School of Management and the Department of Economics at the University of Toronto. He has served as Associate Dean (Social Sciences) of the School of Graduate Studies, Director of the Institute for Policy Analysis, and the acting dean of the Faculty of Management. His research activities have been in the fields of inter-industry input-output analysis, macroeconomics, and business-cycle analysis.

ROBERT W. SEXTY is a professor in the Faculty of Business at the Memorial University of Newfoundland. He is a past president of the Administrative Sciences Association of Canada. A prolific writer, he is the author of several books, including *Canadian Business in the New Stakeholder Society* and *Canadian Business and Society: Understanding Social and Ethical Challenges* (1995). He consults for business, government, and not-for-profit organizations.

Index